Wounds of Memory

German memories of the Second World War are controversial, and they are used to justify different positions on the use of military force. In this book, Maja Zehfuss studies the articulation of memories in novels in order to discuss and challenge arguments deployed in political and public debate. She explores memories that have generated considerable controversy, such as the flight and expulsion of Germans from the East, the bombing of German cities and the 'liberation' of Germany in 1945. She shows how memory retrospectively produces a past while claiming merely to invoke it, drawing attention to the complexities and contradictions within how truth, ethics, emotion, subjectivity and time are conceptualised. Zehfuss argues that the tensions and uncertainties revealed raise political questions that must be confronted, beyond the safety net of knowledge. This is a compelling book which pursues an original approach in exploring the politics of invocations of memory.

MAJA ZEHFUSS is Professor of International Politics at the University of Manchester. She is the author of *Constructivism in International Relations: The Politics of Reality* (Cambridge, 2002) and has written articles for a number of journals, including the *European Journal of International Relations, Millennium*, the *Review of International Studies, Third World Quarterly, International Relations* and *International Politics*.

T0370680

Wounds of Memory: The Politics of War in Germany

Maja Zehfuss

CAMBRIDGE
UNIVERSITY PRESS

CAMBRIDGE UNIVERSITY PRESS

Cambridge, New York, Melbourne, Madrid, Cape Town, Singapore, São Paulo, Delhi, Dubai, Tokyo, Mexico City

Cambridge University Press
The Edinburgh Building, Cambridge CB2 8RU, UK

Published in the United States of America by Cambridge University Press, New York

www.cambridge.org
Information on this title: www.cambridge.org/9780521174466

First published 2007
First paperback edition 2011

A catalogue record for this publication is available from the British Library

ISBN 978-0-521-87333-8 Hardback
ISBN 978-0-521-17446-6 Paperback

In Erinnerung an Gerhard Zehfuß (1942–2004)

Contents

Abbreviations	*page*	ix
Preface		xi

1 Speaking of war and memory — 1
Speaking of war and memory: political debate — 4
Speaking of war: novels — 13
Reading memory — 20
Speaking of the Second World War (and not the Holocaust) — 26

2 Forgetting to remember? — 32
The significance of remembering — 33
The significance of forgetting — 37
How to remember (and forget) — 40
Memories of the flight and expulsion from the East: Grass's
Im Krebsgang — 41
Multiple memories — 55
The imperative to remember and the desire to forget — 60
Forgetting to remember — 63
The reframed war revisited — 68
Concluding thoughts — 71

3 Wounds of memory — 76
Don't mention the war? — 77
The year of remembrance 1995: time to mourn? — 79
Air war and literature: the (im)possibility of truth in fiction — 81
Der Brand: inappropriate sentimentality? — 87
The problem of victimhood — 92
Ledig: *Vergeltung* — 96
Mulisch: *Das steinerne Brautbett* — 101
Victims and perpetrators in one — 108
Memories of strategic bombing and the Iraq war — 116
Concluding thoughts — 121

4 The truth of memory — 126
Never again German war — 127
Forgotten Wehrmacht atrocities: the exhibition — 129
Recreating immediacy: Ledig's *Die Stalinorgel* — 141
Impossible authenticity: Walser's *Ein springender Brunnen* — 146

Representing war and the political context   151
The truth of fiction   155
Beyond truth? Emotion and ethics   161
Representing war: the other political context   166
Concluding thoughts   171

5   Times of memory   175
Memory and temporality: between past and present?   176
When we remember: Johnson's *Jahrestage*   182
Different times: Vonnegut's *Slaughterhouse 5*   189
Tensions of time   197
Thinking time differently   208
The future of ethics   213
Concluding thoughts   218

6   Memory, uncertainty, responsibility   221
Challenges of memory   221
The spectre of horror   228
The spectre of the Holocaust   242
War and the spectre of its Other   251
Speaking of war and memory: uncertainty and responsibility   259

Bibliography   267
Index   285

Abbreviations

BBC	British Broadcasting Corporation
CDU	Christlich Demokratische Union (Christian Democratic Union)
CSU	Christlich-Soziale Union (Christian-Social Union)
EDC	European Defence Community
FDP	Freie Demokratische Partei (Free Democratic Party)
FRG	Federal Republic of Germany
GDR	German Democratic Republic
NATO	North Atlantic Treaty Organisation
PDS	Partei des Demokratischen Sozialismus (Party of Democratic Socialism)
POW	Prisoner of War
RAF	Royal Air Force
SA	Sturmabteilung
SD	Sicherheitsdienst
SPD	Sozialdemokratische Partei Deutschlands (Social Democratic Party of Germany)
SS	Schutzstaffel
UK	United Kingdom of Great Britain and Northern Ireland
UN	United Nations
UNPROFOR	United Nations Protection Force in the former Yugoslavia
USA	United States of America

Preface

When I grew up, war was bad. Unconditionally bad. What was particularly bad was Germans being involved in any war. 'We' had started two world wars, after all. Although Germans are still seen as profoundly biased against war, war has been able to dramatically improve its reputation. Germans still hesitate to call it that when they are involved – *Kampfeinsatz* (combat mission) being the most martial terminology thinkable – but war, in some guises, has become acceptable. And I am still struggling to understand. What is perhaps most astonishing is that the Second World War – the very reason war was so assuredly bad – came to be instrumentalised in justifying this shift, in justifying the permissibility of war.

One of the intriguing aspects about the debates I explored for my previous book,[1] in which I trace this shift, was that from the Gulf War onwards the Second World War and memories of it were invoked in order not only to make sense of the problem of using force today but to argue for it. In other words, *the* bad war was used to argue that war wasn't so bad after all. At the same time, it was used, of course, to warn against war. This is intriguing, especially since – even though the Second World War was mentioned time and again – not very much was said at all about that war and Germans' experiences in it. Although politicians, intellectuals, scholars and 'ordinary' Germans often seem strangely certain about what 'Germans' remember, I found myself wondering about what the Germans know or remember of the war – and about whether that is the right question to ask. As it happened, once I had started on the project, these questions were drowned out by a flurry of interest in the war amongst the German public: interest in Allied bombing against German cities, the flight and expulsion of Germans from the East, the rape of thousands of women at the end of the war and Stalingrad. Suddenly, the Second World War was 'in', and this led to heated debate, not least about how Germans may today relate to those events: does

---

[1] Maja Zehfuss, *Constructivism in International Relations: The Politics of Reality* (Cambridge: Cambridge University Press 2002).

remembering suffering amount to construing Germans as victims of the Second World War, to playing into the hands of the far Right? In its almost ritualistic insistence on this concern, the debate seemed similar to the invocations of Second World War memories in order to support or reject the use of military force. The two, in my view, are related, and both are stuck in an unproductive pattern. Reading them together also demonstrates that the focus on an appropriate relation to the past may translate into an unintended, and to some unwanted, programme in relation to war today.

I am of course a member of 'Generation Golf', the generation that, as Florian Illies observed, could not be moved by successive debates on the Third Reich because we had already seen the film material disturbing the nation in our history classes at school when we were barely teenagers, the generation that always takes into account the 'dark side' of history which was on the syllabus in pretty much every grade. Illies seems to think that this generation has a relation to this history which is relaxed and emotionless, which makes nervous those who still had to fight against the silence surrounding the Third Reich, and who presume this to be a sign of forgetting the past, of ignorance and worse.[2] Although I recognise Illies's humorous description of the Germany of my youth, I do not share his conviction that we are 'cool' about our history. Yet he captures something significant. I was astonished when I first read the argument that recent German interest in civilian suffering in the Second World War meant that Germans were construing themselves as victims 'again'. Having grown up with what Illies describes, I really did not understand the 'again'. Although I now know what is meant, I remain surprised that this alleged return to the 1950s is so unproblematically assumed, denying the experience of those who were not around at the time, and that the 'generation of the grandchildren' is often represented as ignorant and in need of education in these debates. The grandchildren, of course, are hardly children any more and, following Illies, probably know quite a bit about this past.

Yet we don't *remember*. Or do we? Politicians today, over sixty years after the war, still invoke the Germans' memory, the horrors they have experienced. Do I, born several decades after the war, remember? I am bemused that politicians should claim my memory of a time before my birth, but I am just as astonished when I am told that I do not remember or am admonished, invariably by someone really well-meaning who happens not to be German, that I should no longer worry about it. Accordingly, this subject raises for me the question of memory. What does it mean

---

[2] Florian Illies, *Generation Golf: Eine Inspektion* (Berlin: Argon 2000), pp. 174f.

to remember, and what does remembering tell us about how we understand the reality we live in? Memory retrospectively produces a past while claiming merely to invoke it, drawing attention to numerous complications regarding how we conceptualise truth, ethics, emotion, subjectivity and time. So whilst my argument is motivated by a concern over the ways in which memories of the Second World War have been discussed and instrumentalised, in particular – and not unrelatedly – in ways that make difficult a serious engagement with the Germans' suffering in war and that justify war today, its core is the profound uncertainty that marks our world and the significance of acknowledging this, particularly in scholarship. Although this book is an intervention in debates about Germans' memories of the Second World War, these debates will continue anyway. If there is a small contribution that I would wish to make it is to destabilise the certainty with which much is claimed – not least about what Germans do and should remember – which is always at risk of translating into a dangerous self-righteousness. Because 'we' Germans got it so dreadfully wrong in the past, because we remember, we have privileged knowledge about how we should act in the present. It is the burden of my argument that knowledge, whether or not it is possible, is actually not the point.

The shock at discovering that 'Germany's conscience',[3] Günter Grass, had served in the Waffen-SS as a 17-year-old and had neglected to inform the people he had been cajoling into admitting the crimes of the Third Reich of the fact underlines the desire that we should be able to clearly distinguish Good from Bad. Grass was meant to be Good. Personally, I am cheered to know that it is more complicated. Life has a way of being so, and we need to find the courage to acknowledge, certainly when it comes to memory and to war, that we cannot opt simply for the Good, because it is not on offer. Thinking that we can is nothing but a dangerous illusion. This is not because those of us who are German ought to be anguished about being German. During the 2006 World Cup I actually found myself cycling across Munich with a German flag attached to my backpack. The flag had been given to me by Linus, who had made it himself, reflecting his enthusiasm for the tournament and, of course, Germany's successes. Linus's mother, my friend Susi, had recognised my unease at the gift and my surprise at their house being decorated with flags; but was she meant to explain the Holocaust to her 6-year-old son? Cycling off with my flag, I felt self-conscious at first, but quickly realised that anyone seeing me would have assumed nothing more than that I was supporting my country's football team: a perfectly normal thing to do. No one would have derived any view as to my political positions from seeing me with the

[3] Tim Adams, 'Germany's conscience', *Observer*, 10/02/02, 25.

flag. Politics and our responsibility within it involves agonising, whatever our histories. But maybe, just occasionally, it might also help not to take ourselves too seriously.

It should perhaps be noted that I no longer live in Germany, although I do not feel any less German for that. My questions about the politics of war in Germany certainly predate my move to the UK, but some issues were brought to my attention in a different way. Some of my thoughts on strategic bombing, for example, were prompted by a Masters seminar at the University of Wales, Aberystwyth, and one may certainly speculate about how far being exposed to the British way of remembering the same war, which happens to be no less idiosyncratic, has affected my thoughts on the matter. More importantly, however, as a German resident in the UK, I am neither fully inside the issues raised here nor outside, and at the same time, of course, simultaneously both. I am both at a distance and very much caught up in what is after all part of how I construe who I am. This has not made writing this any easier, but it may just have made it possible.

I still cannot believe that I have written this book. My profound thanks go to the many people who discussed with me the issues raised here and who encouraged me to carry on when I despaired at the impossible task. Above all, I would like to thank Jenny Edkins, whose contribution is impossible to acknowledge adequately: her friendship and intellectual generosity were crucial in writing this book; Susanna Rieder, whose enthusiasm and detailed comments persuaded me to carry on; Steve Smith, whose advice at crucial junctures of this project was indispensable; and Hidemi Suganami, whose favourable, if critical, comments on the first paper towards this book made me persist in what appeared to be a daunting project. I am also grateful to Jay Winter and an anonymous referee for Cambridge University Press for their critical but constructive comments on the manuscript, and to Duncan Bell and Stuart Elden for commenting on a particular chapter. I owe a debt of gratitude to Ingo Leiß and Helmut Schmitz, who both generously shared their expertise in German literature, and to Roland Bleiker, Stef Craps and Eduardo Mendieta who drew my attention to specific texts. Work towards this book was presented in a number of settings: at the invitation of the Aberystwyth PostInternational Group and the Cambridge International Studies Association, at several ISA conventions, at the Cambridge Centre of International Studies and at the 'Future of Memory' conference in Manchester. I received fruitful feedback each time. My thanks for their productive comments go in particular to Tarak Barkawi, David Campbell, James Der Derian, Aida Hozic, Naeem Inayatullah, Debbie Lisle, David Smith and Annick Wibben. I would particularly like to thank Josef Ansorge for his searching questions and for sharing his thoughtful reflections on Germany's past. For stimulating discussions about Derrida's work my thanks go especially to Dan Bulley and Nick Vaughan-Williams. As always, I am grateful to Horst Zehfuß for keeping me in touch with the German press, but this time also for sharing his memories.

I would like to thank the University of Warwick for two terms' study leave in 2003–04 which enabled me to start this project. I am also grateful to Jackie and Graeme Smith and to Véronique Pin-Fat for their hospitality, which enabled me to finish it.

Bernhard A. Eble of the Gedenkstätte Weiße Rose at the Ludwig-Maximilians Universität München kindly assisted me in discovering the context of the plaque 'Wunden der Erinnerung' on the university's main building. The plaque, which inspired the title of this book and is briefly discussed in Chapter 3, is part of a European project by artists Beate Passow and Andreas von Weizsäcker. For a description of the project see www.dhm.de/ausstellungen/Wunden_der_Erinnerung.html.

Parts of Chapter 2 have appeared as 'Remembering to Forget/ Forgetting to Remember' in Duncan S. A. Bell (ed.), *Memory, Trauma and World Politics: Reflections on the Relationship between Past and Present* (Basingstoke: Palgrave Macmillan 2006); this material is reproduced with permission of Palgrave Macmillan. Other material appearing in this book, in particular in Chapter 4, has been published as 'Writing War, against Good Conscience', *Millennium: Journal of International Studies* 33, 1 (2004), 91–121. I gratefully acknowledge permission to use this material here.

Although my wonder at how we speak about and remember war was significant, this book also has another origin. My thanks are to the participants of a memorable conversation on family histories in Larry George's kitchen, Costas Constantinou, Erin Manning and, especially, James Der Derian, who pressed me to write about my own. Although I have not done that in any direct way, his insistence set me off on what proved to be a treacherous but fascinating path.

I would not write without the support of Edith, Horst and Ulrich Zehfuß, who are there for me always: thank you. Finally, I also owe a debt of gratitude to Gerhard Zehfuß who, in his inimitable way, was and remains an inspiration to me: this book is dedicated to his memory.

1   Speaking of war and memory

> Never again do we want to send our sons to the barracks. And if again somewhere this insanity of war should break out, and if fate should want it that our land becomes a battlefield, then we shall simply perish and at least take with us the knowledge that we neither encouraged nor committed the crime. Carlo Schmid (1946)[1]

When, several decades after Carlo Schmid's impassioned plea, the Germans[2] were confronted with the question of war, they seemed to follow his lead. They seemed to want nothing to do with war. Many objected strongly to the 1991 Gulf War; thousands took to the streets. Most prominently, Foreign Minister Hans-Dietrich Genscher asserted that war could not under any circumstances be a means of politics,[3] a view that was shared by opposition politicians.[4] This forceful rejection of war in general and the Gulf War in particular was often illustrated, underlined and justified with references to and memories of the Second World War. In his statement on the Gulf War Chancellor Helmut Kohl mentioned, first of all, the Germans' experiences of war, their memories and their resulting ability to understand the suffering of people caught up in war.[5] These experiences, Kohl asserted, 'have been deeply ingrained in the memory of our people as a whole'.[6] Later, when the Federal Republic of Germany

---

[1] Carlo Schmid, *Erinnerungen* (Bern 1979), p. 490, quoted in Donald Abenheim, *Reforging the Iron Cross: The Search for Tradition in the West German Armed Forces* (Princeton: Princeton University Press 1988), p. 43. Carlo Schmid was one of the 'fathers' of the Basic Law (the constitution of the Federal Republic of Germany).

[2] The notions of 'the Germans', 'German' and 'Germany' are used with some (self-)irony in this book. Evidently, none of these are homogeneous, circumscribable entities; it is superfluous to repeatedly draw attention to this by putting them in quotes.

[3] 'Die Deutschen an die Front', *Der Spiegel*, 04/02/91, 19.

[4] Heidemarie Wieczorek-Zeul (SPD) in Deutscher Bundestag, *Plenarprotokoll*, 12/2, Bonn, 14/01/91, 41; Willi Hoss (Bündnis/Die Grünen) in Deutscher Bundestag, *Plenarprotokoll*, 11/235, Bonn, 15/11/90, 18849.

[5] Deutscher Bundestag, *Plenarprotokoll*, 12/3, Bonn, 17/01/91, 46.

[6] Ibid. All translations from the German are mine unless otherwise noted. (Translations below from German novels are likewise mine, and not from the standard published translations.)

when we face an ethico-political question and what is needed is a decision. The responsibility of scholars then lies in acknowledging this gap and the irresolvability of uncertainty.

This book explores some key debates on war memories and offers detailed readings of seven novels which depict the German experience of the Second World War. Although the argument revolves around the politics of war in Germany, most of the book does not concern itself directly with the debates on whether and in what way the FRG should deploy its military.[9] Indeed, it deliberately moves away from the seemingly coherent arguments about the significance of the past for the present and towards the bewildering complexity that emerges from examining articulations of memory. Doing so raises questions not merely about the Germans' memories of the Second World War and their political implications but also about our understandings of truth, ethics, subjectivity, emotion and time. This first chapter sets out the context.

Speaking of war and memory: political debate

The 1991 Gulf War raised the question of war for the newly unified FRG. Using military force was bound to be a problematic proposition, given that the last war was remembered as such an unmitigated disaster. Indeed, throughout the Cold War the FRG had maintained armed forces expressly in order not to use them.[10] Therefore widespread opposition against the war might have been expected, but the fierceness and passion with which it was rejected was perhaps surprising: after all, the FRG was not making any direct military contribution. Yet thousands demonstrated against the war, prompting Michael Schwab-Trapp to comment that Germany seemed to be 'identical' with the peace movement.[11]

Politicians shared the people's consternation that the celebration of the end of the Cold War had so quickly been superseded by what many in Germany saw as the very worst. On the day after US fighting commenced, Hans-Jochen Vogel of the SPD noted in a speech to the Bundestag that he had been a soldier half a century earlier: 'With many of my generation I know what war means. The images of that time are in front of our eyes . . . We feel and suffer with the victims in the entire region, with the people who are dying there.'[12] Otto Graf Lambsdorff of the FDP made

---

[9] These debates are explored in detail in Zehfuss, *Constructivism*.
[10] See Detlef Bald, *Militär und Gesellschaft 1945–1990* (Baden-Baden: Nomos Verlagsgesellschaft 1994), p. 91.
[11] Michael Schwab-Trapp, *Kriegsdiskurse: Die politische Kultur des Krieges im Wandel 1991–1999* (Opladen: Leske und Budrich 2002), p. 98.
[12] Deutscher Bundestag, *Plenarprotokoll*, 12/3, 17/01/91, 47f.

the same gesture: 'Herr Vogel has mentioned it: Herr Dregger and I, we all belong to those who have still personally experienced the last war. We know what we are talking about. None of us wish that the younger people have this experience: war is not the father of all things, it is the father of all horrors.'[13]

Articulations of Second World War memories continued in later debates, when the issue was whether the Bundeswehr should participate in operations abroad. In 1995, speaking about the German contribution to enforcing the peace treaty in Bosnia-Herzegovina, Chancellor Kohl noted that '[i]n many families, also in our own, the memory of the terrible, bitter experiences of the Second World War is still alive'.[14] On the same occasion Elisabeth Altmann of Bündnis90/Die Grünen (hereafter the Greens) referred to her early childhood experience of war: 'I was born in 1943. The first years of my life I spent mostly in the air-raid shelter.'[15] The Bundestag representative for Bosnia, Freimut Duve, when addressing the people's situation there, noted that many members of parliament had had experience of six years of war and hence knew what war meant.[16]

Whilst some politicians invoked war memories mainly to appeal to their audience to imagine the Bosnians' suffering, others explicitly linked them to their position on the question of Bundeswehr deployment. Günter Verheugen of the SPD noted that many of his parliamentary colleagues had experienced the Second World War and the immediate postwar years, and 'know what the German people thought as a consequence of the experience of a terrible war: Away with the weapons!'[17] Jens-Uwe Heuer of the PDS contextualised his opposition to the government's plans with his own memory: 'I belong to that generation that consciously experienced the Second World War as a youth. In the old Federal Republic it was called the generation of the Flak [anti-aircraft battery] assistants. At the time we said after the war: Never, never do we want to carry arms, never again do we want war.'[18] His colleague Gerhard Zwerenz similarly spoke of being in the war and his feeling, as a result, of a 'lifelong unforgettable culpability' that made it impossible for him to agree to any war.[19]

Schmid referred to war as an 'insanity' in which Germans never again would want to have any part; they would, he said, be prepared simply to die if war were to engulf their country as long as they could take with them 'the knowledge that [they] neither encouraged nor committed the crime'. Schmid's words of 1946 reflect the shock at the time about the horror

---

[13] Ibid., 51.   [14] Deutscher Bundestag, *Plenarprotokoll*, 13/76, Bonn, 06/12/95, 6632.
[15] Ibid., 6670.   [16] Deutscher Bundestag, *Plenarprotokoll*, 13/48, Bonn, 30/06/95, 3996.
[17] Ibid., 3988.   [18] Deutscher Bundestag, *Plenarprotokoll*, 13/76, 06/12/95, 6672.
[19] Deutscher Bundestag, *Plenarprotokoll*, 13/48, 30/06/95, 3997.

and destruction of the Second World War, but scholars still identify a strong aversion to war amongst Germans. According to Omer Bartov, Germans see any war as hell.[20] Richard J. Evans observes that the 'bitter experience of the destructive effects of war has left the Germans with a strong and healthy distaste for military adventurism'.[21] And Thomas U. Berger asserts that '[i]n the case of Germany, many contend that the legacy of the Holocaust and other Nazi atrocities has inflicted such deep wounds on the German psyche that large sections of the population are unwilling to once again sanction the use of force in the name of the nation and the state'.[22] Indeed, at the time of unification Chancellor Kohl cited 'never again war' together with 'never again dictatorship' as principles that were fundamental to the Basic Law.[23]

The Germans' allegedly negative attitude towards war is, in view of their past, perhaps understandable. It was an intended outcome of re-education after the Second World War. However, after the end of the Cold War it quickly became a nuisance,[24] for it translated into opposition against international military operations to which 'friends and partners' desired a Bundeswehr contribution.[25] In other words, the German aversion to war came to be out of sync with partners' expectations. Hence politicians and analysts alike asserted the need for the FRG to become more 'normal',[26] to be less focused on and inhibited by the past. Apparently, this happened: from Somalia via Bosnia to Kosovo and Afghanistan the Bundeswehr participated in ever more war-like operations. Therefore the point-blank refusal to contemplate any involvement in the war against Iraq beyond permitting the USA to use their bases on German soil and fly through German airspace looks like a relapse – and one that can be explained away as an election gambit: Chancellor Gerhard Schröder made a populist decision in refusing to participate in an unpopular war. Until then, the FRG had after all been, or so it appeared, on a trajectory

---

[20] Omer Bartov, *Germany's War and the Holocaust: Disputed Histories* (Ithaca: Cornell University Press 2003), p. 12.

[21] Richard J. Evans, 'The New Nationalism and the Old History: Perspectives on the West German *Historikerstreit*', *Journal of Modern History* 59 (1987), 796.

[22] Berger, *Cultures of Antimilitarism*, p. 3.

[23] Deutscher Bundestag, *Plenarprotokoll*, 11/228, Berlin, 04/10/90, 18019.

[24] Actually, it turned out to be a nuisance much earlier, in the early 1950s, when rearmament was at issue. See Abenheim, *Reforging the Iron Cross*; Berger, *Cultures of Antimilitarism*, Chapter 2.

[25] See Zehfuss, *Constructivism*, Chapter 2.

[26] See, for example, Klaus Kinkel, 'Verantwortung, Realismus, Zukunftssicherung', *Frankfurter Allgemeine Zeitung*, 19/03/93, 8; William Horsley, 'United Germany's Seven Cardinal Sins: A Critique of German Foreign Policy', *Millennium: Journal of International Studies* 21 (1992), 225; Franz-Josef Meiers, 'Germany: The Reluctant Power', *Survival* 37 (1995), 82–103.

towards a less historically anguished approach to the use of force. Wolfram Wette claimed that the German contribution to the operation against the Taliban was the first 'war without Hitler' and that it therefore represented a certain normalisation.[27]

Yet the FRG's participation in increasingly war-like operations does not in itself mean that Second World War memories have become less significant in the context of imagining and debating war. Although references to this war have perhaps become less frequent in Bundestag debates on military deployments, they have not disappeared. In the debate over the deployment of Bundeswehr troops to Afghanistan, Foreign Minister Joschka Fischer recalled the destruction that the Second World War had brought to Germany and that was still visible on the Reichstag in which he was speaking. He also referred to the 'never again war' principle and its importance.[28] Friedrich Merz of the CDU/CSU noted the memories of the older generation and their significance to the question of war,[29] and Kerstin Müller of the Greens talked about the 'historical lessons of the catastrophe of Nazi rule and the world war'.[30] 'Historical concerns' also featured in relation to the question of a possible Bundeswehr deployment to Lebanon.[31] Reports of the waning of memory, or of any loss of the significance of this past in political debate, appear premature.

Whilst the memories often led to invoking the 'never again war' principle,[32] some argued that the point was *not* to avoid war at all costs but rather what was conceptualised as 'taking responsibility'. According to Foreign Minister Klaus Kinkel, it was precisely because Germany had 'broken the peace in the past [that] it is morally–ethically obliged to participate in the defence of peace with all its power now'.[33] Hence Germans had to help people who suffered under dictatorship and oppression, even militarily. This meant that 'never again Auschwitz', the other lesson from

---

[27] Wolfram Wette, 'Ein Hitler des Orients? NS-Vergleiche in der Kriegspropaganda von Demokratien', *Gewerkschaftliche Monatshefte* 45 (2003), 239. Chancellor Gerhard Schröder represented the operation as not really a war; he explicitly noted that it involved neither participating in air strikes nor deploying combat troops on the ground. Friedrich Merz (CDU/CSU), however, described it as the 'most dangerous deployment' of the Bundeswehr so far. Deutscher Bundestag, *Plenarprotokoll*, 14/198, Berlin, 08/11/01, 19285 and 19288.

[28] Deutscher Bundestag, *Plenarprotokoll*, 14/198, Berlin, 08/11/01, 19293f.

[29] Deutscher Bundestag, *Plenarprotokoll*, 14/202, Berlin, 16/11/01, 19859.

[30] Ibid., 19869.

[31] See, for example, Ralf Beste et al., 'Abenteuer Nahost', *Der Spiegel*, 21/08/06, 27.

[32] See, for example, Alice H. Cooper, 'When Just Causes Conflict with Acceptable Means: The German Peace Movement and Military Intervention in Bosnia', *German Politics and Society* 15 (1997), 100; see also Zehfuss, *Constructivism*, Chapter 3.

[33] Deutscher Bundestag, *Plenarprotokoll*, 12/240, Bonn, 22/07/94, 21166.

that past, had come to be in tension with 'never again war'.[34] The need to stand up against oppression and dictatorship in the world was an alternative interpretation of the significance of the past for the present and one that could be used to support Bundeswehr participation in international missions. This view increasingly gained ground, especially after the Federal Constitutional Court ruled in 1994 that deployments abroad were not in conflict with the Basic Law. Arguably, the controversial 1995 decision to contribute to a rapid-reaction force in Bosnia constituted a turning-point; later parliamentary decisions in favour of deployments commanded larger cross-party support.[35] This decision is, moreover, of particular interest because Kinkel's speech recommending it to parliament offered a reframing of Second World War memories that was to prove powerful.

Supporting the deployment to Bosnia meant overcoming, or interpreting away, two implications of Second World War memories. Firstly, war in general was remembered as horrible and therefore as something to be avoided; secondly, the war in the Balkans was recalled as particularly cruel. Therefore, or so the argument went, it would be counterproductive and indeed outright dangerous to deploy German soldiers there. This idea that Bundeswehr soldiers could not be sent to the Balkans where Wehrmacht troops had caused havoc during the Second World War was termed the 'Kohl doctrine'.[36] The following statement by Hermann-Otto Solms of the FDP captures the gist of it: 'There must not be under any circumstances any deployment of German troops in the area of the former Yugoslavia – neither on the water nor on the ground nor in the air. This is imperative if only for historical reasons.'[37] The reasoning behind the Kohl doctrine was not necessarily concern for the wounds that might be ripped open for people in the former Yugoslavia at the sight of German troops but rather a fear of escalation and worries about the safety of German soldiers.[38]

In order to overcome both the general rejection of war and its own promise not to deploy soldiers to the Balkans, the government did not downplay Second World War memories but instead reframed them. In June 1995 the UN Security Council issued a mandate for an additional

---

34 Cooper, 'When Just Causes Conflict', 104.
35 Robert H. Dorff, 'Normal Actor of Reluctant Power? The Future of German Security Policy', *European Security* 6 (1997), 56 and 65.
36 Josef Joffe, 'Abschied von der "Kohl-Doktrin"', *Süddeutsche Zeitung*, 16/12/94, 4.
37 Deutscher Bundestag, *Plenarprotokoll*, 12/151, Bonn, 21/04/93, 12941.
38 Klaus Kinkel, 'Peacekeeping missions: Germany can now play its part', *NATO Review* 42/5 (1994), 3–7; 'Länger verheddern', *Der Spiegel*, 02/10/95, 37; 'Wir haben eine neue Rolle übernommen', interview with Volker Rühe, *Der Spiegel*, 16/10/95, 24.

rapid-reaction force to enable UNPROFOR troops already stationed in the former Yugoslavia to fulfil their mission; the Federal Government decided to contribute to the protection and support of this force.[39] In the Bundestag debate about this decision Foreign Minister Kinkel delivered a crucial speech in which he construed the proposed operation as analogous to the Allied 'liberation' of Germany in 1945.[40] Kinkel made it clear that he saw the decision which the Bundestag was about to make as one of historical significance. For him, there was only one possible outcome: 'We want to and have to show solidarity.'[41] In Kinkel's argument the need to contribute to the deployment was based not least on the need to show solidarity with friends and partners, with the countries that had been carrying the burden of casualties in an effort to help other human beings, in particular France and Great Britain, and with those 'innocent' people who were dying cruel deaths in the former Yugoslavia.[42] This claim that solidarity necessitated participating in the operation was embedded in a narrative of the past which comes to its dramatic head in the Allies' liberation of Germany. Kinkel argued that Germans had 'a political and moral obligation to help, also and particularly in view of [their] history'.[43] Crucially, he stressed that the Germans had been freed from Nazi dictatorship by the Allies' use of military force; this had made the new democratic beginning possible. He claimed that what had been forgotten too quickly was that the Germans had not liberated themselves from the regime.

This argument links the deployment under discussion to the duty to oppose oppression and, significantly, represents today's Bundeswehr troops as analogous to the Allied liberators. The parallel created in Kinkel's speech between the heroic liberators and the Bundeswehr is presumably designed to break the more obvious link that had previously been significant: that between Wehrmacht and Bundeswehr. Kinkel had to overcome the Kohl doctrine which entailed implicit reference to the Wehrmacht's conduct on the Eastern front and in the Balkans in particular. Kinkel's argument shifts the focus from the barbarity of the German war to the goodness of the Allied war. Crucially, this shift was apparently successful in terms of justifying the FRG's use of military force:

---

[39] The cabinet decision is printed as 'Europäische Truppe schützen und stützen', *Süddeutsche Zeitung*, 27/06/95, 5. See also 'Deutsche "Tornados" sollen in Bosnien zum Schutz der europäischen Eingreiftruppe eingesetzt werden', *Süddeutsche Zeitung*, 27/06/95, 1.

[40] See also Chapter 2. For a detailed analysis of this speech and its use of norms, see Zehfuss, *Constructivism*, Chapter 3.

[41] Deutscher Bundestag, *Plenarprotokoll*, 13/48, 30/06/95, 3956.

[42] Ibid., 3955f.   [43] Ibid., 3957.

Germany's liberation by the Allies was invoked time and again to underline the need to intervene militarily in situations of human rights abuse and dictatorship.[44] Kinkel himself deployed the same argument again, in relation to Kosovo, in 1998.[45]

Thus, despite the claim that Germans are irretrievably biased against war owing to their past, Second World War memories are used to argue both *for* and *against* war. To put it differently, the same memories that were invoked to reject war were crucial in constructing the possibility of using force abroad. Examining more closely the phenomenon of the Germans' contextualisation of war in relation to their memories of the Second World War, it becomes clear that – far from necessarily biasing them against war for all time – war memories have been used all along to argue both for and against German contributions to military operations.[46] Once Kinkel's argument is made, this is not surprising, for although the Second World War was a catastrophe for Germany, it also eventually made possible a new democratic beginning, at least in the FRG. In other words, the experience and memory of the war are deeply ambiguous. On the one hand, there are the memories of defeat, destruction and suffering; on the other, the Allied liberators – retrospectively speaking – 'brought' peace, freedom and prosperity. Following Kinkel's reframing of the Second World War the Germans, crudely put, had to fight now, because liberation from the Nazi regime had only been achieved through war and outside intervention. They had to be ready to liberate others from oppression and war by violent means, just as the Allies had liberated them. This argument is problematic. Firstly, it assumes that it is possible to end oppression and indeed war itself through war. Secondly, and more fundamentally, the political reasoning is removed from the actual case at hand and instead related to Germany's relation to its past. In other words, the argument is not about the wars in Bosnia or Kosovo; rather, it is about the Germans' role and experience in the Second World War and their alleged meaning for military policy today. Elsewhere I have objected to this argument because of this focus on the self.[47] However, by simply rejecting the argument as problematic an opportunity is lost to examine its implications. Hence I here approach the issue by taking seriously what is said regarding the past and Germans' memories.

---

[44] See Werner Schulz (Bündnis90/Die Grünen) in Deutscher Bundestag, *Plenarprotokoll*, 13/76, 06/12/95, 6665; Guido Westerwelle (FDP) in Deutscher Bundestag, *Plenarprotokoll*, 14/187, Berlin, 19/09/01, 18310.

[45] Deutscher Bundestag, *Plenarprotokoll*, 13/248, Bonn, 16/10/98, 23129.

[46] For a detailed analysis of this phenomenon, see Zehfuss, *Constructivism*, Chapter 3.

[47] Ibid., p. 219.

Clearly, there is no agreement on what the past means in terms of (particular) military deployments today. What, however, remains unsaid in these debates is that there has always been considerable controversy in Germany over how the past should be remembered in the first place. Despite the fundamental significance of Second World War memories to political debate about the military instrument, there was often little or no elaboration of what the experiences that were being invoked actually were. For example, in his contribution to the debate on the deployment to Bosnia, Zwerenz spoke of his 'dreadful' experiences in a Red Army hospital in Minsk in 1944, but left to our imagination what these might have been. He also noted the significance of his contact with White Russians from whom he learnt about German actions in Minsk and the surrounding area in 1941, again without expanding on what these were.[48]

War memories are generally invoked in this way in the political debate. They are called up in one or two sentences, often using established phrases, and their meaning for the political question at issue is asserted. Given the Germans' alleged obsession with their past, particularly in relation to the military, it is tempting to conclude that the brevity of these invocations of memory is at least in part due to the expectation that the memory is shared. However, this expectation, if that is what it is, appears mistaken. In this particular case, despite Zwerenz's confident reference to the Wehrmacht's actions in White Russia, there was an outcry when the exhibition 'War of Extermination: Crimes of the Wehrmacht 1941 to 1944' showed pictures of atrocities committed by the Wehrmacht in White Russia and Serbia.[49] Germans seemed not to share Zwerenz's memory, or indeed the memory implicitly invoked by the Kohl doctrine, which relied on the idea that the Balkans was a particularly unsuitable region for Bundeswehr deployments because of events during the Second World War, sometimes summed up in the acknowledgement that the Wehrmacht had 'wreaked havoc' there. The question as to what extent the Wehrmacht was involved in atrocities indeed turns out to be highly controversial. Many seemed persuaded by what is often called the myth of the 'clean' Wehrmacht: although individual soldiers may have committed atrocities, the Wehrmacht as an institution did not support Nazism and its crimes. Therefore most ordinary soldiers merely fought for the fatherland and remained 'decent'.

Ironically, despite the apparent popularity of this myth, many Germans nevertheless opposed deploying Bundeswehr troops to the Balkans, ostensibly because the Wehrmacht had 'wreaked havoc' there.

---

[48] Deutscher Bundestag, *Plenarprotokoll*, 13/48, 30/06/95, 3997.
[49] See Chapter 4, pp. 129–41.

A similar tension is apparent when the memories called up by Kinkel are examined. He asserted that the Allies liberated the Germans, and nobody challenged him, certainly within the Bundestag debate. Yet at the same time a controversy was raging in Germany about whether the memory of 'liberation' was appropriate at all.[50] Closely exploring German memories of the Second World War thus challenges what is presented as obvious in the debates over the use of the military. The issue is not, however, what the Germans really remember, nor what the lessons are of this past; these questions cannot be answered, nor are they particularly interesting. This book does not offer yet another attempt to ascertain the Germans' memories and explain, understand or predict their resultant political choices, but instead examines significant tensions in and the implications of speaking of memories.

Although politicians from across the political spectrum have referred to the past as significant, one may suspect that Second World War memories are becoming increasingly less important. References to the past were perhaps most noticeable in the Bundestag in the context of the 1991 Gulf War, the deployments to Bosnia and the Kosovo operation, yet they have not disappeared from the debate. Memories in particular of the bombing of German cities seeped into discussions about the Iraq war.[51] The Second World War and its horror continue to be invoked, and not only by those who fought in it or experienced its effects on civilians. Kohl, who was born too late to have been a soldier, pointed out that Germans of the older generation still remembered the horrors of war. But he went further: he claimed that these 'experiences have been deeply ingrained in the memory of our people as a whole'. Therefore Germans, he argued, empathise in a special way with people's suffering in war.[52] He also asserted that Germans were particularly able to understand people's fear of war 'because we have . . . experienced the horrors and sufferings of war on our own bodies'.[53] Duve similarly noted, albeit in a different context, that '[t]his war haunts all of us – those who experienced it as soldiers or children and those who were born after its end'.[54] Thus Kohl and others treated war memories as something that did not merely concern the generation who experienced the war; rather they are something akin to expert knowledge that has been passed on to succeeding generations. Memories of the Second World War are construed not only as crucial for

---

[50] See Chapters 2 and 5.

[51] See Chapter 3, pp. 116–21; by 'the Iraq war' (or 'the war against Iraq') I mean the conflict that began in 2003, as opposed to the 1991 Gulf War.

[52] Deutscher Bundestag, *Plenarprotokoll*, 12/3, 17/01/91, 46.

[53] Deutscher Bundestag, *Plenarprotokoll*, 12/5, 30/01/91, 67.

[54] Deutscher Bundestag, *Plenarprotokoll*, 13/163, Bonn, 13/03/97, 14718. See Chapter 4.

the current attitude to war of the generation that actually experienced that conflict but are also cited as important to the German people more broadly, even those who did not experience the war at the time.

Similarly, whilst it is tempting to see all this talk of the Second World War as one more unsurprising expression of the Germans' obsession with their difficult past, the phenomenon is not confined to Germany. In other countries there are, intriguingly, also references to memories of the Second World War. The war against Iraq, for example, has been construed by Americans in the context of the 'liberation' of Germany and Japan.[55] Although such 'analogies' are controversial, and often seem not to work, it is difficult not to see a link between the enthusiasm with which the six-tieth anniversary of D-Day was celebrated – highlighting the glory of the fight against Nazi barbarity – and the claim that the war against Iraq is part of a larger fight for freedom. The Second World War indeed 'haunts all of us', even if in fundamentally different ways. Americans, as opposed to Germans, remember a 'Good War'.[56] Therefore what is interesting is not so much that Germans, in the context of war, refer to memories of the Second World War. Others do, too. If the Germans' references to memories of the past are different at all, this may be because they remember the other side of the fight. Theirs are memories tainted by guilt, defeat, destruction and misery. This makes it interesting to examine them, as their problematic character means that questions about what it means to articulate them are raised. Thus what is examined here is neither a transient phenomenon that is likely to disappear as war survivors die, nor a uniquely German issue. This is important. The conviction that the deployment of memories of the Second World War in political debate is a peculiarly German phenomenon, and one that may be on the wane, implies that it need not be seriously investigated. Yet 'I remember', or indeed 'we remember', is a powerful claim, and one that therefore does need to be examined.

Speaking of war: novels

In exploring Second World War memories and their political implica-tions this book does not examine merely political controversy and public

---

[55] James Dao, 'Experts debate meaning of regime change', *New York Times*, 22/09/02; Representative Skelton in United States Department of Defense, *Testimony of U.S. Sec-retary of Defense Donald Rumsfeld before the House Armed Services Committee regarding Iraq (Transcript)*, 18/09/02.

[56] Dagmar Barnouw, *The War in the Empty Air: Victims, Perpetrators and Postwar Ger-mans* (Bloomington: Indiana University Press 2005), p. 173f; Trevor B. McCrisken and Andrew Pepper, *American History and Contemporary Film* (New Brunswick: Rutgers University Press 2005), Chapter 4.

debates over appropriate forms of remembering. Rather, it explores a number of novels in detail. To some this may appear to be a detour, and perhaps it is. A good detour is, of course, as much about the significance of the particular route taken as it is about arriving at the final destination. Nor can one explain a detour: it must be taken in order to reveal its attractions. In this section I nevertheless outline why I consider this 'detour' fruitful, why novels constitute an intriguing way of speaking of war and memory.

Novels and war

Novels are closely associated with war. According to Jost Hermand, war literature has existed ever since there has been any literature at all.[57] Rainer Emig categorically states that war is today perceived through literary and cultural fiction.[58] Yet writing about war faces profound problems. For example, as Jochen Pfeifer notes, the 'realistic depiction of atrocities is a dramatic problem of the first order for the war novel in general'.[59] Indeed, any representation would be inadequate. On the other hand, fictional representation may actually be necessary to approach the horrors of the war. This is suggested, for example, by references to literature in factual depictions of war, such as to Hans Erich Nossack's work, in order to describe the situation in Hamburg during the bombing raids.[60] Inasmuch as it is possible at all to represent what war is 'really like', fiction, ironically, may be needed.

Representing war appears to present a particular problem when it comes to depictions of the Second World War. Margot Norris states categorically the impossibility of representing this war.[61] She argues that the 'census of the war dead resists and exceeds both representation and attempts at signification'.[62] In this view, the catastrophe of the Second World War was too enormous to allow for representation. The novels discussed here engage with the German experience of this war, which is

---

[57] Jost Hermand, 'Darstellungen des Zweiten Weltkrieges', in: Jost Hermand (ed.), *Literatur nach 1945 I: Politische und regionale Aspekte* (Wiesbaden: Akademische Verlagsgesellschaft Athenaion 1979), p. 11.

[58] Rainer Emig, *Krieg als Metapher im zwanzigsten Jahrhundert* (Darmstadt: Wissenschaftliche Buchgesellschaft 2001), pp. 39f.

[59] Jochen Pfeifer, *Der deutsche Kriegsroman 1945–1960: Ein Versuch zur Vermittlung von Literatur und Sozialgeschichte* (Königstein/Ts.: Scriptor 1981), p. 201.

[60] Ulrich Schwarz, 'Überall Leichen, überall Tod', in: Stephan Burgdorff and Christian Habbe (eds.), *Als Feuer vom Himmel fiel: Der Bombenkrieg in Deutschland* (Munich: Deutsche Verlags-Anstalt 2003), p. 80. See also Chapter 4.

[61] Margot Norris, *Writing War in the Twentieth Century* (Charlottesville: University Press of Virginia 2000), p. 2.

[62] Ibid., p. 3.

arguably even more problematic. With two exceptions, Kurt Vonnegut's *Slaughterhouse 5* and Harry Mulisch's *Das steinerne Brautbett* (*The Stone Bridal Bed*), they are also written by Germans. All portray war in some way, though some are not war novels in a narrow sense. The portrayal of a war that had not only been lost but that was started and conducted in a brutal and criminal way by a totalitarian regime poses a challenge. Hans Wagener claims that the only possible German war novel would have to be an anti-war novel.[63] Indeed, it is worth noting that the main theme of German war novels may be the futility of war.[64] Yet Wagener's claim, though intuitively persuasive, is problematic for two reasons. Firstly, as Wagener is aware, the claim is inaccurate. Novels published in the 1950s were often heroic in tone, praising the accomplishments of the Wehrmacht. As Wagener himself points out, many early Second World War novels were – surprisingly from today's perspective – in the tradition of the adventure story.[65] These novels helped establish and consolidate the myth of the 'clean' Wehrmacht. Secondly, and more fundamentally, one might ask whether a war novel can ever be an anti-war novel. The war novels (in the narrow sense) explored here seem to be *intended* as anti-war novels, but Vonnegut's *Slaughterhouse 5*, discussed in Chapter 5, explicitly notes the danger of unwittingly making war attractive, even in an 'anti-war novel'. It is, in other words, by no means clear that it is possible to write such a thing as an anti-war novel.

Given the anti-war attitude in Germany and the problem of whether a war novel may ever truly be an anti-war novel, it is perhaps surprising that there are German Second World War novels at all. One might expect war to have been so discredited and the experience of this war so problematic that silence is the only possible response. Indeed, this is suggested by Klaus Harpprecht in relation to the bombing of German cities,[66] and there certainly seems to be no equivalent for the Second World War to Erich Maria Remarque's famous First World War novel *Im Westen nichts Neues* (*All Quiet on the Western Front*).[67] Still, after a brief

---

[63] Hans Wagener, 'Soldaten zwischen Gehorsam und Gewissen: Kriegsromane und -tagebücher', in: Hans Wagener (ed.), *Gegenwartsliteratur und Drittes Reich: Deutsche Autoren in der Auseinandersetzung mit der Vergangenheit* (Stuttgart: Reclam 1977), p. 242.

[64] Alan Bance, 'Germany', in: Holger Klein (ed.) with John Flower and Eric Homberger, *The Second World War in Fiction* (London: Macmillan 1984), p. 101.

[65] Wagener, 'Soldaten', p. 242.

[66] See Volker Hage, *Zeugen der Zerstörung: Die Literaten und der Luftkrieg: Essays und Gespräche* (Frankfurt am Main: S. Fischer Verlag 2003), pp. 118f.

[67] Erich Maria Remarque, *Im Westen nichts Neues*, Edited by Brian Murdoch (London: Routledge 1984). See also Elisabeth Domansky, 'A Lost War: World War II in Postwar German Memory', in: Alvin H. Rosenfeld (ed.), *Thinking about the Holocaust: After Half a Century* (Bloomington: Indiana University Press 1997), pp. 241f.

period of silence, the first West German war novels appeared in 1949.[68] There was a considerable amount of writing on the war until the mid-1950s, and some of the books were popular successes. Hans Hellmut Kirst's light-hearted trilogy *08/15*, for example, sold 1.8 million copies.[69] According to Alan Bance, a smaller number of significant war novels were written after 1955, though 'the popular, adventure-story kind of war book still thrived'.[70] Pfeifer similarly observes that 'after 1960 few significant war novels were published, and these are clearly different from those of the 1950s'.[71] There is, in other words, a gap after the 'early' war novels, a period in which there appears to have been little writing about the Second World War, though Bance acknowledges some publications and republications in the 1970s.[72] Volker Hage also observes this gap but, with respect specifically to writing on bombing against German cities, he asserts that the gap was one in reception, not production.[73]

Novels and politics

The 'gap' – whatever its reason – and the discussion of it in the secondary literature is interesting insofar as it points to a link between the questions society is exposed to and the literature that is written or, at least, read. Indeed, Wagener asserts a relationship between the 'slowly swelling flood of war novels in West Germany' shortly after the Second World War and the debate about rearmament, the EDC (European Defence Community) Treaty signed in 1952 and the possible implications of nuclear war. He supports this claim by observing that fewer such novels were published after 1955, when the FRG had become integrated into NATO.[74] This reasoning also seems to be supported by Gert Ledig's insistence that his *Die Stalinorgel* (*The Stalin Organ*) – a novel stressing the senselessness and horror of war – was merely a *Kampfschrift*, that is, a text written to support a particular (political) goal.[75] The interaction between political questions and literature is further emphasised by political debates about war and memory which novels are seen to have sparked off.[76]

It is important, however, to acknowledge the widespread criticism of German Second World War fiction. The secondary literature on

---

[68] Wagener, 'Soldaten', p. 241.
[69] Walter Nutz, 'Der Krieg als Abenteuer und Idylle: Landser-Hefte und triviale Kriegsromane', in: Hans Wagener (ed.), *Gegenwartsliteratur und Drittes Reich: Deutsche Autoren in der Auseinandersetzung mit der Vergangenheit* (Stuttgart: Reclam 1977), p. 265; Hans Hellmut Kirst, *08/15* (Munich: Wilhelm Goldmann Verlag n.d.).
[70] Bance, 'Germany', p. 92.   [71] Pfeifer, *Der deutsche Kriegsroman*, p. 9.
[72] Bance, 'Germany', p. 94.   [73] See Chapter 3, p. 85.
[74] Wagener, 'Soldaten', p. 241.   [75] Quoted in Hage, *Zeugen der Zerstörung*, p. 45.
[76] See Chapter 2.

German postwar war fiction focuses on the political implications of the texts, often leaving to one side the question of literary merit; it largely objects to the novels' alleged politics. Wagener analyses West German war novels in order to examine the representation and criticism of the Third Reich in the most important texts. He explores a series of themes: the moral dilemma of fighting for the wrong cause, the failure of the officer caste, doubts and insights in war diaries and reports, and the politics of omission. He concludes that in 'most war novels a serious analysis of the Third Reich only takes place in brief dialogues'.[77] In novels depicting the Second World War there is little discussion of the causes of or reasons for the war, or other questions of policy. The war presents itself to the characters as inevitable; what is at issue is how they cope with the war, not how they came to be in it in the first place. Generally, the books zoom in on individuals' experiences. Pfeifer argues that 'through objectification the individual can more easily be represented as victim of the powerful conditions', especially where the narrative perspective is that of the lower military ranks. As a result, German writing on the war has – aptly, according to Pfeifer – been termed *Obergefreitenliteratur* (literature of the lance corporals): the main characters rarely hold a higher military rank.[78] This conveniently provides a reason not to have them discuss war aims or policy. In Lothar-Günther Buchheim's book *Das Boot* (*The Boat*), for example, famous owing to its cinematic rendition, political debate is, Wagener claims, intentionally excluded.[79] Bance, who is concerned particularly with how 'the central questions of the Eastern campaign' – basically the topic of atrocities – are 'deflected in war literature', sums up this problematic:

Common to most war books (but particularly useful when dealing with the war in the East) is the limitation of perspective to that of the small man, a 'corporal's point of view' which permits a very limited grasp of the war as a whole, concentrates on the individual, and rules out extensive discussion of German policy or war aims.[80]

In other words, the 'kind of life lived by the ordinary soldier on active service is a good alibi (in terms of faithfulness to reality, mimesis) for the writer's own limitation of his perspective'.[81] In some ways this perspective is justifiable: it reflects the authors' military experiences. The

[77] Wagener, 'Soldaten', p. 242.   [78] Pfeifer, *Der deutsche Kriegsroman*, p. 60f.
[79] Wagener, 'Soldaten', p. 258; Lothar-Günther Buchheim, *Das Boot* (München: Piper Verlag 1973).
[80] A. F. Bance, 'The Brutalization of Warfare on the Eastern Front: History and Fiction', in: Ian Higgins (ed.), *The Second World War in Literature* (Edinburgh: Scottish Academic Press 1986), p. 106.
[81] Ibid., p. 107.

criticism is, however, that the situation of the lower ranks is universalised and too easily accepted, and, as a result, the Germans appear to have had no hand in bringing about the situation that is experienced as so horrible. This affects how readers relate to the events depicted. Pfeifer argues that the perspective of the lance corporal 'prevents a historical interpretation, as well as insights into essential connections of the war. It makes easier the identification of the reader with the depicted suffering and the conflicts of the soldiers.'[82] To put it bluntly, soldiers in these novels are victims rather than culpable agents. For example, the 'theme of betrayal of German troops (by their leaders, by the regime) is almost ubiquitously present',[83] whilst few novels engage the German soldiers' deep-seated blind obedience.[84] Whilst Heinrich Böll's title *Wo warst du, Adam? (And where were you, Adam?)*[85] could be read as a demand for individual accountability, the answer 'I was in the world war' can also be seen as an escape from responsibility. Ernestine Schlant argues that this answer, given in the epitaph to the book, 'takes refuge in an alibi that seemingly submerges the individual in the enormity of the world war'.[86]

Overall, Pfeifer complains that German war novels disconnect war from politics, even when they take a clear position against war and include typical episodes from politics.[87] In a similar vein, Bance asserts that '[i]n fiction as in reality, the tendency in the *Bundesrepublik* has been to separate the fighting aspect of the Second World War from its political context'.[88] Wagener agrees that the omission of political questions must be criticised.[89] Hermand, more drastically, reasons that, after 1952/3, with the emerging Cold War, an increasing justification of the war experience turned more and more into an 'open apology for the past'.[90] The gist of these criticisms is that the exclusion of the political context performed in the novels is impossible, and that it is therefore itself political. Put differently, 'any German war novel . . . is inevitably received as a political statement'.[91] The political statement allegedly implied by the novels is then problematic, inasmuch as it excludes or denies not only the larger political context of the Third Reich but also the immediately relevant matter of the armed forces' role and conduct.

---

[82] Pfeifer, *Der deutsche Kriegsroman*, p. 61. See also Bance, 'Germany', p. 107.

[83] Bance, 'Brutalization of Warfare', p. 107.   [84] Pfeifer, *Der deutsche Kriegsroman*, p. 118.

[85] Heinrich Böll, *Wo warst du, Adam? und Erzählungen* (Cologne: Friedrich Middelhauve Verlag 1967).

[86] Ernestine Schlant, *The Language of Silence: West German Literature and the Holocaust* (New York: Routledge 1999), p. 30. Schlant's 'critical' expectations are problematic, as Barnouw observes, *War in the Empty Air*, p. 267, n. 41.

[87] Pfeifer, *Der deutsche Kriegsroman*, p. 111.   [88] Bance, 'Brutalization of Warfare', p. 105.

[89] Wagener, 'Soldaten', p. 261.   [90] Hermand, 'Darstellungen', p. 30.

[91] Bance, 'Germany', p. 107.

Pfeifer observes that 'in most of the novels there are no Nazis at all'.[92] Where Nazis in the Wehrmacht are depicted, they are often represented as an isolated group, shunned by the majority. This is well illustrated by a memoir that found a wide readership. Peter Bamm's *Die unsichtbare Flagge* (*The Invisible Flag*) construes the soldiers, particularly those who are part of the medical profession, as adhering to an ethos that sets them apart from the Nazis. Interestingly, the Nazis are only ever referred to as 'the others' in this book.[93] Christian Graf von Krockow notes in relation to the debate about Wehrmacht atrocities that such a book would be unthinkable today. Although it does not conceal the fact that there were crimes, they are represented as 'not really amongst the ranks of the Wehrmacht'. The criminals thus were not 'us' but 'the others'.[94] In other words, Bamm's book, and arguably novels about the Second World War more generally, confirm the myth that most soldiers were basically decent and at best misguided. Bance stresses the reluctance, in German literature, to acknowledge Wehrmacht barbarity.[95] Two points are important here. Firstly, Bance's observation is pertinent in terms of the memory of the Wehrmacht as the organisation that remained 'clean' during the Third Reich, an untenable but persistent myth that literature could be seen as complicit in creating and maintaining. Secondly, Bance sees in this complicity an outright failure of literature to fulfil its role in society:

This failure of the West German writer – on the whole – to perform his proper function and go against the grain (which is what a free democratic society is supposed to pay writers to do) only indicates, perhaps, that you cannot have instant democracy. Yet, since war novelists otherwise faithfully respected the circumstantial detail of authentic reporting, realistic time-scale and historical accuracy, their omission or evasion of certain aspects of the Second World War amounted to an even more successful hidden persuasion practised upon a willing public.[96]

Thus Bance expects writers not simply to reflect attitudes of the population but to go 'against the grain'. Below I discuss related points about literature and counter-memory, and the idea that literature is an institution that is, in principle, free from constraint.

In sum, the concerns over the political bias evident in German war novels which allegedly suppress the involvement of the Wehrmacht in the Nazi regime and its atrocities might be seen to suggest that one is ill advised to engage with this literature, in particular in any study related

---

[92] Pfeifer, *Der deutsche Kriegsroman*, p. 135.
[93] Peter Bamm, *Die unsichtbare Flagge* (Frankfurt am Main: Fischer Bücherei 1957).
[94] Christian Graf von Krockow, 'Zwei Pole, die das Verhängnis bargen', in: Heribert Prantl (ed.), *Wehrmachtsverbrechen: Eine deutsche Kontroverse* (Hamburg: Hoffmann und Campe 1997), p. 153.
[95] Bance, 'Brutalization of Warfare', p. 112.   [96] Ibid., p. 99.

to political questions. Crucially, the seriousness of the allegation against German war novels – essentially of making the war and the regime look better than they were, not least by concealing crimes – is not denied here. It must therefore be clarified from the outset that the reading of novels in this book is undertaken not to tease out their political 'message' or to discover what some of them claim to offer: insights into what the war was 'really like'. Rather, it is crucial to tease out how novels, which speak in a different voice, may disturb the official memory of war and other certainties (such as, at times, what appears to be their own intended 'message').

Reading memory

Novels dealing with the Second World War can be seen as one way of coming to terms with the past.[97] In doing so, they may challenge or go beyond officially enacted memory, though art may equally reinforce official political messages or support problematic ideas about the past, such as the myth of the 'clean' Wehrmacht. Reiko Tachibana explicitly explores literature as counter-memory of the Second World War in Japan and Germany, focusing on the experiences of Hiroshima and Nagasaki and the Holocaust respectively.[98] She argues that the writing she examines 'seeks a liberation of the reader from a dogmatic perspective on, or blindness toward, the legacies of World War II, aiming instead at provocation toward an active participation in history'.[99] Tachibana notes that one quality of narratives about the war is 'an awareness of the process of writing itself'.[100] She asserts that 'postwar narrative in both countries has a strong tendency to become writing about writing, as well as writing about the war: words are a means of remembering and revisioning history'.[101]

In offering counter-memories novels constitute a form of testimony; this may be seen to be in tension with their fictionality. This tension and the novels' reflection on what they do are crucial to what is argued here. In other words, what makes examining novels a fruitful move is the double function of literature. It not only reflects the preoccupations of society but may also challenge them. It not only offers up particular memories – sometimes as testimony – but also reflects upon and raises questions about what it means to remember. Unlike the political debate which seems to simply assume that we know what it means to

---

[97] Pfeifer, *Der deutsche Kriegsroman*, p. 6.
[98] Reiko Tachibana, *Narrative as Counter-Memory: A Half-Century of Postwar Writing in Germany and Japan* (Albany: State University of New York Press 1998).
[99] Ibid., p. 2.   [100] Ibid., p. 253.   [101] Ibid., p. 254.

remember – and that this is unproblematic – novels tell memories and at the same time challenge their possibility. This has the potential to provoke critical thinking or, as Tachibana puts it, the reader's active participation.

Some of the novels discussed here suggest that we cannot speak of the past in the way in which we do, whilst at the same time doing precisely that. Memory may be profoundly problematic, but it is also unavoidable. We have to take account of the way the past 'now imposes itself',[102] even if it never existed in the way it now appears. Despite, or perhaps because of, this problematic character of memory, it has ethico-political implications. Tim Woods argues that memory is 'a key for the ethical representation of the past, and literature, as a mechanism for collective memory which opens up the past to scrutiny, can act ethically by resisting dogmatic, fixed, closed narratives'.[103] In other words, literature is a particularly interesting memory practice, one which may not only depart from officially enacted memory but present what Tachibana, following Michel Foucault, calls 'counter-memory', that is, a necessary opposition to the reassuring stability of traditional history. There are two aspects to this. One is, crucially, the ability of literature to disturb what is accepted. Woods puts this beautifully when he says that 'literature is a site/territory where "noise" may be fed into the efforts to "quieten" history'.[104] The other is the intimate relation between literature and memory in the first place. Aleida Assmann claims that 'memory and literature have always been connected to each other in the closest possible way'.[105] Indeed, it appears to be difficult to find a novel that does not engage the question of memory. Unsurprisingly, then, reading literature as memory is an accepted feature of Holocaust studies and the study of war and memory.[106] Thus my use of novels to explore German Second World War memories is not unusual.

---

[102] Martin Walser, *Ein springender Brunnen* (Frankfurt am Main: Suhrkamp 2000), p. 9.
[103] Tim Woods, 'Mending the Skin of Memory: Ethics and History in Contemporary Narratives', *Rethinking History* 2 (1998), 346.
[104] Tim Woods, 'Spectres of History: Ethics and Postmodern Fictions of Temporality', in: Dominic Rainsford and Tim Woods (eds.), *Critical Ethics: Text, Theory and Responsibility* (Basingstoke: Macmillan 1999), p. 119.
[105] Aleida Assmann, *Erinnerungsräume: Formen und Wandlungen des kulturellen Gedächtnisses* (Munich: Verlag C.H. Beck 1999), p. 103.
[106] See, for example, Lawrence L. Langer, *The Holocaust and the Literary Imagination* (New Haven: Yale University Press 1975); Shoshana Felman and Dori Laub, *Testimony: Crises of Witnessing in Literature, Psychoanalysis, and History* (New York: Routledge 1992); Dominick LaCapra, *History and Memory after Auschwitz* (Ithaca: Cornell University Press 1998); Paul Fussell, *The Great War and Modern Memory* (Oxford: Oxford University Press 1975); George L. Mosse, *Fallen Soldiers: Reshaping the Memory of the World Wars* (Oxford: Oxford University Press 1990); Winter, *Sites of Memory*.

Generally speaking, memory, and its significance to politics, has attracted increasing interest. The role of memory in 'imagining community'[107] has been noted, and memorials and commemorations have been analysed in terms of their political significance, for example.[108] Jenny Edkins in particular has highlighted both the state's desire and power to impose particular memories and individuals' resistance to this.[109] In other words, how the past is remembered is a crucial site of political struggle, and one that cannot be passed over when examining how the remembered past is invoked in political debate. This book approaches the intersection of war, memory and literature in the spirit of a 'general strategy of deconstruction'.[110] What is at issue is not discovering what is being remembered and how that might affect political choices, but interrogating the logic within which articulations of memory operate. Jonathan Culler explains that to 'deconstruct a discourse is to show how it undermines the philosophy it asserts, or the hierarchical oppositions on which it relies, by identifying in the text the rhetorical operations that produce the supposed ground of argument, the key concept or premise'.[111] Deconstruction relies on simultaneous inversion and displacement. This double movement is designed to address the oppositions and contradictions necessarily involved in language without either neutralising them or reaffirming them. As Derrida explains:

On the one hand, we must traverse a phase of *overturning*. To do justice to this necessity is to recognize that in a classical philosophical opposition we are not dealing with a peaceful coexistence of a *vis-à-vis*, but rather with a violent hierarchy. One of the terms governs the other (axiologically, logically, etc.), or has the upper hand. To deconstruct the opposition, first of all, is to overturn the hierarchy at a given moment. To overlook this phase of overturning is to forget the conflictual and subordinating structure of the opposition.[112]

This phase of overturning is crucial in order not to neutralise the opposition, which in practice would leave the hierarchy in place. It is only possible to intervene in a field of signification by going through this phase.

---

[107] Benedict Anderson, *Imagined Communities: Reflections on the Origin and Spread of Nationalism*, Revised edn (London: Verso 1991).
[108] For example Winter, *Sites of Memory*.
[109] Jenny Edkins, *Trauma and the Memory of Politics* (Cambridge: Cambridge University Press 2003).
[110] Jacques Derrida, *Positions*, Translated and annotated by Alan Bass (London: Athlone Press 1987), p. 41.
[111] Jonathan Culler, *On Deconstruction: Theory and Criticism after Structuralism* (London: Routledge 1983), p. 86.
[112] Derrida, *Positions*, p. 41. See also Jacques Derrida, *Limited Inc* (Evanston: Northwestern University Press 1988), p. 21.

Indeed, one has to go through this phase continuously, as the hierarchy of binary oppositions always re-establishes itself.[113] Although the overturning is necessary, it is not sufficient. It is crucial to move towards a new term which is no longer part of the previous regime.[114] Deconstruction therefore works through a 'double gesture',[115] a reversal and a displacement. In Culler's words, to 'deconstruct an opposition is to undo and displace it, to situate it differently'.[116] This explanation stresses how deconstruction may be deployed in reading a text. Significantly, however, deconstruction is 'an event that does not await deliberation, consciousness or organisation of a subject'; rather, it 'takes place'.[117] It is not a question of adding something to the text: the text already undermines itself, falls apart under the weight of its own assumptions. As Derrida observes, 'there is always already deconstruction, at work *in* works, especially in *literary* works'.[118] The text produced by how the past is spoken of in political discourse similarly comes apart.[119] The way in which we speak of the past is, as will be shown, undermined by its own assumptions.

Showing how texts are undermined by their own assumptions, are always already deconstructing, involves engaging in what Derrida calls a 'nontranscendent reading'.[120] In such a reading one is not concerned to find the meaning of the text or a presumed referent – which at any rate do not exist – but rather to tease out the multiple significations of the text, for '[m]eaning [*sens*] and effect are never produced or refused absolutely; they always keep a reserve at the disposition of a potential reader, a reserve that has less to do with a substantial wealth and more with an aleatory margin in the trajectories, an impossibility of saturating a context'.[121] In such a reading authorial intention is not decisive. The act of reading is important; it is, one might say, another act of writing. Derrida explains that:

---

[113] Derrida, *Positions*, p. 42.   [114] Ibid., pp. 42f.
[115] Derrida, *Limited Inc*, p. 21.   [116] Culler, *On Deconstruction*, p. 150.
[117] Jacques Derrida, 'Letter to a Japanese Friend', in: David Wood and Robert Bernasconi, *Derrida and Difference* (Coventry: Parousia Press 1985), p. 5.
[118] Jacques Derrida, *Memoires for Paul de Man: The Wellek Library Lectures at the University of California, Irvine*, Revised edn, Translated by Cecile Lindsay, Jonathan Culler, Eduardo Cadava and Peggy Kamuf (New York: Columbia University Press 1989), p. 123.
[119] 'Text', of course, does not just mean written words; it 'implies all the structures called "real", "economic", "historical", "socio-institutional", in short: all possible referents'. Derrida, *Limited Inc*, p. 148.
[120] Jacques Derrida, *Acts of Literature*, Edited by Derek Attridge (London: Routledge 1992), p. 44.
[121] Jacques Derrida, *Points . . . Interviews, 1974–1994*, Edited by Elisabeth Weber, translated by Peggy Kamuf and others (Stanford: Stanford University Press 1995), p. 175.

literature depends on reading and the right conferred on it by an experience of reading. One can read the same text – which thus never exists 'in itself' – as a testimony that is said to be serious and authentic, or as an archive, or as a document, or as a symptom – or as a work of literary fiction that simulates all of the positions that we have just enumerated.[122]

This has two significant implications. Firstly, it is impossible to distin-guish – once and for all – between fiction and non-fiction: 'the border between literature and its other becomes undecidable'.[123] Secondly, read-ing has significant implications and thus calls on responsibility.

Fiction may be read as testimony, and some Second World War novels are, although fictitious, offered as such; they respond to a desire to know. The undecidability of the boundaries between genres does 'not in the least invalidate the exigency of truthfulness, sincerity or objectivity, any more than it authorizes a confusion between good faith and false testi-mony. But the chaos remains (*demeure*), from which alone a right (*juste*) reference to truth emerges'.[124] Indeed, Derrida argues, literature is nec-essary to testimony, if such a thing exists: 'if the testimonial is by law irreducible to the fictional, there is no testimony that does not struc-turally imply in itself the possibility of fiction, simulacra, dissimulation, lie, and perjury – that is to say, the possibility of literature, of the innocent or perverse literature that innocently plays at perverting all of these dis-tinctions'.[125] Testimony may never be entirely separated from literature, for that would entail its disappearance: 'In order to remain testimony, it must therefore allow itself to be haunted. It must allow to be parasitized by precisely what it excludes from its inner depths, the *possibility*, at least, of literature.'[126] Thus any testimony structurally implies the possibility of fiction. It is therefore not possible to exclude fiction from testimony by focusing on other practices of truth-telling such as documentary writing, interviewing witnesses or television reports. Fiction is necessary for any such representation to be possible.

Crucially, fiction is not only a symptom, a sign of its times, but a simulation, self-reflective, designed to create an effect. Derrida observes that:

Even given that some texts appear to have a greater potential for formalization, literary works *and* works which say a lot about literature and therefore about themselves, works whose performativity, in some sense, appears the greatest pos-sible in the smallest possible space, this can give rise only to evaluations inscribed

---

[122] Jacques Derrida, *Demeure: Fiction and Testimony*, in Maurice Blanchot, *The Instant of my Death*/Jacques Derrida, *Demeure: Fiction and Testimony*, Translated by Elizabeth Rottenberg (Stanford: Stanford University Press 2000), p. 29.
[123] Ibid., p. 92.   [124] Ibid.   [125] Ibid., p. 29.   [126] Ibid., p. 30.

in a context, to positioned readings which are themselves formalizing and performative. Potentiality is not hidden in a text like an intrinsic property.[127]

The text is performative, but what is being performed is not exhausted within the text itself: it requires reading. Given that readings are 'themselves formalizing and performative', reading calls for responsibility: 'A reader is not a consumer, a spectator, a visitor, not even a "receiver".'[128] Indeed, 'there is no text before and outside reading'.[129] Rather, the process is marked by 'a duel of singularities, a duel of writing and reading'.[130] Or, to put this differently, both reader and writer are engaged in writing, together and simultaneously against each other. Neither 'writer' nor 'reader' controls the process, nor may either of them evade responsibility. Derrida argues that the writer, in one sense, has a 'duty of irresponsibility, of refusing to reply for one's thought or writing to constituted powers' which he sees as 'perhaps the highest form of responsibility'.[131] Writing does not have one pre-determined meaning that must be discovered; rather, multiple readings are possible. I take this not only as a licence to read the novels under discussion in ways that raise interesting questions but also as a reminder of the responsibility of *my* reader.

This is particularly significant, because Derrida considers literature to be the institution which 'gives *in principle* the power to say everything, to break free of the rules'. Literature 'implies that licence is given to the writer to say everything he wants to or everything he can, while remaining shielded, safe from all censorship, be it religious or political'.[132] This is important in relation to a topic as sensitive as German Second World War memories. Some of the limitations of political debate have already become apparent and will be discussed throughout this book. Literature may go beyond such constraints, although some believe that there was a prohibition against writing about German suffering, for example. Literary critic Marcel Reich-Ranicki rejects such a view in relation to Allied bombing against German cities. According to Reich-Ranicki, there are no taboos in literature, much as Derrida asserts that literature may in principle address anything: 'The writer may depict everything – but he may not flee from the question why he has depicted it.'[133] Reich-Ranicki concedes that many writers are not up to some topics; literature as such, however, is equal to all topics.[134]

---

[127] Derrida, *Acts of Literature*, pp. 46f.   [128] Ibid., p. 51.   [129] Ibid., p. 58.
[130] Ibid., p. 69.   [131] Ibid., p. 38.   [132] Ibid., p. 37.
[133] 'Als das Ghetto brannte', interview with Marcel Reich-Ranicki, in: Volker Hage, *Zeugen der Zerstörung: Die Literaten und der Luftkrieg: Essays und Gespräche* (Frankfurt am Main: S. Fischer Verlag 2003), p. 243.
[134] Ibid.

Literature may thus be crucial due to its ability – in principle – to tackle any topic and its freedom – in principle – to say anything. Crucially, however, Derrida warns that 'the freedom to say everything is a very powerful political weapon, but one which might immediately let itself be neutralized as a fiction'.[135] In other words, it is important not to dismiss reading literature as an interesting endeavour but one that does not contribute to or challenge the serious business of politics. Clearly, my readings cannot claim for themselves that they are final, correct. Their point is not so much to make an argument, although that is of course part of any academic endeavour. Mindful both of the power of fiction and the ever-present danger of its neutralisation, it is to make an intervention.

Speaking of the Second World War (and not the Holocaust)

This book zooms in on memories of the Second World War, especially as represented by novels. They involve, amongst other things, German soldiers shot to pieces, civilians barbecued in fire storms set off by Allied bombing and children drowning in the freezing Baltic Sea. We do not, in contrast, find in the novels German soldiers massacring civilians, executing 'partisans' and setting villages alight, nor is there any discussion of the Holocaust. Therefore the emerging picture of the Second World War is one of a cruel but 'normal' war. Although historical accuracy is not the point, it is necessary to comment on what is not an accidental omission but a deliberate strategy, a strategy that I embark upon realising that in the eyes of some this puts me in a 'revisionist' camp, intent on exculpating the Germans.

In his *Wages of Guilt: Memories of War in Germany and Japan* Ian Buruma claims that the 'German war was not only remembered on television, on the radio, in community halls, schools and museums; it was actively worked on, labored, rehearsed. One sometimes got the impression, especially in Berlin, that German memory was like a massive tongue seeking out, over and over, a sore tooth.'[136] Although his title suggests otherwise, Buruma's book is actually about memories of the Holocaust. Buruma explains that he focuses on the war against the Jews 'since it was that parallel war, rather than, say, the U-boat battles in the Atlantic, or even the battle of Stalingrad, that left the most sensitive scar on the collective memory of (West) Germany'.[137] Buruma is arguably not alone

---

[135] Derrida, *Acts of Literature*, p. 38.
[136] Ian Buruma, *Wages of Guilt: Memories of War in Germany and Japan* (Vintage: London 1995), p. 8.
[137] Ibid., p. 10.

when he says 'war' but chiefly means 'the Holocaust'. Indeed, Elizabeth Domansky diagnoses a 'displacement of World War II by the Holocaust' in German politics of memory from the late 1960s onwards.[138] Dagmar Barnouw even claims that the war has been, for Germans, 'a terra incognita, inaccessible for want of information except the Evil of Nazi persecutions'.[139] She argues that the 'nearly total exclusion from historical memory of German wartime experiences, among them large-scale air raids, mass deportations, and warfare involving millions of conscripts, has over the decades created a serious loss of historical reality'.[140] In Barnouw's view the Germans have not just forgotten the war, 'they forgot having forgotten'.[141]

Thus one might conclude that the war has, for the Germans, disappeared behind the Holocaust, and this would appear to be confirmed by the enormous interest in the Holocaust in history, journalism and literature that was, until recently, not matched by an equivalent interest in the war. But memories of the Second World War, whether or not they had ever disappeared, have now re-emerged in the public domain. The Second World War is 'in', Robert G. Moeller alleges.[142] Some articulations of Second World War memories have an air of grievance about them, fuelling concerns that the Germans are in the business of construing themselves as victims of the war. Yet the possibility of German self-pity is a poor reason to shy away from scrutinising Second World War memories; this accusation prevents engagement with the political and ethical issues involved. Crucially, the Second World War is being offered as (implicit) justification for wars today; we have to start taking seriously questions about whether it may legitimately provide the moral certainty that it is invoked to convey.

In some ways, the war – if such a distinction can be made at all – is indeed more ethically challenging than the Holocaust. What I mean by this is that the Holocaust is in one sense ethically trivial: there is agreement that exterminating civilians on a large scale is bad. The war, however, is not so simple. This is exemplified in the myth of the 'clean' Wehrmacht which is possible precisely because fighting for one's country is often seen not only as acceptable but imperative, whether or not one's country is in the wrong. One may, of course, have doubts as to whether fighting on behalf of a country that is engaged in exterminating an entire people, and thereby supporting this policy, could ever be

---

[138] Domansky, 'A Lost War', pp. 246 and 251–8.
[139] Barnouw, *War in the Empty Air*, p. xii.   [140] Ibid.   [141] Ibid., p. xiv.
[142] Robert G. Moeller, 'On the History of Man-Made Destruction: Loss, Death, Memory, and Germany in the Bombing War', *History Workshop Journal* 61 (2006), 103.

justified – but that is precisely the point: this discussion is likely to be more difficult than that about whether exterminating another people can be justified.

The Second World War memories articulated in the German context illustrate the horror of war; it seems inappropriate to dismiss them because the suffering they recall was set off not by those who inflicted it but by the aggressive policies of the Third Reich. The suffering does not cease to exist, become less painful to remember or indeed less relevant to situations of war today because it occurred in response to a war of aggression or because the German people at the same time committed unimaginable atrocities. Thus my focus on the Second World War as a war – that is, an armed conflict, rather than an adjunct to the Holocaust – is not an inevitable outcome of the use of novels which are seen to be guilty of excluding the Holocaust and its political context, but is in the spirit of a Derridean overturning, a necessary phase. We tend to consider the Holocaust as primary, as crucial to any understanding. Here, I turn this around, setting aside the Holocaust and treating the war as central. Of course, it will become apparent that it is not possible to separate the two. Not least the debate about Wehrmacht atrocities discussed in Chapter 4 shows that the spectre of the Holocaust lurks not beyond but within the war. In Chapter 6, therefore, I bring the Holocaust back in, highlighting the inseparability of the two, and consider how the phase of overturning has changed our understanding of the ethico-political stakes.

The desire to exclude on ethical grounds Second World War memories that focus on German suffering is a recurrent theme in Chapters 2 and 3, which explore the expulsions of Germans from Eastern territories and the Allied bombing of German cities respectively. In other words, concerns are expressed about alleged attempts to construe Germans as victims of the Second World War. Chapter 2 takes its cue from accusations of forgetting. Through a reading of Günter Grass's *Im Krebsgang* (*Crabwalk*) it explores the tension between the need to remember and the desire to forget in the context of the expulsions, which are often construed as having been taboo or forgotten in the FRG in recent decades. Given the value attached to remembering, particularly in relation to the Third Reich, forgetting comes itself to be an ill to avoid. This not only leads to an ironic performative contradiction when it is claimed that remembering the expulsions is problematic. The chapter also shows that the matter is more complex, that forgetting is an inevitable part of remembering. The implications of this are pushed further by exploring how Wehrmacht atrocities are simultaneously forgotten and remembered in the justification of Bundeswehr operations abroad.

Chapter 3 explores perhaps the most 'unwelcome' of German memories of the Second World War, those of the bombing of cities by the British and Americans. These memories remain difficult to address not only because of the ever-present fear of representing Germans as victims but also because of the thorny question of how to speak of the horrors inflicted upon German civilians by the heroic liberators. The chapter shows recent debates to be caught up in, and limited by, such concerns and explores two novels in a bid to go beyond such confines. Gert Ledig's *Vergeltung (Retaliation)* draws the reader into the sheer horror of an air raid in which both German civilians and Allied airmen die in the cruellest ways, thereby ignoring the sensitivities about constructing victimhood. Harry Mulisch's *Das steinerne Brautbett* also raises the question of whether inflicting such horrors may ever be ethical. Relating the memories of Allied strategic bombing through reading these novels to the question of the current war against Iraq, the chapter highlights the painfulness of such memories. Emotion, which lies beyond what we commonly understand to be knowledge, but is inextricably linked to remembering the Second World War, is then explored as an important aspect of our engagement with war today.

Chapter 4 considers another emotional debate, that about the exhibition on Wehrmacht atrocities. It turns to two novels that are very different from each other, but that are both accused of excluding the political context; they also do not really engage with Wehrmacht atrocities. Nevertheless, they raise significant questions. Ledig's *Die Stalinorgel*, which can be seen to artistically re-create the immediacy of war, confronts the reader not only with its horror but also with the deep confusion experienced by soldiers in combat. In Ledig's representation war is hell, no matter what its purpose or which side one may be on. In contrast, Walser's *Ein springender Brunnen (A Gushing Fountain)* approaches war from the perspective of a young boy who is keen to be called up and prove himself at the front, though he never actually is. Walser contextualises his story within reflections on the problematic of memory, in particular that when we remember we no longer are who we were. Taken together these two texts not only undermine the idea of the Allied 'Good War' but also engage in interesting ways with problems of truth and ethics in the context of fiction and memory. Fiction which is often construed as the opposite of truth is, ironically, at the same time *necessary* to representations of war. The chapter explores the question of the ethics of truth, the need to make decisions in the face of ethico-political questions and the problem of how emotions relate to these issues.

Chapter 5 explores how our understanding of temporality is in question when it comes to memory. Memory is often seen to be *in* the present but *about* the past; memories may therefore change over time but not their allegedly objective referent, the past that is remembered. This clear distinction between the remembering and the remembered on the basis of an equally clear distinction between the past and the present is, however, problematic. Although the end of the war is now remembered by many Germans as 'liberation', this is actually a controversial interpretation. The chapter treats this not as a problem of *whether* or not Germany was liberated, but of *when*. Uwe Johnson's *Jahrestage* (*Anniversaries*), with its multiple layers of time, provides the opportunity to further reflect upon these issues, whilst Kurt Vonnegut's *Slaughterhouse 5* undermines our trust in the naturalness of our linear conception of time by introducing a different temporality in which each moment is permanently present. Although on balance this latter idea actually reinforces linearity, the idea that linearity is not the only way to think time is significant, as our understanding of ethics is based on linearity.

Chapter 6, finally, explores the wider implications of the arguments that have been made. It discusses the challenges raised by thinking through the problematic of memory and speaking of the past, and takes further the implications of these challenges for the role of Second World War memories in arguments about the use of military force by the FRG. The chapter reconsiders the problematic of right-wing versions of memory and brings the Holocaust back in. This leads to a discussion of the problematic boundary between war and atrocity. Finally, the chapter brings out the significance of uncertainty and relates it to the problem of responsibility not merely in politics narrowly conceived but also in scholarship.

Despite the problems associated with Second World War memories, they have been ever-present in debates about use of the military instrument in the FRG since the end of the Cold War. The question of whether it is part of Germany's responsibility to participate in international military operations has often been contextualised with such memories, not only by those who had themselves been in the war. Whether German troops should be sent to the Balkans where the Wehrmacht had wreaked havoc, in particular, involved considerable soul-searching and agonising. Of course, given the past, given the awful memories of the Second World War, Germans can be expected to agonise about war and in particular their own involvement in it. However, the reverse, which I noted at the beginning of this chapter, is less often considered: such memories, in all their difficulty, might be experienced as relevant when the situation faced is one of agony. War, with its inextricable link to death, confronts us with stark choices. Under what circumstances, if any, should we expose fellow citizens to the clear danger of being killed? Under what circumstances, if any, should we ask them to kill others on our behalf? Which others may be killed, and under what circumstances? Most of us presumably find these questions difficult when we are confronted with them in particular contexts. At the same time, war has been invested with overtly ethical purposes, has been deployed as a 'solution' to ethical problems: defending Kuwait, stopping civil war, human rights abuses and even genocide in the Balkans, and liberating Iraq have been some of the supposed aims of going to war since the 1990s. Frequently, and although war has undoubtedly changed fundamentally since the Second World War, these problems are conceptualised with reference to memories of that war.

2   Forgetting to remember?

In 1995 almost 300 'Conservatives and critical Liberals'[1] published an appeal under the heading '8 May 1945 – Against Forgetting'. It cited the first President of the FRG, Theodor Heuss: 'Basically, this 8 May 1945 remains the most tragic and questionable paradox for every one of us. Why? Because we were saved and destroyed at the same time.'[2] The advertisement asserted that, in contrast to Heuss's apt characterisation, the date of the unconditional surrender of the German Reich had increasingly come to be represented as 'liberation' by politicians and the media. This meant, according to the campaign, that there was a danger of forgetting that this day had marked not only the end of the National Socialist terror regime but also 'the beginning of the terror of expulsion and of new oppression in the east and the beginning of the division of our country'. That was a problem, because an 'image of the past that conceals, suppresses or qualifies these truths cannot be the basis for the self-conception of a self-assured nation that we Germans have to become in the European family of peoples in order to rule out comparable catastrophes in future'.[3] This implies that the Germans must remember the 'full truth'. This apparently simple demand, however, poses serious problems. In later chapters I address the question of truth as an issue of representability; this chapter explores something related but different, namely the question of the suppression, silencing or forgetting of (aspects of) the past in memory.

The reasoning presented in the advertisement campaign could be questioned on a number of levels. I am interested specifically in one aspect: the rhetoric *against* forgetting and by implication *for* remembering. This concern may be surprising, for on the surface it may appear obvious that we should strive to remember, particularly where violence and oppression are concerned. Three reasons for this spring to mind: firstly, because we

---

[1] '8. Mai 1945 – Gegen das Vergessen', *Frankfurter Allgemeine Zeitung*, 28/04/95, 3.
[2] '8. Mai 1945 – Gegen das Vergessen', *Frankfurter Allgemeine Zeitung*, 07/04/95, 3.
[3] Ibid.

have a duty towards the victims; secondly, because hope for reconciliation may be found in acknowledging the past; and finally, because we may learn from the past. As a result, exploring memories – especially the kind that have been suppressed – and preserving them is often seen as a progressive move. Such arguments are, however, problematic. They assume that there is a particular memory we must work towards, that what must be remembered may be clearly identified, such as the 'truths' referred to in the advertisements. Klaus Neumann observes in relation specifically to the Holocaust that those 'who admonish Germans today not to forget seem often to assume that what needs to be remembered is self-evident'.[4] That, however, is not the case. This chapter explores how, more fundamentally, remembering always already entails forgetting. Thus the opposition of remembering versus forgetting, that values the former over the latter, is more problematic than is acknowledged. The chapter starts by looking at arguments about the significance of remembering and forgetting, and then reads closely Grass's novella *Im Krebsgang*, which explores the sinking of a ship carrying thousands of German refugees in 1945.

The significance of remembering

With their 1995 campaign 'against forgetting' the Right in Germany caught up with the *Zeitgeist*. In the 1980s *Historikerstreit* (Historians' Dispute) they had been accused of wanting to 'draw a line' under the past, though it is not clear that they had actually argued against remembering.[5] The campaign against forgetting, at any rate, implies that remembering is good, even that it is crucial in order to prevent history from repeating itself. It acknowledges that the memory of the horrors of National Socialist rule must be kept alive, but states satisfaction at having set off a public debate about the 'crimes of expulsion'.[6] In other words, the rhetoric is one of more memory – not less – and this expresses widely held convictions, for, in recent decades, the assertion of the necessity and value of remembering has been powerful in relation to the history of the Third Reich.

In 1985, in his famous speech on the fortieth anniversary of the end of the Second World War in Europe, Federal President Richard von Weizsäcker – urging incidentally that 8 May 1945 should be seen as liberation – cited the cabbalistic saying inscribed at Yad Vashem: 'Wanting

---

[4] Klaus Neumann, *Shifting Memories: The Nazi Past in the New Germany* (Ann Arbor: The University of Michigan Press 2000), pp. 7f.
[5] See '*Historikerstreit': Die Dokumentation der Kontroverse um die Einzigartigkeit der national-sozialistischen Judenvernichtung* (Munich: Piper 1987).
[6] '8. Mai 1945 – Gegen das Vergessen', *Frankfurter Allgemeine Zeitung*, 05/05/95, 3.

to forget prolongs the exile, and the secret of redemption is remembering.'[7] Von Weizsäcker argued that Germans had to face the truth about their country's past as best they could. The saying – usually cut short into 'the secret of redemption is remembering' – subsequently gained prominence in the German discourse on the Third Reich. In Helmut Dubiel's view it became clear from this reception that von Weizsäcker's discussion had not been differentiated enough. The saying had been 'stripped of its Jewish origin' and now strangely referred to 'the possibility of a moral emancipation of the perpetrator through memory of guilt'.[8] Klaus Naumann also criticised the fact that von Weisäcker seemed unaware that the cabbala deals with 'the victims of historical injustice', not the perpetrators.[9] Despite these criticisms, faith in redemption through remembering evidently persisted. Ten years later Federal President Roman Herzog's speech on the fiftieth anniversary of the bombing of Dresden invoked community through recalling the dead and hinted at the motive of salvation.[10]

Despite the struggle over the particular form remembering should take, as indicated by the campaign 'against forgetting', the belief in the value of remembering is widely shared. The motif of remembering appears not only in relation to commemorations of the Holocaust and the Second World War but also in debates about current politics, particularly when the issues are seen to touch on the 'lessons' of this past. This is the case with questions about the use of military force and war. Chapter 1 showed how Foreign Minister Kinkel, in a 1995 Bundestag debate about deploying troops to Bosnia, contextualised the decision within an understanding of the past and thereby underlined the significance of remembering. Two aspects of his argument will be revisited here: firstly, his reference to the Allied 'liberation' of Germany – precisely what is questioned by the advertisement campaign mentioned above – and, secondly, his reconfirmation of the Kohl doctrine.

To recall briefly, Kinkel argued that Germans had a political and moral duty to help in Bosnia, in particular because of their past. He asserted that they had 'forgotten too quickly' that the Allies had used military force to liberate the Germans from the Nazi regime and to make the

[7] Richard von Weizsäcker, 'Zum 40. Jahrestag der Beendigung des Krieges in Europa und der nationalsozialistischen Gewaltherrschaft', 08/05/85, www.dhm.de.

[8] Helmut Dubiel, *Niemand ist frei von der Geschichte: Die nationalsozialistische Herrschaft in den Debatten des Deutschen Bundestages* (Munich: Carl Hanser Verlag 1999), p. 213. See also Ute Frevert, 'Geschichtsvergessenheit und Geschichtsversessenheit revisited: Der jüngste Erinnerungsboom in der Kritik', *Aus Politik und Zeitgeschichte* B40–1 (2003), 6.

[9] Klaus Naumann, *Der Krieg als Text: Das Jahr 1945 im kulturellen Gedächtnis der Presse* (Hamburg: Hamburger Edition 1998), pp. 232f.

[10] See Chapter 3, pp. 80–1.

new democratic beginning possible.[11] The Bundeswehr should do what the Allies did: assist people in distress. Kinkel invoked a memory of the outcome of the Second World War as 'liberation' to support his particular political choice. Although this was – surprisingly – not challenged, in referring to the Second World War he still faced a problem: the Kohl doctrine, that is, the idea that, owing to the past, no German troops could be deployed to the former Yugoslavia. Kinkel affirmed this principle – the decision, he said, was not about *ground* troops – but seemed to overturn its spirit.[12]

This was where Kinkel's opponents took their cue. Rudolf Scharping, the leader of the opposition, argued that, although the Germans wanted to support the UN in Bosnia-Herzegovina, they did not want to participate in implementing this mandate. He represented this as living up to 'a human and political duty towards this part of Europe which had to suffer under the dreadfulness of the Second World War'.[13] Scharping recalled Chancellor Kohl's view that German soldiers should not be deployed to the former Yugoslavia because 'the memory of the atrocities in the Second World War could only lead to an escalation of the conflicts and an irresponsible endangering of German soldiers', and warned against changing this policy.[14] Clearly, both sides to the argument portrayed the past as pertinent. Although they drew different conclusions, they agreed on the need to remember the past, not merely in the context of commemoration but in that of making policy choices. They argued about which 'lesson' to draw, not, however, about what it means to remember in the first place. This latter question is significant, nonetheless, in order to consider the implications for invocations of memory in political debate.

The question of remembering – and indeed of confronting painful memories – is not exclusive to German discourse. Andreas Huyssen notes the 'emergence of memory as a key concern in Western societies', set off by the increasing debate about the Holocaust and media interest in the fortieth and fiftieth anniversaries of events during the Third Reich.[15] Moreover, the 'recurrence of genocidal politics in Rwanda, Bosnia, and Kosovo in the allegedly posthistorical 1990s has kept the Holocaust memory discourse alive'.[16] But Huyssen sees the 'memory boom' as a much

---

[11] Deutscher Bundestag, *Plenarprotokoll*, 13/48, 30/06/95, 3957.
[12] Note that in the formulation of the Kohl doctrine cited in Chapter 1 deployments 'in the air' are explicitly ruled out as well.
[13] Deutscher Bundestag, *Plenarprotokoll*, 13/48, 30/06/95, 3959. [14] Ibid., 3960.
[15] Andreas Huyssen, 'Present Pasts: Media, Politics, Amnesia', *Public Culture* 12 (2000), 21f.
[16] Ibid., 23.

wider phenomenon ranging from 'the historicizing restoration of old urban centers', to a 'popular obsession with "self-musealization" by video recorder', to work 'related to genocide, AIDS, slavery, and sexual abuse', to name but a few of his examples.[17]

One may ask why there is such a surge of interest in memory now.[18] One reason is frequently noted: the passing away of those who lived through the Holocaust.[19] Crucially, this 'explanation' already takes as given that we want, or ought, to remember. Earlier I noted as possible reasons for this conviction our duty to the victims, the hope of reconciliation and the idea that we may – and must – learn lessons from the past. Herzog indeed asserted a common motivation for remembering when he said that '[o]ne's own history teaches one the best lesson'.[20] As noted in Chapter 3, Herzog – like von Weizsäcker – displayed a belief in redemption and reconciliation through memory.

Avishai Margalit observes that the Truth and Reconciliation Commission in South Africa was also 'established with the hope that it would bring social catharsis – that the truth about the past will, by being revealed, bring reconciliation'.[21] Margalit is concerned with 'the healing power of truth in the case of communal memories'[22] and, more broadly, the question of whether there is an ethics of memory.[23] He examines whether or not there is an obligation to remember the past.[24] This is no doubt an important question. However, my concern is different: it is not whether there is an imperative to remember, or why, but a closer exploration of how we already remember. This includes examining the implications of supporting the imperative to remember, whether or not it is possible to defend it ethically or morally. I have noted possible reasons for the imperative to remember. These assume not only that remembering is beneficial but, more fundamentally, that it is possible to recall the truth about the

---

[17] Ibid., 24f.

[18] This is also evidenced in the growing literature on memory, particularly in the context of war and atrocity. See, for example, Paul Antze and Michael Lambek (eds.), *Tense Past: Cultural Essays in Trauma and Memory* (New York: Routledge 1996); Edkins, *Trauma and the Memory of Politics*; Winter, *Sites of Memory*; James E. Young, *The Texture of Memory: Holocaust Memorials and Meaning* (New Haven: Yale University Press 1993).

[19] See, for example, Jan-Werner Müller, 'Introduction: The Power of Memory, the Memory of Power and the Power over Memory', in: Jan-Werner Müller (ed.), *Memory and Power in Post-War Europe: Studies in the Presence of the Past* (Cambridge: Cambridge University Press 2002), pp. 13f; Frevert, 'Geschichtsvergessenheit', 7.

[20] Roman Herzog, 'Dresden – A Warning for the Future: Speech by the Federal President in Dresden on 13 February 1995', in: *Remembrance and Perpetual Responsibility* (Bonn: Press and Information Office of the Federal Government 1995), 6.

[21] Avishai Margalit, *The Ethics of Memory* (Cambridge, MA: Harvard University Press 2002), p. 5.

[22] Ibid.   [23] Ibid., p. 6.   [24] Ibid., p. 7.

past. And yet there are those, like Huyssen, who are critical of the trend towards more and more remembering: 'Total recall seems to be the goal. Is this an archivist's fantasy gone mad?'[25]

The significance of forgetting

Margalit points out that 'memory breathes revenge as often as it breathes reconciliation'.[26] Thus the benign political implications of remembering are in question. As Ilana R. Bet-El notes in relation to the former Yugoslavia, '[w]ords of the past became weapons of war'.[27] This danger of memory may appear even more acute given the alleged scope for manipulation, but distortion is often by no means necessary to incite a desire for revenge. Significantly, the charge of manipulation implies that there is a 'correct' memory from which manipulated memories deviate. In the context of the passing away of Holocaust survivors Aleida Assmann identifies a shift from individual to what she calls cultural memory. She sees this as problematic 'because it brings with it the danger of distortion, reduction, instrumentalisation'.[28] She seems to assume that individual memory and cultural memory are somehow distinct and that the former is not distorted, reduced and instrumentalised. Yet both these assumptions are untenable.[29] Crucially, the fear of manipulation seems to suggest not so much that we should liberate ourselves from dangerous memories, but that the more we remember the better, for surely those who know more about the past are less easily manipulated.

Yet some really do not want to be part of the current memory-fest, whatever its reasons. Friedrich Nietzsche is often cited as the great champion of forgetting.[30] He is indeed concerned that the past must not become the 'gravedigger' of the present.[31] Nietzsche's championing of forgetting, however, has to be read in its context, namely the discussion of the relevance of history to human life, in which he suggests that there are three types of history: monumental, antiquarian and critical. The critical

---

[25] Huyssen, 'Present Pasts', 25; though also see 37.   [26] Margalit, *Ethics of Memory*, p. 5.
[27] Ilana R. Bet-El, 'Unimagined Communities: the Power of Memory and the Conflict in the Former Yugoslavia', in: Müller, *Memory and Power in Post-War Europe*, p. 206.
[28] Assmann, *Erinnerungsräume*, p. 15. On a similar distinction between communicative and cultural memory, see Jan Assmann, *Das kulturelle Gedächtnis: Schrift, Erinnerung und politische Identität in frühen Hochkulturen* (Munich: Verlag C.H. Beck 2002).
[29] For a powerful study that undermines both assumptions, see Alistair Thomson, *Anzac Memories: Living with the Legend* (Melbourne: Oxford University Press 1994).
[30] See, for example, Assmann, *Erinnerungsräume*, pp. 64f, 131, 167f; Edith Wyschogrod, *An Ethics of Remembering: History, Heterology, and the Nameless Others* (Chicago: The University of Chicago Press 1998), p. xi.
[31] Friedrich Nietzsche, *Unzeitgemäße Betrachtungen* (Stuttgart: Alfred Kröner Verlag 1964), p. 104.

attitude towards the past – which calls for the strength to break with and dissolve the past in order to be able to live – becomes necessary from time to time when knowledge of the past threatens to rule over life.[32] Nietzsche asserts that '[f]orgetting belongs to all actions: as to the life of everything organic belongs not just light, but also darkness'. Indeed, according to Nietzsche, it is possible to live with hardly any memory but 'it is entirely impossible to live without forgetting altogether'.[33] Nietzsche dismisses here, with characteristic verve, the necessarily positive connotation of remembering. In fact, remembering may wear us down, may stop us from action and may be pernicious. Nietzsche is often read to be saying 'Forget!'[34]

Inevitably, there is a problem with the instruction to forget: it only serves to remind us, and hence we remember. Unsurprisingly, it is therefore difficult to find advocates of concrete forgetting in politics. The conservative historians of the *Historikerstreit*, who are seen as having wanted to 'draw a line' under the past (of the Third Reich), actually seem to suggest that the Germans ought to remember differently, with more positive attachment to the nation. Michael Stürmer, in a contribution to the debate, complained that '[a]nything is possible in a country without memory'. The search for the 'lost past', he argued, is 'morally legitimate and politically necessary'.[35] If anything, then, he claimed to be advocating more – not less – remembering. Similarly, in the 1997 Bundestag debate about the exhibition on Wehrmacht crimes Alfred Dregger – who is seen as a key proponent of a memory of the Wehrmacht that 'forgets' its involvement in atrocities – seemed motivated by reminding Germans of the situation of ordinary soldiers in the Second World War,[36] that is, by a desire to remember the fate of the *Landser* (privates). In sum, those accused of (promoting) forgetting actually regard themselves as (promoting) remembering.

Even novelist Martin Walser's high-profile polemic against the (Holocaust) memory culture in his acceptance speech for the 1998 Peace Prize of the German Book Trade, for which he was accused of a 'refusal of memory',[37] does not break with this pattern. Walser said that he closes himself to all ills which he cannot help remove, that he 'had to learn to

---

[32] Ibid., p. 124.   [33] Ibid., p. 103.

[34] This is of course an oversimplification of Nietzsche's position, which is close to Derrida's, discussed below.

[35] Michael Stürmer, 'Geschichte in geschichtslosem Land', in: *'Historikerstreit'*, p. 36.

[36] See his second intervention in the Bundestag debate, discussed in Chapter 4, pp. 133–4.

[37] Micha Brumlik, Hajo Funke and Lars Rensmann, 'Einleitung', in: Micha Brumlik, Hajo Funke and Lars Rensmann, *Umkämpftes Vergessen: Walser-Debatte, Holocaust-Mahnmal und neuere deutsche Geschichtspolitik* (Berlin: Verlag Das Arabische Buch 1999), p. 7.

look away'.[38] Not only that. He asserted that his reaction to the 'unbearable' was proportionate, unavoidable and justified: 'I do not have to bear the unbearable.' He raised this in the context of ills continuously projected by television into his life, but developed the argument further in relation to Germans' attitude to their past: 'Everyone knows our historical burden, the everlasting disgrace, no day on which we are not reproached with it.' He alleges that this 'cruel service of memory' might be part of the illusion that a little bit of exoneration is possible, something he excludes altogether. However, he wants to resist the 'permanent representation of our disgrace', for which he suspects there are instrumental, if worthy, reasons in the present.[39]

For all the controversy that the speech set off[40] Walser nowhere actually so much as mentions a desire to forget. He observes that, when confronted with filmic representations of concentration camps, he has 'looked away' at least twenty times. Walser's image, however, is telling. Looking away is already a looking somewhere else: there is no escape from memory as such. It is also interesting to note that the planned Holocaust memorial that he criticised as a 'monumentalisation' of German disgrace[41] has also been derided as a *Kranzabwurfstelle* (a place to dump wreaths).[42] In other words, official commemoration may actually conceal forgetting: the laying of wreaths by politicians creates no more than an illusion of remembering. As has been noted about remembrance in Dresden, 'Memory was seen to by the appropriate official authorities';[43] ordinary people were not involved. In Assmann's view, symbolic commemoration is indeed closer to forgetting than to active memory work.[44] Memorials and museums, for example on the sites of concentration camps, as spaces of memory may 'obstruct memory'.[45] The 'memory boom' might be in danger of inadvertently allowing people to forget, as they trust that the memorials and the 'appropriate authorities' take care of the business of remembering.[46] Thus it is not only unclear whether remembering is necessarily

---

38 Martin Walser, 'Dankesrede zur Verleihung des Friedenspreis des Deutschen Buchhandels in der Frankfurter Paulskirche', 11/10/98, www.dhm.de. For more on Walser see Chapter 4.
39 Walser, 'Dankesrede'.
40 See Frank Schirrmacher (ed.), *Die Walser-Bubis-Debatte: eine Dokumentation* (Frankfurt am Main: Suhrkamp 1999); Brumlik, Funke and Rensmann, *Umkämpftes Vergessen*.
41 Walser, 'Dankesrede'.
42 This is noted in Michael Geyer, 'The Place of the Second World War in German Memory and History', Translated by Michael Latham, *New German Critique* 71 (1997), 37.
43 Jens Schneider, 'Im brüchigen Rahmen der Erinnerung', *Süddeutsche Zeitung*, 10/02/05, 3.
44 Assmann, *Erinnerungsräume*, p. 335.   45 Ibid., p. 333.
46 See, however, Edkins's study of memory practices that looks beyond the memorials to how people respond to them. Edkins, *Trauma and the Memory of Politics*.

'better' than forgetting; remembering and forgetting are also not easily distinguished.

How to remember (and forget)

Nietzsche's argument upsets the widespread conviction that we must strive to remember. Remembering and forgetting are still opposed in his conceptualisation, but the latter is valued over the former. However, despite accusations that certain groups are forgetting, in the debates considered here no one seems to actually embrace forgetting as a positive goal. Indeed, apart from Nietzsche himself perhaps, it is difficult to find any outright advocates of forgetting.[47] Thus Nietzsche's intervention – his overturning of the dichotomy remembering/forgetting – appears to have failed: the privileging of remembering is fully intact. Yet, significantly, the distinction between (promoters of) remembering and (promoters of) forgetting is not clear, and cannot be. Huyssen therefore argues that the issue 'is not whether to forget or to remember, but rather how to remember and how to handle representations of the remembered past'.[48] Thus, the argument 'against forgetting', which implies the imperative to remember, is a move in the struggle over *how* to remember. Similarly, von Weizsäcker's speech promotes a particular version of memory.

Von Weizsäcker's pronouncement, although made from the authority of office, notes the context of struggle; he refers to 'debates about the past', but his call for honesty implies that this has been lacking. He reiterates several times that 8 May is a 'day of memory' and that it calls for truthfulness.[49] Despite criticisms that von Weizsäcker's truthfulness is limited,[50] his argument is important. He refers to the diversity of experiences on 8 May 1945, many of them marked by hopelessness. Yet he concludes: 'And nevertheless what it is today necessary to say for us all together became clearer day by day: 8 May was a day of liberation.' This is not to say that the suffering that began on this day should be forgotten, merely that it should be related to its reason: the start of the war and the beginning of the Nazi regime. Overall, memory must be kept alive, not least because it is relevant to policy choices today, for example those concerning political asylum and relations with neighbouring countries. Von Weizsäcker sees

---

[47] See, however, Maja Zehfuss, 'Forget September 11', *Third World Quarterly* 24 (2003), 513–28. But note that this, too, is a *conditional* appeal to forget.

[48] Andreas Huyssen, *Twilight Memories: Marking Time in a Culture of Amnesia* (New York: Routledge 1995), p. 214.

[49] Von Weizsäcker, 'Zum 40. Jahrestag'.

[50] See, for example, M. Lane Bruner, *Strategies of Remembrance: The Rhetorical Dimensions of National Identity Construction* (Columbia: University of South Carolina Press 2002), Chapter 2.

a 'danger of forgetting' and appeals to his fellow Germans: 'Let us look truth in the face on today's 8 May as best we can.'[51] Von Weizsäcker thus opens up the question of the multiplicity of memories when he notes the diversity of experiences at the end of the Second World War. At the same time his speech enacts interpretative authority in arguing that, whatever these experiences, all Germans should now remember 8 May 1945 as a day of liberation, disregarding the fact that this might be difficult for those who, for example, lost their possessions and, often, their loved ones as a result of flight or expulsion from Eastern territories.

Clearly, which memory is appropriate is a controversial issue. In debates about using military force, however, the past is unproblematically used as a shared repertoire through which to interpret the present and act for the future. Despite the continuing struggle over how to properly characterise 8 May 1945 – with the campaign 'against forgetting' forcefully rejecting von Weizsäcker's portrayal of the date as 'liberation' – Foreign Minister Kinkel confidently referred to Allied liberation in his justification of the Bundeswehr deployment to Bosnia. This raised no objection, certainly within the Bundestag debate. Thus Kinkel apparently expected people to share his understanding of the outcome of the Second World War as essentially liberating, and those who might object to such a representation in commemorations of the Second World War accepted – or at least acquiesced in – this interpretation in the context of current policy choices. In other words, even though this memory was controversial, it was possible to deploy it in political debate without attracting criticism.

Memories of the flight and expulsion from the East: Grass's *Im Krebsgang*

Although Kinkel's argument revolved around the notion that the Germans had been liberated by the Allies, the 'conservatives and critical liberals' seem not to have criticised it; they were in favour of the deployment he was justifying, as well as the wider aim of making possible Bundeswehr participation in international operations. Yet I want to take seriously their complaint that the portrayal of 8 May 1945 as liberation excludes 'the beginning of the terror of expulsion' and investigate the supposedly suppressed memory of the expulsions. Recent German interest in Second World War memories has revolved around two allegedly forgotten themes that seem to be particularly pertinent to the concerns of this book: the Allied bombing of German cities, addressed in Chapter 3, and the flight and expulsion of Germans from what is often called 'Ostgebiete' (Eastern

---

[51] Von Weizsäcker, 'Zum 40. Jahrestag'.

territories) towards the end of the war.[52] Interest in the latter is sometimes seen as having been set off by Grass's 2002 novella *Im Krebsgang*. Significantly, examining the novella closely makes it possible to discuss not only memories of the flight and expulsion but what it means to remember in the first place.[53]

Im Krebsgang revolves around the sinking of the *Wilhelm Gustloff* on 30 January 1945. The ship, which was carrying several thousand German refugees from the port of Gdingen, was torpedoed by a Russian U-boat. The narrator, Paul Pokriefke, and his mother, Tulla, are survivors of the disaster: Paul is born that same day. Tulla always wanted Paul to tell the world, to bear witness to the events of that day, but Paul has resisted this idea. Paul's son Konrad eventually takes up the task, with tragic consequences. Grass's characters might be said to be straightforward to the point of being stereotypical, representing different generations and their attitudes to the events. The narrative, however, is complex; it shifts between different levels and narrative strands. If the events of 30 January 1945 and their memory are read as central, several narrative elements can be seen as grouped around them. Firstly, there is the nexus of information about historical events and figures, such as Wilhelm Gustloff, his murderer David Frankfurter, the U-boat commander Alexander Marinesko, the refugees aboard the ship, the history of the *Wilhelm Gustloff* up to 30 January 1945 and finally the events of that day. To complicate matters this 'information' emerges from the interplay of Konrad's postings on a website in honour of the Nazi Gustloff and Paul's reflections upon them. Secondly, there is the story about Tulla as the survivor of the disaster. And thirdly, the story in the present of the novella tells of Konrad becoming obsessed with Gustloff and his memory, and eventually murdering another boy. The link between the three is the sinking of the *Gustloff*, though there is a subtle, but significant, shift from the *Gustloff* to Gustloff in the narrative present. Bringing together these different levels makes it clear that *Im Krebsgang* is not simply a novella about the sinking of the *Gustloff* or about the flight of Germans from East Prussia. Such an interpretation is unable to account for the continuous reflection on memories and their effects in the novella.

---

[52] Note also interest in the defeat at Stalingrad, which, however, does not seem to have generated the same intensity of public debate. See, for example, Wolfram Wette and Gerd R. Ueberschär (eds.), *Stalingrad: Mythos und Wirklichkeit einer Schlacht* (Frankfurt am Main: Fischer 1997); Guido Knopp, *Stalingrad: Das Drama* (Munich: C. Bertelsmann 2003); Bernd Ulrich, *Stalingrad* (Munich: Beck 2005); and the German edition of Antony Beevor, *Stalingrad*, Translated by Klaus Kochmann (Munich: Goldmann 2001).

[53] This chapter leaves to one side memories of the flight and expulsion as maintained by expellee organisations and the political aims they pursue.

That *Im Krebsgang* is both a contribution to memory and a reflection on it is clear immediately. The dedication page reads simply 'In memoriam' and the text itself begins: '"Why only now?" said someone, who was not me.'[54] Why, that is, has Paul not written about this earlier? Paul mentions someone 'who does not like excuses' pointing to his profession as a journalist: he had, after all, written on just about anything else. Paul replies equivocally.[55] Significantly, that Paul has not written about the *Gustloff* is considered nothing less than a failure because of a general lack of such reports. Paul later complains that no one had wanted to hear about it.[56] Thus the book reflects upon the context of its articulation of memory. It represents itself as disrupting an uncomfortable silence – a lack of memory, one might say – and the reaction it has provoked, as is shown below, appears to confirm this view.

There are two further immediate indications that what is at issue is memory, not the Germans' sufferings at the hands of the Allies. Firstly, the narrative time is the present of the unified FRG – and therefore when memory is seen to be and not when the past was.[57] Secondly, the narrator asserts that Schwerin is the 'place of origin' of his story.[58] Wherever one might choose to look for the origin of German suffering in the Second World War, Schwerin – a town in Mecklenburg-Vorpommern – is not a likely candidate. Schwerin is, however, Gustloff's birthplace and Tulla's home town after the war. It is, crucially, where Konrad lives with his grandmother and from where he posts information about the sinking of the ship on the Internet. It is this information on the web that is more literally the origin of the story, though one could also see it in the 'old writer' employing Paul, on Tulla's request, to write about his birth. The reference to Schwerin as the origin permits several interpretations. It is important that the narrator does not locate the origin in the Baltic Sea, where the ship was sunk. The story thus originates from Gustloff, Tulla or Konrad – or, more probably the fictional interplay of all three – and not simply from the events of 30 January 1945.

Writing, especially as a German, about the sinking of the *Wilhelm Gustloff* – a particular event in the flight and expulsions of Germans from the East – raises questions. Although Moeller forcefully argues that there has been a public memory of the expulsions since the 1950s,[59] this topic was considered taboo, or at least unpopular, later. Writing about this is inevitably confronted with the question whether it is permissible, and how

---

[54] Günter Grass, *Im Krebsgang* (Göttingen: Steidl 2002), p. 7.   [55] Ibid., p. 7.
[56] Ibid., p. 31.   [57] On the temporality of memory, see Chapter 5.
[58] Grass, *Im Krebsgang*, p. 8.
[59] Robert G. Moeller, *War Stories: The Search for a Usable Past in the Federal Republic of Germany* (Berkeley: University of California Press 2001).

the topic may be addressed at all, issues that Grass's novella foregrounds. The novel starts with what turns out to be a double move of distancing: Paul, the narrator, who is depicted as employed by Grass's alter ego in the novel, the old writer,[60] to tell the story 'in his place'[61] – one could also say invented by the fictional Grass – discusses why he is only now telling this story. Although Paul is the most lively and complex of the characters, and probably shares some views with Grass, Grass makes clear the distance between him and the narrator by inserting another 'false' Grass into the novella. Paul cannot 'represent' Grass, because this place is already taken. This move at the same time blurs the boundary between reality and fiction: Grass appears to be in the novella, although he cannot be.

The novella is disrupted throughout to grapple with the issue of how, when and why this story should be told – often in conversations between Paul and the old writer. Clearly, there are no easy answers; the matter is difficult to approach. The narrator finds it difficult to get started. He says that the 'words still have difficulties with me',[62] though this relationship later changes: then *he* 'is searching for words'.[63] Whether language is in charge of the narrator or vice versa in this evidently difficult endeavour, the matter is approached 'crabwise', that is, obliquely rather than directly. There are numerous references to this 'crabwise' approach in the text, most obviously, of course, in the title.[64] 'Krebsgang' is the movement of a crab: sideways, oblique.

Clearly, Grass approaches his topic with care and what appears to be trepidation. Nevertheless, *Im Krebsgang* has provoked debate about whether recent German literature, and in particular Grass's book, has played down the Germans' responsibility for the Holocaust and the Second World War.[65] The *Guardian* greeted its publication with surprise and, it seems, dismay that 'the literary guru of the European left' is embracing 'causes that were previously associated with the right, if not the far-right'. In this view his novella has 'clearly tuned into a new, more considered, less reflexive approach to the past among Germans'.[66] The lengthier review in the *Observer* found much to admire in Grass and his book, but also described the novella as 'sympathetic to some of the historical imperatives of the Right'.[67] Ulrich Raulff in the *Süddeutsche Zeitung*

---

[60] The alter ego, the old writer, is identified as the author of *Hundejahre* – that is, Grass. Grass, *Im Krebsgang*, p. 77.
[61] Ibid., p. 99.   [62] Ibid., p. 7.   [63] Ibid, p. 99.
[64] For example, Grass, *Im Krebsgang*, pp. 30, 88, 107, 176 and 216.
[65] Volker Hage, 'Unter Generalverdacht', *Der Spiegel*, 08/04/02, 178–81.
[66] John Hooper, 'Günter Grass breaks taboo on German war refugees', *Guardian*, 08/02/02, 16.
[67] Adams, 'Germany's conscience'.

put his finger on the problem when he presented the novella not as good literature but as a work on memory, a kind of excavation of the German store of suffering that tunes into an increasing interest in the topic.[68] It is the focus on German suffering that arouses concern: are the Germans construing themselves as victims (again)?

In 1944/5 many Germans either fled from or were forced to leave Eastern territories, within what was then the German Reich and beyond. What exactly happened is controversial, though detailed historical work and a range of popular history books on the subject exist.[69] Overall 10–14 million Germans were expelled from the East or fled; roughly 2 million of them are believed to have died in the process.[70] Although – whatever the precise figures – a large number of Germans in the postwar Germanies were affected by these events, it arguably became increasingly less possible to speak about them in public. In his detailed study of fiction on the flight and expulsion, Louis Ferdinand Helbig raises the question of how these events may even be named:

Who still knows today the variety of fates, the spontaneous and the official terms for what was happening? Was it 'only' the fear of being expelled, and therefore flight? Was it the 'unofficial expulsion' [*Vertreibung*], the expulsion [*Ausweisung*] already before the Potsdam Agreements? Was it an at least outwardly humane 'resettlement' [*Aussiedlung*], a euphemistic 'transfer' quasi under international law, brutal 'deportation', a throwing-out, an ideologically veiled 'resettlement' [*Umsiedlung*]? Of course, in the moment of the events – often there was immediate danger to life – there was nothing less important than concern about the word, the legalistic explanation. The event itself took on an enormous dimension that pushed everything else to the background. There are few undisputed terms.[71]

These difficulties of expression point to questions of appropriate representation and to the problematic of the political context. In the German Democratic Republic (GDR) memories of the expulsion were frowned upon, because they implied accusations against the Soviet Union; in the FRG reference to the expulsions came to be seen as an attempt to obscure

---

[68] Ulrich Raulff, 'Untergang mit Maus und Muse', *Süddeutsche Zeitung*, 05/02/02, 13.
[69] See, for example, Wolfgang Benz (ed.), *Die Vertreibung der Deutschen aus dem Osten: Ursachen, Ereignisse, Folgen*, updated edn (Frankfurt am Main: Fischer Taschenbuchverlag 1995); Stefan Aust and Stephan Burgdorff (eds.), *Die Flucht: Über die Vertreibung der Deutschen aus dem Osten* (Stuttgart: Deutsche Verlags-Anstalt 2002).
[70] Michael Schwartz, 'Vertreibung und Vergangenheitspolitik: Ein Versuch über geteilte deutsche Nachkriegsidentitäten', *Deutschlandarchiv* 30 (1997), 178; Helga Hirsch, 'Flucht und Vertreibung. Kollektive Erinnerung im Wandel', *Aus Politik und Zeitgeschichte* B40–1 (2003), 18f; Eric Langenbacher, 'Changing Memory Regimes in Contemporary Germany?', *German Politics and Society* 21 (2003), 47; Hans-Ulrich Wehler, 'Einleitung', in: Aust and Burgdorff, *Die Flucht*, pp. 10 and 14.
[71] Louis Ferdinand Helbig, *Der ungeheure Verlust: Flucht und Vertreibung in der deutschsprachigen Belletristik der Nachkriegszeit*, 3rd edn (Wiesbaden: Harrasowitz Verlag 1996), p. 172.

German guilt – and indeed, at least until unification, if not beyond, it was associated with revanchist desires to change the borders.[72]

There can be no doubt that the expulsions involved what we would today describe as serious human rights violations, atrocities even. These were, however, committed against the 'people of perpetrators', which made it difficult for them to speak about the matter for fear of being seen to count up German victims against victims of the Germans.[73] Even almost sixty years after the events, the novella of a firmly leftist German writer, rather than leading to messages of support for his contribution to remembering, set off a debate in the mainstream press about the danger of styling Germans as victims. Obviously, Grass's novella disturbed the established discourse on memory. In order to understand this it is necessary to examine the book in detail.

'*I only live for this, that my son . . . will bear witness*': Tulla

In *Im Krebsgang* different attitudes towards the memory of the sinking of the *Gustloff* are represented by different characters. Tulla is a survivor of the disaster. She is an *Umsiedlerin*, an ethnic German who in 1945 left – or was forced to leave – the East and came to live in Schwerin, in the GDR. Tulla escaped on the *Gustloff*. To Grass's readers, she is an old acquaintance. She appears not only in *Katz und Maus* (*Cat and Mouse*) and *Hundejahre* (*Dog Years*) but is even mentioned as probably drowned with the *Gustloff* in *Die Rättin* (*The Rat*).[74] In *Im Krebsgang* Tulla complains about what 'this Russian' could possibly have been thinking when he attacked the ship. Her understanding of the events is not affected by historical scholarship on the matter: that the U-boat commander believed the ship to be carrying troops, for example, and that there were not only civilian refugees on board.[75]

---

[72] Hirsch, 'Flucht und Vertreibung', 14; Hans-Werner Rautenberg, 'Die Wahrnehmung von Flucht und Vertreibung in der deutschen Nachkriegsgeschichte bis heute', *Aus Politik und Zeitgeschichte* B53 (1997), 34–46; Hans-Joachim Noack, 'Die Deutschen als Opfer', in: Aust and Burgdorff, *Die Flucht*, p. 18. Attempts to reclaim property, for example in Poland, underline the idea that memories of the expulsion lead to unpalatable political aims. See, for example, Berthold Kohler, 'Nachkriegszeiten', *Frankfurter Allgemeine Zeitung*, 14/09/04, 1.

[73] Wehler, 'Einleitung', p. 10. See Chapter 3.

[74] Günter Grass, *Katz und Maus* (Frankfurt am Main: Luchterhand Literaturverlag 1988); Günter Grass, *Hundejahre* (Neuwied am Rhein: Luchterhand 1963); Günter Grass, *Die Rättin* (Darmstadt: Luchterhand 1986). See Hubert Spiegel, 'Das mußte aufschraiben!', *Frankfurter Allgemeine Zeitung*, 09/02/02, 56.

[75] The *Gustloff* counted as a warship because it was armed and had military personnel on board. It was 'fair game' in the context of the conduct of war by the Third Reich. Clemens Höges et al., 'Die verdrängte Tragödie', in: Aust and Burgdorff, *Die Flucht*,

It is extremely important to Tulla that the story of the *Gustloff* is told, despite – or because of – the failure of both German states to show any interest. As she puts it: 'I only live for this, that my son one day will bear witness.'[76] To Paul she says: 'You must write it down. You owe it to us as a lucky survivor.'[77] She continuously goes on about the sinking, in particular about the drowning of the children. However, it is also important to note what she does *not* go on about: the loss of her *Heimat*. Tulla does not want to change the borders as, arguably, expellees' organisations did for a long time, or even insist on her right to return;[78] she simply wants the story of this disaster told. *Im Krebsgang* seems to be a response to the lack of engagement with the flight and expulsion of Germans from the East which both Tulla and, as noted above, the narrator observe.

According to Moeller, the situation had been different, at least in the FRG, in the late 1940s and early 1950s. The 'women, men, and children who had left or been driven out of eastern Europe by the Red Army at the war's end, and those in uniform for whom captivity in the Soviet Union followed German surrender' had then been the 'most important representatives of German victimhood'.[79] He argues not only 'that a selective past, a past of German suffering, was in fact ubiquitous in the 1950s';[80] pointing out that 'trauma and suffering are among the most powerful forces capable of shaping "communities of memory"', he claims also that, in the '1950s, most west Germans created such communities by focusing on their own experiences, not on the trauma and suffering they had caused for others'.[81] Thus Moeller's work challenges the claim that stories such as Tulla's have not been told in the FRG, though he says little about the years after the 1950s, which are not the subject of his study. Helmut Dubiel's exploration of Bundestag debates confirms Moeller's assessment, but also demonstrates the gradual disappearance of the expellees from official memorialisation as the theme of Germans as victims of the Second World War became increasingly unacceptable.[82] Thus, whilst Moeller is probably correct that remembrance of the expulsions was intense in the first years of the FRG's existence, and even

---

p. 60. See also Uwe Klußmann, 'Attacke des Jahrhunderts', in: Aust and Burgdorff, *Die Flucht*, pp. 69–70.

[76] Grass, *Im Krebsgang*, p. 19.   [77] Ibid., p. 31.

[78] Note, however, Tulla's favourable words about Axel Springer, the newspaper tycoon, whom she describes as 'revanchist', supportive of the expellees. Grass, *Im Krebsgang*, p. 31. The proposed motto of the 1985 meeting of the organisation representing Silesian expellees had been '[F]orty years of expulsion – Silesia remains ours'. Rautenberg, 'Wahrnehmung von Flucht und Vertreibung'. See also Naumann, *Krieg als Text*, p. 74.

[79] Moeller, *War Stories*, p. 3.   [80] Ibid., p. 18.   [81] Ibid., p. 12.

[82] Dubiel, *Niemand ist frei*.

constitutive of its understanding of itself as a community, there may still be the omission in public memory that is alleged in *Im Krebsgang*.

With respect to literary representations of the expulsions, the assessments of different scholars contradict each other. Norris detects a lack of such representations.[83] Yet Helbig demonstrates the wealth of such literature.[84] Nevertheless, Helbig also diagnoses a taboo, a lack of reception by the general public which he contrasts with the magnitude of the event: 'The number of refugees and expellees had grown until about 1958 to one-fifth of the West German population: about 10 million compared with 40 million locals.'[85] In other words, almost anyone in the FRG had some direct or indirect relation to the expulsions. Nevertheless, Helbig agrees that 'expulsion' was 'for long periods of the last four postwar decades – and it is still – a taboo, but at least an emotive word in the media culture of the Federal Republic'.[86] Moreover, in addressing the topic one has to be mindful not only of the historical context of German atrocities but also of previous memorialisations. In the 1950s memories of those events were used to create an image of German victimhood and to evade or lessen German guilt. It is presumably because of such previous politics of memory that addressing those events is immediately seen in the light of a problematic desire to represent Germans as victims.

Unsurprisingly, Paul has little time for Tulla's continuous telling of the past. She is described not merely as stuck in the past politically – as, in other words, not having learnt the lessons the German collective has supposedly learnt, as still holding opinions at least close to Nazism.[87] In Paul's view, Tulla, who clings to her East Prussian dialect, also whines as though all this time had not passed since then.[88] Paul's jibe indicates that she is fundamentally stuck in the past. Tulla says: 'One can't forget something like this. It never stops. I don't only dream about it, how, when it was all over a single cry went up over the water. And all the little children between the ice floes . . .'[89] For her, this event is permanently present. Paul also notes, of those at a meeting of *Gustloff* survivors, that '[f]or them the war had never ended'.[90] He regards their world as 'narrowed'.[91] This is

---

[83] Norris, *Writing War*, p. 6.
[84] Helbig, *Der ungeheure Verlust*. See also Jörg Bernhard Bilke, 'Flucht und Vertreibung in der deutschen Belletristik', *Deutsche Studien* 32 (1995), 177–88.
[85] Helbig, *Der ungeheure Verlust*, p. 6. See also Hirsch, 'Flucht und Vertreibung', 18f.
[86] Helbig, *Der ungeheure Verlust*, p. 53.
[87] Tulla's political views are ambiguous. In line with her GDR background, she is a declared 'anti-fascist' (Grass, *Im Krebsgang*, p. 40), and when Konrad talks of racial purity Paul is (fairly) sure that this does not come from his mother (ibid., p. 106), but she later claims that 'David' behaved 'like a real Jew' in constantly speaking of the Germans' disgrace (ibid., p. 182).
[88] Ibid., p. 11.   [89] Ibid., p. 57.   [90] Ibid., p. 97.   [91] Ibid., p. 115.

presented as a criticism, but it is also a pertinent observation of how Tulla sees the issue. For her it is an experience 'out of time' and sui generis. She is not interested in how it might relate to other matters. Tulla does not perceive her memory of the sinking of the ship as linked to political questions, though she criticises the lack of interest and even suppression of memory. For her, it is a matter primarily of telling what was, of bearing witness. She does not care whether this might be politically problematic.

'I did not want to': Paul

Paul is embarrassed that his mother continuously goes on about the *Gustloff*. He has to admit, he says, that 'mother has always said many things too loudly and at the wrong time'.[92] Yet he refers to himself as a 'survivor of a tragedy that has been forgotten by the whole world',[93] a status which he does not enjoy.[94] Paul came to West Berlin just before the Wall was built.[95] Tulla claims that she 'sent' the boy to the West so that he would make something of himself, but she really wanted something specific. In her Eastern dialect she asserts that 'I only live for this, that my son one day will bear witness.'[96] He, however, resisted his mother's wish. He was not only critical of his mother's attitude; he also found it impossible to see 'as who' he should have 'reported': 'As "child of the Gustloff"? Or as someone who is, due to his profession, disinterested?'[97] Paul instead sent Tulla books. One is a documentary-style account of the disaster, 'written quite factually but too disinterestedly', even in Paul's view. Therefore it is no surprise that Tulla rejected this account: 'All this is not experienced in a way that is personal enough in my view. It doesn't come from the heart!'[98] Tulla's memory is at least in part affective, and she does not recognise it in these books.

Paul, as a journalist, had bought a computer with a modem as soon as they were on the market, surfed the net and finally came across homepages on which those stuck in the past 'but also new young Nazis ["frischgebackene Jungnazis"] aired their mindlessness on pages of hatred. And suddenly – with the name of a ship as the search term – [he] had clicked the right address: www.blutzeuge.de.'[99] Blutzeuge, an old German term for martyr that has the ring of Nazi terminology, is to become important in the story. It is also clear that the sinking of the *Gustloff* will be central – but neither why nor how. The 'origin' of Paul's narrative remains ambiguous. Of course, there is the peculiarity of Paul's birth during the sinking of the *Gustloff* and his mother's continuous

---

[92] Ibid., p. 39. [93] Ibid., p. 41. [94] Ibid., p. 70. [95] Ibid., p. 18.
[96] Ibid., p. 19. [97] Ibid., p. 93. [98] Ibid., p. 94. [99] Ibid., p. 8.

reminders of this fact. The idea of 'surfing the net' and 'suddenly' coming across the web page suggests that it all happens accidentally, whilst the reference to a 'search term' and this being the 'right' address mark it as a purposive endeavour. Paul is, despite protestations to the contrary, displaying an interest in the *Gustloff* that, however, he seeks to conceal.

It later transpires that Paul has been employed by an 'old' writer who believes that his generation should have told this story but has failed to do so.[100] Yet this does not settle the 'why': why did Paul agree, given that he had always resisted his mother's demands that he 'must write this down'? The reader is none the wiser, and it is not clear whether Paul knows himself. He also claims still not to know *how*, if at all, the story should be told: whether chronologically or whether 'he must cross time's path obliquely more or less in the manner of crabs which feign the reverse gear, swinging out sideways, but make headway quite quickly'.[101] The novella is structured on the latter pattern: it interweaves historical elements about Gustloff and his murderer, the sinking of the ship and the flight of Germans at the end of the war with Tulla's life and the story about Konrad (and his narrator father) in the present of the novella. As the title suggests, the 'crabwise' approach to these matters, that perhaps reflects how memory works, namely in ways that challenge chronology,[102] has won out.

This 'crabwalk' finds expression in frequent disruptions of the story in the narrative present with information about Tulla, reflections on the website, thoughts about Paul's own role as narrator and suchlike. For example, Paul claims that he once took a class in 'creative writing' but was told he lacked talent. Now, however, one of his teachers has made him re-emerge: 'the origin of my screwed-up existence was a unique event, exemplary and therefore worth telling'. The former teacher employs the narrator as a ghost-writer, but after a few pages Paul says that he 'does not want to continue in the crabwalk'.[103] He is stuck and does not think it is worth the effort. Nevertheless, Paul pursues the trail of the website because of his mother, he believes, who never let up. She had always told him about it, about how cold the sea was and how the children drowned. 'You must write it down. You owe it to us as a lucky survivor', she said. But, he claims, 'I did not want to. After all, no one wanted to hear about it, not here in the West and much less in the East. The *Gustloff* and its damned story were taboo for decades, in an all-German way, so to speak.'[104] This representation of his refusal is already part of telling the story. His attitude towards the memory of the *Gustloff* is therefore ambivalent. On the one hand, he recognises that there has been

---

[100] Ibid., pp. 77f.   [101] Ibid., pp. 8f.   [102] See Chapter 5.
[103] Grass, *Im Krebsgang*, p. 30.   [104] Ibid., p. 31.

a silence and that this is problematic; on the other, he finds his mother's preoccupation with her memory irritating and does not, at first, want to intervene in the silence. His leftist inclination makes him fearful of the political consequences. For Paul, the question of this memory is part of wider considerations, and he is torn.

'I have sworn . . . to bear witness': Konrad

Because Paul refused, Tulla hoped that her grandson, Konrad, would write about the sinking of the *Gustloff* some day.[105] According to Paul, Tulla started working on Konrad as soon as she had the opportunity, after the fall of the Berlin Wall, when the boy was 10 or 11 years old: she 'filled him up with stories about refugees, stories about atrocities, stories about rapes, which in fact she had not experienced in person'.[106] Tulla thus goes beyond her experience – into areas of which she has no more knowledge than anyone else, but using her survivor status – in her bid to win her grandson over to bear witness to the events of 30 January 1945.

Whilst surfing the net Paul finds a site celebrating Wilhelm Gustloff, born in 1895 in Schwerin. He lived in Switzerland and used his talent for organisation: 'he became a member of the [Nazi] party' and by 1936 had attracted 5,000 new members in Switzerland. He reportedly once said that he most loved in this world his wife and his mother, but if his Führer ordered him to kill them he would, although this quotation is disputed on the website as a 'Jewish' invention.[107] For the purposes of the novella, however, Gustloff is established as a true-believing Nazi. The reader is more likely to trust the narrator with historical information than a fictional Neo-Nazi web page. Throughout the novella the postings are indeed never allowed to speak 'for themselves'; they are always mediated by Paul's commentary and his introduction of corrective historical detail. Neo-Nazi views can apparently not appear without comment, whatever taboos are broken.

Through the combination of Paul's reports of what he finds on www.blutzeuge.de and his own account we learn about David Frankfurter, Gustloff's murderer. Frankfurter, born in 1909 to a rabbi, suffered from chronic suppuration of the bone marrow and had five unsuccessful operations. He went to Germany to study medicine and experienced the excesses against Jews after the Nazis had come to power. He escaped to Switzerland. After his mother's death he once again travelled to Germany and saw his own relatives mistreated. Frankfurter was probably depressed for several reasons – his unsuccessful studies, the loss of his mother, constant physical pain and the political developments – and, towards the end

---

[105] Ibid., p. 94.   [106] Ibid., pp. 100f.   [107] Ibid., pp. 10f.

of 1935, started considering suicide.[108] Eventually, Frankfurter visited Gustloff in Davos and shot him dead.[109] Afterwards, he turned himself in, telling police officers and later, in the same words, the court: 'I shot because I am Jewish. I am fully aware of what I have done and I do not regret it on any account.'[110] Some saw his deed as an act of resistance, others as a cowardly murder. Gustloff, in any event, became a martyr of the Nazi movement, whilst his murderer was forgotten. A ship, maintained by the regime to provide classless holidays to the German people under the heading 'Kraft durch Freude' ('strength through joy'), was named after Gustloff:[111] the *Gustloff* which was sunk on 30 January 1945.

In the midst of all the celebration of Gustloff on the Internet, one chatroom-user corrects the use of the term 'front-line soldier' to describe Gustloff who, he points out, had not served in the First World War.[112] The story then develops further around two characters on the net, Gustloff's admirer, who promotes Nazi views, and his counterpart, who champions Frankfurter. The two call themselves 'Wilhelm' and 'David', and the latter claims to be Jewish. 'Wilhelm' and 'David' begin chatting like friends.[113] The narrator, who is convinced that these are young people and not unreconstructed Nazis, cannot understand why they are so keen on Gustloff.[114] He also begins to suspect that the site is not maintained by a group of Neo-Nazis but by a smart loner[115] and even believes 'David' to be invented by 'Wilhelm'.[116]

Paul regularly visits www.blutzeuge.de and increasingly becomes aware that 'Wilhelm' is his son. After the border to the GDR was opened, Konrad insisted on visiting his grandmother, Tulla, in Schwerin. Eventually, he moved in with her. Tulla, unsurprisingly, told Konrad about her life in Danzig and about the sinking ship, and Konrad became 'her great hope'.[117] Konrad starts his web page, interestingly dedicated, as the Internet address indicates, to Gustloff rather than the *Gustloff*. The desire to bear witness on behalf of his grandmother blurs with Neo-Nazi thought in Konrad's writings. He refers to his 'dear grandmother to whom I have sworn, in the name of the Kameradschaft Schwerin on her white hair to bear witness to the truth and nothing but the truth: it is the Jewry of the world that wants to chain us Germans to the pillory for all time and eternity . . .'[118] Tulla's memories are not affected by such anti-Semitism. Her stories have come to be politicised in a particular way. It is this particular politicisation – the return of Nazi ideology[119] – that seems to mark the

---

[108] Ibid., pp. 15–17.   [109] Ibid., pp. 26–8.   [110] Ibid., p. 28.   [111] Ibid., pp. 28f.
[112] Ibid., p. 36.   [113] Ibid., pp. 48f.   [114] Ibid., p. 50.   [115] Ibid., p. 18.
[116] Ibid., p. 89.   [117] Ibid., p. 44.   [118] Ibid., pp. 73f.
[119] 'The Jew' is, in the last analysis, responsible for the sinking of the ship, according to the webpage. Ibid., p. 14.

intended centre of the novella. This leads to a peculiar tension between the desire to tell the expellees' story and the desire, discussed below, to escape memory, to forget.

The webpage calls to mind[120] the date of the sinking as proof of fate rather than an accident: 'on 30 January 1945 the ship named after Gustloff began to sink, exactly fifty years to the day after the birth of the martyr [*Blutzeuge*], and thereby to mark the general downfall twelve years after the seizure of power, again exactly to the day'.[121] This indicates once more Konrad's Neo-Nazi tendencies, which set him apart from Paul's much-criticised mother. On 30 January 1990 Tulla puts down flowers at the site of the former Gustloff memorial. However, she says she did not do this for Gustloff, but for the sunken ship and the drowned children.[122] She is interested in the human tragedy and her memory of it, not the ideology that Gustloff stood for. On the other hand, with her focus on the drowned children, she shares an important omission with Konrad. She only ever speaks of the refugees and the children and, consequently, she cannot understand what 'the Russian' was thinking when he torpedoed the ship.[123] Similarly, Konrad wants to make the *Gustloff* known to Internet users 'just as a refugee ship'. As Paul points out, Konrad – like Tulla – 'suppresses' the 1,000 U-boat sailors, 370 women navy auxiliaries and the operating crew for the anti-aircraft guns who were also on board. Konrad mentions the wounded soldiers in passing but, despite noting the amount of flour and dry milk on board, fails to say anything about the Croat war volunteers used to complement the crew. Paul cannot understand why Konrad lies 'to himself and others':[124] 'Why did he deny what had been available for years and what was hardly disputed any more even by' those who were stuck in the past? He wonders whether Konrad's desire for a 'clean balance of victims was so urgent' and can only suspect what might have led Konrad to cheat: 'the desire for a clear concept of the enemy'.[125] At any rate, for Konrad the matter is clearly political, as further events in the novella show.

Killing in the name of memory

The relationship between 'Wilhelm' and 'David' takes on a new dimension when the two decide to meet. 'David' comes to Schwerin, and they eventually go to the site of the former Gustloff memorial. There, 'David' declares that, 'as a Jew', he can 'only think of this' and spits three times

---

[120] The German phrase 'in Erinnerung rufen', which Grass uses, is to call to 'memory' rather than to call to 'mind'.
[121] Grass, *Im Krebsgang*, p. 11.   [122] Ibid., p. 91.   [123] Ibid., p. 11.   [124] Ibid., p. 103.
[125] Ibid., p. 104.

onto the spot.[126] Konrad immediately shoots him and – imitating Frankfurter's killing of Gustloff – proceeds to turn himself in, using the words
he later also says in court: 'I shot because I am German.'[127] Konrad
admits the deed but sees himself, as Paul observes, 'beyond any guilt'.[128]
During the trial it turns out that 'David' was not Jewish. His real name
was Wolfgang. Neither Tulla nor Konrad are impressed by this, though
Tulla is upset by the news: he behaved as a Jew, in Tulla's opinion – a
rare display of anti-Semitic views – as he had 'always only talked of our
disgrace'. Konrad simply claims that it had been up to him to decide
whether 'David' had 'spoken and acted' as a Jew.[129]

Konrad argues that he does not hold anti-Semitic views, though he
considers it preferable for the Jews to go to Israel.[130] 'David's' 'execution' had not been about anti-Semitism; it had been about the failure to
honour Gustloff's memory and perhaps about the sinking of the *Gustloff*, for which – upon reflection – Konrad places the responsibility not
with the submarine commander but with Grand Admiral Karl Dönitz,
the commander of the Third Reich's navy, who had permitted military
personnel to go on board the refugee ship. Konrad describes shooting
'David' as his way of commemorating 'the martyr'.[131] It had had little to
do with 'David': 'It was and is about something bigger . . . Schwerin has to
finally honour its great son by name.'[132] Bearing witness for the drowned,
Tulla's motivation, which she hoped to pass on to Konrad, appears at best
secondary. It is unclear how the shooting could contribute to that aim.

The novella finally descends into a morality play, what Barnouw calls 'a
superfluous, noisily pedagogical finale',[133] on the danger of Neo-Nazism.
Paul considers his mother to be the guilty party.[134] Tulla, however, styles
herself as a victim: what happened was painful for her.[135] She does not
link Konrad's deed to her stories about the *Gustloff*, but instead argues
that 'something like this could only happen because for decades one "was
not allowed to speak about the *Gustloff*. Obviously not here in the East.
And where you are in the West, when they spoke of the past at all, then
they spoke continuously only of other bad things, of Auschwitz and such
like."'[136] In the trial, she blames Konrad's parents, whom she considers
unable to love, and the computer which had led Konrad astray. But then
she is back to her favourite theme, 'the ship about which up to now
no one had wanted to know anything' and which had been a source of
endless questions for her grandson.[137] Several explanations are offered

[126] Ibid., p. 174.   [127] Ibid., pp. 175 and 189.   [128] Ibid., p. 178.
[129] Ibid., pp. 181f.   [130] Ibid., p. 196.   [131] Ibid., pp. 191f.   [132] Ibid, p. 192.
[133] Barnouw, *War in the Empty Air*, p. 91.
[134] Grass, *Im Krebsgang*, p. 193; though see also p. 184.
[135] Ibid., p. 179.   [136] Ibid., p. 50.   [137] Ibid., p. 180.

for Konrad's actions, including the failure of his school to engage with his Nazi-inspired views. Paul notes that, in contrast, little was said about Wolfgang, the 'actual victim of the deed';[138] there was more compassion for the perpetrator.[139] Konrad is sent to jail. He changes some of his views towards the end of the novella, but remains committed to Gustloff. Paul eventually goes onto the Internet again and finds a website championing his son as a role model. The text ends with Paul's desperation: 'It does not stop. It will never stop.'[140]

Multiple memories

Each of the main characters of the novella represents a different attitude towards remembering the sinking of the *Gustloff*. For Tulla, remembering the events is both inevitable and crucial. It is perhaps important that she does not allege that they could not be mentioned, but rather that no one wanted to hear. Indeed, the novella repeatedly makes reference to publicly available information about the sinking. Heinz Schön, a crew member, had written a well-researched volume about the *Gustloff* which was published in the FRG but not the GDR. Even in the West there was allegedly no public reaction to the book, no debate. Similarly, a 1950s film and a much later television documentary are portrayed as having fallen on deaf ears.[141]

Paul is sure that Tulla would like the book by Schön – a fellow survivor; he eventually sends it to her.[142] Yet she is dissatisfied with such books. Evidently, they fail to represent her experience. About a documentary-style account written by three Englishmen she says: 'It doesn't come from the heart!'[143] Tulla thus objects to the lack of emotion in historical representation. Her stories revolve around the image of the drowning children. They had jumped or fallen into the water wearing lifebelts, but many of them ended up head down in the water, with their legs sticking up into the air. It is this image of the 'poor children' that does not leave Tulla.

One may wonder whether Tulla is at all interested in *information* about what happened. After all, she already knows what she remembers. Assmann interestingly argues that affective memory is unresponsive to correction or amendment. It is the 'vividness of the affective impression' that is decisive.[144] However, this is not quite the issue here. Apart from Paul's dubious claim that Tulla is lying about the precise circumstances of his

---

[138] Ibid., p. 196.   [139] Ibid., p. 197.   [140] Ibid., p. 216.
[141] Ibid., pp. 61f and 113.   [142] Ibid., pp. 62 and 94.   [143] Ibid., p. 94.
[144] Assmann, *Erinnerungsräume*, p. 274.

birth, there is no suggestion that her memory is faulty. Tulla's negative reaction to Schön's book points rather to its failure to represent 'what it felt like' and to speak to her emotions now. Tulla wants Paul to bear witness on behalf of the 'poor children', to commemorate and mourn them. Thus for her the sinking is a matter of the heart. That is why she wants Paul to write about it. It might also be why his account is fictional, rather than 'factual': better able to depict, as well as evoke, emotions.

Paul has a less affective relationship to the events. He seems to think that if all the available information about the past were out in the open, politically objectionable constructions of memory would become impossible, an attitude he shares with the 'old writer'. In the old writer's view, the disaster of the sinking of the *Gustloff* has become open to abuse, in particular by Neo-Nazis, because it has not been appropriately remembered in the first place. So the obvious solution is to provide more information to the public about what happened, in order to create a more differentiated memory that cannot be so easily instrumentalised. Paul puts this into practice when, throughout the book, he supplements the information he reports from his son's website with further historical detail, in what appears to be an expectation to be able to amend and correct the picture of the past. His apparent view that if only everything was known about the past, it would no longer be open to right-wing manipulation has to contend with the question of whether memory is open to amendment through knowledge, and indeed with the radical impossibility of knowing and making known the past, that is, the impossibility of representing the past simply as it was.

The latter is something Paul is very aware of. With reference to the number of people on board, Paul observes that 'no one knows anything precise',[145] as the mechanisms for registering passengers had broken down under the onslaught of people desperately seeking to leave. His comment could also be read as a wider comment on the impossibility of knowing what exactly happened when the ship went down and few were able to save themselves in lifeboats. Paul reflects that the 'number will always remain uncertain. But what do numbers tell? Numbers are never correct. Six thousand six hundred people were registered, among them five thousand refugees.'[146] It is not known how many were actually on board and Paul undermines our trust in figures: 'If I mention figures, they are not correct', he says. It is not just impossible to be precise; it is not clear what the figures mean: 'How much does one life more or less count?'[147] In the end, figures hinder rather than help the difficult process of representing what happened: 'death disappears behind rows of

---

[145] Grass, *Im Krebsgang*, p. 105.   [146] Ibid., p. 104.   [147] Ibid., p. 152.

numbers'.[148] Detailed statistical information is not the solution in terms of representing the events.

Of the mass flight from East Prussia the narrator says: 'I cannot describe it. No one can describe that.'[149] However, he is of course at the same time describing it.[150] Although it may be impossible to represent it, it is equally impossible not to do so. In writing a book about the memory of the *Gustloff* the story inevitably arrives at some point – even after many digressions – at the sinking itself, which is portrayed as not representable:

> what happened inside the ship cannot be grasped by words . . . Therefore I do not try to imagine the terrible and to force the atrocious into fully painted images, however much my employer presses me to string individual fates together, to make the grand connection with epically sweeping calmness and strained empathy and thus, with words of horror, to do justice to the extent of the catastrophe.[151]

Even Tulla has no words for it, though she says that she could tell stories of epic length about the general events of her flight.[152] Interestingly, though Tulla ceaselessly speaks of these events, she never attempts to write them herself; she wants someone to do it in her place. Paul, who eventually does, escapes into describing how the 1950s film represented the situation; this is, of course, despite the claim to the contrary, also a representation of what happened.

The old writer is convinced that Paul is unable to 'grasp with words the thousand-fold dying',[153] but also that Paul's 'report has got what it takes to be a novella'. Paul claims that this 'literary assessment' means nothing to him, because he is 'merely reporting'.[154] He thus enforces a distinction between genres, the difference in the status or purpose of texts, what Paul Ricoeur notes as the difference in 'the implicit contract between the writer and the reader'.[155] Paul's insistence that he is 'merely reporting' is thus an implicit claim to factuality, which is, however, undermined not only by the reflections on the impossibility of knowing and representing what really happened but also by claims which turn the fictional world into the 'real' reality and thereby draw attention even more clearly to the fictionality of the text. The old writer's identification as Grass through acknowledging him as the author of *Hundejahre* could be seen as shrinking the distance between fiction and reality. The old writer becomes Grass, and therefore the 'real' Grass seems to enter the novella. However, quite apart from the problem that the historical Grass per definitionem cannot be in the

[148] Ibid., p. 136; see also pp. 134f.   [149] Ibid., p. 102.
[150] See also ibid., pp. 99 and 101f.   [151] Ibid., p. 136; but see p. 132.
[152] Ibid., pp. 136 and 157.   [153] Ibid., p. 139.   [154] Ibid., p. 123.
[155] Paul Ricoeur, *Memory, History, Forgetting*, Translated by Kathleen Blamey and David Pellauer (Chicago: The University of Chicago Press 2004), p. 261.

novella, if the old writer were Grass, he should be in charge. But this relationship seems to be overturned when he reports that he, who has known Tulla for a long time, would never have thought that Tulla 'would develop in such a banal direction, for instance into a party functionary and an activist who solidly meets the target'.[156] Moreover, though the old writer is depicted as the employer, and on occasion as forcing the narrator to carry on, it is 'not him' but 'mother' who forces Paul. Paul even claims the old writer is compelled by Tulla.[157] Thus Tulla has control over the old writer, the fictional Grass.

Whilst the boundary between the fictional world of the novella and the supposedly real world of Grass's authorship of *Hundejahre* is deliberately blurred, the fictionality of the text is actually underlined. Grass disturbs the reader's desire to simply identify him with the narrator by appearing as a false Grass. The text inserts a distance between itself and the reader's potential faith in the information it presents: knowledge about the past is not only profoundly problematic, it is also not what is presented here. This is fiction. Readers are not to simply believe what they are told; they have to think for themselves, accept what was highlighted in Chapter 1 as the responsibility of the reader.

Nevertheless, the narrator repeatedly presents historical information as secure and relevant. The problems with Paul's 'neutral' provision of information become most obvious when he intervenes on his son's web page. Konrad enthuses about the young girls whose innocence was to be protected from the reach of the Russian beast. This is a reference to the justification for the Wehrmacht's continuation of the lost fight on the Eastern front: it was to protect German civilians from the alleged barbarity of Soviet troops.[158] Paul points out that, whether innocent or not, these girls had been in uniform complete with swastika, militarily drilled and under oath to the Führer.[159] Whilst this additional information may be correct, one wonders how it is thought to have the potential to affect Konrad's beliefs. Is Paul really implying that it was acceptable – or at least more tolerable – for women to be raped as long as they were in German uniform, drilled and sworn in? Besides, Paul is offering not suppressed historical detail – as he seems to suggest – but an alternative, and frankly questionable, interpretation of information already available. Paul's comment thus undermines his own belief that the problem with the memory of the *Gustloff* has been a lack of information.

---

[156] Grass, *Im Krebsgang*, p. 100.   [157] Ibid., p. 99.
[158] On this, see, however, Heinrich Schwendemann, 'Tod zwischen den Fronten', in: Aust and Burgdorff, *Die Flucht*, esp. pp. 78–80.
[159] Grass, *Im Krebsgang*, p. 105.

Paul's attitude towards and relationship with the past is different from Tulla's. For Tulla, portrayed as the only one to have personal memories of the events, no time seems to have passed between then and now. There is no question: the memory of the sinking must be preserved. Paul, who was there, nevertheless has no recollections of his own: he was only born on the day and, though he insists that his mother is lying about his birth having taken place after her rescue from the *Gustloff*, he could not possibly remember.[160] This merely underlines Paul's unreliability as a provider of information, the fictionality of the story. Both Paul and Tulla point out that there are increasingly fewer witnesses to the events,[161] and this might change the character of the memory.[162] This problematic is illustrated in Konrad. Although Konrad says he wants to bear witness for his grandmother, he appears motivated by other considerations. He is more interested in Gustloff and his memory than in the memory of the sinking of the ship, even if both come together on the website. Konrad, unlike Tulla, needs an extraneous reason for keeping the memory alive: love for his grandmother, perhaps, or his political views. The memory must *become* relevant, though Konrad proclaims a clear attitude towards the past as such: 'Those who forget the history of their people are not worthy of it!'[163] However, Konrad offers not the history of his people but rather only those aspects of the past which he thinks should be remembered. Therefore his father's sole intervention on the website must fail not only because it is bizarre but because it misses the point: Konrad is not interested in an account of the past that is complete and accurate, even if such a thing was possible.

Im Krebsgang discusses the impossibility of doing what it does: representing the past. Reflection upon the status of the representation offered is a characteristic move in fiction, and one that clearly sets it apart from political rhetoric. This is crucial; for it highlights the fact that the problem with political rhetoric that relies on interpretations of the past in order to justify particular courses of action is not merely that such interpretations remain controversial but that it is impossible to invoke a memory that would fully and accurately represent the past. Yet the case cannot simply be closed by observing the impossibility of appropriately depicting the past – arguing, for example, that the Germans should get over it and concentrate on their responsibilities in contemporary international politics, for the past is always represented. Hence it becomes necessary to explore how, if at all, the (im)possibility of representation is acknowledged.

---

[160] Ibid., p. 146.   [161] Ibid., p. 94.
[162] See, for example, Assmann, *Erinnerungsräume*, pp. 12–15.
[163] Grass, *Im Krebsgang*, p. 160.

The imperative to remember and the desire to forget

Paul's attitude towards the past is most ambiguous, even contradictory. Whilst one might expect Paul to be on 'David's' side, he is not satisfied with the boy's attempt at correcting Konrad's representations of the past. Paul roundly criticises 'David' for merely setting in motion 'his anti-fascist prayer wheel'.[164] Paul clearly wants to find for himself some ground *between* his son who is affected by Neo-Nazi ideas and 'David' who represents a shooting over the mark in the other direction: full identification with the victims of the Third Reich. Paul's ambivalent attitude concerns not only how the past should be remembered but whether memory is necessary or desirable at all. Towards the beginning of the novella, he notes that everything is 'past, blown away'.[165] However, the whole drift of his narrative is about the inescabability of the past, including the last sentence: 'It will never stop.'[166]

The profound exasperation with this situation finds its expression in the unfortunate claim that 'history is a blocked-up loo. We flush and flush, and yet the shit comes up.'[167] In other words, all efforts of *Vergangenheitsbewältigung* (coming to terms with the past) have been in vain: the Nazi past always catches up with us again, and history repeats itself.[168] When Konrad shows his father a model *Gustloff* which he built in the correctional facility, Paul thinks: 'Does this not stop? Does this hi/story always start anew?'[169] The phrasing is such that in German the term 'Geschichte' is indeterminate between its two possible but usually grammatically clearly distinguishable meanings. 'Story' and 'history' blur into each other: it is not clear whether Paul fears the recurrence of the story or a repetition of history. Is the concern about Germany descending into oppression, aggression and large-scale human rights abuses, or is it about individual youngsters expressing their views through a violence that is shocking but not comparable?

Whichever the case may be, in an ironic twist on the positions in the *Historikerstreit* Paul, the leftist journalist, ends up wishing that the past would go away (though he also wants to memorialise the Germans' flight from the East: his son has expressed his own 'forbidden' thoughts).[170] He cannot understand that Konrad should be interested in such 'old stories'[171] and groans that this never ends, expressing implicitly his desire that it would. In the *Historikerstreit* it was the Right who were seen to argue that the past was being kept present artificially by the Left and that the Germans should now be allowed to draw a line under the past

---

[164] Ibid., p. 134.   [165] Ibid., p. 37.   [166] Ibid., p. 216.   [167] Ibid., p. 116.
[168] Ibid.   [169] Ibid., p. 208.   [170] Ibid., pp. 210f.   [171] Ibid., p. 76.

and concentrate on the future, whilst the Left opposed such a desire to dispose of the past.[172] In *Im Krebsgang* Paul ends up arguing for disposing of the past, whereas Konrad champions remembering. This reflects the positions as portrayed in the advertisement campaign 'Against forgetting'. In the novella, this swapping of roles remains tenuous, however, for each side stresses the need to remember different aspects of the past. How remembering is valued appears to depend crucially on *what* is to be remembered. Yet this struggle at the same time highlights the fact that forgetting and remembering are not separable in the way suggested by the advertisements, and indeed by accusations from the Left that it is the Right who would like to forget.

The novella seems to end with a challenge to the consensus that it is imperative to remember. Von Weizsäcker had called on Germans to remember the war and the Holocaust; this need to remember was not disputed. There is indeed often concern about the waning of memory, the ease of forgetting. However, the end of *Im Krebsgang* points to the inescapability of memory: it always comes back. What is more, the last lines speak of a palpable desire to escape the grasp of memory. Yet it is not so simple, for escaping memory is, according to the novella, neither possible nor desirable. Despite the final lines, *Im Krebsgang* is obviously intended as a contribution to memory and one that overcomes or at least addresses the suppression of particular memories. Grass construes the space into which he launches his book, within the text, as a silence or even taboo. For example, the 1995 survivors' meeting in the novella was, for the first time, able to include those from the former East Germany, where previously, on official instructions, the sinking of the ship had to be covered in silence.[173] But it is not merely a matter of suppression in the GDR. Paul refers to himself as a 'survivor of a tragedy that has been forgotten by the whole world'.[174] He says that he had not wanted to write about the disaster, because no one was interested in either German state, that the story of the *Gustloff* had been 'taboo' in both Germanies.[175] In the GDR the topic had been ruled out altogether – the brotherly Soviet Union could never have committed such an atrocity against the Germans – and in the FRG it was mentioned but always tarnished by the idea that remembering or commemorating such suffering could only ever serve to make appear less horrendous the crimes committed by the Germans. In other words, Grass seems to agree with the advertisement 'Against forgetting' that the suffering of Germans at the end of the war, in particular in the context of flight and expulsion, has been forgotten. Yet it is

---

[172] 'Historikerstreit'.   [173] Grass, *Im Krebsgang*, p. 92.   [174] Ibid., p. 41.
[175] Ibid., p. 31.

precisely the political exploitation of this topic by the Right that Grass's text seeks to disrupt: the taboo is problematic in Paul's eyes because it creates an opportunity for right-wing manipulation. Paul describes the *Gustloff* at one point as 'a ship which did not only sink, but which is a legend because [this wás] suppressed'.[176] Despite everything, memory persisted, but it could not be publicly discussed, leading to the development of a legend.

Grass's alter ego in the novella, the old writer, has a veritable guilt complex about not having dealt with this dangerous suppression earlier. Although, because of his connections to Danzig, he would have been ideally placed to write the story, he could not:

Unfortunately, he said, he did not find that sort of thing easy. His omission, regrettable, even more: his failure. But he did not want to talk his way out of it, merely admit that, towards the mid-sixties, he had been fed up with the past, that the voracious present which was constantly saying nownownow had prevented him from [reacting] in time over roughly two hundred pages . . . Now it was too late for him. He had not actually invented me as an alternative but found me after searching for a long time amongst the lists of survivors like a piece of lost property. As a person of rather pathetic image, I was nevertheless predestined: born as the ship was sinking.[177]

The old writer considers that it would have been the 'task of his generation' to 'give expression to the misery of the East Prussian refugees'. One should never have been silent about 'so much suffering, just because one's own guilt had been so overpowering and the professed remorse urgent'; one should never have allowed the 'avoided topic' to be left to the right-wingers. This 'omission was indescribable'.[178]

Im Krebsgang enacts a paradox: it is about the memory of the *Gustloff* and as such inevitably contributes to this memory. In view of the criticism in the text of the suppression of this memory the contribution to such a memory appears to be an important function of the text. However, the text itself – the development of the plot, for example – expresses the negative effects of the very memory that is being constructed, and the desire to escape what is represented as inescapable. On the one hand, it could or even must be seen as a contribution to the fight against (official) silencing – if that is what it is – of the memories of the expellees' suffering: the 2 million dead, the violence even against those who survived, their loss of their *Heimat* and their difficult integration into an unwelcoming environment, at least in the FRG. In fact, Grass has written exactly the 'roughly two hundred pages' that his alter ego claims not to be able to

---

[176] Ibid., p. 63.   [177] Ibid., pp. 77f.   [178] Ibid., p. 99.

produce.[179] On the other hand, the novella speaks of an urgent desire to escape this memory because of the possibility of right-wing abuse. This tension becomes palpable by reading the dedication page and the last two sentences of the novella together: 'In memoriam' it all starts, only to end with 'It does not stop. It will never stop.'[180]

Forgetting to remember

A 'common-sense' definition of forgetting might be 'being unable to remember'.[181] However, the issue is more insidious. Bartov insists, in relation to French memories of the Holocaust, 'that one cannot forget what one does not remember'.[182] In order to forget, one has to remember in the first place. Conversely, in order to remember, one has to forget. Assmann argues that forgetting is necessary for the process of remembering.[183] She claims that what 'is selected for memory is always defined by the edges of forgetting'.[184] Remembering without forgetting is impossible. As Derrida points out, a 'limitless memory would in any event be not memory but infinite self-presence'.[185] This means that any simplistic opposition of remembering versus forgetting, and by implication simply valuing one over the other, is impossible. Derrida and Bernard Stiegler claim, in the context of the politics of the archive, that the 'very fact that there is a politics of memory already poses a problem. It is necessary to have memory, we think spontaneously, and memory is better than amnesia.'[186] Yet it is, they suggest, not as simple as that: 'Why is it necessary to have memory, in the end? You are never going to prove that memory is better than nonmemory. What is more, memory includes forgetting. If there is selectivity, it is because there is forgetting.'[187]

Remembering versus forgetting is a false opposition. The commitment to remembering as such, apparent in debates both about the past and about using military force, means little. Indeed, opposing remembering to forgetting offers a false choice. In *Im Krebsgang* as in public debates in Germany the problem is not so much whether to remember or to forget

---

[179] On this, see also Volker Hage, 'Das tausendmalige Sterben', in: Aust and Burgdorff, *Die Flucht*, p. 41.
[180] Grass, *Im Krebsgang*, p. 216.
[181] *Collins English Dictionary*, 3rd updated edn (Glasgow: HarperCollins Publishers 1994), p. 604.
[182] Bartov, *Germany's War*, p. 170.   [183] Assmann, *Erinnerungsräume*, pp. 19 and 411.
[184] Ibid., p. 408.
[185] Jacques Derrida, *Dissemination*, Translated by Barbara Johnson (London: Athlone Press 1981), p. 109.
[186] Jacques Derrida and Bernard Stiegler, *Echographies of Television: Filmed Interviews*, Translated by Jennifer Bajorek (Cambridge: Polity Press 2002), p. 63.
[187] Ibid., p. 64.

but rather *how* to remember; memory, in some form, and its implications are inescapable. Tulla, Paul and Konrad all remember the sinking of the *Gustloff* in some way, but each does so differently. *Im Krebsgang* suggests that Konrad's version of memory is profoundly problematic; it leads him to kill an innocent boy. Paul's criticism, which the 'old writer' approves of, is that Konrad's information about the past is incomplete. This, however, is not an effective challenge. *Im Krebsgang* itself suggests that it is impossible to represent the past accurately and completely. Equally, it is impossible to remember everything about the past; forgetting is always part of remembering.

Thus it is not enough to simply affirm a belief in remembering. The struggle between Paul and Konrad indicates that, although remembering and forgetting are inextricably linked, this does not mean that any memory is perceived to be as good as any other. Nor can we freely select what to forget, simply pick and choose, because it is anyway impossible to remember everything. Memories may appear unbidden. And even if intentional forgetting, as Nietzsche championed it, were possible, matters are more complicated. Firstly, different *appropriate* memories may be possible, though Grass construes Konrad's to be beyond the pale. Secondly, and crucially, although Paul objects that Konrad's memory excludes important facts, it is actually the political implications of these omissions that Paul is concerned about. The problem is not a potential duty towards the omitted victims of Nazi atrocities, but the fear of what Konrad and young people like him may do. In other words, the issue is that memory does not merely mark a relation to the past, but one to the present and indeed the future.

The implications of memory for the present have been explored in relation to identity:[188] memory is about a past that is in some way (produced as) 'ours' and therefore inextricably linked to representations of who we are. Memories are not only about where 'we' come from but about where 'we' might go. They are thus part of our inventions of community. This is evident in how Konrad uses the past, envisioning 'the Germans' in light of this past. The way in which *Im Krebsgang* has been co-opted into public debate reacts to precisely such an alleged attempt at identity construction; identification with the group of the remembered – the expellees from the East – is assumed, and thus a return to a German self-image as victims of the Second World War is diagnosed. This interpretation leaves to one side something crucial, however: the implied criticism of precisely this

---

[188] See, for example, Anderson, *Imagined Communities*; Assmann, *Erinnerungsräume*; Gerd Knischnewski and Ulla Spittler, 'Memories of the Second World War and National Identity in Germany', in: Martin Evans and Ken Lunn (eds.), *War and Memory in the Twentieth Century* (Oxford: Berg 1997), pp. 239–54.

process in the figure of Konrad. The novella is, at any rate, seen as having set off a wider debate about whether Germans are construing themselves as victims of the Second World War (again). Grass, it is alleged, through focusing on German suffering, becomes part of the 'transformation of the society of perpetrators into one of victims'.[189]

Hubert Spiegel, in his review of *Im Krebsgang*, calls the novella an 'important book', although he argues that a number of criticisms can be raised. He acknowledges the difficulty of speaking about the sinking of the *Gustloff*, even if information about the disaster has always been available. Spiegel notes the consensus in the FRG not to count up 'German suffering and injustices committed against Germans' against the Nazis' crimes. He claims that one could say that Grass's termination of this consensus comes too late, when reference to German suffering in the Second World War no longer requires much courage. This argument is perhaps more interesting for what it says about the reviewer's views than for what it elucidates about the novella. There is, in the review, a continuous subtle shifting between 'mentioning German suffering' and 'counting up victims against each other'. It seems to me that Grass can be seen to terminate the consensus on never doing the latter only if this consensus does not exist – in other words, if the reviewer already considers the suffering represented in the novella something that may be used to reduce, in some way, the Germans' responsibility for the crimes of the Third Reich.

This is decidedly more shocking an attitude than anything expressed in *Im Krebsgang*. It is the inevitable possibility of memories being co-opted into such political argumentation that makes their telling difficult, if no less necessary. Spiegel raises questions that invariably arise in relation to fiction on this topic: 'Is it permissible for there to be victims on the German side, on the side of the perpetrators? And may their suffering be the object of artistic representation?'[190] However, the problem is not so much the representation of German suffering as the immediate link to victimhood, and in particular the supposed 'balance sheet' on which victims of the Holocaust are counted up against German victims of the expulsions.[191] The worries about recourse to the memory of the expulsions are based on the fear of an unwarranted construction of Germans as victims. If this were the case, and for some it will invariably be, this would certainly be a matter of concern in terms of an appropriate relation to an unpalatable past. The concern is that memories of suffering lead to Germans encountering themselves as victims in the past, and that this would be not merely inappropriate but politically dangerous. Grass's

---

[189] See Hage, 'Unter Generalverdacht', 178, which is critical of such critiques.
[190] Spiegel, 'Das mußte aufschraiben!'.
[191] This problem is further discussed in Chapter 3.

choice of the sinking of the *Gustloff* to represent the fate of the refugees and expellees perhaps heightens such concerns: after all, the sinking of a ship full of refugees, mainly women and children, could be described as a massacre, though it was not a war crime.[192] The focus on the drowning of thousands of children – the image of innocence – may be seen to obscure why they escaped onto the ship in the first place: the war of aggression, the war of extermination and the Holocaust, all perpetrated by their compatriots.

However, two points seem important here. Firstly, Grass, unlike the political discourse, of which his novella is seen by some to be a part, and indeed some official commemoration, does not make it easy for Germans to take on the guise of 'victims'. Not even the navy auxiliaries – young girls – count as 'innocent' in *Im Krebsgang*, as Paul's unfortunate but telling intervention shows. Roman Bucheli observes about Second World War memories in Grass's *oeuvre*: 'It is painful wherever you look; you were perpetrator and victim in one; you felt shame for both. This synchronicity of guilt and disgrace, which cannot be offset against each other, represents a basic constant of his work.'[193] Secondly, it may be worth asking whether there is something at work here other than construing Germans as victims. Perhaps the current concern with the experiences of ordinary Germans in the Second World War is more to do with a concern with the fate of civilians in war generally. With Germany willing to use its military again, interest in the situation of a civilian population caught up in war is not merely reactionary. Although warfare has changed profoundly since the Second World War, civilians still become victims of attacks. From this angle, the *Gustloff* seems an interesting case, as there might not be such a large difference between the Soviets sinking this ship in the belief that it was carrying troops and NATO bombing refugees mistaken for a military convoy, for example.[194]

No convincing explanation has been offered for why the Germans now – sixty years after the end of the war – should be so keen to redefine themselves as victims. In other words, we lack a response to the question that *Im Krebsgang* raises but never really addresses: 'Why only now?'[195] If remembering German suffering was such a grand strategy of exoneration, one would think that the Germans would have used it before. Whilst memories of suffering were popular and important in the 1950s, they had become politically unacceptable. The idea that these memories are used for an exculpatory 'balance sheet' seems to miss more

---

[192] Höges et al., 'Die verdrängte Tragödie', p. 60.

[193] Roman Bucheli, 'Die verspätete Erinnerung', *Neue Zürcher Zeitung*, 09-10/02/02, 63.

[194] Press conference by Jamie Shea and Brigadier General Giuseppe Marani, *NATO Press Conferences*, 15/04/99 (www.nato.int/kosovo/press/p990415a.htm).

[195] Grass, *Im Krebsgang*, p. 7.

than it explains. The function of the 'balance sheet' is supposedly to diminish the Germans' guilt and responsibility. The question, however, remains: why should this suddenly be so important sixty years after the war, when today's Germans could so simply thwart any accusations of guilt by pointing to their date of birth? Why, in the context of an unprecedented – if perhaps still inadequate – level of acceptance of involvement in and responsibility for the Third Reich, should the Germans exhume the memory of their dead civilians in defence of their ancestors' actions? Although it might make Germans feel good not just to be the villains of the piece and have some proper victims, too, that hardly offers an explanation; claiming that it does hints at a nervousness over the political implications of such memories. The question remains: why is the fate of the expellees more relevant to the wider public in Germany today than it has been for decades?

The idea that Germans are construing themselves as victims *again* in a bid to exonerate *themselves* betrays an atemporal understanding of the matter. Today's Germans are simply equated with the Germans of the 1950s (*again*) and the Germans of the Third Reich (*themselves*). This trivialises the matter, even in view of the responsibility of the German community for their past. Memory is often thought of as located in the present and thus as able to change over time – an issue to be explored in Chapter 5. Grass's representation fails to address this temporal element. Although Tulla, Paul and Konrad could be seen as embodying different memories in time, in themselves each of their memories remains static, and therefore Grass's text provides little by way of an answer to the question it poses: 'Why only now?' Just like related public debates, *Im Krebsgang* largely conceptualises the memories of the sinking of the *Gustloff* in the context of the Third Reich and the fear of a return of Neo-Nazi thinking. This, however, provides no indication as to why Germans now desire to remember this event, if indeed they do. In fact, *Im Krebsgang* represents a lost opportunity in that – with the figure of Konrad – it remains stuck in the idea that an interest in these aspects of German history is indicative of Neo-Nazi tendencies. In that sense, the pedagogical finale is not so much superfluous as problematic. *Im Krebsgang* fails to address the phenomenon of widespread interest in the expulsions and strategic bombing amongst the German population and in particular amongst the 'generation of the grandchildren'.[196]

---

[196] For a different rendering of the implications of the *Gustloff* sinking, see a novel by a member of the 'generation of the grandchildren': Tanja Dückers, *Himmelskörper* (Berlin: Aufbau-Verlag 2003). For a reference to the interest of this generation in this history, see Christian Habbe and Hans-Ulrich Stoldt, 'Tief in jedem Hinterkopf', interview with František Černý, in: Aust and Burgdorff, *Die Flucht*, p. 129.

The reframed war revisited

Maurice Halbwachs points out that we recall and localise our memories in relation to society. He argues that 'most frequently, we appeal to our memory *only* in order to answer questions which others have asked us, or that we suppose they could have asked us'.[197] In other words, the recollection of memories is already a response. Apart from being consequences of the policies and actions of the Third Reich, the expulsions of Germans from the East and the strategic bombing of German cities share their connection with war. It is therefore not inconceivable that at least some recent interest in these events stems not from a new wish to excuse the Nazi regime and ordinary Germans' involvement in it, but rather from what is experienced as a 'return' of war.

Apart from the existence of the Bundeswehr, the highest purpose of which was described, during the Cold War, as ensuring it would not be used,[198] the FRG had no involvement with war until the 1990s. It did not participate in the 1991 Gulf War, but the conflict set off the debate about deployments abroad. Such operations started with a deployment of paramedics in Cambodia and reached their climax so far, depending on interpretation, with the participation in the bombing in relation to Kosovo or with the deployment of special forces in Afghanistan. In other words, the FRG was confronted with the possibility of using – or even the imperative to use – their armed forces for military purposes and ultimately war. At the same time, war became a more frequent issue for 'the West' more generally, in particular since the events of September 11, 2001 and the US reaction to them. In this context, it is an obvious move to ask about Germans' experiences in war. Until recently, the Second World War was the last war Germany had been involved in, and certainly the last one a large section of the population had experienced, particularly as civilians. Second World War memories were invoked from the start in political debate about the usage of the military instrument, and these references may have contributed to the recent interest.

Thus, through the question of war, Second World War memories have become important in a double way: on the one hand because they were referred to by politicians in order to illustrate and justify their claims about war, and on the other hand because it was increasingly significant to understand what war is like. I showed in Chapter 1 how politicians explicitly linked the use of military force to Second World War memories.

---

[197] Maurice Halbwachs, *On Collective Memory*, Edited, translated and with an introduction by Lewis A. Coser (Chicago: The University of Chicago Press 1992), p. 38 (italics added).
[198] See Bald, *Militär und Gesellschaft*, p. 91.

Foreign Minister Kinkel's reframing of the Second World War so as to make central the accomplishment of the liberators rather than Wehrmacht atrocities or German aggression was highlighted. Kinkel's argument in support of a Bundeswehr deployment in Bosnia was based on invoking memory and on arguing that Germans had 'forgotten too quickly' that they had been liberated through the use of force. In other words, Kinkel asserted that it is necessary to remember in order to identify the right course of action today. His argument thus implies that it is good to remember, that he remembers, and that, based on remembering, he is able to tell what the FRG should do.

Yet Kinkel's narrative is also clearly marked by forgetting. Obviously, Kinkel 'left out' what the conservatives raise in their advertisement campaign, the expulsions of Germans from the East and the division of Germany, and thus information that may have raised doubts as to whether the Germans had been 'liberated'. More significantly, his argument is haunted by another absence. Kinkel referred to the Kohl doctrine – that German soldiers should not be deployed in the Balkans – without ever spelling out *why*. In other words, the reason for the Kohl doctrine is left out. Of course, for Kinkel's argument it is crucial that Wehrmacht atrocities are de-emphasised or forgotten.

One might, however, have expected the opposition to clarify just why the Bundeswehr could not be deployed in the Balkans as Kinkel conspicuously failed to respond to shouts of 'Why?' from the opposition during his speech in the Bundestag.[199] Opposition leader Scharping referred to 'good reasons' for not participating in the implementation of the UN mandate in Bosnia and the 'dreadfulness' of the Second World War. This 'dreadfulness' appears at first only in the passive voice: this 'part of Europe' had to 'suffer under the dreadfulness of the Second World War'.[200] There is no indication as to how this 'dreadfulness' came about. Still, it might be too obvious to say so. Scharping referred several more times in the abstract to 'the historical situation' and the 'German past' which meant that a deployment of German soldiers in the former Yugoslavia was ill-advised.[201] But matters become interesting when he starts spelling out why 'the German past is at work in the heads of the Serbian soldiers'. Firstly, there is the issue of propaganda and thus not per se of the previously cited German past but its – obviously illegitimate – instrumentalisation by Serbian groups. Secondly, there are particular circumstances of German actions in Yugoslavia and especially Bosnia that go beyond the generic dreadfulness of the Second World War. As an

---

[199] Deutscher Bundestag, *Plenarprotokoll*, 13/48, 30/06/95, 3957.
[200] Ibid., 3959.   [201] Ibid., 3962.

example Scharping cited the co-operation of the SS leadership with Muslim Bosnians. These Bosnians perpetrated atrocities 'that confused even those who otherwise had little objection to cruelty'.[202] So, in Scharping's representation, the problem lies not, as one might have expected, with crimes committed by Germans but with unreasonable propaganda and the Germans' unfortunate association with overzealous and barbarous Bosnians. The Germans *themselves* are not represented as perpetrators in Scharping's argument at all.

Further opposition statements remained in the abstract. Joschka Fischer asserted that 'memories of a warring Germany' should not be refreshed anywhere, and particularly not in the former Yugoslavia.[203] He provided an explanation: he opposed deployments to areas where 'the Wehrmacht caused havoc in the cruellest way in the Second World War'.[204] Gregor Gysi made a similar point.[205] Still the audience is left to fill in a large blank: what precisely is meant by the Wehrmacht 'causing havoc'? 'Causing havoc' might be seen as an ordinary part of war, especially if one believes that war is hell, as Bartov argues Germans do.[206] The outrage over the 1997 exhibition on Wehrmacht crimes suggests that the atrocities committed by the Wehrmacht were not specifically remembered[207] and had therefore been anything but too obvious to mention. The reconfirmation of the Kohl doctrine thus revolves around a simultaneous remembering and forgetting. Wehrmacht atrocities are remembered inasmuch as they form the centre of the doctrine, but they are at the same time forgotten: entirely left out in Kinkel's case, curiously defined away in Scharping's and abstracted in Fischer's and Gysi's.

This is not dissimilar to both the advertisement campaign 'against forgetting' and indeed Grass's novella, for closer investigation of the flight and expulsion of Germans from the East leads to questions as to why they were forced to leave, why they were treated in ways that led to a large number of deaths and why many of them chose to run before they could be forced to leave.[208] Grass's narrator Paul is shocked by the one-sided focus of his son's web page on atrocities committed by Soviet forces against German civilians. The website refers to the 'Russian beast' from which girls and women were fleeing.[209] Paul notes that at the time the 'acquired contempt of the Russian ["des Russischen"] turned into fear

[202] Ibid., 3963.   [203] Ibid., 3982.   [204] Ibid., 3974.   [205] Ibid., 3980.
[206] Bartov, *Germany's War*, p. 12.   [207] See Chapter 4, pp. 129–41.
[208] Of course, one can explain this with reference simply to the territorial changes agreed by the Allies which foresaw the transfer of populations and to the Russian way of warfare. For the latter, see the controversial Andreas Hillgruber, *Zweierlei Untergang: Die Zerschlagung des Deutschen Reiches und das Ende des europäischen Judentums* (Berlin: Siedler 1986).
[209] Grass, *Im Krebsgang*, p. 103.

of the Russians'.[210] What remains unsaid despite Paul's intervention is how Soviet troops and civilians had been treated by the Wehrmacht and other German units during occupation and war. The 'conservatives and critical liberals' of the advertisement campaign are keen to remind us of the expulsions; they allege this has been forgotten. But they make no reference to what preceded it.

Thus one may conclude that we see here an apologist attitude to the German past that does not cease to cause concern: what is left out are some of the worst Nazi crimes. So should we not appeal to the imperative to remember, and remember *everything*, in order to undermine such politically motivated exclusions? My argument has left us unable to have faith in such an option. Forgetting is an inevitable part of remembering. It makes no sense to aim for a 'complete' memory. Such a thing does not exist. Forgetting is not simply the opposite of remembering. Rather, remembering is structurally dependent on forgetting, is always already marked by forgetting. We always remember and forget at the same time. This means that the idea of getting memory to conform more closely to the 'full truth' is not only a narrow concern but one doomed to fail. Quite apart from the radical impossibility of 'true' knowledge about the past, this ignores the inextricable relationship of remembering and forgetting.

Little is thus gained by demonstrating that, for example, the memory of the Second World War invoked by Kinkel entails forgetting, for forgetting is inevitable. One may, of course, be concerned about *what* is forgotten and which political purposes such forgetting serves. Yet what is crucial is the move that conceals the forgetting in the first place, namely the way in which full remembering is portrayed as both necessary and possible. Indeed, it is rendered as telling 'the truth' about the past, obscuring the inevitable forgetting. In other words, the political discourse plays on the power of the 'we remember'; it does not admit its limitations. It is important to challenge this by acknowledging precisely that remembering everything is not possible, by acknowledging the ambiguity of memory. Rather than asserting a different, more appropriate memory, it is actually recognising the inevitable uncertainties involved that may allow us to challenge the way in which the supposed 'knowledge' about the past is presented as an answer to an ethico-political question in the present: we know what is right because we remember.

Concluding thoughts

This chapter has started to challenge the closure that is effected by how Second World War memories are spoken of in political discourse. Literary

---

[210] Ibid., p. 102.

writing is interesting not only because it may present an alternative vision of what is or should be remembered but also because it presents memories differently and reflects on what it means to articulate memories. Unlike official acts of commemoration, which necessarily seek to paper over struggles about memory in a bid to invent and maintain community, literature can bear the tension between different possible memories. Von Weizsäcker noted the diversity of memory, but only to immediately close down the issue. In contrast, *Im Krebsgang* is organised around a diversity of memories which both overlap and diverge. Although Konrad's version of memory is condemned in the novella, Paul is not able to convince Konrad. Paul's memory may be portrayed as superior to Konrad's, but it is not without its own problems. There is nothing to suggest that his is the 'solution' to the problem of remembering the expulsions. Moreover, Tulla's in many ways problematic memories are nevertheless not obviously illegitimate. Despite Grass's at times overly transparent morality tale, a multiplicity of possible memories emerges, and readers have to judge for themselves. This is difficult for at least two reasons: firstly, because the tricky question of political implications must be confronted; and, secondly, because there is no pretence that there are easy grounds for such judgement.

German memories of the flight and expulsion are politically unwelcome owing to the alleged possibility of instrumentalisation. The nervousness over interest in Second World War memories is telling. That Grass embraces expellees' memories demonstrates, if nothing else, that there is no straightforward link between memories and political positions. Konrad, who tries to use the sinking of the *Gustloff* to promote his political convictions, makes a mess of it, but since he persuades himself enough to shoot another boy the danger seems to be confirmed. However, through Paul's reflections it becomes clear that simply forgetting or suppressing memories is not a solution. This is arguably what previously happened, and still the past is rearing its ugly head. So Paul attempts his rationalist solution: he aims to amend his son's memory through (historical) knowledge. If only everyone knew the full story, instrumentalisation for unpalatable political purposes would fail. And yet this does not work. Memory is not, and cannot be, about knowing everything. It relies on forgetting for its very possibility, and thus it does not, in any trivial sense, represent an overcoming of forgetting. Indeed, the issue of what we should remember, how we should remember, is, unsurprisingly, not one about knowledge alone. Grass is reproached for playing into the hands of the Right, but *not* with presenting any false information about the past.

As a result, the problem of right-wing politics may not be solved through the promotion of the 'right' memory. It is not possible to identify such a thing, nor would the 'right' memory necessarily lead to the 'right' political convictions. And yet the 'crabwise' approach of fiction to the issue of memory is important. Hage observes that the 'many-voiced access to the tragedy gives Grass the possibility of addressing aspects beyond the politically correct'.[211] It is not just that literature may present a multiplicity of positions without necessarily judging between them.[212] By stressing the fictionality of what might appear to be information and reflecting upon the necessarily imperfect act of representation, literature, more fundamentally, disturbs our faith in (the possibility of) knowing and thereby keeps open the question of memory. By refusing an answer as to what constitutes appropriate memory, it places us where we should be – and inevitably always are – with respect to difficult memories. We may have all the available information, but we still know that we don't know: we know neither what the past was nor what we should do.

It is useful to reflect here upon Derrida's discussion of the limitation of knowledge. Although knowledge incurs our trust, knowledge is not only imperfect but also fails to provide solutions to the most difficult problems that we are faced with. These call instead for responsibility, decisions:

If there are responsibilities to be taken and decisions to be made, responsibilities and decisions worthy of the name, they belong to the time of a risk and of an act of faith. Beyond knowledge. For if I decide because *I know*, within the limits of what *I know* and *know I must do*, then I am simply deploying a foreseeable program and there is no decision, no responsibility, no event.[213]

When confronted with an ethico-political question we may *want* to turn to the relative security of knowledge. What Derrida argues is that this move cannot succeed. This type of question cannot be answered through knowledge; the call for responsibility is a call beyond knowledge. We need to make a decision – which is different from just a choice between pre-given options – in a condition of risk, of radical insecurity. Yet this does not mean that we may shun knowledge. Despite the need to go beyond it, knowledge remains important. Derrida points out that 'to go beyond does not mean to discredit that which we exceed'.[214] In Derrida's words,

For there to be decision and responsibility, I am not saying that one needs ignorance or some form of not-knowing; not at all, on the contrary, one needs to know

---

[211] Hage, 'Das tausendmalige Sterben', 45.
[212] On the advantages and disadvantages of such multiplicity, see Barnouw, *War in the Empty Air*, pp. 34f.
[213] Jacques Derrida, 'Autoimmunity: Real and Symbolic Suicides', in: Giovanna Borradori, *Philosophy in a Time of Terror: Dialogues with Jürgen Habermas and Jacques Derrida* (Chicago: The University of Chicago Press 2003), p. 118.
[214] Ibid., p. 133.

and one needs to know as much as possible and as well as possible, but between one's knowledge and the decision, the chain of consequence must be interrupted. One must, in some way, arrive at a point at which one does not know what to decide for the decision to be made. Thus a certain undecidability, contrary to what one says and often pretends to think, the undecidability – this one, in any case – is the condition or the opening of a space for an ethical or political decision, and not the opposite.[215]

Thus we are stuck between the necessity of an impossible knowledge and the inadequacy of knowledge, even if we could have it, to the task that we are confronted with. In other words, we are in a position of considerable uncertainty when we confront questions that require a responsible decision, for example about how we should remember the Second World War or about whether military force should be deployed. It is therefore the pretence or illusion of certainty created by the invocation of memory and the claiming of lessons from the past that is the problem.

It is important to undermine such certainty. Taking into account the public struggle over memory and its political implications, and in particular the doubts that literature may raise, may do so. It would be no mean feat to disturb the confidence of those asserting not only the need to remember but their clear view of *how*. The confident use of memory as knowledge to address the problem of military intervention is based on such certainty. This move is undermined by any deeper reflection on memory. How we should remember is a significant ethico-political question, one that reaches in some way beyond knowledge, particularly when memories are deployed in political debate. This, of course, is already a concern both of the debate about memories and of Grass: the controversy is not about what we know but about what we think we ought to do, politically.

Inasmuch as the imperative to remember is an expression of the need to *know* it fails to appreciate that the question of how we should remember reaches beyond knowledge. The problem of 'unwelcome' memories – such as of the suffering of German expellees – cannot be solved through an appeal to knowledge. Trying to do so obscures what is important: the inevitable tension between different experiences of and perspectives on these events, the impossibility of arriving at a representation that does justice to everyone. This impossibility might be vexing to some, but it is at the same time what keeps open the space for politics.[216] Insofar as Grass's exploration of different memories does not offer grounds for

---

[215] Jacques Derrida, *Negotiations: Interventions and Interviews 1971–2001*, Edited and translated by Elizabeth Rottenberg (Stanford: Stanford University Press 2002), p. 298.

[216] As Grass's text reminds us, events could easily have turned out differently. See *Im Krebsgang*, p. 174.

judgement between them, it leaves us with a tension. This irresolvability is important not least because the question of war has been addressed in the context of these memories which have been dealt with in ritualistic but eminently 'acceptable' ways – in other words, in ways that apparently solve and thereby conceal the ethico-political questions involved. Recognising the tensions, the uncertainty and the lack of universally acceptable grounds for judgement would be an important step towards repoliticising the problem, towards acknowledging that what is at issue is a decision that is pre-determined neither by the past nor by anything else.

3   Wounds of memory

Kinkel's reinterpretation of the implication of Second World War memories asserted not only that it was possible for Germans to contribute to international military operations but that it was imperative. Chapter 2 showed that his argument was problematic. Nevertheless, it paved the way for an increasingly assertive use of force by the FRG. Yet in the summer of 2002 the government and the people categorically refused to consider any involvement in the proposed war against Iraq. This was perhaps particularly surprising in view of the claim that Iraq would be liberated as Germany and Japan had been in 1945, an idea that should have sat nicely with the justifications for using military force that Kinkel had offered. These revolved around the Germans' responsibility, as a result of Allied liberation and the guilt of the Nazi regime, to actively contribute to wars against oppression. Yet there was widespread agreement in the FRG that the war against Iraq was unjustifiable. Thus, whilst others were debating the pros and cons of invading Iraq, the Germans had a debate about a different war: the Second World War, and in particular their memory of the bombing of cities.

This chapter explores memories of this 'strategic bombing'. It starts by observing the scale of the destruction wreaked upon German cities and then explores three occasions for discussing the so-called 'air war':[1] firstly, the 'year of remembrance' 1995 and in particular the federal president's speech on the fiftieth anniversary of the bombing of Dresden; secondly, a debate about the failure of German writers to adequately represent the air war; and thirdly, a recent book by a historian that led to considerable controversy. The common theme that emerges from these three different reflections on German experiences and memories of strategic bombing is the worry that they imply that Germans were victims of the Second World War, and that this is unacceptable in view of their guilt. This theme, already encountered in Chapter 2, seems to revolve around set arguments.

---

[1] The German debate refers to *Luftkrieg*, air war. This is a misnomer, as it suggests that it took place only or primarily in the air.

In order to shed more light on why these agreed and politically acceptable terms of the debate might be problematic this chapter explores two novels, Ledig's *Vergeltung* and Mulisch's *Das steinerne Brautbett*.

Don't mention the war?

In his novel *Slaughterhouse 5* Vonnegut has the narrator read out a letter from the US Air Force in response to his request for information about the results of the bombing of Dresden. The information, the letter says, is 'top secret still', prompting the narrator's wife to exclaim: 'My God – from *whom*?'[2] This is a good question. Nothing seems less secret than the destruction done to German cities by American and British bombing. The images of destroyed cities and in particular of ruined churches – some of which, like St Nikolai in Hamburg, have been preserved as memorials[3] – are familiar, and the scars in urban environments remain visible today.[4]

The bombing had very serious consequences. All statistics are subject to debate, but they give an indication of the impact. According to Mark Connelly, 3.37 million residential buildings were flattened;[5] Wolfram Bickerich claims that within the boundaries of the old FRG 41 per cent of pre-war flats had been destroyed.[6] W.G. Sebald claims that 7.5 million Germans were rendered homeless.[7] According to Hans Mommsen, 80 per cent of people in the old Reich changed their residence during the war, and of those at least 7 million had been affected by air raids.[8] Two million children were evacuated as part of the *Kinderlandverschickung*,[9]

---

[2] Kurt Vonnegut, *Slaughterhouse 5, or The Children's Crusade: A Duty-Dance with Death* (London: Vintage 2003), p. 8.

[3] See also Jochen Bölsche, 'So muss die Hölle aussehen', in: Stephan Burgdorff and Christian Habbe (eds.), *Als Feuer vom Himmel fiel: Der Bombenkrieg in Deutschland* (Munich: Deutsche Verlags-Anstalt 2003), p. 19. The Frauenkirche in Dresden has recently been restored.

[4] Though note the 'second destruction' of postwar urban planning. Rudy Koshar, *Germany's Transient Pasts: Preservation and National Memory in the Twentieth Century* (Chapel Hill: The University of North Carolina Press 1998), p. 290. See also Jörg Friedrich, *Der Brand: Deutschland im Bombenkrieg 1940–1945* (Munich: Propyläen Verlag 2002), p. 519.

[5] Mark Connelly, 'Die britische Öffentlichkeit, die Presse und der Luftkrieg gegen Deutschland, 1939–1945', in: Lothar Kettenacker (ed.), *Ein Volk von Opfern? Die neue Debatte um den Bombenkrieg 1940–45* (Berlin: Rowohlt 2003), p. 72.

[6] Wolfram Bickerich, 'Die Moral blieb intakt', in: Burgdorff and Habbe, *Als Feuer vom Himmel fiel*, p. 208.

[7] W. G. Sebald, *Luftkrieg und Literatur: Mit einem Essay zu Alfred Andersch* (Munich: Carl Hanser Verlag 1999), p. 11.

[8] Hans Mommsen, 'Wie die Bomben Hitler halfen', in: Burgdorff and Habbe, *Als Feuer vom Himmel fiel*, p. 119.

[9] Katharina Stegelmann, 'Ein Riesenspaß, ein Alptraum', in: Burgdorff and Habbe, *Als Feuer vom Himmel fiel*, p. 215. *Kinderlandverschickung* means literally 'sending children to the countryside'.

though this was done not only to protect them from air raids but also to 'educate' them in the spirit of Nazism. The number of civilians killed in air raids appears to have been between 370,000 and 600,000.[10] The figure is uncertain not only because remains were often not found, for example owing to fire storms, which made counting difficult, but figures also differ depending on whether forced labourers and concentration camp inmates were included in the count or not. Even on the basis of these imprecise numbers it is worth noting that 'only' about 1.5 per cent of the population of cities actually died in the air war.[11] Although the death toll could therefore be seen as surprisingly low, many more were, as the above statistics indicate, seriously affected. Yet it is unclear whether the bombing achieved its aims, not least because there was a running dispute at the time as to what those aims actually were. Two alternatives were proposed as the main target: industry or arms production on the one hand and German morale on the other. What does appear relatively clear is that neither of these was destroyed.[12]

Despite its scale and impact, there appears not to have been much debate about the air war and its significance in the FRG until recently.[13] Jochen Bölsche even sees strategic bombing as 'one of the last taboo topics' which is now being wrested from forgetting.[14] In this sense, and this is often noted, it is similar to the flight and expulsion of Germans from the East. Perhaps the bombing of German cities was not discussed because, as Hage suggests, the sight of the destruction was intimately connected with the 'culpable aggression of the generation of their parents', at least for those born after the war.[15] Perhaps it was because Germans could not possibly ask the Allies to explain their actions. It has been suggested, in

---

[10] Sebald, *Luftkrieg und Literatur*, p. 11 speaks of 600,000 dead; Friedrich, *Der Brand*, p. 63, says the estimates range between 420,000 and 570,000; Olaf Groehler, *Bombenkrieg gegen Deutschland* (Berlin: Akademie Verlag 1990), p. 320, puts the German dead at 370,000 to 390,000.

[11] Friedrich, *Der Brand*, p. 63.

[12] Tom Bower, *The Pledge Betrayed: America and Britain and the Denazification of Postwar Germany* (New York: Doubleday & Company 1982), p. 304. See also Schwarz, 'Überall Leichen', p. 75; Stephen A. Garrett, *Ethics and Airpower in World War II: The British Bombing of German Cities* (New York: St Martin's Press 1993), pp. 158 and 161f; and A. C. Grayling, *Among the Dead Cities: Was the Allied Bombing of Civilians in WWII a Necessity or a Crime?* (London: Bloomsbury 2006), p. 106f. For a discussion of what the target was, see Garrett, *Ethics and Airpower*, esp. Chapter 6, and Richard Overy, 'Die alliierte Bombenstrategie als Ausdruck des "totalen Krieges"', in: Kettenacker, *Ein Volk von Opfern?*, pp. 27–47.

[13] Until recently one had to consult the English-language literature to find any discussion of the ethicality of strategic bombing. See, for example, Garrett, *Ethics and Airpower*; Michael Walzer, *Just and Unjust Wars: A Moral Argument with Historical Illustrations*, 2nd edn (New York: Basic Books 1992), Chapter 16; Grayling, *Among the Dead Cities*.

[14] Bölsche, 'So muss die Hölle aussehen', p. 22.   [15] Hage, *Zeugen der Zerstörung*, p. 52.

any case, that the 'collective injury'[16] has, despite an apparently consistently large number of local commemorations at the sites of destruction, not been sufficiently or adequately remembered by the Germans. This alleged failure to remember is interesting, particularly in the context of the Germans' supposed obsession with this past.[17] Now there are claims that after sixty years the Germans have 'rediscovered' the air war as a dark chapter of their recent history.[18] There is an intriguing tension between the ubiquitous reminders and the assertion that the air war had been forgotten. Yet there seems little point in asking whether or not 'the Germans' really remember; it is not clear what this would mean. Remembering and forgetting, as shown in Chapter 2, are closely intertwined. However, it is interesting to explore the debates set off by contributions to remembering strategic bombing, not only in order to grasp more about the Germans' reaction to Iraq but also to pursue further questions about the (im)possibilities of remembering.

The year of remembrance 1995: time to mourn?

The year 1995, with its sequence of fiftieth anniversaries of events at the end of the Second World War, was marked by a frenzy of remembering. In his study of the 'year of remembrance 1995' as it was stage-managed and reported in the press,[19] Klaus Naumann finds that 'an almost unending sequence of place names, numbers of victims and reports of contemporary witnesses runs through the year of remembrance. It is about the suffering and dying of the civilian population, about its encounter with total war, with the air war and area bombing.'[20] Despite this focus on suffering, many texts were, according to Naumann, at the same time labouring with a problem which they 'felt to be a taboo: how to write about Allied violations of the norms of civilised conduct of war' without setting off one group of dead against another?[21] This worry that remembering German suffering is in danger of counting up German victims against victims of the Germans arises time and again in discussions of the air war in particular and German experiences in the Second World War in general.

Naumann notes that in 1995 for the first time since German unification 'the air war was the focus of public memory [*Gedenken*] and for the first

---

[16] Thomas W. Neumann, 'Der Bombenkrieg: Zur ungeschriebenen Geschichte einer kollektiven Verletzung', in: Klaus Naumann (ed.), *Nachkrieg in Deutschland* (Hamburg: Hamburger Edition 2001), pp. 319–42.

[17] Buruma, *Wages of Guilt*, p. 8.

[18] Christian Habbe, 'Vorwort', in: Burgdorff and Habbe, *Als Feuer vom Himmel fiel*, p. 9.

[19] Naumann, *Krieg als Text*, p. 10.   [20] Ibid., p. 33.   [21] Ibid., p. 34.

time a national site of remembrance [*Gedächtnisort*] could establish itself –
Dresden'.[22] Federal President Herzog's speech at the 'central hour of
commemoration' on the anniversary of the air raid reveals, according to
Naumann, the theme of the commemorations:

It was about the self-image of the now unified nation in remembrance of its (air)
war victims. By remembering the dead, one was speaking at the same time about
oneself. *Self-reconciliation* with 'the history' (Herzog) was the background theme
that had already announced itself in the press reports about the air war, the attack
on Dresden and its assessment.[23]

After some introductory words, Herzog's speech starts with a lamenta-
tion for the victims: 'We are here first and foremost to mourn, to lament
the dead.'[24] Yet he immediately pauses and clarifies that there must be
no counting up of different groups of war victims against each other, a
warning that is repeated four more times.[25] Indeed, the first lamenta-
tion is prefaced with a clarification: 'No one present in this room wants
to indict anyone or expects anyone to show remorse or indulge in self-
accusation. No one wants to offset the wrongs committed by Germans
in the Nazi state against anything else.'[26] Herzog in fact explicitly objects
to 'mourning being seen as an attempt to square the suffering of the victims of crimes committed by Germans against people of other nations,
and against fellow countrymen, with the suffering of German victims
of war and expulsion'.[27] This explicit and rather belligerent rejection of
an unattributed and therefore presumably imagined criticism is remarkable. Firstly, the self-assurance with which a right to mourn German
victims is expressed is noteworthy in itself. Secondly, this right to mourn
is expressed *as against* a supposedly critical Other that is never named;[28]
it is not the Germans' failure to mourn that is at issue but the Other's
apparently active prevention of such mourning. Finally, this means that
the German identity promoted is not only based on shared mourning but
also on a shared rejection of unreasonable suppression of this mourning
by an imagined Other, that is, on what amounts to asserting a new German victimhood. In other words, the Germans generously refrain from
reproaching the Allies with the death and destruction caused by strategic bombing, but they certainly won't tolerate any interference with their
memorial practices.

---

[22] Ibid., p. 35.   [23] Ibid., p. 51.   [24] Herzog, 'Dresden', p. 5.
[25] Naumann, *Krieg als Text*, p. 52.   [26] Herzog, 'Dresden', p. 5.   [27] Ibid., p. 6.
[28] This is similar to Walser's claim, cited in Chapter 2, that there is 'no day on which
[Germans] are not reproached with' their disgrace, which also does not indicate who is
doing the reproaching. Walser, 'Dankesrede'.

Naumann's reading of the speech is interesting. He notes that 'there is a suggestion of the Christian idea of salvation. A new community constitutes itself in the face of mass death.' He argues that Herzog not only gives us to understand that 'before the bombs everyone is equal'; the speech also suggests that a coming to terms between the victims of the bombs and the enemies in the war would reconcile the 'we-group of the Germans who can only then "find peace"'.[29] There is a strong emphasis on 'healing' the wounds of the war – both those suffered and those inflicted by Germans – and an unspoken assumption that such healing is possible, despite the boundary aggressively enforced around identity. On the other hand, what is also important is Herzog's willingness to confront the issue of emotions – the need for a space to mourn. This is intriguing, because emotionality, as shown below, also comes to be derided as sentimentality in relation to memories of the air war. Finally, Herzog's reading of 'Dresden' explicitly addresses the question of war. Dresden, he argues, is 'above all a beacon against war' and 'Dresden reflects the utter senselessness of modern wars'.[30] Herzog's categorical rejection of war – a reaffirmation of the 'never again war' principle – was significant because of the then ongoing wars in the Balkans and the fact that the Bundeswehr would be deployed there only a few months later. He claims: 'Only this is certain: it is war *as such* that we must resist, that we must hate.'[31] It soon turned out that nothing was in fact less certain.

Air war and literature: the (im)possibility of truth in fiction

Given the focus in 1995 on commemoration, including of the air war, it is surprising that someone should claim two years later that 'the experience of a national humiliation without comparison that had been undergone by millions in the final years of the war has never really been put into words and has been neither shared amongst those who experienced it nor passed on to those born later by those immediately affected'.[32] Yet Sebald, a German literary scholar who lived in the UK, did precisely that in a lecture series in Zurich in 1997, published in book form in 1999. When Germans look back, in particular at the period from 1930 to 1950, he claimed, it is 'always a looking and looking away at the same time'.[33] He particularly bemoans an 'inability of a whole generation of German

---

[29] Naumann, *Krieg als Text*, p. 54. The German word translated here as 'peace' is *Ruhe*, meaning 'rest'.
[30] Herzog, 'Dresden', p. 8.   [31] Ibid. (italics added).
[32] Sebald, *Luftkrieg und Literatur*, p. 6.   [33] Ibid.

writers to record and bring into our memory [*Gedächtnis*] what they had seen'.[34]

Sebald starts with the difficulty of imagining the destruction of Germany and the related horror of the final years of the war. He uses statistics from the UK Strategic Bombing Survey – that the RAF used 1 million bombs in 400,000 sorties, that of the 131 cities and towns that were attacked some were destroyed almost entirely, that 600,000 civilians died, that 3.5 million flats were destroyed, that at the end of the war 7.5 million were homeless, that per inhabitant there was 42.8 cubic metres of rubble in Dresden; but he points out that we do not know what all this means 'in truth'.[35] In other words, the recent commemorations do not mean that we understand, in any meaningful sense, the horrors of such bombing. Sebald emphatically argues that Germans need to grasp how horrific this bombing was, but claims that the destruction appears to have left almost no 'trace of pain in the collective consciousness' of the German people, a paradoxical situation in view of the number of people who were exposed to the bombing campaign and its consequences.[36]

Sebald argues that postwar German literature does not address the experience of strategic bombing. He suggests that older authors were busy establishing their reputations and younger ones were so 'fixated on their own reports of their experiences in the war which time and again slid into sentimentality' that they did not seem to notice the 'horrors of the time'.[37] This certainty about what were the 'horrors of the time' is illustrative of Sebald's attitude: he construes himself as knowing and able to judge. This is astonishing in itself, but perhaps particularly so given the widespread idea that 'having been there' is necessary to such knowledge.[38] Sebald, born in 1944 in the Southern German countryside, beyond the reach of the bombers, counteracts this way of thinking with remarkable conviction. In his view, even the *Trümmerliteratur* ('literature of the rubble'), which supposedly addressed what the authors found when they returned from the war, was marked by individual and collective amnesia. The 'real situation of material and moral destruction' could not be described.[39] It is significant to note the appeals to 'truth', the 'real situation' and such like – conceptions that are crucial to Sebald's argument – as well as the demand that literature represent what cannot be represented.

Sebald claimed that the air war had remained a 'disgraceful family secret that was covered by a kind of taboo'.[40] In his view, Hans Erich Nossack was the only exception to the general literary silence in the

---

[34] Ibid., p. 7.   [35] Ibid., p. 11.   [36] Ibid., pp. 11f.   [37] Ibid., p. 17.
[38] See Chapter 4, pp. 155–6.   [39] Sebald, *Luftkrieg und Literatur*, p. 17.   [40] Ibid.

immediate postwar years, though later in the text he offers a list that includes Heinrich Böll, Hermann Kasack and Peter de Mendelsohn.[41] However, he criticises both Kasack and Nossack for making the reality of the horrors disappear behind an art of abstraction and metaphysical fraud. He takes issue with Nossack's 'rhetoric of fatefulness'.[42] In the end, though, Nossack is, in Sebald's view, primarily interested in 'pure facticity', for example the weather, the sound of the aircraft or the glow of the fire on the horizon – a project that Sebald clearly approves of, for Sebald believes that the ideological inflexibility reflected in some writing may be compensated by a 'steadfast gaze at reality'.[43] With reference to Nossack's work, Sebald asserts that 'in the face of the total destruction, *the ideal of truth* . . . turns out to be the only legitimate reason for continuing with literary work. In contrast, the production of aesthetic and pseudo-aesthetic effects out of the rubble of a destroyed world is a method with which literature withdraws its own justifiability.'[44]

Literature is thus obligated by the ideal of truth; a focus on aesthetics is objectionable. He cites de Mendelsohn's work as an example of the latter, which consists, in Sebald's view, of a series of embarrassments.[45] Discussing Arno Schmidt's *Aus dem Leben eines Fauns* (*From the Life of a Faun*) as a 'similarly dubious literary treatment of the reality of the destruction', he questions what he calls the 'dynamic language actionism with which Schmidt here produces the spectacle of an air raid'.[46] Sebald complains that he is unable to see the scene that is represented; rather, he sees the author, doggedly working on his sentences. As a result, he rejects what he calls Schmidt's 'demonstrative avant-gardism' as inappropriate.[47] In sum, those few representations that exist are, according to Sebald, 'questionable'.[48] There is a significant tension in Sebald's reflections: he is suspicious of the artistic element in depictions of such terrible human suffering, but at the same time he sees literary writing as fundamentally necessary. On the surface, Sebald resolves this tension through an apparent belief that it is possible to come down on the side of truth, to judge literature with respect to its truthfulness. Apart from bemoaning the alleged lack of memory, this appears to be the impetus behind the lectures.

It is important to note the slight, but significant, change of tack in a chapter added to the lectures in the book: Sebald here more readily admits that there *are* literary representations of the air war, but criticises them as inappropriate. His ability to judge thus becomes even more central.

---

[41] Ibid., pp. 37 and 52.   [42] Ibid., p. 56.   [43] Ibid., p. 57.
[44] Ibid., p. 59 (italics added).   [45] Ibid.   [46] Ibid., pp. 63f.
[47] Ibid., pp. 64f.   [48] Ibid., pp. 18f.

He claims that he expected that reactions to his lecture series would disprove, with references to examples that he had been unaware of, his thesis that the destruction of German cities had found no space in the consciousness of the newly formed German nation. Instead, the letters he received confirmed his view that 'future generations would be unable to imagine the course, the extent, the nature and the consequences of the catastrophe visited upon Germany by the air war if they were to rely on the testimony of writers'.[49] This is crucial, because 'literariness' might actually be necessary to depict the air raids. Although he claims that '[a]ny treatment of the real scenes of horror of the destruction has until today something illegitimate, almost voyeuristic' about it, which even his own notes may not avoid,[50] relying on eyewitness accounts does not hold the solution. Sebald argues that the 'apparently undamaged continued functioning of normal language in most eyewitness reports calls up doubts about the authenticity of the experience that they preserve'.[51] The idea that a radical shift in language is necessary is intriguing, though one wonders on what grounds Sebald asserts this. At any rate, eyewitness reports are therefore of limited use and must be complemented with what appears under a 'synoptic, artificial view'.[52] Thus, in Sebald's argument, literature about the air war is both suspect *and* necessary.

In sum, Sebald claims that he does not question that there is some memory of the destruction; but he does not trust its form or its articulation, and does not believe that it has much affected public consciousness in the FRG.[53] His claims generated a lot of interest.[54] There was some agreement with the thrust of his argument, though it has been noted that matters are not as straightforward as he makes out. Walser, for example, strongly objected to Sebald's criticism; he found this discontent against authors who have not written about the air war 'absurd'.[55] Peter Schneider, another German writer, sees one obvious reason for the alleged reluctance to engage the issue: 'the project of describing the people of perpetrators also as victims of the world war it had set off appeared to be a moral and aesthetic impossibility'.[56] Schneider asks – and notes that Sebald did not ask – whether this topic may be treated *at all* in the form of a novel.[57] In contrast, Hage argues that that was precisely the question Sebald was concerned with; he points out that Sebald was less interested

[49] Ibid., p. 75.   [50] Ibid., p. 104.   [51] Ibid., p. 32.   [52] Ibid., p. 33.   [53] Ibid., p. 87.
[54] Hage, *Zeugen der Zerstörung*, p. 113. For a summary of Sebald's argument and the debate, see Barnouw, *War in the Empty Air*, Chapter 4.
[55] Martin Walser, 'Bombenkrieg als Epos', in: Kettenacker, *Ein Volk von Opfern?*, p. 130.
[56] Peter Schneider, 'Deutsche als Opfer? Über ein Tabu der Nachkriegsgeneration', in: Kettenacker, *Ein Volk von Opfern?*, p. 159.
[57] Ibid., p. 165.

in the asserted lack of portrayals of the air war than in the problematic of using this experience for aesthetic effect.[58] This, however, seems too subtle a reading of Sebald's polemic.

According to Hage, the 'gap' between the significance of the air war and its limited expression in literature asserted by Sebald is 'less one of production than one of reception'.[59] Hage notes that much of the literature on the air war published up until the beginning of the 1960s came to be forgotten, even though some of the books had been popular successes.[60] The early wave of novels both about the front and the air war had been narrated in a conventional way and without much reflection, leaving few texts that were noteworthy in a literary sense. In the 1960s and 1970s there were few attempts to depict the air war.[61] However, according to Hage, if one pays attention, one finds an 'echo' of the air war in the texts of many authors who were children or teenagers during the war.[62] Yet it seems to me that in the famous postwar novels the air war appeared, if at all, on the margins. In Grass's *Die Blechtrommel* (*The Tin Drum*), for example, there is a brief comical scene in which Oskar makes love to Roswitha during a raid,[63] though Walser's 1991 novel *Die Verteidigung der Kindheit* (*Defence of Childhood*) addresses it in detail in the story of a man who lived through the destruction of Dresden as a child and who is obsessed with remembering, and indeed preserving, the past.[64]

Three related reasons for the apparent 'gap' between the impact of the bombing and its limited representation in literature are raised: firstly, the question of a need to tell the memories of the air war; secondly, the possibility of doing so; and, thirdly, the danger of depicting Germans as victims. Walter Kempowski, for example, wonders whether there was less writing on the air war than some now suspect because everyone had experienced it: there was no one to tell such stories *to*.[65] Yet Dieter Forte, who published a trilogy about the air war in the 1990s, notes that even immediately after the war a large part of the population had no clue about what it had meant to experience air raids, but those who had 'had no more

---

[58] Volker Hage, 'Berichte aus einem Totenhaus', in: Burgdorff and Habbe, *Als Feuer vom Himmel fiel*, p. 104.

[59] Hage, *Zeugen der Zerstörung*, p. 119.   [60] Ibid., p. 34; Hage, 'Berichte', p. 107.

[61] Hage, *Zeugen der Zerstörung*, p. 85.   [62] Ibid., p. 89.

[63] Hage, 'Berichte', p. 111. See Günter Grass, *Die Blechtrommel* (Darmstadt: Luchterhand Literaturverlag 1989), pp. 402f.

[64] Hage, 'Berichte', p. 111. See Martin Walser, *Die Verteidigung der Kindheit* (Frankfurt am Main: Suhrkamp 1991).

[65] 'Das hatte biblische Ausmaße', interview with Walter Kempowski, in: Hage, *Zeugen der Zerstörung*, p. 195.

words for it'.[66] What is more, '[t]hose who had experienced it did not need to talk about it any more. They knew what had happened. Those who had not experienced it did not believe you.'[67] Thus, whilst those who did not know might have needed to hear, those who did were unable to speak, unable at any rate to speak in such a way that they would be understood. Forte portrays the experience as fundamentally unrepresentable. There is, he says, 'horror beyond language, an unspeakable terror'. He argues that it is wrong to believe, as we do, that we may 'write down and record everything'.[68] What he tried to do, when he finally wrote about it over forty years later, was to approach the 'horror beyond language', to find images.[69] Yet the idea that it is possible to pass on the experience, he thinks, is an illusion. Despite his own doubts over the possibility of telling these experiences, Forte is concerned about forgetting: 'There was from the beginning a silent agreement to forget. No memory. Forgetting. That is really sinister.'[70] Nevertheless, he suggests that perhaps it is necessary to be silent for one's whole life 'in order to remember again'.[71] As survivors such as Forte are finally finding their voice, a new way of looking at this past has, according to Hage, become not only possible but also necessary: fewer and fewer people who experienced the war are still alive.[72] The argument is that memory is returning precisely because it is, together with the eyewitness generation, about to pass away: now there is a new need to tell about these experiences. The need for remembering, however, does not mean that there is an acceptable way of doing so. Writer Monika Maron argues that there is the 'feeling that we Germans should not complain. Others have suffered more than we have. And this feeling worked as a prohibition, in my case in a way that was not reflected any more.'[73] The need to tell these experiences and the possibility of doing so are thus linked and yet at the same time in tension. The tension, unsurprisingly, is marked by the issue of depicting Germans as victims.

Whatever the reason, there appears to be some evidence that, considering the extent of the catastrophe, the air war has remained 'a rather neglected literary subject'.[74] The debate about Sebald's intervention discusses reasons that go beyond a potential lack of acceptability: that people

---

[66] Dieter Forte, *Schweigen oder sprechen*, ed. Volker Hage (Frankfurt am Main: S. Fischer 2002), pp. 49f.

[67] Ibid., p. 49.   [68] Ibid., p. 33.   [69] Ibid., p. 47.

[70] 'Alles Vorherige war nur ein Umweg', interview with Dieter Forte, in: Hage, *Zeugen der Zerstörung*, p. 164.

[71] Forte, *Schweigen oder sprechen*, p. 36.   [72] Hage, *Zeugen der Zerstörung*, p. 100.

[73] 'Der Fisch und die Bomben', interview with Monika Maron, in: Hage, *Zeugen der Zerstörung*, p. 217.

[74] Volker Ullrich, 'Weltuntergang kann nicht schlimmer sein', in: Kettenacker, *Ein Volk von Opfern?*, p. 111.

did not want to hear or already knew, and, crucially, that the horror could not be expressed. In contrast, for example, to Herzog, who points to reasons that are extraneous, these are all reasons that come from within the German community, the inability to express the horror coming even from the survivors themselves. Finally, the question that we encountered in relation to the 1995 commemorations recurs: whether the people of perpetrators has the right to be concerned about its own victims,[75] whether memories of the air war would represent Germans as victims and to what extent this is permissible. Such memories are haunted by these questions that appear again in the debate around Friedrich's *Der Brand* (*The Blaze*).

Der Brand: inappropriate sentimentality?

Friedrich's *Der Brand: Deutschland im Bombenkrieg 1940–1945* (*The Blaze: Germany in the Air War 1940–1945*), published in 2002, became something of a bestseller and was also serialised in the German tabloid *Bild*. Reactions to the text were heated, both in Germany and the UK.[76] Friedrich's book did not seem to be covered by the positive connotation attached to remembering the past. His contribution to memory instead caused considerable concern. The main reason is no surprise: some of the debate is collected in a volume tellingly entitled *Ein Volk von Opfern?* (*A People of Victims?*).[77] This title neatly summarises the concern, on both sides of the Channel, that Friedrich's book in particular but also wider recent developments signal a self-conceptualisation of the Germans that increasingly – or again – renders them as *victims* of the Second World War. Whether or not the articulation of memories of strategic bombing has ever been taboo, the topic has now become a mainstream interest.

Der Brand seems an awkward book to have become a bestseller. In well over 500 pages Friedrich describes the air war under idiosyncratic headings – 'Weapon', 'Strategy', 'Land', 'Protection', 'We', 'I', 'Stone' – in minute and at times tedious detail. Yet the detail is also what makes the book interesting. For example, where most texts merely mention numbers Friedrich explores the technicalities of death. The detailed description of course means that Friedrich's representations are occasionally graphic, something that he has in common with the novels considered below. He cites, for example, a report of the destruction of Wuppertal which

---

[75] Hage, *Zeugen der Zerstörung*, p. 129.
[76] I focus on the debate in Germany. For English summaries of and contributions to the debate, see Barnouw, *War in the Empty Air*, Chapter 4, and Moeller, 'On the History'.
[77] Lothar Kettenacker (ed.), *Ein Volk von Opfern? Die neue Debatte um den Bombenkrieg 1940–45* (Berlin: Rowohlt 2003). On the reaction in the UK, see also Michael Sontheimer, 'Schillerndes Ungeheuer', *Der Spiegel*, 02/12/02, 56–7.

notes that 'the charred bodies' were only about 50 centimetres long[78] and asserts that the phosphor used in bombing to ignite fires made the bodies 'shrink into small mummies'.[79] Friedrich also notes that, according to American researchers, the cause of death in the air war was only in about 5 to 30 per cent of cases explosion, pressure or impact of rubble; 5 to 15 per cent died owing to the heat of the air, but 60 to 70 per cent from carbon monoxide poisoning.[80] Most died where they had sought refuge: in the cellars.[81] One of the problems, Friedrich claims, was that people expected to be killed by bombs, not by the gases emitted by their own supplies of coal catching fire.[82] Insufficient or faulty protection from the attacks, he argues, contributed to the deaths.

Another set of details deals with the idea of undermining morale through bombing cities and the implied expectation that the Germans would somehow overthrow their government or force it to abandon the war. Friedrich describes the situation of the Germans thus:

What had previously been a family might look in 1944 as follows: the father works in Dortmund, the mother lives with a toddler in the Allgäu [in the countryside in Southern Germany], the twelve-year-old daughter is with the *Kinderlandverschickung* in Thuringia, her fourteen-year-old sister in a training camp of the *Volkswohlfahrt* [People's Welfare] in Franconia, the nineteen-year-old son is laying siege to Leningrad. Everyone is thinking of nothing else than seeing each other again, the Führer is paying for the free tickets, and everyone is permanently on the road. In this situation people do not revolt, rather they make travel plans.[83]

Friedrich clearly puts us in a position to imagine in more detail what life and death were like during the air war. Inevitably this has an emotional effect. It is not surprising that such history writing attracts criticism.

Some contributions to the debate over Friedrich's book, such as Horst Boog's, are largely concerned with alleged errors of historical fact – a line of critique that Boog claims Friedrich sees as pedantic.[84] To begin with, the question whether bodies shrank in the way Friedrich, and indeed some literary representations, make out is controversial.[85] Hans-Ulrich Wehler more broadly attributes an 'insecurity of historical judgement'

---

[78] Friedrich, *Der Brand*, p. 19.   [79] Ibid., p. 479.   [80] Ibid., p. 378.
[81] Ibid., p. 388.   [82] Ibid., p. 386.   [83] Ibid., p. 460.
[84] Horst Boog, 'Ein Kolossalgemälde des Schreckens', in: Kettenacker, *Ein Volk von Opfern?*, pp. 131–6.
[85] Shrunk bodies are also mentioned in Sebald, *Luftkrieg und Literatur*, p. 35; Bölsche, 'So muss die Hölle aussehen', p. 22; Christian Habbe, 'Mit dem Rechen des Todes', in: Burgdorff and Habbe, *Als Feuer vom Himmel fiel*, p. 152, and Nicholas Stargardt, 'Opfer der Bomben und der Vergeltung', in: Kettenacker, *Ein Volk von Opfern?*, p. 56. Boog, however, claims that the shrinkage was generally no more than 10 to 15 per cent: 'Ein Kolossalgemälde', p. 132.

to Friedrich.[86] There is, in other words, concern about the information Friedrich presents in his book. This also applies to Friedrich's exclusive focus on the bombing of German civilians: it is as though only Germans had been exposed to these air raids.[87]

Another line of critique is less concerned with what is represented in the book than with how. Friedrich's language indulges in pathos, and the critics claim that in places he uses Nazi terminology.[88] For example, he says that the *Gefallenen* – a term that usually refers to soldiers killed in action – of the raids on Hamburg in July 1943 are 'ciphers of the worst that force of arms has inflicted on the creature. Not because of the rivers of blood that were shed but because of the way in which living things were wiped off the face of the earth by a deadly breath.'[89] The 'deadly breath' oozes an almost comical pathos, but the critics were more concerned that Friedrich calls the civilian dead of the air war *Gefallene*,[90] something the Nazi regime had done.[91] Hage objects to this terminology as Nazi propaganda, but in contrast to other critics he is not particularly concerned about Friedrich's use of 'crematoria' to denote air-raid shelters.[92] There was unease over this comparison of the cellars in which civilians were seeking refuge to 'crematoria'[93] owing to the inevitable associations with Auschwitz,[94] even though Friedrich explicitly rejects any analogy between the destruction of the Jews and the destruction by bombs.[95] Ute Frevert, moreover, notes the closeness between *Der Brand (The Blaze)* and the meaning of 'Holocaust' and accuses Friedrich of 'historical relativism'.[96] In sum, Friedrich is seen implicitly to assert a comparison between strategic bombing and the Holocaust, along with other crimes of the Third Reich. This is perhaps particularly apparent in his use of the phrase 'war of extermination', also noted with concern by the critics.[97] Yet Sebald had also used the term *Vernichtungskrieg* for the air war.[98] It is, moreover, a term one finds in Clausewitz;[99] it cannot therefore be seen as reserved exclusively for the German war on the Eastern front, as

---

[86] Hans-Ulrich Wehler, 'Wer Wind sät, wird Sturm ernten', in: Kettenacker, *Ein Volk von Opfern?*, p. 143.
[87] Stargardt, 'Opfer der Bomben', p. 60.
[88] Ibid., pp. 58f; Wehler, 'Wer Wind sät', p. 143.   [89] Friedrich, *Der Brand*, p. 193.
[90] See, for example, ibid., pp. 193, 197 and 388.
[91] Friedrich acknowledges this. Ibid., p. 409.
[92] Hage, *Zeugen der Zerstörung*, p. 129, n. 233.
[93] Friedrich, *Der Brand*, pp. 194 and 388.
[94] See, for example, Wehler, 'Wer Wind sät', p. 143 and Ralph Giordano, 'Ein Volk von Opfern?', in: Kettenacker, *Ein Volk von Opfern?*, p. 168.
[95] Friedrich, *Der Brand*, p. 342.   [96] Frevert, 'Geschichtsvergessenheit', 12.
[97] Wehler, 'Wer Wind sät', p. 143.   [98] Sebald, *Luftkrieg und Literatur*, p. 19.
[99] Herfried Münkler, *Über den Krieg: Stationen der Kriegsgeschichte im Spiegel ihrer theoretischen Reflexion* (Weilerswist: Velbrück Wissenschaft 2003), p. 94, n. 8

the critics argue it is, though the term certainly does evoke the atrocities there. It must be noted that 'war of extermination' does seem inappropriate, if simply because of the small percentage of the German population actually killed in the air raids.

Finally, Friedrich is charged with sentimentalising the air war. Eric Langenbacher asserts that the book was 'new in emphasizing the human dimension of the suffering and in the use of provocative and melodramatic prose'.[100] Similarly, Willi Winkler argues that Friedrich's success belongs to 'the wave of sentimentalisation which is apparently necessary'.[101] In this argument, even with 'love of the detail' a historical study could not, for example, have accomplished the public engagement with the Holocaust that was achieved by the American television series *Holocaust*, also aired in Germany.[102] Thus Friedrich's book could be seen as creating an opportunity to mourn, that is, as working towards what Federal President Herzog claimed to be necessary. On the other hand, and worryingly, in Winkler's view, '[s]uddenly the sentimentalised is the only representational form for addressing the Allied air raids and the expulsion of the Germans from Eastern territories'.[103] In Boog's judgement, too, *Der Brand* is about re-experiencing the air war 'in an affective and easily remembered way'.[104] Boog criticises Friedrich for leaving 'the reader in an emotionally heated empty space'.[105] In other words, Friedrich provides no guidance as to how to deal with the gruesome detail about the various forms of dying he describes. He does not engage the question of what, if anything, it all means.

Wehler sees a danger in Friedrich's book. There appears to be a 'new basic current in the German public, perhaps some kind of psychological turn of the tide. German victims of the Second World War suddenly move to the centre of attention.'[106] Friedrich's book with its 'passion for the helpless victims of the Allied air war' could 'support the fashionable cult of the victim that has already been causing a sensation in the United States'.[107] This, significantly, makes reference to trends outside

---

[100] Langenbacher, 'Changing Memory Regimes', 60.
[101] Willi Winkler, 'Nun singen sie wieder', in: Kettenacker, *Ein Volk von Opfern?*, p. 105. This is perhaps also what Bollmann means when he objects that Friedrich works through suggestion rather than argument. Ralph Bollmann, 'Im Dickicht der Aufrechnung', in: Kettenacker, *Ein Volk von Opfern?*, p. 139.
[102] Winkler, 'Nun singen sie wieder', p. 105. Frevert also mentions the personalisation and emotionalisation effected by this series. Frevert, 'Geschichtsvergessenheit', 7.
[103] Winkler, 'Nun singen sie wieder', p. 105.   [104] Boog, 'Ein Kolossalgemälde', p. 131.
[105] Ibid., p. 133.   [106] Wehler, 'Wer Wind sät', p. 140.
[107] Ibid., 143; see also Wehler in Stephan Burgdorff and Christian Habbe, 'Vergleichen – nicht moralisieren', interview with Hans-Ulrich Wehler, in: Burgdorff and Habbe, *Als Feuer vom Himmel fiel*, p. 44.

Germany, rather than understanding the development merely as part of the history of dealing with the Third Reich and of revisionist constructions of German identity. Wehler's concern is that, whilst he does not object to comparisons between atrocities in war, 'moralising judgements' lead to nothing but a 'moral reproach for the other'.[108] Yet some see Friedrich precisely as moving beyond such moralising. According to Cora Stephan, Friedrich's book destroys 'all illusions which may be linked to the hope that evil may be clearly distinguished from good'.[109] The point of the book, she says, is neither to relativise nor to justify, only to acknowledge.[110] Walser similarly believes that Friedrich 'has stylistically gone beyond the perpetrator–victim division'; he is, in Walser's view, 'equally close to everyone'.[111] And Schneider argues that perhaps now, after accepting the horrors that the Germans visited upon others, it is possible to acknowledge 'the extent to which they themselves became the victim of the destruction that had been unleashed by them'.[112] This, however, remains controversial.

Friedrich's book is credited – whether one approves of it or not – with setting off another debate about the air war.[113] Interestingly, an earlier work on the topic, published in 1990 by East German military historian Olaf Groehler, did not generate such widespread debate.[114] A link is sometimes made between Friedrich's *Der Brand* and an entirely different book said to have had a similar effect: Grass's *Im Krebsgang*.[115] As discussed in Chapter 2, this novella is seen to have led to public discussion of the suffering of the expellees. What is considered to connect the two is the representation of 'Germans also as victims of the Second World War'.[116] Significantly, Lothar Kettenacker employs the term 'also', thereby implying that the debates do not construe the Germans 'only' – but merely 'also' – as victims. One might naively assume then that there is

[108] Wehler in Burgdorff and Habbe, 'Vergleichen', p. 43.
[109] Cora Stephan, 'Wie man eine Stadt anzündet', in: Kettenacker, *Ein Volk von Opfern?*, p. 96.
[110] Ibid., pp. 97f.   [111] Walser, 'Bombenkrieg', p. 127.
[112] Schneider, 'Deutsche als Opfer?', p. 165.
[113] Lothar Kettenacker, 'Vorwort des Herausgebers', in: Kettenacker, *Ein Volk von Opfern?*, p. 10. *Der Spiegel*, for example, published a series of articles on the air war under the title 'Als Feuer vom Himmel fiel', 06/01/03, 13/01/03, 20/01/03, 27/01/03, and later expanded this material into a book: Burgdorff and Habbe, *Als Feuer vom Himmel fiel*.
[114] Groehler, *Bombenkrieg*. This book must, however, also have found a significant readership, as Bölsche points out that it was soon sold out. Bölsche, 'So muss die Hölle aussehen', p. 24.
[115] Grass, *Im Krebsgang*. This link to the debate set off by Grass's novella is made, for example, by Stargardt, 'Opfer der Bomben', pp. 57f; Ullrich, 'Weltuntergang', p. 111; Wehler in Burgdorff and Habbe, 'Vergleichen', p. 43.
[116] Kettenacker, 'Vorwort des Herausgebers', p. 10; see also Ullrich, 'Weltuntergang', p. 112; Frevert, 'Geschichtsvergessenheit', 9.

no problem. Against the background of the acknowledged responsibility of the German people for the Holocaust and the Second World War, it seems, one might think, not only possible[117] but in fact necessary to ask about the impact of the war on Germans. Certainly, if war experiences are claimed as shared knowledge with respect to which military intervention abroad may be justified, as they are, it is necessary to explore these experiences.

The problem of victimhood

In commemoration as well as public debate about memories of the bombing, the question of whether remembering these events does not mean portraying Germans as victims of the Second World War is prominent. Kettenacker raises this question in the preface to his collection in relation to Friedrich's *Der Brand*: 'May the Germans, too, regard themselves as victims in the face of the disaster that they visited upon the world?'[118] In his analysis of the 1995 commemorations in the press, Naumann argues that '[a]ll texts revolve around the victim status'.[119] The problem is posed in two main ways. One deals with the question of the 'cause' of the Allied bombing, the other with the question of whether remembering German suffering implies a form of exonerating the Germans. Indeed, the previous reticence about addressing this topic is attributed to the fear of counting up one group of victims against another.[120]

The sensitivity of the issue of whether the Germans are depicting themselves as victims may perhaps only be understood in the context of German attitudes in the decades immediately after the war. Through a reading of parliamentary debates Dubiel shows how the Germans constructed themselves as having suffered first from the 'scourge' of the Nazi regime and then from the war. This story neatly turns the Germans from perpetrators into victims, first of Hitler and then of the Allies.[121] As Moeller notes, in this account 'all Germans were ultimately victims of a war that Hitler had started but everyone lost'.[122] Denazification and the Soviet Union's failure to return POWs further contributed to this myth of German victimhood. Conspicuously absent was any concern for the

---

[117] This is implied by Heribert Seifert, 'Rekonstruktion statt Richterspruch', in: Kettenacker, *Ein Volk von Opfern?*, p. 153.

[118] Kettenacker, 'Vorwort des Herausgebers', p. 11.

[119] Naumann, *Krieg als Text*, p. 321.

[120] Wehler in Burgdorff and Habbe, 'Vergleichen', p. 43. Barnouw represents this fear as one that Germans would want to forget the victims of the Nazi regime if they were to remember their own; she rejects this concern as unfounded. *War in the Empty Air*, p. 29.

[121] Dubiel, *Niemand ist frei*, Chapter 1.   [122] Moeller, *War Stories*, p. 3.

victims *of* the Germans, in particular the murdered Jews. The self-conception as victim was crucial for the constitution of the new West German state:

One of the most powerful integrative myths of the 1950s emphasized not German well-being but German suffering; it stressed that Germany was a nation of victims, an imagined community defined by the experience of loss and displacement during the Second World War. The stories of German victims, particularly expellees and POWs in Soviet hands, were central to shaping membership in the West German polity. Remembering what had been was of great significance for envisioning what was to come.[123]

In the context of such early constructions of German victimhood, which never entirely disappeared, accusations of styling the Germans as victims acquire both meaning and a powerful emotionality. Naumann, however, questions whether, as Moeller suggests, the discourse of victimhood of the immediate postwar decades is simply being taken up again now.[124] Significantly, the concern about German self-representation as victims sees recent debates and commemorations not just in the context of the past which they are apparently about but also in the context of earlier renderings of this past. Put differently, today's memory is interpreted not merely in the context of what it is thought to remember – the air war – but of earlier memories.[125]

What the 1950s representations of Germans as victims excluded was not only consideration for the Germans' victims but also the Germans' role in bringing about the events that were thought to have victimised them. Inevitably, then, more recent public debates about the air war refer to the significance of bearing in mind what is considered its cause. According to Ralph Giordano, who asserts quite simply that the Germans would prefer to see themselves as victims, the responsibility, causality and chronology of events 'must remain the basis of any discussion',[126] an argument that implies the pertinence of this supposed cause-and-effect relationship. In a crude summary of this position one might say that the German civilian war dead were not victims of the Allies but rather of their own – or their fellow citizens' – prior crimes. In this view, the attack on Coventry 'triggered' the retaliation by the British.[127] This idea is reflected in Thomas Mann's 1942 BBC broadcast from exile in California in which

[123] Ibid., p. 6.   [124] Naumann, *Krieg als Text*, p. 321.

[125] According to Jeffrey K. Olick, '[l]ater versions of the past, either implicitly or explicitly, are always responses to earlier ones'. *In the House of the Hangman: The Agonies of German Defeat, 1943–1949* (Chicago: The University of Chicago Press 2005), p. 3.

[126] Giordano, 'Ein Volk von Opfern?', pp. 166 and 168.

[127] Michael Schmidt-Klingenberg, 'Wir werden sie ausradieren', in: Burgdorff and Habbe, *Als Feuer vom Himmel fiel*, p. 58.

he expressed regret that his home town, Lübeck, had been destroyed, but asserted that he thought of Coventry and had 'no objection against the lesson that everything has to be paid for'.[128]

Many contributions to the debate insist that the Germans had *started* it and that Allied bombing had to be seen as a *response* – 'retaliation', as in Ledig's title *Vergeltung*. Therefore the Germans had to accept the destruction wreaked over their country as something they themselves were responsible for. Kettenacker's collection indeed starts with a contribution that construes the bombing of Wielún, a small town in Poland with no notable industry, infrastructure or military installations, on 1 September 1939 as the origin of the air war, the 'when and where everything started',[129] though it also makes reference to the earlier destruction of Guernica. Seventy per cent of Wielún was destroyed; 1,200 people died. Overall, 20,000 people were killed in early bombing raids on Poland.[130] The implication is that the Germans only suffered the consequences of what they started. Their dead are therefore not 'victims' in the same way as, say, the British or Polish civilian dead; they lack the necessary 'innocence'.

It is important to note the double meaning of the German term *Opfer*. Dubiel claims that the category *Opfer* became a semantic medium of suppression, and that this might in part be due to its etymology. *Opfer* means both the 'innocent subject to whom a disastrous event happens without his own assistance' – what in English would be termed a 'victim' – and the 'ritual practice which is meant to give a higher, transcendent meaning to an act' – what in English would be called 'sacrifice'. It is therefore impossible in German, Dubiel argues, to adequately express senseless suffering that is not self-incurred ('victim'), and this lack of semantic differentiation came to be used in the postwar years.[131] Any reference to sacrifices made could be read as one to victimhood. Nicholas Stargardt notes that the rhetoric of 'helpless and passive suffering' which easily led on to Christian ideas of martyrdom and redemption and of national reconstruction only appeared after the collapse of the Nazi regime. It was only then, he argues, that the German 'readiness to make sacrifices' became a popular myth that was meant to clarify how the German people had been seduced by Nazi propaganda and then destroyed by Nazi extremists and the Allied terror against defenceless civilians. During the war, Stargardt notes, the Germans had not so much wanted to be victims as make a sacrifice: the

---

[128] Schwarz, 'Überall Leichen', p. 71; see also Hage, 'Berichte', p. 101.
[129] Joachim Trenkner, 'Wielún, 1. September 1939: "Keine besondere Feindbeobachtung"', in: Kettenacker, *Ein Volk von Opfern?*, p. 23.
[130] Ibid., pp. 20 and 22.   [131] Dubiel, *Niemand ist frei*, p. 74.

double meaning of the word *Opfer* 'served as a call to arms'.[132] The civilian population made sacrifices and was, in some sense, sacrificed by the regime in a senseless war, but this 'sacrifice' slides into 'victimhood' with its presumption of innocence.

The argument that draws attention to German aggression as the 'cause' of Allied bombing highlights the way that the suffering German civilians lack the innocence required for the meaning of *Opfer* as victim. This reasoning is popular, and there is some plausibility to it. However, a concern simply for who started it hardly makes for a sophisticated moral argument. Wolfgang Sofsky indeed refers to it as children's morality.[133] Schneider similarly questions as simplistic the idea that the air war was legitimate because the 'fascist aggressor' had started 'the logic of destruction'.[134] Above all, the temporal sequence is uncritically translated into causality. This is a questionable argumentative strategy. Mann construed the destruction in the UK as an explanation for the destruction in Germany. Yet this is dangerously close to – implicitly – counting up British civilian dead to excuse the killing of German civilians, making it difficult to argue that the Germans should be prohibited from doing the same, even if the Germans set the whole process off in the first place.[135] Thus this argument ties itself into a knot: the acknowledgement of the alleged cause of the bombing turns out to offer precisely the kind of justification for the Allies that it is meant to reject for the Germans. In other words, it seems to be little more than a reversed kind of offsetting. Ironically, this opens up the possibility not perhaps of exoneration for the Germans but of ready-made atonement. Naumann notes this ploy, which seems inextricably related to the obsession with acknowledging the 'cause' of the bombing. He concludes that the 'chapter of the air war against Germany is written as a tragedy of vengeance' in the 1995 press. The texts are 'in the end in agreement: the Germans have atoned' for their crimes.[136] In other words, if the bombing was a result of and punishment for similar bombing raids, and indeed even the

---

132 Stargardt, 'Opfer der Bomben', p. 63. See also Siobhan Kattago, 'Representing German Victimhood and Guilt: The Neue Wache and Unified German Memory', *German Politics and Society* 16 (1998), 99f.
133 Wolfgang Sofsky, 'Die halbierte Erinnerung', in: Kettenacker, *Ein Volk von Opfern?*, p. 126.
134 Schneider, 'Deutsche als Opfer?', p. 161; see also Overy, 'Alliierte Bombenstrategie', p. 45.
135 What is at issue here is the construction of arguments within the German debate; I am not offering a view as to whether the British count up their victims to justify the bombing. Grayling seems concerned that comparisons have obscured the moral assessment of area bombing. *Among the Dead Cities*, p. 6.
136 Naumann, *Krieg als Text*, p. 50.

Holocaust, then it may also have delivered the Germans from some of their guilt.

In sum, the idea of acknowledging the cause runs the danger of not only implicitly suggesting that the bombing was something it was not – a reaction to Nazi crimes[137] – but also follows the same logic as the notion of offsetting one set of victims against another that is, on the surface, so vehemently rejected. Naumann moreover notes that the general acknowledgement of guilt with respect to starting the war and conducting it in criminal ways actually obscures another important point: the shame about the senselessness of the deaths that occurred because Germany had not ended the war sooner.[138] Thus the policing of the debate that sees acknowledging the cause and avoiding any offsetting as crucial fails, because the two are logically related. It is interesting, in this context, to consider Stephan's claim that:

A 'But the others also . . .' does not exonerate. On the contrary: it robs us of the conception of the Good and Right. That is sad, and yet at the same time an anchor for current and future policy – for it demands turning away from moral self-righteousness [*Selbstgewissheit*] which believes its means to be justified because of the horribleness of the enemy.[139]

It is crucial, in other words, to undermine the certainty of ethical categorisation. It is in this spirit that the following reading of two novels is undertaken.

Ledig: *Vergeltung*

Ledig, who was wounded twice as a soldier, was sent back to Germany in 1942 and therefore experienced air raids against German cities.[140] His 1956 novel *Vergeltung* ('Retaliation') depicts the 69 minutes of an air raid against an unnamed German city in July 1944. Obviously, most of those affected are civilians, mainly women, children and older men. However, there are also soldiers in this story: those in charge of the boys operating the anti-aircraft guns, some Soviet soldiers and the crew of a US bomber that is shot down. Every death described – and there are many – is gruesome. As is noted in the prologue, '[i]n these 60 minutes [people were] torn apart, crushed, suffocated'.[141] This list excludes other notable ways

---

[137] Moeller notes that the bombing was not a response to the Holocaust. 'On the History', p. 109.

[138] Naumann, *Krieg als Text*, p. 70.   [139] Stephan, 'Wie man eine Stadt anzündet', 101.

[140] Volker Hage, 'Nachwort', in: Gert Ledig, *Vergeltung* (Frankfurt am Main: Suhrkamp Verlag 2001), pp. 203f.

[141] Ledig, *Vergeltung*, p. 11.

of dying: at least one woman burns 'like a torch',[142] and a squad leader is 'barbecued'.[143] A girl is trapped underneath the rubble together with a man, raped by him and left to die next to his body after he commits suicide by cutting his wrists.[144] Although being barbecued in fluid tarmac perhaps goes beyond anything described in Ledig's *Die Stalinorgel*, discussed in Chapter 4, the deaths in *Vergeltung* are not generally more terrible. However, these are the deaths largely of civilians – women, children, old men – the deaths, in other words, of those whom we would not normally find on a battlefield. So these horrific deaths might be harder to accept owing to *who* is dying and their location in our understanding of war.

The events in *Vergeltung* are difficult to grasp. The reader learns what is happening in a number of places – in a US bomber, in a shelter and at an anti-aircraft position, for example – at the same time. The story of the ongoing events in any one of these places is frequently interrupted, only to be taken up again, without warning, after parallel events have been told. Hage notes that in this novel Ledig has intensified 'the literary method of a mosaic-like montage of synchronous events'.[145] Although the basic technique is similar, *Vergeltung*, in contrast to *Die Stalinorgel*, which confronts the reader with the horror of battle without any commentary, offers more critical reflection on available interpretative frames: Christian ideas, commitment to the fatherland and the problem of retaliation. *Vergeltung* juxtaposes the horrific dying with interpretative frameworks that claim to make sense of war and death. In other words, war and the dying in it are *supposed* to make some kind of sense, and *Vergeltung* fundamentally challenges this idea.

The book contains an opening scene, thirteen chapters and a closing scene. Each of the chapters is prefaced with a statement from one of the book's characters: various German civilians and soldiers, one Russian and one US airman. These usually contain a summary of the life of the person in question. Maria Weinert, born 1925, for example, reports that she used to work as a clerk, that her favourite colour was blue and that she would have liked to learn dancing. She also recalls her childhood when she was Snow White in a school play.[146] These sections focus on the ordinariness of life, but also contain critical observations on the Third Reich. Maria's regret at not having learnt to dance is contextualised with the observation that dancing had been prohibited during most of her youth. Werner Hartung, a teacher, notes that the relationship with his

---

[142] Ibid., p. 10.   [143] Ibid., p. 128.
[144] Ibid., pp. 96–9, 121f, 131, 142–4, 157–9 and 174f.   [145] Hage, 'Nachwort', p. 205.
[146] Ledig, *Vergeltung*, p. 13.

students was strained because, owing to a shortened leg, he was not called up for military service: 'I was not a patriot in their sense [of the word].'[147] In some cases, there is direct criticism of war. Alfred Rainer observes:

> In the event of my death the choral society was supposed to sing the soldiers' chorus from *Margarete* [sic] and I wanted to be cremated. On 2 July 1944, between one and two in the afternoon, I died. My death was probably pointless. It did not harm anyone or help anyone, but I do not cry out in accusation because of that.[148]

Vergeltung thus offers some reflection on the political situation in Germany and the war.

Ledig challenges the idea that the deaths he depicts might make sense. He notes, acidly, the inscription on soldiers graves: 'You did not die in vain.'[149] *Vergeltung* has no time for the old favourite for justifying death in war – dying for the fatherland. As Viktor Lutz, a sergeant in a special unit, who had to kill forty POWs, puts it, '[f]atherland, heroism, tradition, honour are hollow phrases'.[150] The book, moreover, dismisses a powerful alternative for finding meaning in death: Christian thought.[151] *Vergeltung* starts with a morbid play on a Christian idea: 'Suffer the little children to come unto me.'[152] The children in question are dead – suffocated two days earlier in a cellar – and thrown against the wall of the cemetery by a blast. They had been placed in the cemetery because 'their fathers were fighting at the front and their mothers had yet to be searched for'.[153] Only one mother had been found: crushed by rubble. The Christian motif is taken up again towards the end of the book. At the close of the last chapter people can be heard reciting together the section of the Lord's Prayer dealing with forgiving those who trespass against us. The chapter ends: 'For they know not what they do. Amen!'[154] The closing scene starts: 'May God be with us.' Yet it notes that God was with the others, too. 'After the seventieth minute the bombing continued. Retaliation was doing its work.' It was unstoppable, but it was not the Last Judgement.[155]

This last comment, as some others in the novel, might be read as critical of the Allied bombing. For example, a man in the shelter says: 'This must be repaid.'[156] It is not clear what he means, though one suspects it is revenge for the air raid. This is interesting because the term he uses – *vergolten* – is related to *Vergeltung* (retaliation), that is, to what the air raid

---

[147] Ibid., p. 31.   [148] Ibid., p. 43. *Margarethe* is an opera by Charles Gounod.
[149] Ibid., p. 10.   [150] Ibid., p. 106.
[151] *Die Stalinorgel* seems to leave open the possibility of metaphysical hope, however tenuous. See Chapter 4 below.
[152] Ledig, *Vergeltung*, p. 9.   [153] Ibid.   [154] Ibid., p. 197.
[155] Ibid., pp. 198f.   [156] Ibid., p. 161.

is supposed to be in the first place, as the title of the book suggests. Thus there is an allusion to the vicious circle of retaliation. The first scene – dead children thrown against the cemetery wall whose fathers are at the front and whose mothers have vanished – observes: 'This is what retaliation looked like.'[157] This opening move, the definition of 'retaliation' through the description of such misery, might suggest that what is to follow will be a *j'accuse* against the Allies who unleashed such destruction upon civilians. It would be impossible to describe the horrors of an air raid with such passion and not be critical of those who decided to drop the bombs. However, there is no trivial placing of responsibility at the Allies' door, and individual Allied airmen are not singled out for blame, but rather are depicted as entangled in the same hellish war as the Germans. Captain Strenehen, one of the main characters, is portrayed as intentionally dropping his bombs on the cemetery because he assumes that this way only the dead would be hit.[158] He was, the text observes, in that sense, human. However, after he is shot down he is treated cruelly by the Germans, tortured and excluded from the shelter; eventually, he dies.[159] As Reich-Ranicki observes, *Vergeltung* 'is not a book about Germans or about Americans, who also appear in it; it is a book about the sufferings of people at this time, and therefore I believe that this book will not be passé for a long time yet'.[160] Although some characters are ordinary, even 'human', not all Germans are portrayed favourably. Some are overwhelmed by the horror, some selfish, some outright cruel.[161] The memory of the air raids invoked is, then, one not merely of suffering but also of guilt. Although *Vergeltung* graphically depicts the sheer horror of being subjected to an air raid, the idea of Germans as innocent victims is, if anything, made problematic by this close-up view.

It is important to read the book in the context of its title. *Retaliation* suggests that in the final analysis the responsibility for the insanity of this bombing lies not with the Allies, who are merely retaliating, even if in ways that we might not accept as permissible, but with the Germans who provided the reason to do so. In this sense, it is in tune with public debates about the bombing. Whilst much of the secondary literature asserts that Ledig excludes the political context,[162] Hage points out that the title shows the attempt to look at the events not just from a German perspective: the title indicates that, in Ledig's view, the air war had a 'reason, a past history'.[163] Forte concurs with this. He says that it would have

---

[157] Ibid., p. 9.   [158] Ibid., p. 11.   [159] Ibid., pp. 91, 107–9, 186–8 and 195–7.
[160] 'Als das Ghetto brannte', p. 241.
[161] For example, Ledig, *Vergeltung*, pp. 15–17, 91 and 186–8.
[162] See Chapter 1, pp. 16–20.   [163] Hage, *Zeugen der Zerstörung*, p. 47.

been superfluous to say 'and there was Auschwitz'. In his view, when one
writes of retaliation the cause is assumed. It is, he argues, self-evident
that there was Auschwitz, as that is why there were bombs. These issues
are, in Forte's view, inseparable,[164] though one may doubt whether there
was any link between the Holocaust and strategic bombing. The notion
of retaliation is, at any rate, ambivalent. Here the term is used to give
meaning to the Allied raids on German cities even if this use is also criticised. But 'Vergeltung' is what the Nazi regime implicitly claimed for
their own attacks on British cities, too. The V-1 and V-2, rockets used
to attack targets in England in the last year of the war, were known as
Vergeltungswaffen, weapons of retaliation. So retaliation is ambivalent: who
gets to decide what may count as retaliation and what is permissible under
that heading? This ambivalence is important to the overall critique of war
in the text; it is not a question of condemning one side.

Significantly, *Vergeltung* produces unease about the horrific dying *despite*
acknowledging the context of retaliation against the brutality of German
warfare. It is something of a manifesto against war, but it does not simply
demonise the Allies, nor does it in any way heroicise the Germans, not
even as victims. Whereas *Die Stalinorgel*, as will be shown in Chapter 4,
stresses the absence of sense in the hell of war, *Vergeltung* highlights the
tension between possible ways of interpreting the events in meaningful
ways and the 'experience' of the events. In other words, it demolishes
any sense one might propose. *Vergeltung* juxtaposes the horrors of the
destruction caused by the air war with brief life stories of the main characters and thereby highlights how coherent life becomes senseless in the
face of the absurdity called war.[165] *Vergeltung*, Hage says, was 'unique':
nobody had previously depicted the air war with such clarity, hardness
and directness.[166] According to Hage, there is no self-pitying and no
heroicising gesture in Ledig's work. The book was originally rejected on
the grounds that it not only exaggerates the horror but also fails to offer
a positive perspective for the future.[167] Sebald suggests that Ledig's work
was excluded from the collective memory because it went too far.[168] Yet
precisely for those same reasons – the lack of a metaphysical solution and
the representation of war as hell – *Vergeltung* won recognition again in the
1990s.[169]

On the face of it, *Vergeltung* pursues what Tachibana calls the 're-
creation of immediacy',[170] but there are also elements of reflection – such

---

[164] 'Alles Vorherige', 173.   [165] Hage, *Zeugen der Zerstörung*, p. 49.   [166] Ibid., p. 44.
[167] Ibid., p. 46.   [168] Sebald, *Luftkrieg und Literatur*, p. 103.
[169] Hage, *Zeugen der Zerstörung*, p. 49; Hage, 'Berichte', p. 110.
[170] Tachibana, *Narrative as Counter-Memory*, p. 7.

as upon the memory of the air war – that imply distance: 'Later someone claimed: it had not been so bad. Some were always left alive.'[171]
Ledig thus criticises the suppression of the horrors of the raids. Those
who knew just how bad it had been did not speak about it. As was noted
above, they might have felt that people did not want to know or indeed
did not believe them. It was difficult to speak about the air raids, and not
merely because it was hard to adequately portray their horrors. There was
also the problem of how to speak about an injury that had been delivered
by what were now the closest allies, particularly during the Cold War.
In *Vergeltung* Ledig notes this tendency to 'forget' about the events: 'An
hour was enough and horror triumphed. Later some wanted to forget it.
The others no longer wanted to know it. Allegedly they had been unable
to do anything about it.'[172] It is not clear who 'they' are: the Germans
whose government started the war, who remained loyal to it throughout
these events and who failed to push for an end to the war, or the British
and Americans who dropped the bombs. The observation seems relevant
in relation to both.

Vergeltung seems to undermine the idea that there is any sense in the
dying in war, firstly by zooming in on it and thereby implicitly raising the
question of whether this kind of dying may reasonably be said to make
sense. The problem is with who is dying as much as it is with how they
are dying. Secondly, *Vergeltung* dismisses the possible reasons for which
death might be seen to make sense. It produces a profound unease about
the events, despite placing them in the context of retaliation. This raises
questions about how we are to remember the air war: as a collective
injury, a crime, punishment, or a senseless hell? These issues point to
ethical questions that are also reflected in Mulisch's novel.

Mulisch: *Das steinerne Brautbett*

Mulisch, a Dutch writer who repeatedly addressed the implications of
war and occupation, published his novel *Het stenen bruidsbed* in 1959.
The German translation appeared as *Das steinerne Brautbett* in 1960. The
novel is set in 1956, in the midst of the destruction that was postwar
Dresden. Mulisch seems concerned with the question of the ethicality of
bombing civilians. In 1997 Sebald pointed out that, as far as he was aware,
the question of whether such an unlimited air war could be strategically
or morally justified had never been a topic of public debate in Germany
since 1945, presumably 'because a people who had murdered and tortured to death millions of people in camps could not possibly demand

---

[171] Ledig, *Vergeltung*, p. 11.   [172] Ibid., p. 199.

information from the victorious powers about the military-political logic which dictated the destruction of the German cities'.[173] German writers might have stopped short of demanding an explanation for this horror, but Mulisch focuses on the effects that the bombing had both on German civilians and Allied aircrews, and crucially on the questions that this raises.

Mulisch's main character is the 35-year-old dentist Norman Corinth from Baltimore. In 1956 Corinth is invited to a dental convention in the GDR, and, because it is in Dresden, he decides to go, despite the context of the McCarthy era.[174] Corinth's face is marked with scars and dead skin,[175] and he has no eye lashes.[176] His face, which he believes reminds others of a baboon, is a recurring theme in the novel.[177] This scarred face is a permanent, though for the time being enigmatic, reminder of the bombing of Dresden and Corinth's involvement.

The scale of the destruction is evident in the novel. Travelling around Dresden, Corinth passes ruins and signs prohibiting access. Günther, the driver, gets lost; he recognises 'ruins, heaps of rubble, streets' but he doesn't know how they fit together.[178] He also mentions that there are (in 1956!) still tens of thousands of bodies in the ruins.[179] Corinth, perhaps unsurprisingly, suffers from 'stage fright' before setting eyes on Dresden for the first time on this trip.[180] The chapter in which this is described is entitled 'A historical place',[181] generating an expectation that there will be reference to the destruction of Dresden by Allied bombing on 13 February 1945. There is, but only in the sense that Corinth notes the failure by his German interlocutor, at particular junctures in their conversation, to mention it. Ludwig, the owner of the bed-and-breakfast in which Corinth is staying, explains to him the historical character of the precise place as he sees it: it is where Napoleon won his last battle. To Corinth's surprise, he makes no reference at all to what is most on Corinth's mind: the panorama of ruins and heaps of rubble.[182] Later Ludwig mentions a fire 'that we had here', making Corinth again think of the air raids that set off a fire storm. Ludwig, however, merely reports a hotel fire in which Maria Förster, a model and '[o]ne of the most beautiful women of the GDR' was killed.[183] Thus Mulisch opposes the American

---

[173] Sebald, *Luftkrieg und Literatur*, p. 21. There has been consideration of such questions in the English-language literature. See n. 13.

[174] Harry Mulisch, *Das steinerne Brautbett*, Translated by Gregor Seferens (Frankfurt am Main: Suhrkamp Verlag 1995), pp. 10f; see also p. 53.

[175] Ibid., p. 9.   [176] Ibid., p. 11.

[177] Ibid., pp. 20, 30, 38 and 87; see also pp. 22, 29, 46, 60, 88, 90, 92, 152 and 168.

[178] Ibid., p. 37.   [179] Ibid., p. 38.   [180] Ibid., p. 15.   [181] Ibid.

[182] Ibid., p. 17.   [183] Ibid., p. 24.

Corinth, whom everything reminds of the air raids, to the German Ludwig, who appears not to think of them and not to notice the panorama of destruction. Corinth had apparently expected to be challenged – though the Americans' involvement in the destruction of Dresden appears to be unknown to the locals[184] – but finds a disconcerting and perhaps more difficult silence on the issue. Referring to a host of dead and dying flies on a window-sill Ludwig suddenly asserts: 'There is a tradition of dying on a grand scale in Dresden.'[185] Corinth winces but no more is said about it. It is unclear whether Ludwig still means Napoleon or whether he has finally brought up the topic Corinth cannot stop thinking about.

Corinth obviously suffers from great unease in relation to the bombing, and the failure to raise the topic does not help. Ludwig always *seems* to refer to the destruction of Dresden only to then turn out to be speaking about something else altogether. Readers can never be sure whether Ludwig deliberately refers to the issue or whether he is so preoccupied with other matters that he has indeed forgotten and makes these references accidentally. Much later in the novel, when he finally addresses the matter openly, it becomes clear that Ludwig assumes that Corinth considers the destruction of Dresden to have been justified:

You are right, of course, Rotterdam, London, Coventry – well, Hitler wanted to wipe out the English cities, and we all shouted hurrah. Therefore we cannot be surprised now that our cities have been wiped out. And anyway, imagine, all of Europe reduced to rubble, except for Germany. That would have been a little bit unjust. History is always just.[186]

This alludes to the already familiar theme of retaliation. Ludwig still does not speak about the actual events. Corinth explains Ludwig's resistance to remembering the bombing of Dresden in this way: he argues that, unlike the bombing of Hiroshima or the destruction of Carthage, it had no purpose. Therefore history books about Dresden will have pages on a couple of hundred dead of Napoleon's soldiers, 'but the massacre will be noted in small print in a footnote, because it does not belong in the text'.[187] Because it makes no sense, it does not fit into the text of Dresden's history. Indeed, the senselessness of the bloodbath of Dresden puts it, for Corinth, into close proximity to Auschwitz: 'We destroyed Dresden because it was Dresden, just like the Jews were slaughtered because they were Jews. Beyond that: nothing.' And he even claims, because of his own involvement: 'For one night I was a member of the Waffen-SS.'[188]

---

[184] Ibid., p. 71.   [185] Ibid., p. 25.   [186] Ibid., p. 108.   [187] Ibid., p. 110.
[188] Ibid., p. 111.

Corinth does not voice these reflections, and Ludwig proceeds to give something of a speech, worth quoting at length:

But even if it was a hundred times understandable and furthermore our own fault, that does not change the fact that inexcusable things happened. Why, for example, were people who were running through the streets, burning, also shot at with machine guns? Perhaps to deliver them from their sufferings? Or take the people who were standing in the Elbe. You have to know that the heat [*Gluthitze*] in the city was so great that people jumped into the river, people who had nothing left but their lives and their wounds. You really could no longer term them enemies, don't you agree? Those in the river, on 13 February 1945, really could no longer endanger an English parliament. But no: tack, tack, tack. It's an enigma to me what kind of guys these were. Subhumans out of the slums of London, professional criminals. Please understand me correctly, I do not say anything against the bombing, war is war, and Hitler himself proclaimed total war. But when the Allies [used] his methods, which they themselves . . . that . . .[189]

Ludwig stops himself before he can formulate his precise complaint, presumably that the Allies used Hitler's methods, which they claimed to be fighting against. He stops, in other words, when he realises that he is doing what Sebald acknowledged as profoundly problematic: asking the Allies, as a German, to justify their conduct. The matter is not taken any further within the story; Corinth has fallen asleep. Mulisch, it seems, shies back from formulating the question directly and indeed from offering possible answers.

Mulisch introduces the horrors of the bombing of Dresden gradually, through a conversation between the West German Schneiderhahn and some survivors. In a pub, Schneiderhahn asks a couple to tell him about their experiences, but the man asks what purpose there is in talking about it: 'It is over, after all.'[190] Schneiderhahn, however, wants to hear about it; it is, he says, 'without precedent':[191] 'The biggest crime in history: 250,000 dead within an hour, and the Russians were in Bohemia as well, and the war had been lost a long time ago.'[192] 'Won', Corinth thinks.[193] This ambiguity over whether the war was lost or won here shows merely the difference of perspective of a German versus an American. Yet this ambiguity has actually become a political issue, namely of how Germans today are to regard the end of the war: whilst their fatherland lost, the values they are now seen to subscribe to 'won'. Thus, retrospectively, Germans appear not to have been defeated, but liberated. This ambiguity

---

[189] Ibid., pp. 112f.   [190] Ibid., p. 68.   [191] Ibid., p. 69.
[192] Ibid. Schneiderhahn's number is far too large. Groehler estimates the number of dead as between 35,000 and 40,000. Groehler, *Bombenkrieg*, p. 412. See also below.
[193] Mulisch, *Brautbett*, p. 69.

has been used in justifying the Germans' return to using the military instrument.[194]

Finally, the couple starts their tale of 13 February 1945, the day of the bombing. Corinth 'listened, tried to listen, but there was something between him and the words, and he thought, I cannot understand anything of what he says'. The text, probably as part of Corinth's inner monologue, then specifies: 'Those who did not experience it will never be able to understand. The city was dead before it died.'[195] 'Having been there' is often portrayed as crucial to understanding.[196] However, in their report of the night of the bombing the couple go against the rules of this claim to knowledge and authenticity: each speaks for the other, the wife for the husband and the husband for the wife. They never describe the experience from their own position. They speak precisely not on the basis of 'having been there'; their reports already involve a distance. The wife starts by explaining that her husband had stood in the window on the roof; he had not gone to the shelter. Dresden had been spared throughout the war because, they thought, it was a metropolis of art. There had been air-raid alarms many times, but nothing had ever happened. She reports that he sometimes says that he simply could not believe that the English would do this. Schneiderhahn asks whether it was the English. The husband explains that at night it was always the English. Corinth, who knows better, does not intervene. When the husband finally arrived at the shelter, his wife could see that he was half crazy from fear.[197] But he did not tell the others what he had seen. They heard the planes, but they were used to that. 'And the war was really also over, after all.' She then talks of the building shaking, 'heaven crashing down', the building collapsing into the cellar, but interjects 'I have forgotten it' and 'I no longer know.'[198] She fundamentally rejects the notion of 'having been there' as an appropriate claim to truth: 'Afterwards one no longer knows how everything happened.'[199]

Her husband then describes how his wife fled with their child 'between the walls of fire'. Hair and clothes were burnt off her body, and the smoke was choking her. There was a smell of burnt flesh. He explains that '[b]ombs fell between the Bohemian refugees who were crawling in a muddle like bloody maggots. People with their bodies cut in half dragged themselves into the fire in order to just die fast, a man beat to death on the cobbles a child that had been torn to pieces.'[200] She fled through the fire storm until she finally reached the River Elbe. Many were already cooling down in the river when a plane arrived and fired at them from

---

[194] See Chapters 2 and 5.   [195] Mulisch, *Brautbett*, p. 70.
[196] See Chapter 4, pp. 155–6.   [197] Mulisch, *Brautbett*, p. 71.
[198] Ibid., p. 72.   [199] Ibid., pp. 72f.   [200] Ibid., p. 73.

about 10 metres distance. He – who was of course not there to witness this – asserts that 'she already was not really aware of what happened any more'.[201] Her child slid from her arms into the water, and she could not find it.[202] Finally, the husband says that perhaps the child had been dead already and adds that they 'agreed . . . that [the child] was already dead right at the beginning of the attack'[203] – as if it was a question of coming to an agreement. The 'agreement' is crucial, however; it is, one suspects, the only way to bear what happened.

Finally, the man asks whether Schneiderhahn wants to hear more interesting events: 'How I was able to save myself from the cellar after 48 hours and strangled a girl who asked me to? How we ripped the tracks from the streets and burnt bodies with flame-throwers for days?'[204] Schneiderhahn declines the offer. When wife and husband leave, Corinth sees her wooden leg and feels himself inwardly jump up after them 'to do what? To plead? To beg? To throw himself on the floor?'[205] Yet he again does and says nothing. Readers find out only later that Corinth was not just involved in bombing Dresden, but had also gunned down people seeking refuge from the fire in the river.[206] Earlier in the story, he reflects whether the Americans should 'perhaps *not* have flown here to reduce the nest to rubble?'[207] The 'perhaps' does not, however, indicate an admission of an alternative, but is rather an emphasis in what is, in the context, a rhetorical question. Although Corinth is at times consumed by guilt over what he has done, he believes the air raids to have been 'right': it was necessary to destroy the Third Reich.

Hella, the party minder assigned to the dentists convention, asks Corinth whether the memory of his involvement in the bombings still weighs upon him. Despite his continuous preoccupation with the raid on Dresden, he denies this and crudely asks whether she, who had been put in a concentration camp as a communist by the Nazi regime, would have preferred to stay there for another year. She explains that she had meant Dresden in particular, and he claims that that had been the English. He does not want to admit that the second wave of attack was flown by the Americans.[208] The fact that he is physically marked comes into tension with his claim that he never thinks of the raid and with what the reader knows: that he is obsessed with the memory, and everything in Dresden reminds him of his involvement. He denies that these memories haunt him not out of shame but because he wants to have sex with Hella and

---

[201] Ibid., p. 74.   [202] Ibid.   [203] Ibid., p. 75.   [204] Ibid.   [205] Ibid., pp. 75f.
[206] Ibid., p. 95. Note that it is not historically accurate to suggest that bombers shot at people in this way; it would have been fighters, that is, different planes. I am grateful to Tarak Barkawi and Philip Towle for pointing this out.
[207] Ibid., p. 29.   [208] Ibid., p. 89.

fears her reaction. Therefore he claims that it is 'as if it never happened' and that he never thinks about it. She, however, asks whether he does not find this more disturbing than if it still weighed upon him. He shakes his head, but is immediately gripped by a mysterious seizure.[209] Towards the end of the book, Corinth has a breakdown.[210] He can no longer cope with the past in the way he had.

Significantly, it is not only the Germans who are scarred by the events. Corinth is physically marked by his involvement, an outward sign of the memory haunting him. His guilt is not only about what he did but also, apparently, about what he felt. The narrative is interrupted with 'songs', stylised recollections of Corinth's involvement in the bombing. In the first song, Corinth has an erection when joining the attack, and there is reference to the 'enjoyment of arousal floating through his body'.[211] This lust for killing appears, of course, entirely inappropriate in the context of the story the two Germans tell in the pub. It is interesting that this aspect, although it is not taken further, is nevertheless not denied or excluded. There is indeed a similar scene in Ledig's *Vergeltung*, when Strenehen takes out a German fighter and shouts: 'I've killed him! I've killed him!'[212] The text continues: 'He was happy. For a second boundlessly happy. Until he saw the blood on his hands, then he got sick.'[213]

In an interview Mulisch explains that he had wanted to write a book about a German war criminal but, after visiting Dresden in the 1950s, he decided to write a book about an American war criminal. 'That is,' he adds, 'you are of course only a war criminal if you lose a war.'[214] The question was how to represent this; he picked on the idea of an American who only discovers what he has done by reading the paper the next day. What interested Mulisch was what would happen to someone like that.[215] He says that this structural idea was necessary because one cannot just attempt to write about the horrible,[216] a problem also discussed in Vonnegut's *Slaughterhouse 5*, which is explored in Chapter 5. Mulisch's remark seems to acknowledge, when he suggests the necessity of reading the paper, the – controversial – claims of bomber crews that they did not actually know what they were doing. Yet Corinth did not need to rely on the media. Rather more dramatically, when his plane is attacked and the starboard engines catch fire, the crew decide not to parachute over German territory for fear of being lynched. Instead, they try to fly to somewhere behind Russian lines. They throw overboard everything they

---

[209] Ibid., pp. 89f.   [210] Ibid., pp. 181–3.   [211] Ibid., p. 33.
[212] Ledig, *Vergeltung*, p. 30 (English in original).   [213] Ibid.
[214] 'Tanz unter den Ruinen', interview with Harry Mulisch, in: Hage, *Zeugen der Zerstörung*, p. 225.
[215] Ibid.   [216] Ibid., pp. 225f.

no longer need, including the body of a crew member.[217] As they flee they go back towards Dresden: 'It was as if he had expected to see [Dresden] again unhurt: as if the attack had not really happened, but had only been an arranged game, which they had accepted with a wink, a game without duties, without consequences.' But when Corinth looks down on the city he realises that '[i]t had really happened. [Dresden] no longer existed.'[218] In an interview Mulisch explains that, on a visit to Dresden after the war, he had been impressed by the river and the city: 'That is: the city was simply not there! Completely gone! Something incredible, like a dream.'[219] For him, what was horrible was that as a Dutch child in the inhuman situation of occupation and war he had become inhuman as well, because he had been happy about the destruction. As a result, he argues that the question of guilt is more complex than people admitted at the time. Those hiding in the shelters in Hamburg or Dresden had, after all, not started the bombing.[220]

The memory of the air war represented in *Das steinerne Brautbett* is both painful and inescapable, as epitomised in Corinth's scarred face. It is so for both 'sides', those who were bombed and those who dropped the bombs. Just because people do not speak about the events does not mean that they have forgotten, that the memory has vanished. There is, in this depiction, a powerful undercurrent that insists that the bombing was right, in a larger sense, but there is also a struggle to accept this in the face of individual experiences. One further aspect is worth noting in relation to the question of memory. Although Corinth clearly remembers – he 'had been there', after all – he experiences a need to return which is powerful enough to make him go to the GDR during the McCarthy era, a difficulty specifically noted. His memory seems to need confirmation. Remembering is a social activity; it is not just about recalling. The couple who survived the destruction of Dresden are evidently presenting an agreed version of their past; they need each other to confirm that this is what happened, although they were not together when those events occurred.

Victims and perpetrators in one

In the debate about *Der Brand*, Boog asserted that he would have preferred it to be identified in a subtitle as a 'novel', 'drama' or 'tragedy'. In that case one could have judged it to be 'magnificent'.[221] Given the criticisms of the book – styling Germans as victims, sentimentalisation, use of

---

[217] Mulisch, *Brautbett*, p. 163.   [218] Ibid., p. 164.   [219] 'Tanz unter den Ruinen', p. 229.
[220] Ibid., p. 233.   [221] Boog, 'Ein Kolossalgemälde', p. 136.

Nazi language – this is disturbing; it is unclear why he should approve of these in fiction. What Boog, who criticised *Der Brand* for mistakes relating to historical detail, seems to suggest is that in fiction it is all right to get the occasional 'fact' wrong because information is not the point.[222] In other words, fiction would be in some sense 'freer' in the way it approaches the topic. Clearly, publicly expressed memory is constrained by concerns over an unwarranted and exculpatory construction of Germans as victims. The debate about *Der Brand* has constantly revolved around this problem, Federal President Herzog's speech on the fiftieth anniversary of the bombing of Dresden alluded to it, and a number of writers have also noted this difficulty in their response to Sebald. Public debate seems stuck on this theme.

There are two sets of opposed categories at work in this worry about speaking of Second World War memories: perpetrators versus victims on the one hand, and Germans versus non-Germans on the other. It is considered important to align the two to form one dichotomy: German perpetrators versus non-German victims. Whilst this distinction may be clear in the abstract, it appears to be threatened by the particular as invoked by war memories.[223] The concern about the interest in such memories betrays the fear that the distinction is less secure than is claimed; it must be policed, precisely because it no longer seems obvious when German civilians' experiences are taken into account. It does not seem to be clear what it means to say that a woman who burns 'like a torch'[224] and a man who is 'barbecued' were not victims of the bombing, even if the latter was a squad leader.[225] And what of the 'child that had been torn to pieces', but does not die before being beaten to death?[226] That there were German victims (and non-German perpetrators) seems obvious, whether or not one is prepared to accept that civilians exposed to bombings or indeed expellees constituted victims of a kind. Mulisch points out that the people killed in shelters in Hamburg or Dresden had hardly been the ones to start the war. Significantly, the problem is *not* that the sufferings described in Ledig's *Vergeltung*, Mulisch's *Das steinerne Brautbett* and Friedrich's *Der Brand* did not take place or were less gruesome than is suggested; the problem is precisely that they were – people were crushed, torn apart, barbecued, suffocated – and this endangers the clarity of the distinction, which must therefore be upheld differently. In other words, if this suffering is acknowledged at all, then the demand is that it must be

---

[222] This is an idea similar to what Ricoeur notes as the difference in the implicit contract between writer and reader for historical versus literary writing. *Memory, History, Forgetting*, p. 261.

[223] See also Barnouw, *War in the Empty Air*, p. 17.   [224] Ledig, *Vergeltung*, p. 10.

[225] Ibid., p. 128.   [226] Mulisch, *Brautbett*, p. 73.

made clear that the Germans were not victims *despite* the suffering. It is inappropriate to speak of this suffering without noting the alleged cause, the Germans' crimes, precisely because, looking at their experiences, they *appear* to have been victims. This is why Ledig's alleged failure to include the 'political context' is considered so objectionable.

However, whilst official commemoration and the debates about memories of the bombing of German cities may be concerned with *German* suffering, this is not what the novels considered are necessarily about. They already do what Moeller has challenged scholars to do: they start by 'deconstructing the "*Wir*" (we)'.[227] They portray both Germans and Allied combatants and take into account a multiplicity of perspectives. Mulisch's central figure is the former bomber pilot Corinth, who has not only been physically disfigured in the bombing of Dresden but also traumatised. He may not have died a gruesome death, but he clearly suffers. Whilst in Mulisch's novel there seems to be a clear difference between British and Americans in the sky and Germans on the ground, exposed to the bombs, Ledig breaks up this distinction. He depicts not only the fate of civilians but also of airmen and soldiers; crucially, he tells of Russian and American combatants, too. Captain Strenehen, in particular, is a key figure in the novel: he actively aims to avoid German casualties by dropping his bombs on a cemetery, but when he is shot down the Germans do not show the same humanity: he is mistreated, some want to lynch him, and he eventually dies after being thrown out of a shelter. This is crucial: in Ledig's story, not all Germans are passive victims, awaiting their fate in the cellars like sheep on the way to the slaughterhouse. Rather, they commit cruel deeds even whilst mayhem is unfolding around them. Considering such behaviour undermines their simplistic categorisation as 'victims' of the air raids. Just because they are cruelly bombed, they are not necessarily innocent, beyond reproach.

Thus Ledig ignores the victim–perpetrator distinction, but the thrust of his depiction is not the feared exculpatory attitude. He draws attention to the possibility of being a perpetrator at the same time as being a victim. Germans are construed as always also perpetrators, especially but not only in the sense noted by the title: having given cause for this 'retaliation' in the first place. They also cruelly lynched bomber pilots, and sometimes did not help those who needed assistance. Even though *Vergeltung* does not explicitly speak of the Holocaust, the memory performed by Ledig seems marked by guilt and shame. The intention does not appear redemptive, like that suggested in Herzog's speech, not least

---

[227] Moeller, 'On the History', 119. Moeller does not, as far as I can see, mean 'deconstruct' in a Derridean sense.

because Ledig rejects all efforts to make sense of the dying. Although reading Ledig's text undermines the security of the perpetrator–victim distinction, it does not offer a positive view or emotion about what happened and about what this means for today.

Novels challenge the neatness of the distinction, but they do not support the politically worrisome constructions of the past that are supposed to be avoided through upholding the distinction. The worry that the clear categorisation of perpetrators versus victims is being questioned seems to implicitly rely on assuming that Germans remember *as Germans* and thereby invent and support their identity as Germans. It does not take into account the possibility, as arguably enacted in both novels, of remembering without remembering as Germans. However, even if all remembering *by* Germans was remembering *as* Germans, it seems doubtful that knowing more about the German experiences referred to in political debate makes being German a less anguished affair. It is not clear a priori that representing the war, even representing Germans as victims of the bombing of cities or expulsions from the East, supports the creation of a less problematic, historically detached German identity, as was arguably the thrust of conservative arguments in the *Historikerstreit*.

The recognition that perpetrators and victims may not be safely separated from each other, certainly not along national lines, making all Germans purely perpetrators, is crucial for overcoming the impasse created by the requirement that appropriate war memories may in no sense render Germans as victims, for the claim that such clear categorisation is possible leaves us with two equally unsatisfactory, and indeed unrealistic, labels for German experience. Whilst, immediately after the war, Germans arguably saw themselves primarily as having been victims of both Nazism and the war, they later had to recognise that they had been perpetrators, a process – as the debate over Wehrmacht atrocities to be explored in Chapter 4 shows – that is still ongoing. However, this classification then ruled out an acknowledgement of distressful wartime experiences as part of official memory. When, from the 1990s on, interest in civilian experiences during wartime is expressed again, concerns are raised about whether this means that the Germans are beginning to see themselves as victims *rather than* perpetrators: conceptually, there is nowhere else to go. Perpetrator and victim are the only categories available, and they are mutually exclusive. However, thinking about this past in a way that requires a 5-year-old girl who died in the Hamburg fire storm to be categorised as first and foremost a member of the perpetrator community seems problematic. It is precisely this shortcoming that allows those who wish to do so to promote the myth of Germans as victims and to use it to create a positive attachment to the nation: it appears that the categorisation denies the emotive example of the 5-year-old girl, allowing the far Right to construe an image of Germans forbidden their truest memories and therefore 'victimised' by the Left and the victorious powers.

Following this reasoning, the problem does not seem to be so much that Germans remember and have started to publicly discuss memories of suffering in the Second World War, but the perhaps at one stage politically useful, yet by now profoundly unhelpful, classification into victims and perpetrators. This categorisation also carries a further danger, noted in Chapter 2: that of an atemporal application. Barnouw points out that 'the Germans *are* neither victims nor perpetrators', though they were one or the other during the Second World War.[228] The terminology of 'victim' or 'perpetrator', Barnouw suggests, has now become politicised, generalised, and is therefore beyond rational discussion.[229] Thus it seems imperative to overcome this problematic and politically unhelpful categorisation. Laurel Cohen-Pfister observes that '[c]urrent literary texts suggest that the singularity of being either perpetrator or victim is a paradigm inconsistent with collective memory, because these texts construct a framework flexible enough to contain the paradox of experiences and contested memories of several generations'.[230] It appears that literature is able to raise doubts as to the mutual exclusivity and universal applicability of these categories, that it highlights the way that the intractable issue is precisely that people are rarely ever just one or the other but are often, to use the phrase again, 'perpetrator and victim in one'. This is an important contribution to understanding war memories as an ethico-political problem. It is no longer enough to abide by a politically correct formula for remembering, which at any rate never worked.

It is worth noting that what the critics are really afraid of – a return of Nazi thinking and politics – relies on the same problematic categories which the critics vehemently defend as a panacea against them. Both suggest that a correct memory is possible and both – explicitly or implicitly – assume the memories in question to be German, intimately connected to German identity. The worries about the interest in war memories, as discussed so far, assume that what is at issue is Germans remembering *as Germans*. This leads to concerns about attempts to exploit the suffering of German civilians for particular identity constructions and political purposes. The linkage of past German suffering and current German

---

[228] Barnouw, *War in the Empty Air*, p. 56.   [229] Ibid., p. 98.

[230] Laurel Cohen-Pfister, 'The Suffering of the Perpetrators: Unleashing Collective Memory in German Literature of the Twenty-First Century', *Forum of Modern Language Studies* 41 (2005), 131.

identity is, of course, a trademark right-wing move. Yet attempts by Neo-Nazis to instrumentalise the bombing of Dresden for their purposes have been widely rejected. Some survivors make efforts to counter attempts to 'abuse and instrumentalise people's suffering'.[231] They are as puzzled by the idea that they were all perpetrators as they are outraged by Neo-Nazis' attempts to deploy the memory of the destruction for their political purposes. It makes no sense to them that even infants and children of refugees who happened to be in the city should be regarded as perpetrators.[232] Jens Schneider portrays one survivor as objecting to the abuse of her memories as a vehicle for their ideologies by both Left and Right and suggests that the citizens of Dresden have tried to reclaim dealing with the past from the politicians. In a response to Neo-Nazi marches on the 2004 anniversary, survivors, representatives of the churches and other citizens developed a 'frame for remembering' for the sixtieth anniversary, in which they rejected the abuse of memory as well as what they considered to be a mocking of the victims.[233] On the sixtieth anniversary itself 60,000 commemorated the dead and demonstrated against any abuse of memory.[234]

Chapter 2 showed how difficult it is to amend memories that are considered to be an abuse of the past with historical knowledge. As with the expulsions, there are also areas of uncertainty relating to strategic bombing. There has, for example, always been considerable disagreement about how many were killed in the bombing of Dresden. The mayor of Dresden appointed a commission of historians in an attempt to end speculation. However, even before the commission reported it was clear that a precise number could not be established because no one knows how many refugees were in the city at the time.[235] Nor will the correct figure solve much: 'Death had conquered the city – what do we need a number for?'[236] Such efforts might make it possible to reveal as historically incorrect the numbers claimed by the far Right, but it seems difficult to reject, on the grounds of inaccuracy, their references to 'Allied bombing terror', for it is true that the Allies bombed German cities and that this induced terror amongst the population. As Forte notes in reference to air raids, there was 'an unspeakable terror'.[237] We may prefer not to call

---

[231] Gerhard Schröder, 'Erklärung von Bundeskanzler Gerhard Schröder zum 60. Jahrestag der Zerstörung Dresdens', 13/02/05, www.bundeskanzler.de.
[232] See, for example, Schneider, 'Im brüchigen Rahmen'.   [233] Ibid.
[234] 'Dresden setzt Zeichen gegen Rechtsextremismus', Süddeutsche Zeitung, 14/02/05, 1. See also Jens Schneider, 'Eine Kultur der Erinnerung', Süddeutsche Zeitung, 14/02/05, 3.
[235] See Schneider, 'Im brüchigen Rahmen'.   [236] Ibid.
[237] Forte, Schweigen oder sprechen, p. 33.

114 Wounds of Memory

it 'Allied bombing terror', but that is a different matter. Crucially, it is a fallacy to think that the correct memory would allow us to disempower right-wing political positions. Despite the tendentiousness and exaggeration in memories peddled by the far Right, it is crucial to remember that it is their political goals that are worrying.[238]

Chancellor Schröder tried a different tack. He found it necessary to make a statement in the context of the sixtieth anniversary of the bombing of Dresden in which he stressed that all attempts at re-interpreting the past would be rejected, noted again the relationship of cause and effect, and underlined the impermissibility of offsetting some groups of victims against others. Like Herzog ten years earlier, Schröder sought to overcome the danger of commemorating German suffering by making it clear that the occasion is one of *mourning* for 'the victims of war and National Socialist tyranny in Dresden, in Germany and in Europe'.[239] Thus Schröder tried to transcend the German-ness of the memory in order to undermine the possibility of an interpretation that would support the politics of the far Right. This move challenges the categories, in that it tries to overcome the German-ness of what is at issue. Yet it ends up merely expanding the category of victim, lumping together those who experienced the horrors of war with those who were cruelly and systematically murdered by the Germans. This is the move that, some fear, makes everyone a victim (though Schröder commemorated all victims, he did not assert that everyone was a victim, a significant difference that the critics tend to ignore), raising concerns about the impropriety, indeed outrageousness, of members of the 'perpetrator community' sharing a category with the victims of the Nazi regime[240] and more broadly concerns about the suppression of the significance of, or even denial of, the Holocaust. There is rightly concern about not adding to the violence against those who suffered most at the hands of Germans, but also about other political implications. These usually focus on how Germans supposedly do or should feel about themselves as a nation. This is a debate that seems to be always ongoing – the *Historikerstreit*,[241] the controversy about Daniel Jonah Goldhagen's *Hitler's Willing Executioners*,[242]

---

[238] For more on this, see Chapter 6.   [239] Schröder, 'Erklärung'.
[240] See the debate over the Neue Wache memorial and its inscription. Kattago, 'Representing German Victimhood'.
[241] *'Historikerstreit'*; Dan Diner (ed.), *Ist der Nationalsozialismus Geschichte? Zu Historisierung und Historikerstreit* (Frankfurt am Main: Fischer Taschenbuch Verlag 1987), and Charles S. Maier, *The Unmasterable Past: History, Holocaust, and German National Identity* (Cambridge, MA: Harvard University Press 1988).
[242] Robert R. Shandley (ed.), *Unwilling Germans? The Goldhagen Debate* (Minneapolis: University of Minnesota Press 1998), and Norman G. Finkelstein and Ruth Bettina Birn, *A Nation on Trial: The Goldhagen Thesis and Historical Truth* (New York: Henry Holt 1998).

the Walser–Bubis debate,[243] the debate about the Holocaust memorial[244] – and others have commented at length on these issues.

What is proposed here is not a more inclusive victim category, an admittance of (some) Germans into the fold of victimhood. Rather, my argument challenges the *possibility* of such a category. At issue is not that (some) Germans were victims rather than perpetrators, but that it is possible to be both at the same time. Therefore the categories do not work as they are supposed to. Of course, such talk of being victim and perpetrator in one is bound to raise fears of inappropriate apologetics and even moral relativism. Although Olick argues in his own way for reconsidering 'mnemonic orthodoxies', he urges that it is important to do so 'without abandoning moral distinctions, making it seem as if everyone is simultaneously victim and perpetrator'.[245] This, of course, is not at issue here in the first place: the issue is not whether *everyone* was both, but that – certainly applied to 'the Germans' as a community, but also applied to many individuals – the distinction is unhelpful. The categories are not working; it is not a question of my argument undermining them. Crucially, the idea that one may be 'victim and perpetrator in one', that one is neither one nor the other and yet simultaneously both, does not make anything that happened less horrible or morally repulsive. The point is merely, as Heribert Seifert notes in the context of increased interest in the war particularly amongst the younger generations, that where 'light and darkness had been so easy to distinguish, the areas of twilight, in which the good and the bad cannot always be recognised without a doubt, are expanding'.[246]

Given the apparent impossibility of a clear boundary between victims and perpetrators in war, one wonders what is at stake in policing against German constructions of themselves as victims. Of course, this may not be just about German identity. The memories in question highlight the distressing character of the experiences of those who suffer air strikes, whilst the Germans are now supposed to be concentrating on delivering them, like the heroic Allied liberators. This is an unwelcome tension. Yet it is important not to paper over the cracks appearing in the story about why Germans should go to war today by stigmatising the war memories that might encourage critical thinking about the effects of war on ordinary people, for the supposedly good Allied war is in danger of being translated into a programme for the future.

---

[243] Schirrmacher (ed.), *Die Walser-Bubis-Debatte*, and Brumlik, Funke and Rensmann, *Umkämpftes Vergessen*.

[244] Caroline Wiedmer, *The Claims of Memory: Representations of the Holocaust in Contemporary France and Germany* (Ithaca: Cornell University Press 1999), and Edkins, *Trauma and the Memory of Politics*, pp. 132–4.

[245] Olick, *In the House*, p. 340.   [246] Seifert, 'Rekonstruktion', p. 153.

Memories of strategic bombing and the Iraq war

The far Right construes remembering the bombing in a particular way: it is about remembering Dresden's dead as Germans. Yet neither remembering nor mourning are necessarily or obviously national affairs. Others see a link between events in Dresden and those in Baghdad, New York or Grosny.[247] This brings us back to the starting-point of this chapter: the Germans' reaction to the proposition of war against Iraq. In what was an apparent deviation from a trend towards greater willingness to use the military, the German government, in agreement with the people, refused to contemplate the idea. Franziska Augstein argued in January 2003 that the 'vast majority of Germans do not want a war against Iraq' because 'they do not see the point'.[248] They simply did not 'buy' the asserted Iraqi threat.

There was something else, however. Intriguingly, Iraq persistently intruded into the debate about the Allied strategic bombing of German cities during the Second World War that had been set off by Friedrich's *Der Brand*.[249] In a panel on 'The air war against Germany – a morality play for the present?' at the 2003 Leipzig Book Fair, Carola Stern claimed, on the one hand, that there were no parallels, because the Allies' war against Germany had been a defensive war. On the other hand, she argued that aerial bombing is part of modern war, and the question is again whether the end justifies the means.[250] Bölsche, in his discussion of the Allied air war, similarly cited a range of specific questions that made a connection possible and necessary: 'Whether a war against terror may be conducted also with terror attacks; under which circumstances it may be permitted to incinerate women, old people and children; when so-called collateral damage must be regarded as a war crime.' In sum, he claims, looking back 'at the air raids of 1943 throws up very similar questions to the debates about US air raids in Iraq or the Russian bombing of the Chechen capital Grosny'.[251]

Remembering strategic bombing against Germany has in turn, according to Stargardt, been stimulated by the recent war against Iraq. In Chapter 2 I argued, noting Halbwachs's claim that 'most frequently, we appeal to our memory only in order to answer questions which others have asked

---

[247] Schneider, 'Im brüchigen Rahmen'.

[248] Franziska Augstein, 'Rumsfelds Logik', *Süddeutsche Zeitung*, 18–19/01/03, 13.

[249] See, for example, Mommsen, 'Moralisch, strategisch, zerstörerisch', in: Kettenacker, *Ein Volk von Opfern?*, p. 150, and Seifert, 'Rekonstruktion', p. 157.

[250] Carola Stern in 'Bombenkrieg macht alle gleich', in: Burgdorff and Habbe, *Als Feuer vom Himmel fiel*, p. 141.

[251] Bölsche, 'So muss die Hölle aussehen', p. 21.

us, or that we suppose they could have asked us',[252] that the resurgence of interest in Second World War memories may be related to what is experienced as a return of war. Stargardt similarly links the 'literary success' of Grass's *Im Krebsgang* and Friedrich's *Der Brand* to the FRG's current policies. It 'coincides', he says, 'with a time after Bosnia, in which the German Federal Government decides more freely than ever before in its history about military and foreign policy questions'. Yet the memories allegedly fuelled by increasing use of the military in turn lead to a less than happy attitude towards war. As Stargardt points out, if the German government 'takes a fundamentally negative attitude towards the American war plans in Iraq, it can trust that war is not popular in Germany – and for good reasons. We all should listen carefully to the experiences of those who were bombed. Their voices have been silent for all too long.'[253] Thus Stargardt claims political relevance for the allegedly forgotten memories, which are at the same time in danger of being politically sidelined owing to the ever-present worry that they are about nothing more than an implicit exoneration of the Germans through construing them as victims and are therefore associated with the political aims of the Right.

Unsurprisingly, some in Germany made clear that their opposition to the Iraq war was based on their own wartime experiences. Former GDR civil rights campaigner Wolfgang Ullmann argued in his appeal to Chancellor Schröder not to support US President George W. Bush's war plans that those who had, like him, 'experienced the bombing of the almost completely defenceless population of Dresden' must be 'convinced forever' that 'there cannot be a thinkable legitimation for using weapons in this way'.[254] Ullmann seems to be in agreement with former Federal President Herzog, who had asserted that 'Dresden reflects the utter senselessness of modern wars'.[255] Despite Ullmann's and Herzog's conviction, such wartime experience does not, however, necessarily translate into an unconditional rejection of air raids. In fact, songwriter Wolf Biermann was extremely critical of the Germans' attitude to the war against Iraq. Creating an explicit parallel between Joseph Goebbels and Gerhard Schröder, he spoke of today's German government asking 'Do you want total peace?' and the Germans once again replying 'Yessss!'[256] He was, in other words, not convinced that the lesson of strategic bombing was, above all, to avoid such usage of the military instrument. Biermann, whose Jewish father was murdered in Auschwitz, was saved by his mother,

[252] Halbwachs, *On Collective Memory*, p. 38.
[253] Stargardt, 'Opfer der Bomben', p. 58.
[254] Quoted in Bölsche, 'So muss die Hölle aussehen', pp. 21f.
[255] Herzog, 'Dresden', p. 8.
[256] Wolf Biermann, 'Brachiale Friedenliebe', *Der Spiegel*, 24/02/03, 144.

at the age of 6, from the fire storm in Hamburg set off by Allied air raids in the summer of 1943; she swam through the river with him on her back. Biermann sees this event as decisive in his life.[257] Yet unlike Ullmann, Biermann concludes that such military action may at times be necessary. The experience of being exposed to the most horrible aspects of strategic bombing does not provide an answer to the question of whether war – or bombing – is ever morally justified or whether Germany should contribute to this particular war against Iraq.

As noted at the outset, the question cannot be which position on war memories support. Rather, memories provide a context within which we conceptualise war. Second World War memories have the potential to provide an illustration for a certain suspiciousness about easy categorisations and categorical arguments. This has already been shown above in relation to the supposedly clear distinction between victims and perpetrators. The discourse of good versus evil emanating from the White House is another case in point; it led to considerable disconcertion in Germany, certainly because of its religious overtones and the implication that Bush decides who is evil and against whom one, as a consequence, has to fight.[258] Crucially, the clear opposition of good versus evil in the context of air raids must constitute a problem for Germans owing to their memories of strategic bombing. There can be no doubt that (most) Germans today recognise without qualification that their country – and by implication, though this is harder to swallow for some, their compatriots – were at fault and on the wrong side in the Second World War. In Bush's dichotomy, they were on the side of evil. However, this does not automatically mean that it was permissible to incinerate 'their' women and children, to come back to Bölsche's question. This raises a serious problem: if the horrors of air raids against cities were perhaps an unreasonable means in the fight 'against Hitler', then it must be even more so in the fight against what can only ever be lesser villains. Of course, the US administration never proposed or implemented anything like the incineration of cities in Iraq on the model of Hamburg or Dresden. On the contrary, they insisted that their fight was against the regime, not the people, of Iraq and that civilian casualties would be kept as low as possible.[259] However, despite precision-guided weapons, 'collateral damage'

---

[257] See 'Die Lebensuhr blieb stehen', interview with Wolf Biermann, in: Hage, *Zeugen der Zerstörung*, pp. 135–50.

[258] See Herfried Münkler, 'Moralphilosophie auf dem Kriegspfad', *Blätter für deutsche und internationale Politik* 47 (2002), 1335.

[259] See Secretary Colin Powell in 'U.S. Policy towards Iraq: Administration Views', *Hearing before the Committee on International Relations, House of Representatives*, 107th Congress, 2nd session, 19/09/02, Serial No. 107–17, 18.

persists, a term that, in view of Second World War memories, inevitably leads to considerable agitation in Germany.[260]

This interest in those on the receiving end of the bombing is also evident in concern over the failure to outlaw such bombing in the aftermath of the Second World War. Mommsen argues that we should stop downplaying the serious consequences for the civilian population by admitting to 'inevitable "collateral damage"'.[261] He also sees the negative attitude towards the Iraq war in this context.[262] Herfried Münkler asserts that 'subliminally' the memory of the Allied bombing of German cities has played a significant role in debates over the last decade about the legitimacy of military intervention and the implications of war. He argues that it is hardly surprising that where there are 'pictures of bombers and fighter planes that are blanket-bombing an area or dropping cluster bombs one almost always sees an identification with the attacked in Germany'.[263] In other words, despite being in terms of political conviction (more) on the side of the Americans – and no amount of accusations of anti-Americanism can obscure that[264] – there is at the same time an emotional identification with those suffering the air strikes.[265] This empathy, which may be strengthened by the kind of fictional representations discussed above, is not subject to any question about the political convictions or previous deeds of those attacked. It cannot be: their record could not be any worse than that of Germans during the Third Reich. Besides, no matter how criminal the regime is, there will always be some 'innocents' amongst the dead and injured. The unease at the carnage in German cities, despite the proposed justification of retaliation, suggests that *explaining* the events is not everything: one may remain dissatisfied at a different level.

Noting the salience of memories of the Allied air war for understandings of the war against Iraq is not to say that these wars are comparable. A historical or strategic comparison would presumably reveal more differences than similarities. At issue is not an analogy between the bombing of German cities during the Second World War and the Iraq war but the impact which the memory of the former may have on our political imagination in relation to the latter. What is crucial is not least the dimension of

---

[260] Münkler, 'Moralphilosophie', 1338.   [261] Mommsen, 'Moralisch', p. 150.
[262] Ibid.   [263] Münkler, 'Moralphilosophie', 1338.
[264] Whether or not Germans are anti-American is not at issue here; what is claimed is that Germans tend to prefer the political system of the USA to that of Saddam Hussein's Iraq.
[265] This is not an identification with Saddam Hussein, despite Dan Diner's claims in relation to the 1991 Gulf War. *Der Krieg der Erinnerungen und die Ordnung der Welt* (Berlin: Rotbuch Verlag 1991).

identification and affect implied in memories. If their memories of strategic bombing entice Germans to subliminally identify with those suffering the air strikes, then they are exposed to a tension. German memories lead to looking at air strikes from the position of those suffering them, that is, with respect to the current situation, from the position of the Other. It is evident from the representations of air raids discussed above that the experience of those exposed to bombing is one of utter mayhem, senselessness and a general failure to see events from the perspective of those who are dropping the bombs. Through this memory, the Other, for example in the war against Iraq, may be recognised as Self: we are able to empathise. We also more easily relate to the problem that, even though civilian populations may not be targeted, they are on the 'battlefield' and therefore always in danger of becoming targets. Given that it is argued that Western populations now are to war what the crowd is to a football game – spectators[266] – this is important. Crucially, particularly in the context of war, Germans are now supposed to identify with the heroic Allied liberators who brought peace and freedom. This is beginning to look like a difficult story, not only because the 'heroic liberators' brought indescribable horror together with their 'gift' of democracy but also because the invocation of this memory in order to justify military involvement today conflicts with the position in which Germans apparently envisage themselves when confronted with the idea of air strikes.

Yet the point here is not simply that the story told in support of war is profoundly problematic, that, in other words, we must tell a better, less contradictory story about the past. Rather, it is that there is no way out of this story: however much marked by contradiction this memory and its relevance to politics are the case. Memory may be instrumentalised in political debate, as is the case in the stories told about the past in relation to military involvement and in those told by the far Right. Yet looking more closely, thinking through how things are supposed to hang together, reveals that this instrumentalisation comes apart. The argument for German military involvement hangs on the idea of liberation, for example, which looks a lot less straightforward once we consider the method of liberation and indeed the fact that a significant part of Germany did not benefit from the supposed gift of democracy. What is more, no correct memory is possible. Most obviously, there is always a multiplicity of memories that may not be reconciled into one coherent account. More fundamentally, memory does not remain the same. Each articulation of memory is different and yet always linked to previous and parallel

---

[266] Colin McInnes, *Spectator-Sport War: The West and Contemporary Conflict* (Boulder: Lynne Rienner Publishers 2002).

articulations. Unfortunately, these include articulations by the far Right and those of the immediate postwar years, both of which zoom in on German suffering in order to exclude from view the political context. As a result, any recollection of this suffering now appears to be a citation of such articulations, making them appear uncomfortably close to versions of memory that are considered politically objectionable.

Concluding thoughts

This chapter, by looking at a particularly painful aspect of German memories of the Second World War, has developed further some of the points presented in Chapter 2. Again, we have found a multiplicity of memories, the complexity of the question of how memories link to political questions and the impossibility of solving this problem by means of reference to knowledge. This chapter has added the problematic of emotion, in particular as an issue of emotional identification with others through memories and as one of the emotional attitude to the memories in the first place. The empathy with people suffering bombing raids generated by remembering one's own people having experienced similar distress is perhaps more obviously political, especially if it motivated Germans to reject the Iraq war. Yet the emotional identification resulting from memories noted by Münkler is apparently not always decisive. After all, the FRG – controversially – contributed to the air raids in relation to Kosovo. Interestingly, Münkler made no reference to Second World War memories in his discussions of the Kosovo operation at the time, despite raising the issue of references to the history of the Third Reich and of images of the victims.[267] Crucially, the point of the Kosovo operation was contextualised in Germany with a comparison to the atrocities committed by the Nazis; the same did not fall on fertile ground with respect to Saddam Hussein.[268] Thus there is no trivial cause-and-effect relationship between the emotions generated by war memories and debates and decisions on war today.

Thus, again, memories do not provide answers, but they may at times provide reasons to ask questions that undermine the certainty articulated in relation to war. In this particular case the memories had the potential to challenge apparently clear arguments. It is important to acknowledge that Second World War memories *can* – not that they *must* – disturb an easy categorisation into good and evil in the context of war against

---

[267] Herfried Münkler, 'Den Krieg wieder denken: Clausewitz, Kosovo und die Kriege des 21. Jahrhunderts', *Blätter für deutsche und internationale Politik* 44 (1999), 679 and 688.
[268] Wette, 'Ein Hitler des Orients?, 233.

oppressive regimes. Moreover, the implications of considering memories in political discourse are, of course, much like anything else, not necessarily good. It is clear that memories may be instrumentalised for the (violent) promotion of particular interests. They may lead to inappropriate navel-gazing that displaces current issues regarding the Other in relation both to the past and to the Self. They may support nostalgic notions of a 'community of the suffering' and therefore serve to again distract us from the particularity of the situation in question. What I have emphasised is how memories may highlight ambiguities and tensions that mark ethico-political problems. This necessitates recognising not only the diversity of memories but also the potential contradictions within them.

Although memories are asserted with confidence in political debate, once we explore them they turn out to be controversial, challenged by alternative memories, impossible to pin down. Survivors of the raid on Dresden have tried to pit their memories against articulations of memory that they find to be unacceptable. The concern that memories of strategic bombing might lead Germans to inappropriately construe themselves as having been victims is prominent but peculiar. Given the imperative to remember, most prominently asserted by von Weizsäcker, it seems bizarre to first 'vet' memories as to whether they assign a politically acceptable role to particular groups of people. Moreover, it is difficult to force people to remember in prescribed ways, even though the state often puts considerable effort into supporting a particular version of memory.[269] People fight to articulate and defend their memories, not least because they think they 'know' because they remember, and, as we saw in the context of Federal President Herzog's speech, because they consider that they have a right to mourn. Not least because people are emotionally involved, they want memories to be as they think they should be.

The danger, then, is that emotions support another unreflected certainty. Ironically, however, such certainty is always under threat precisely because when it comes to memory, everyone is an authority. Therefore, the claim to knowledge implied in memory threatens any particular proposed memory. Formulating any sentence in which memory 'is' anything at all appears impossible, though we nevertheless do it all the time; I certainly do in this book. Despite all efforts of control, in this particular case it was evident that memory happens, whether or not it is politically welcome, whether or not it is able to represent the past, whether or not it is in danger of undermining the convenient but unsatisfactory categorisation into victims versus perpetrators. At the same time, this memory seems to have a powerful hold on those who think they remember: it may

---

[269] See Edkins, *Trauma and the Memory of Politics.*

form the basis of an attachment to this supposed knowledge of the past. It may evoke a desire to mourn. Literary representations are significant in this context not least because they are able to engage with this aspect of emotionality in a different way. Whilst the public debate derides the emotional as 'sentimentality', novels may attempt to both represent and recreate fear, horror, disgust and shame. They thus allow for a different relationship to the past and one that seems to be important. We seem to find ourselves beyond knowledge in a narrow sense, not merely because how we ought to react to particular situations may be an ethico-political question which, as outlined in Chapter 2, requires a decision but also because we – as a matter of fact – react in ways that are not always in tune with what we know. The emotions supposedly evoked by remembering strategic bombing are so unwelcome precisely because they interfere with what is being asserted as the facts about the past. Empathising with or mourning for the dead on the side of the perpetrators is seen as profoundly problematic because they were the ones we know committed the crimes. Again, we find ourselves in a situation of ambiguity, of uncertainty, and the reading of novels has been used to facilitate recognising that.

Memory is not just something to be pulled out of a hat when it suits us. Memory may haunt us. It comes back unbidden, in ways and shapes that we do not foresee and perhaps do not want. It may confront us with 'forgotten' pain and emotion, make us feel uncomfortable, pose questions we would rather ignore. As Assmann points out, 'remembering is not an intentional act; one remembers or one simply does not remember. It would probably be more correct to say that something remembers one.'[270] Mulisch's main character is scarred by his memories. He is playing the same role as Western airmen now: a 'perpetrator' of air strikes with their inevitable civilian casualties. Corinth is permanently reminded of his involvement in the bombing of Dresden owing to the scars on his face which he received when he was shot down. He was operated on by Red Army doctors. Hella claims that nowadays such surgery could be done almost without leaving scars behind.[271] This could be seen as an involuntary comment on the development of air wars, the supposed invulnerability of Western soldiers, the cleanness of surgical strikes. However, even in the context of massive air raids that left permanent scars on Germany's urban environment, Ledig sees memory as already disappearing straight after the war. Forte, as noted, even claimed that there is a conspiracy to forget and deny it ever happened. Mulisch represents the memory as holding out for a bit longer. Hella, in his *Das steinerne Braut-bett*, asserts that '[t]he war is only over when the last person who has

---

[270] Assmann, *Erinnerungsräume*, p. 29.   [271] Mulisch, *Brautbett*, pp. 60f.

experienced it has died'.[272] More than sixty years after the war, these reports of the imminent death of memory are looking greatly exaggerated, and it has been observed that 'the desire to remember' appears not to die with 'the generation of those affected'.[273]

'Wunden der Erinnerung' ('Wounds of Memory')[274] reads a rectangular piece of glass on the main building of the Ludwig-Maximilians University in Munich, pictured above; it covers damage from the Second World War, though this is not explained. Although the broken bricks are easily noticed, the glass with its inscription is inconspicuous. You have to look up to see it, and the students' bicycles parked just underneath are more likely to attract attention. And yet, once seen, the glass with its inscription is intriguing: why is it there? Why has the damage on the building not been fixed? Why this inscription? Nothing is explained. The preservation of the destruction is remarkable in itself, but it is the inscription that interests me. Memory is identified as a wound, suggesting its painfulness. Given the context of the Third Reich, painfulness is to be expected. Interestingly, the inscription is 'wounds of memory', not 'wounds of war'. The pain

---

[272] Ibid., p. 81.   [273] Habbe, 'Vorwort', p. 9.
[274] The glass is signed 'B. Passow and A. v. Weizsäcker'; for more information, see Preface above.

is attributed not to the act of destruction, but to its memory. As Sofsky notes about the bombing of German cities during the war, 'it is not the facts that cause a stir but the memory of them.'[275] In the ordinary course of events, wounds may heal. Yet these 'wounds of memory' are being kept open, preserved and pointed out – if inconspicuously – to the passer-by; these wounds of memory, however painful, are to be confronted.

[275] Sofsky, 'Die halbierte Erinnerung', p. 124.

4 The truth of memory

Talk of the Germans' 'wounds of memory' seems to suggest that their pain results from having suffered in the Second World War. The idea that Germans should 'never again' wage war could be seen to derive from this, from the desire to avoid such suffering in future. The previous chapters perhaps supported such an interpretation. War was represented as something that in some way 'came over' Germans as civilians. This, however, is at best a truncated representation of German memories of the Second World War and the wounds associated with them. This chapter considers a different aspect, and one that some may regard to be 'war itself', namely the experience of soldiers. Memories of the soldiers' war are no less controversial and emotional than are those of the effects of the war on civilians, especially where the issue of Wehrmacht crimes is concerned. Chapter 2 noted that the issue of Wehrmacht atrocities was central to the Kohl doctrine, but was concealed or at least de-emphasised in the argument made in support of Bundeswehr deployments to Bosnia in 1995. This problematic is examined here from a different angle. The atrocities in question and their significance for how Germans remember the Second World War have not been discussed so far. Taking this aspect into account makes it possible to appreciate that the 'wounds of memory' are not just about the suffering which might be seen as inflicted by others but also about the guilt surrounding the Germans' horrific actions in the past.

The chapter starts by briefly reconsidering the 'never again war' principle, which does not derive merely from the destruction that war had brought to Germany. It is also, perhaps even chiefly, an expression of concern about what Germans may do when they use military force. The chapter considers the debate sparked off by the exhibition on Wehrmacht crimes. Two novels are then presented: Ledig's *Die Stalinorgel*, which takes us into the combat zone, and Walser's *Ein springender Brunnen*, which examines the thoughts and experiences of a boy growing up during the Third Reich who eventually trains for war but never gets to see any action. The two texts make it possible to discuss the role of personal experience and political context in representing war and, more fundamentally, to raise questions about what might be meant by the truth.

Never again German war

It would be a mistake to see German aversion to war, even as prompted by Second World War memories, as exclusively based on the suffering endured. Rather, the invocation of the past and articulation of memories suggest that the recollection of Germans as perpetrators is at the root of anti-war sentiments. Berger suggests that '[i]n the case of Germany, many contend that the legacy of the Holocaust and other Nazi atrocities has inflicted such deep wounds on the German psyche that large sections of the population are unwilling to once again sanction the use of force in the name of the nation and the state'.[1] I noted in Chapter 1 Zwerenz's statement in a Bundestag debate about a proposed deployment to Bosnia that, as a result of his war experiences, he felt a 'lifelong unforgettable culpability' that made it impossible for him to agree to any war whatsoever.[2] The problem is authorising the use of military force on behalf of the German state. That is, whilst the ability to imagine just what 'collateral damage' may mean may be *one* aspect of the Germans' anti-war attitude, there is another significant element that this book has so far largely ignored and that might perhaps be summed up by observing that the Germans do not seem to trust themselves with the use of force.

At times, German politicians' views seemed to be inconsistent: they supported a number of international military operations in principle but rejected German participation. Peter Glotz, for example, claimed that the Germans had a right to say that they would help in non-violent ways, for example financially and logistically, but that they wanted nothing to do with war.[3] This was not because the international military operation at issue was wrong, but because Germans had killed so many, and so many Germans had been killed, in the Second World War, that their rejection of war must surely be acceptable and understandable. Some thought such rejection of German involvement in potentially dangerous military operations was cynical: the Germans were apparently ready to fight until the last Frenchman.[4] Yet Glotz's position is not inconsistent

---

[1] Berger, *Cultures of Antimilitarism*, p. 3.
[2] Deutscher Bundestag, *Plenarprotokoll*, 13/48, 30/06/95, 3997.
[3] Deutscher Bundestag, *Plenarprotokoll*, 12/151, 21/04/93, 12969.
[4] Kinkel claimed that his (German) opponents seemed to be ready to fight in Bosnia to the last Frenchman or Briton. Deutscher Bundestag, *Plenarprotokoll*, 13/48, 30/06/95, 3957. For a critique of the idea that Germany was simply free-riding on the provision of security by other states, see Berger, *Cultures of Antimilitarism*, pp. 2f and *passim*.

if the problem is not war itself, but Germans being involved. This worry about the Germans' inability to deal with the use of force seemed to also be expressed in the idea that they should only ever deploy troops in a multilateral context and in the concern that any use of force would initiate a process of militarisation.[5] The repeated confirmation by German politicians at the time of unification that war 'would never again emanate from German soil'[6] also seems based on the Germans' distrust of their own ability to handle military force. In other words, the Germans' allegedly negative attitude towards war, which is often seen to be invested in the so-called 'never again war' principle, may perhaps be better characterised as 'never again German war'.

Whatever the reasons for rejecting German war in particular, the differentiation between supporting a proposed international military operation and agreeing to German participation highlighted that the Germans' relationship to war was thought to be different from that of other peoples. Yet the reasons German war might be more dangerous than war in general remained unspoken. War was portrayed as awful, with little differentiation between different kinds of awfulness. This lack of differentiation might be seen to be evident in Schmid's passionate rejection of any future involvement of the German people in the crime of war cited at the beginning of this book. This seems to submerge the crime of the German Second World War in the idea that every war is the same in the sense of inevitably being a crime. I noted in Chapter 1 Schlant's concern that 'the enormity of the world war' might be abused to provide some form of 'alibi' to the individual who could not be expected to be able to resist or change it.[7] Bartov similarly notes the danger involved in Germans regarding any war as hell:

Paradoxically, this view has in turn legitimized the actions of German soldiers in the war as in no way essentially different from those of all other soldiers. Thus one finds a combination of anti-war sentiment, apologetics, and a sentimental admiration for the men who 'saved' Germany, indeed the whole of Europe, from the 'Bolshevik-Asiatic hordes,' along with a powerful rejection of the notion that the

---

[5] See, for example, Peter Glotz (SPD) in Deutscher Bundestag, *Plenarprotokoll*, 12/151, 21/04/93, 12970; Zehfuss, *Constructivism*, Chapters 2 and 3.

[6] Hans-Dietrich Genscher, speech at the 45th General Assembly of the UN, in: Presse- und Informationsamt der Bundesregierung, *Bulletin*, 115, 27/09/90, 1201; Helmut Kohl, Message on the day of German unification on 3 October 1990 to all governments in the world, in: Presse- und Informationsamt der Bundesregierung, *Bulletin*, 118, 05/10/90, 1227; see also 'Vertrag über die abschließende Regelung in bezug auf Deutschland', reprinted in: *Grundgesetz für die Bundesrepublik Deutschland*, 51st edn, (Munich: C. H. Beck'sche Verlagsbuchhandlung 1993), Article 2.

[7] Schlant, *Language of Silence*, p. 30.

Wehrmacht had served as Hitler's main instrument in implementing his policies of conquest and genocide.[8]

Bartov seems to overstate the extent to which the position he describes is common amongst Germans – a matter discussed in the next section – but his point is important. There is indeed a danger that crimes within war are drowned out by the depiction of war as a crime.[9] The Kohl doctrine referred to the inadvisability of deploying German soldiers in the Balkans because the Wehrmacht had 'caused havoc' there. This was not explained further, leaving open the question whether 'causing havoc' had been a normal part of war, which was after all seen to be hell, or whether this was a reference to war crimes, impermissible even in the context of the hell that is war. Thus, before exploring two novels and the difficulties they raise in depicting what war was 'really like', it is important to gain an understanding of the problematic of Wehrmacht atrocities and Germans' memories of them.

Forgotten Wehrmacht atrocities: the exhibition

In 1995 the Hamburger Institut für Sozialforschung (Hamburg Institute for Social Research) opened an exhibition entitled 'War of Extermination: Crimes of the Wehrmacht 1941 to 1944' that relied heavily on photographs of atrocities. It provoked fierce discussions, unprecedented in relation to an exhibition in the history of the FRG and culminating in a Bundestag debate in March 1997.[10] The exhibition was, amongst other things, accused of being profoundly one-sided,[11] demagogic,[12] indoctrinating[13] and unscientific.[14] It was claimed that there was

---

[8] Bartov, *Germany's War*, p. 12.

[9] Chapter 6 raises the opposite question: whether it might be useful to think of war as always an atrocity. See pp. 254–9.

[10] Heribert Prantl, 'Einleitung', in: Heribert Prantl (ed.), *Wehrmachtsverbrechen: Eine deutsche Kontroverse* (Hamburg: Hoffmann und Campe 1997), p. 23. See also Hannes Heer, 'Von der Schwierigkeit, einen Krieg zu beenden: Reaktionen auf die Ausstellung "Vernichtungskrieg: Verbrechen der Wehrmacht 1941 bis 1944"', *Zeitschrift für Geschichtswissenschaft* 45, no. 12 (1997), 1087.

[11] Gottfried Greiner, no title, in: Hans Günther Thiele (ed.), *Die Wehrmachtsausstellung: Dokumentation einer Kontroverse* (Bonn: Bundeszentrale für politische Bildung 1997), p. 35.

[12] Gerhard Kaiser, 'Aufklärung oder Denunziation?', in: Prantl, *Wehrmachtsverbrechen*, p. 53.

[13] Friedrich Karl Fromme, 'Was bleibt: die Schuld', in: Prantl, *Wehrmachtsverbrechen*, p. 80.

[14] Franz W. Seidler, 'Pauschale Verurteilung verunglimpft einzelne', in: Prantl, *Wehrmachtsverbrechen*, p. 87; Greiner, no title, p. 35. There is controversy about whether the photos are authentic and show what the exhibition claims they show. See, for example, Bogdan Musial, 'Bilder einer Ausstellung: Kritische Anmerkungen zur

'something infamous' about it, that it 'wants to discredit',[15] that it intends a 'wholesale defamation' of all Wehrmacht soldiers,[16] that it 'demonises'.[17] Furthermore, the scientific and moral legitimacy of its authors was questioned.[18]

Although the exhibition had already been to fourteen German and Austrian cities, the controversy became truly acrimonious in 1997 when it came to Munich. This was apparently because it was to be shown in the town hall,[19] which could have been seen as signalling approval of its message by the city, but probably also because Bavaria is notoriously conservative. The *Bayernkurier*, the official publication of the Bavarian Conservative party (the CSU), called the exhibition a 'moral campaign of extermination against the German people', representing an 'intensification of the punishment measures of Nuremberg'.[20] The aim of the organisers was, according to the same article, to 'dispute the honour of millions of Germans'.[21] Such reactions and demonstrations outside the exhibition led to enormous publicity. Ironically, far more people – 88,400 – went to see the exhibition in Munich than anywhere else.[22] Yet owing to public pressure, the exhibition was closed in 1999, to re-open later after being substantially changed.[23] The exhibition has now itself become an event of contemporary history,[24] stimulating research not only about Wehrmacht crimes and their memory but also on the exhibition and its effects.[25]

Wanderausstellung "Vernichtungskrieg: Verbrechen der Wehrmacht 1941 bis 1944"', *Vierteljahreshefte für Zeitgeschichte* 47 (1999), 563–91; Ernst Rebentisch, no title, in: Thiele, *Die Wehrmachtsausstellung*, pp. 58f; Günther Gillessen, 'Kritische Bemerkungen zur Ausstellung "Die Verbrechen der Wehrmacht"', in: Thiele, *Die Wehrmachtsausstellung*, pp. 87–90; Johannes Willms, 'Außer Thesen nichts gewesen', *Süddeutsche Zeitung*, 16/11/00, 15.

[15] Erika Steinbach (CDU/CSU) in Deutscher Bundestag, *Plenarprotokoll*, 13/163, 13/03/97, 14719.
[16] Rebentisch, no title, p. 58.
[17] Günther Roth, no title, in: Thiele, *Die Wehrmachtsausstellung*, p. 70.
[18] Alfred Dregger (CDU/CSU) in Deutscher Bundestag, *Plenarprotokoll*, 13/163, 13/03/97, 14710.
[19] See Heribert Prantl, 'Einführung', in: Prantl, *Wehrmachtsverbrechen*, p. 231 and Herbert Riehl-Heyse, 'Die Geister einer Ausstellung', in: Prantl, *Wehrmachtsverbrechen*, p. 239.
[20] Florian Stumfall, 'Wie Deutsche diffamiert werden', in: Prantl, *Wehrmachtsverbrechen*, p. 252.
[21] Ibid., p. 253.   [22] Dubiel, *Niemand ist frei*, p. 23; Prantl, 'Einführung', p. 233.
[23] Bartov, *Germany's War*, p. xii; Ruth Wodak, '"Wie Geschichte gemacht wird" – zur Entstehung und zu den Absichten eines Projekts', in: Hannes Heer, Walter Manoschek, Alexander Pollak and Ruth Wodak (eds.), *Wie Geschichte gemacht wird: Zur Konstruktion von Erinnerungen an Wehrmacht und Zweiten Weltkrieg* (Vienna: Czernin Verlag 2003), p. 8; Johannes Willms, 'Die glorreiche Provokation', *Süddeutsche Zeitung*, 22/11/00, 15.
[24] Heer, 'Von der Schwierigkeit', 1087.
[25] See, for example, Heer, Manoschek, Pollak and Wodak, *Wie Geschichte gemacht wird*.

What interests me is the violence and absurdity of the reaction to the exhibition. The exhibition did not argue anything new; there was widespread agreement that its substantive claims had long been accepted, at least amongst historians.[26] However, as *Die Zeit* journalist Karl-Heinz Janßen observed, the 'horrible truth' had been known only to experts and those who were interested; it had not overcome the 'wall of mutually agreed silence amongst the German public'.[27] Military historian Wette agreed that the facts had not been 'sufficiently known' by the general public,[28] although, as his colleague Gerhard Schreiber pointed out, this information 'could have been known' by anyone.[29] Indeed, despite the uproar in the CSU, many of the exhibition's claims can be found in history textbooks approved for Bavarian secondary schools.[30]

The forcefully negative reaction to the exhibition indicates that the conviction that Wehrmacht soldiers had courageously fought for their country and had not been tarnished by the atrocities committed by the SS and SD was still widespread. Indeed, the Wehrmacht, or so the story goes, had largely been opposed to National Socialism. In the introduction to the volume accompanying the exhibition, Hannes Heer and Klaus Naumann claim that the 'struggle over memory' started on 9 May 1945. The High Command of the Wehrmacht had suggested the line in its last situation report: 'The unique achievement of front and *Heimat* will find its final appreciation in a later just judgement of history . . . Each soldier may therefore lay down his arms in an upright and proud way.'[31] This laid the foundation for what is called the myth or legend of the 'clean'[32] Wehrmacht, the myth, as Heribert Prantl puts it, of the 'upright, brave, misled Wehrmacht soldier who fulfilled his soldierly task with decency

---

[26] See, for example, Prantl, 'Einleitung', p. 11; see also 'Pressemitteilung des Hamburger Instituts für Sozialforschung vom 24.4.97', in: Prantl, *Wehrmachtsverbrechen*, p. 217.

[27] Karl-Heinz Janßen, 'Als Soldaten Mörder wurden', in: Prantl, *Wehrmachtsverbrechen*, p. 29.

[28] Wolfram Wette, 'Jude gleich Partisan', in: Prantl, *Wehrmachtsverbrechen*, p. 42; see also Till Bastian, *Furchtbare Soldaten: Deutsche Kriegsverbrechen im Zweiten Weltkrieg*, 2nd edn (Munich: Verlag C.H. Beck 1997), p. 9.

[29] Gerhard Schreiber, 'Dokumente einer Vergangenheit, die ehrlich angenommen werden muß', in: Prantl, *Wehrmachtsverbrechen*, p. 172. See also Jan-Philipp Reemtsma, 'Die wenig scharf gezogene Grenze zwischen Normalität und Verbrechen', in: Prantl, *Wehrmachtsverbrechen*, p. 188. Easily accessible paperbacks on the issue include Bastian's *Furchtbare Soldaten*. *Die Zeit* produced a special issue on the topic in 1995: *Gehorsam bis zum Mord? Der verschwiegene Krieg der deutschen Wehrmacht – Fakten, Analysen, Debatte*, *Zeit-Punkte* 3 (1995).

[30] 'Lehrer loben die Wehrmacht-Ausstellung', in: Prantl, *Wehrmachtsverbrechen*, p. 316.

[31] Quoted in Hannes Heer and Klaus Naumann, 'Einleitung', in: Hannes Heer and Klaus Naumann (eds.), *Vernichtungskrieg: Verbrechen der Wehrmacht 1941–1944* (Hamburg: Hamburger Edition 1995), p. 32.

[32] The myth construes the Wehrmacht as having been *sauber*, meaning 'clean' but also 'honest', 'upstanding'.

and who then returned to the *Heimat*, beaten on the battlefield, but untarnished'.[33]

Some of those on the Right of the political spectrum – who are accused of peddling this myth – argue that the supposed legend does not exist; it is rather a 'phantom', a straw man, invented only to be shot down.[34] Yet this is hardly convincing in view of the claims, in particular by veterans, that the Wehrmacht had not been involved in atrocities as they are shown in the exhibition, or at least not systematically. Jan Philipp Reemtsma, the director of the institute responsible for the exhibition, also observed that the reaction of the press to the end of the legend rather confirmed its existence.[35] Whilst critics claimed that the myth did not exist, 'at any rate not in the monumental form which the organisers need for the purpose of ripping the mask off its face with a grand gesture',[36] supporters applauded the exhibition's role in dispatching it once and for all.[37]

Aside from the obvious outrage, Frevert notes the 'deep shock' which the exhibition provoked amongst the population.[38] It was, she argues, the question of personal responsibility that made the exhibition a central event in the politics of the past. She worries, however, about the moralising tendency in conversations with those who experienced the events at the time; this had also paralysed earlier debates.[39] Indeed, the fear of being judged – and the refusal to be judged – by those who did not have to go through the ordeal of the war was palpable in discussions surrounding the exhibition.[40] Yet not all of the younger generation were set on judging. Heer points out that the 'grandchildren ask in a different way [from the sons]: Where were you? How did you get there? As who did you come out of it?'[41] He claims that they do not want to apportion blame: they want to know what happened.

Heer sees in the reaction of veterans' groups a 'last ritual battle' of a generation that is ready to leave the stage.[42] Another such last ritual battle was played out in the Bundestag, confirming the power, sensitivity and emotionality of Second World War memories. Following the pattern already familiar from debates about military deployments, a number of the speakers referred to their own experience of the war: Alfred Dregger,

---

[33] Prantl, 'Einleitung', p. 13.
[34] Günther Gillessen, 'Die Ausstellung zerstört nicht eine Legende – sie baut eine neue auf', in: Prantl, *Wehrmachtsverbrechen*, p. 166.
[35] Reemtsma, 'Die wenig scharf gezogene Grenze', 189.
[36] Gillessen, 'Kritische Bemerkungen', 90.
[37] Frevert, 'Geschichtsvergessenheit', 8; see also Dubiel, *Niemand ist frei*, p. 25.
[38] Frevert, 'Geschichtsvergessenheit', 8.   [39] Ibid., 9.
[40] See, for example, Rainer Stephan, 'Wenn alle nach der Ehre fragen', in: Prantl, *Wehrmachtsverbrechen*, p. 272.
[41] Heer, 'Von der Schwierigkeit', 1093.   [42] Ibid.

Otto Graf Lambsdorff and Gerhard Zwerenz. Dregger's speech in defence of the Wehrmacht is particularly interesting. He claimed that 'soldiers have always been victims of war' and insisted that most soldiers had not been involved in crimes. But, he argued, the question concerned us all because 'how a people treats its soldiers after a lost war says a lot about its moral substance, about its dignity, and its inner strength – or weakness'.[43] Dregger was keen to prove that German soldiers had been honourable, and he quoted French President François Mitterand in order to do so. At the fiftieth anniversary celebrations of the end of the war Mitterand had said: 'And the uniforms and even the ideas that at that time lived in the heads of the soldiers who died in such great numbers mean little to me in this context. They were brave. They accepted the loss of their life for a bad cause. But their attitude had nothing to do with that. They loved their fatherland.'[44] Although Dregger admitted that there had been crimes, he saw the exhibition as a wholesale slander against the troops. According to him, we must remember that the soldiers were identical with the whole population of the time, and the war generation could not be branded as generally members and relatives of a 'gang of criminals'.[45] Therefore he rejected the exhibition, which 'confuses the generation of sons and grandsons'.[46] In sum, Dregger attempted to move the issue away from the problematic of Wehrmacht crimes; he construed it instead as one of the attitude of successor generations, of the respect owed to the soldiers.

This argument led to disconcertion not only on the Left. Dubiel claims that the 'figure of Alfred Dregger towers like a memorial of the 1950s over the political culture of the 1990s. His individual arguments are as old as the Bonn republic: the criticism of Germany's Nazi past damages the unity of the people. Only Hitler and some commanders were responsible, and the Germans were the real victims.' But, Dubiel points out, 'in contrast to fifty years ago Dregger realises that politicians like him today only represent a minority of Germans'.[47] Dregger's argument was obviously problematic, but, intriguingly, it seemed to come from the heart: it was about his feelings. Heer observes that 'behind his attacks the despair about the dead comrades became perceptible'.[48] This is confirmed by Dregger's later intervention, in response to speeches that were profoundly critical of his attitude. He said that he would not dismiss the criticisms out of hand.

---

[43] Deutscher Bundestag, *Plenarprotokoll*, 13/163, 13/03/97, 14710.
[44] Quoted by Dregger in ibid., 14710f. See also Theodor Waigel (CDU/CSU) in ibid., 14727. For two slightly different versions of Mitterand's words, see Naumann, *Krieg als Text*, p. 263.
[45] Deutscher Bundestag, *Plenarprotokoll*, 13/163, 13/03/97, 14711.   [46] Ibid., 14712.
[47] Dubiel, *Niemand ist frei*, p. 26.   [48] Heer, 'Von der Schwierigkeit', 1099.

Crucially, in order to explain his aggressive defence of the Wehrmacht, he pointed out that he had survived only by chance: 'I know many privates who were killed next to me. It pains me when all these privates are being accused as representatives of the Nazi Wehrmacht.'[49] This admission of pain makes it difficult to simply dismiss Dregger's attitude. Clearly, he rejects accepted historical facts. Yet, however historically inaccurate and politically unpalatable his position may be, his feelings and his desire to mourn for his lost comrades are nevertheless powerful.

The fact that politicians from different parties showed how painful the past was for them, if for different reasons, made the debate interesting and also made it possible for Dregger to become involved in something of a dialogue. Dubiel notes that this was the first time in his long years in parliament that Dregger had shown 'signs of thoughtfulness'.[50] This thoughtfulness had been provoked by very personal interventions by Dregger's political opponents. Initially, with Dregger one of the first speakers, the debate had looked set to become unpleasant. However, Otto Schily of the SPD changed the tone – and the stakes – by referring to his family's experiences. Schily observed that 'the debate about the role of the Wehrmacht is difficult and painful'. It was also, he said, 'inevitable'. He warned that the debate should not be conducted in the style of 'self-satisfied morality'.[51] Schily then went on to speak of his family, stopping more than once, overcome by emotion. Firstly, he mentioned his uncle, a group captain in the Luftwaffe, who sought his own death during a raid. He then spoke about his eldest brother, who had refused to join the Hitler Youth but had been unable to flee abroad; he eventually volunteered for the front and was seriously wounded in Russia. Schily further described his father, an opponent of the Nazi regime, who – perversely – had been offended that, as a member of a prohibited anthroposophist society, he was not drafted into the Wehrmacht. Finally, Schily spoke of his wife's father who fought against the Wehrmacht as a Jewish partisan in Russia.[52] According to Schily, only his wife's father had risked his life for a just cause, fighting an army that was effectively protecting the gas chambers, that was leading a war of extermination, that at least did nothing to stop the *Einsatzgruppen* from committing mass murder but in actual fact supported them.

Like Schily, Christa Nickels of the Greens approached the topic in a personal way: she spoke about her father's war experiences. She noted that no one ever talks about what it was like to shoot someone for the first time.

[49] Deutscher Bundestag, *Plenarprotokoll*, 13/163, 13/03/97, 14720.
[50] Dubiel, *Niemand ist frei*, p. 33.
[51] Deutscher Bundestag, *Plenarprotokoll*, 13/163, 13/03/97, 14714.   [52] Ibid.

Although she had asked people, they were still unable to speak about it.[53] She admitted that she only noticed at the time of the Bitburg controversy[54] that in her father's photograph from the war he wears a black uniform with skulls on it.[55] In 1989 she visited Majdanek and broke down, also because of 'what was done to the men' like her father.[56] Like Schily, Nickels, who was born in 1952, portrayed the war as something that causes her, and others, pain. She argued that we should not cover up the wounds. It was not possible to comfort those who were involved by claiming that they should no longer hurt because they had been acting under duress. This, she said, did not help at all.[57] Dubiel observes that Nickels 'can only bear the insight that her father was one of the perpetrators by turning him at the same time into a victim'.[58] However, he suggests that this is fundamentally different from other representations of soldiers as victims, such as Dregger's: 'Her reflection on the conditions under which her father became (was turned into) a perpetrator does not of course serve to morally exonerate him.' It is by bearing this 'ambivalence with respect to her own family' that Nickels wants to develop the Germans' relationship to their own collective after the Holocaust.[59] Thus, even if Nickels's father was a victim, inasmuch as he was possibly forced to do what he did, this does not mean that he was not a perpetrator: he did what he did, and this is not to be excused.

Duve, who also replied directly to Dregger, noted the flip-side of the myth of the 'clean' Wehrmacht: that other groups were easily blamed. He observed how those who were drafted into the Waffen-SS rather than the Wehrmacht had always suffered from having been part of the wrong group. The idea had been: 'You were SS . . .; we were the soldiers.'[60] There had been, in other words, a desire to distinguish between the war in which everyone had been involved in a largely honourable way and the Holocaust which was perpetrated by the few, even if the German people had to bear responsibility for it as a whole. This distinction was not possible; moreover, the matter was one not just for those who were involved at the time: 'This war haunts all of us – those who experienced it as soldiers or children and those who were born after its end.'[61]

---

[53] Ibid., 14719.   [54] See Chapter 6, pp. 246–7.
[55] Deutscher Bundestag, *Plenarprotokoll*, 13/163, 13/03/97, 14719.   [56] Ibid., 14720.
[57] Ibid.   [58] Dubiel, *Niemand ist frei*, p. 31.   [59] Ibid., p. 32.
[60] Deutscher Bundestag, *Plenarprotokoll*, 13/163, 13/03/97, 14718. Note also the recent controversy surrounding Grass's admission that he had served in the Waffen-SS. See, for example, Dirk Kurbjuweit et al., 'Fehlbar und verstrickt', *Der Spiegel*, 21/08/06, 46–66. For a moving exploration of why his elder brother could possibly have volunteered for the Waffen-SS, see Uwe Timm, *Am Beispiel meines Bruders*, 3rd edn (Cologne: Kiepenheuer & Witsch 2003).
[61] Deutscher Bundestag, *Plenarprotokoll*, 13/163, 13/03/97, 14718.

The Bundestag debate showed that the question of Wehrmacht atrocities was extremely sensitive. Jutta Limbach, in her opening speech for the exhibition in Karlsruhe, pointed out that the involvement of the Wehrmacht in mass murders still constituted a 'sensitive spot in the soul [*Gemüt*] of some Germans' that turned those discussing the theme into violators of a taboo.[62] Günther Gillessen agreed that the exhibition 'hits a nerve'.[63] As was repeatedly noted, the Wehrmacht represented more or less everybody at the time; the Wehrmacht was 'the German people in arms'.[64] Reemstma observed:

When one speaks of the Wehrmacht, one speaks . . . of the people [*Volksgemeinschaft*]. The Wehrmacht is the interface of people and regime, and because of that one touches ground that is emotionally the most sensitive, for one speaks not about what everyone actually did but about what everyone might potentially have done. The everyone who is the grandfather, the father, the uncle, the brother.[65]

It is therefore not surprising how strongly the Wehrmacht has been defended. It is clear to historians, of course, that the Wehrmacht 'was involved in the crimes of the Nazi state through active participation and passive toleration'. These well-documented facts, Wolfgang Benz argued, cannot be 'rejected and dismissed as "defamation" of all members of the Wehrmacht'.[66] The 'splitting into good and bad, into a criminal SS and a chivalrous Wehrmacht does not correspond to the complex historical reality'.[67]

And this was, of course, the problem. Suddenly, the 'clean' Wehrmacht was recognised as embroiled in the Holocaust; and the Wehrmacht meant everybody's father, brother, uncle. The reaction to this outrageous idea that loved ones who had perhaps been killed in the war were portrayed as at least indirectly responsible for the Third Reich's worst crimes often manifested itself in a concern for the 'honour of the soldiers'. It was inappropriate, some argued, for later generations, who were lucky enough not to have been involved, to doubt or destroy the soldiers' honour by alleging that they had all been involved in atrocities – or had at least served in an organisation that, as an institution, had been mixed up in

---

[62] Jutta Limbach, 'Rede zur Eröffnung der "Wehrmachtsausstellung" in Karlsruhe am 10.1.97', in: Prantl, *Wehrmachtsverbrechen*, p. 62.
[63] Gillessen, 'Die Ausstellung', p. 169.
[64] Werner von Scheven, 'Gibt es eine Traditionslüge? – Die Wehrmacht in Rußland und die Tradition der Bundeswehr', in: Thiele, *Die Wehrmachtsausstellung*, p. 132.
[65] Jan Philipp Reemstma quoted in 'Die Diskussion in der Arbeitsgruppe 1', in: Thiele, *Die Wehrmachtsausstellung*, p. 83.
[66] Wolfgang Benz, no title, in: Thiele, *Die Wehrmachtsausstellung*, p. 32.
[67] Ibid., p. 32.

the crimes of the war of extermination. Wolfgang Eichwede, however, suggested defining the honour of the soldiers differently, namely that it may only be 'defined in the dignity of the victims'. He means by this that 'we – the Germans then and the Germans today – have to answer to [the victims]. The questions for the Wehrmacht have their roots in the fate of the victims.' A 'strategy of justification that conceals' would not be permissible.[68] Thus the Germans' victims should be the primary referent in thinking about this time.

Originally, it had been envisaged that the Bundestag would sign a cross-party declaration on the Wehrmacht exhibition, but this project was abandoned when the depth of emotion became obvious; a compromise declaration was considered inappropriate. All parties had, however, submitted proposals for such a declaration. In his speech, Zwerenz of the PDS, who had himself been a frontline soldier[69] and admits to having deserted,[70] mocked the 'Wagnerian opera tone' of the proposal by the CDU/CSU and FDP that describes, he said, the Second World War as a tragedy of which millions of German soldiers and civilians had become victims.[71] He regarded as 'typical' the fact that they were thinking of German victims before they mentioned 'a single Jewish, Polish, Russian victim of the German war of extermination'. Zwerenz recalled the millions of dead Russian POWs whose fate was better referred to as 'planned genocide' than the Wehrmacht being 'mixed up in crimes'.[72] He was particularly irritated that arguments defending the soldiers against a blanket judgement did not ask what would have happened if those 18 million men had insisted that they were 'the people' and refused to fight. In sum, Zwerenz pointed out, '[w]ithout this Wehrmacht there would have been no Holocaust, no genocide, no Second World War and its 50 million dead'.[73] Thus the Wehrmacht did not simply defend the fatherland: it shares responsibility for the Holocaust.

The soldier's honour was seen as significant not merely because those who had served the German state were seen to be entitled to today's Germans' respect but also because of the Wehrmacht's relationship to today's armed forces. The Bundeswehr, interestingly, went through different phases in its reaction to the exhibition. At first it publicly ignored it. Then it recommended that soldiers visit it and facilitated a debate between the director of the exhibition, Heer, and high-ranking officers.

[68] Wolfgang Eichwede, no title, in: Thiele, *Die Wehrmachtsausstellung*, pp. 33f.
[69] Deutscher Bundestag, *Plenarprotokoll*, 13/163, 13/03/97, 14717.
[70] Volker Ullrich, 'Den Mut haben, davonzulaufen', *Gehorsam bis zum Mord?*, 67.
[71] Deutscher Bundestag, *Plenarprotokoll*, 13/163, 13/03/97, 14717. For the proposal, see Deutscher Bundestag, *Drucksache*, Bonn 13/7162, 11/03/97.
[72] Deutscher Bundestag, *Plenarprotokoll*, 13/163, 13/03/97, 14717.   [73] Ibid.

However, when controversy and pressure from veterans' and soldiers' groups increased, the Bundeswehr withdrew its public support.[74]

In the Bundestag debate, Defence Minister Volker Rühe explained that '[o]ur responsibility demands that we look at our past critically in order to draw the right lessons for the future'. He acknowledged that the thesis that the Wehrmacht had been the 'largely untarnished refuge of decency and honour in the midst of Nazi barbarity' had been disproved by recent historical research.[75] It was simply wrong, he said, to suggest that debate about the role of the Wehrmacht only started with the exhibition. Historical research had gone much further. Rühe agreed that information about the Wehrmacht and the Second World War was necessary, but also noted the criticisms of the exhibition in terms of its aim, content and scientific methodology.[76] He pointed out that, as defence minister, he had already stated in 1995 that the Wehrmacht as an organisation had been embroiled in Nazi crimes and could not therefore provide the basis for tradition.[77]

Duve stressed that there had not been 'military reform' in the FRG, as Dregger had claimed, but newly founded and democratically legitimated armed forces.[78] This was, he insisted, a significant difference. Because of this he criticised those who were trying to arouse emotions within the Bundeswehr by claiming that today's soldiers must feel offended by this exhibition.[79] Benz agreed that the Bundeswehr 'as a democratic army is not in the tradition of the Wehrmacht'.[80] The two, according to Inspector General Klaus Naumann, must not be equated in any way.[81] Given these arguments, it is of course not clear how the exhibition could possibly serve to link the two armed forces.[82] Yet the matter is not simple. In Theo Sommer's words, the Bundeswehr is 'the successor of the Wehrmacht but not its continuation'.[83] Although it has repeatedly been attempted by governments, it is difficult to declare away the tradition of the Wehrmacht.[84] The question of the relationship between Bundeswehr and Wehrmacht always remains. Colonel Bernhard Gertz admitted that even fifty-two years after the Second World War it was necessary for every

---

[74] Riehl-Heyse, 'Die Geister einer Ausstellung', pp. 237f.
[75] Deutscher Bundestag, *Plenarprotokoll*, 13/163, 13/03/97, 14721.   [76] Ibid., 14722.
[77] Ibid., 14721; see also Hans-Adolf Jacobsen, 'Zur Rolle der Wehrmacht im Rußlandfeldzug 1941–1944', in: Thiele, *Die Wehrmachtsausstellung*, p. 49.
[78] Deutscher Bundestag, *Plenarprotokoll*, 13/163, 13/03/97, 14718.   [79] Ibid.
[80] Benz, no title, p. 32.
[81] Klaus Naumann, 'Erinnern, lernen – nichts kopieren', in: *Gehorsam bis zum Mord?*, 87.
[82] Christine Bernbacher, quoted in 'Die Diskussion in der Arbeitsgruppe 2', in: Thiele, *Die Wehrmachtsausstellung*, p. 140.
[83] Theo Sommer, 'Die Diktatur des Krieges', in: *Gehorsam bis zum Mord?*, 5.
[84] See, for example, Abenheim, *Reforging the Iron Cross*.

Bundeswehr soldier to engage with the role of the Wehrmacht and its soldiers.[85] He argued that those 'who convey the impression to society that
the Wehrmacht altogether was a criminal institution and . . . consequently
all its soldiers criminals, thereby also incriminate the Bundeswehr'.[86] In
contrast to what he perceived as a blanket accusation, he claimed that
'for the mass of Wehrmacht soldiers the assumption continues to be valid
that they served a wrong cause individually in an honourable way',[87]
thus insisting on what others saw as an untenable myth of the 'clean'
Wehrmacht.

Broader connections between the Second World War and wars
today were also repeatedly made, making for a different link between
Wehrmacht and Bundeswehr. Janßen, for example, argued that the photos shown in the exhibition should be seen by those interested in deployments to the Balkans.[88] Naumann observed that with the question of
Bundeswehr deployments abroad 'constellations ("combat missions")
and topographies ("Serbia") appeared in the collective memory that led
to historical reminiscences'.[89] In the Bundestag debate on the exhibition, Heiner Geißler of the CDU/CSU noted that in recent years there
have been 'war crimes such as murder and homicide and rape and slaughter',[90] and Gerald Häfner of the Greens mentioned Bosnia and Rwanda.[91]
Although these references do not actually liken the Bundeswehr to the
Wehrmacht, the possibility of any link was unwelcome, especially to
those on the Right. Ernst Rebentisch rather sourly noted in a workshop on the exhibition that one could 'pass over the exhibition without comment, if it did not pursue political aims which under the pre-
text of information [Aufklärung] are directed against Germany's ability
to defend itself [Wehrfähigkeit] and readiness'.[92] What is at issue, then,
is the political effect of recollections of the past on the present and the
future.

The debate revolved around a series of problems, many of which have
also marred other debates on Second World War memories. The first
point to note is that the claims presented in the exhibition were not new;
indeed, it was criticised for saying 'nothing new'.[93] There appeared, however, to be a discrepancy between what historical scholarship had asserted

[85] Bernhard Gertz, no title, in: Thiele, Die Wehrmachtsausstellung, p. 105.
[86] Ibid., p. 105.   [87] Ibid., p. 106.
[88] Janßen, 'Als Soldaten Mörder wurden', p. 35.
[89] Naumann, Krieg als Text, pp. 143f.
[90] Deutscher Bundestag, Plenarprotokoll, 13/163, 13/03/97, 14725.   [91] Ibid., 14708.
[92] Rebentisch, no title, p. 58.
[93] Fromme, 'Was bleibt', p. 79; Dregger (CDU/CSU) in Deutscher Bundestag, Plenarprotokoll, 13/163, 13/03/97, 14710.

and what the public had been aware of or willing to accept. The matter was sensitive, because the Wehrmacht was seen to be identical with the people and because links were possible to the Bundeswehr. Moreover, not least because 'everyone' has relatives who served in the Wehrmacht, this was a matter for everyone, and therefore no one could, on behalf of others, rule on what would constitute the 'right' memory. In Duve's words, this 'war haunts all of us'.

The controversy was seen to be not just one about the past. The tenuous but inevitable connection between Wehrmacht and Bundeswehr has already been noted. What is more, for Geißler, the point was to shape the future in the right way.[94] He argued that most Wehrmacht soldiers had not been involved in atrocities. Just like the overwhelming majority of soldiers, his brother and father had not been criminals: 'The mourning for those two and many other soldiers was not for criminals but the victims of a world war orgy that had been instigated by political gangsters.'[95] However, in view of the sheer number of dead, Geißler accepts that making myths about a supposedly honourable war is not permissible. Crucially, '[w]e are speaking about the present and the future in the memory of the past'.[96]

The debate underlined the fact that the memory of the Second World War was seen as significant to all Germans, not merely to those who had been involved. In particular, it is worth noting the power of the emotions that were often revealed in contributions to the debate. This was not just about instrumentalising the past for political purposes in the present: this was about how people *felt*. It was not just about the community's appropriate relationship to a difficult past, but was taken to be deeply personal. What touched Dregger was not the arguments fellow parliamentarians made – these had been the same for years – but, if anything, the realisation that the issue was not easy for them either, that they did not lack feelings for those who had had to live through the war. It was these emotions that created the opportunity for communication, however limited.

Although this was important, and although some intriguing points were raised in the debate, it was marred by entrenched positions amongst the Right and Left and the desire to find an 'appropriate' shared version of the past. Again, political and public debate seems to be restricted by recurring concerns and often unspoken prohibitions. There was the difficult question of in what sense, if at all, German soldiers had been victims.

---

[94] Deutscher Bundestag, *Plenarprotokoll*, 13/163, 13/03/97, 14726.
[95] Ibid.   [96] Ibid.

Theo Waigel of the CDU/CSU said he felt that 'justice and compassion towards millions, towards the victims, but also towards the millions of soldiers' were missing.[97] According to Ude, however, the Germans could only speak of the injustices of others – such as the air war – if they acknowledged their own.[98] Whilst it is true that it would be outrageous for the Germans to speak of others' injustices without acknowledging their own, the reverse, as shown in Chapter 3, seems rather more complicated. Moreover, having explored this debate, we still know no more about what the war was actually like, what precisely prompts Dregger's strength of feeling, except that he survived only by chance. The debate offers assessments of the meaning of war experiences, but does not explore what these were. Nickels, for example, speaks of her father having to kill, but tells us nothing of the context, of what actually happened. In contrast, novels depict concrete, if not necessarily factual, experiences. Ledig's *Die Stalinorgel* gives us a glimpse of a combat zone. It must be noted that neither of the two novels explored in this chapter really addresses the issue of Wehrmacht crimes. As in the other chapters, the novels are not read as sources of information, but as reflections upon the problems of remembering and speaking of war, the question of what it might mean to tell the truth about war. This then allows us to throw a different light on the failure to depict Wehrmacht atrocities as part of representations of the war.

Recreating immediacy: Ledig's *Die Stalinorgel*

Many of those who experienced the Second World War referred to the fact in the political debate. There was remarkably little graphic description, however, although this might have helped the opponents of war. Ledig was a soldier, and his *Die Stalinorgel* gives a close-up view of a combat zone. Ledig's two novels about the war, *Die Stalinorgel*[99] and *Vergeltung*, were originally published in 1955 and 1956. The former, an account of the war on the Eastern front, was popular at the time, whilst the latter – a depiction of 69 minutes during an air raid, explored in

---

[97] Deutscher Bundestag, *Plenarprotokoll*, 13/163, 13/03/97, 14727.
[98] Christian Ude, 'Rede zur Eröffnung der "Wehrmachtsausstellung" am 24. Februar 1997 in der Ludwig-Maximilians-Universität', in: Prantl, *Wehrmachtsverbrechen*, p. 262.
[99] 'Stalinorgel'- 'Stalin's organ' – is an expression used by German soldiers to refer to the rocket launchers BM 8 and BM 30 (also known as 'Katyusha') used by the Red Army in the Second World War because of the loud, howling noise they produced. I am grateful to Ken Booth for advice on the colloquial expression in English.

Chapter 3 – was considered too gruesome.[100] The virtual disappearance of both novels until their recent republication[101] is perhaps not surprising.

Die Stalinorgel is a complex but harrowing account of 48 hours of battle over a single hill close to Leningrad. Ledig's account of soldiers' experiences offers no redeeming features. This is not the story of a cruel world confronted through a sense of duty or with heroism. There is 'no mercy', not even for the dead.[102] War is a senseless hell, 'pure madness', an 'absurd spectacle of horror'.[103] *Die Stalinorgel* opens with the image of a lance-corporal, stuck upside down in a tree, both hands shot off and dead. Half an hour later, when the tree is felled by a machine gun, he has also lost a foot: 'When he fell on the ground, he was only half a man.'[104] A minute later what is left of him is flattened by a tank. Then an explosion throws up a mass of scraps of uniform, flesh and blood. 'Then finally the lance-corporal was left alone.'[105] As there is no one alive to report his death, the lance-corporal is counted as missing.

We encounter the lance-corporal only when he is already dead. Like most characters in the novel, he is never given a name. They are referred to by their military rank only, which, given that more than one major or sergeant appears, makes it difficult to follow them as individuals. The storyline jumps between different positions on the German front, as well as into the Russian trenches. This breaking-up of the story seems to reflect the scramble of the senseless battle over the hill, which no one wins. This, and the relentless realism of the description, systematically undermines any simplistic identification with the soldiers. Any act which could potentially be described as altruistic or heroic is contextualised within an account of confusion, egotism, base motives and appalling sanitary conditions. It is not just that no hero walks off into the sunset: it is that there are only characters who have already been brutalised to such an extent by the war that, even where they might commit an act of heroism, it appears futile, if not naive, and certainly does not inspire admiration.

Many elements of Ledig's novel are common to war novels: a commanding officer issuing a senseless command and later coming to regret

---

[100] Florian Radvan, 'Nachwort', in: Gert Ledig, *Die Stalinorgel* (Frankfurt am Main: Suhrkamp Verlag 2000), pp. 203–29; Volker Hage, 'Die Angst muß im Genick sitzen', *Der Spiegel*, 04/01/99, 160; Sebald, *Luftkrieg und Literatur*, pp. 100f; Hage, 'Nachwort', p. 205.

[101] Radvan, 'Nachwort', pp. 203 and 227f; Hage, 'Die Angst', 160; Hage, 'Nachwort', p. 201.

[102] Hage, 'Die Angst', 160.   [103] Ibid., 162.

[104] Gert Ledig, *Die Stalinorgel* (Frankfurt am Main: Suhrkamp Verlag 2000), p. 7.

[105] Ibid., p. 8.

it; small acts of defiance against superior officers ('No soldier may refuse an order, but he may forget about it'[106]); desertion in the heat of battle; a fanatic insisting on shooting one particular deserter as a warning to others whilst hundreds are, against their orders, retreating; amputations under horrific conditions; brutality against captured enemies; orders that make no sense once they reach the front; ambiguous orders and superiors trying to shift responsibility to those they command; appalling conditions; an act of heroism; and death, death and death again. However, unlike in such novels as Erich Maria Remarque's *Im Westen nichts Neues* (*All Quiet on the Western Front*) or Heinrich Böll's *Wo warst du, Adam?*, the point does not seem to be to draw the reader into sympathy with the common soldier in any straightforward way.

The description of grimy, dusty, hairy men vegetating in a hole in the ground, waiting to fulfil an order that will almost certainly result in their deaths, trying to numb themselves with alcohol, shitting onto a spade or into empty tins so that they need not risk their lives by crawling out of the hole,[107] undercuts any notion of underdog heroes. Equally, when engineer Meller – one of the few characters with a name – blows himself up with two hand grenades in order to take out an enemy machine gun and create an opening for his unit which has been surrounded, he does so only because he has already received a fatal stomach wound.[108] Meller's death is described in gruesome detail, and his commanding officer finds himself unable to write the usual letter to the family about the 'shot in the chest and painless death'.[109]

Representations of war are always fraught with difficulties, not least the risk of trivialising the bloodshed and/or heroicising. *Die Stalinorgel* appears to be an attempt to fictionally re-create the carnage without representing the soldiers as heroes. Three points seem worth noting here. Firstly, *Die Stalinorgel* lacks one or several 'heroes' (in the sense of main characters) who might take readers through the confusion of the battle and allow them to identify with someone. Although certain characters appear repeatedly, they neither invite such identification, nor do they reduce the sense of unmitigated mayhem going on around them. Secondly, there is no difference in the portrayal of Russian and German soldiers. *Die Stalinorgel* jumps between both sides of the front;[110] a captured Russian and a captured German both observe that those holding them are much like their fellow soldiers and have the same desire for 'a little food, some warmth, no suffering any more'.[111] However, this is not to conjure up some sentimental notion of a common humanity. The

---

[106] Ibid., p. 29.   [107] Ibid., p. 13.   [108] Ibid., pp. 17–19.   [109] Ibid., p. 19.
[110] Hage, 'Nachwort', p. 205.   [111] Ledig, *Die Stalinorgel*, pp. 45 and 110.

Germans are also described as 'animals' by a Russian,[112] and both are observed in acts of brutality against enemy soldiers.[113] This even-handed treatment, which nevertheless offers no hope, is crucial because of the concern that German war memories portray the Germans as victims, count up German suffering against the suffering of the Germans' victims. Pfeifer observes that *Die Stalinorgel* is an exception to the general rule whereby German war novels treat the Second World War from the German perspective only.[114] In Ledig's work the relentless destruction of war hits both sides, and therefore 'humanity beyond all nationalities appears as victim'.[115] Pfeifer considers this to be problematic – Germans are still construed as victims, even if as part of humanity – but for the moment it is important to note that Ledig's novel is not about *German* soldiers and is therefore arguably of little use to any revisionist construction of German identity that would construe *German* soldiers as the real victims of the war.

Finally, the novel is such a horrific read not just because of all the gruesome detail: it is because no hope whatsoever is offered. The opening scene, for instance, is one of uncontrolled mayhem, in which it is impossible – and it would be irrational – to have the slightest concern for others. There is no comradeship under fire to take the edge off the horror conjured up in the painstakingly detailed description. Towards the end of the book, the major, looking at his men, remembers a time when there might still have been something like that, earlier in the war. But now what he sees is a 'bunch of lonely men. Already they envy one another, coveting what little tobacco remains in their pockets. A crust of bread, hard as a rock. A handful of cartridges, picked up from the dirt.'[116] Everyone only wants to survive for themselves. As the captain thought much earlier on: 'He wanted to live, like they all wanted to live. He had come to the conviction that it was better not to be a hero and instead to stay alive.'[117]

Thus *Die Stalinorgel*, though certainly a war novel, is designed to be an anti-war novel. Yet whereas Remarque, writing about the First World War, could bluntly state that his book was 'meant to be neither an accusation nor a confession. It is only the attempt to report about a generation that was destroyed by the war – even if it escaped its shells',[118] depicting the 'German' experience of the Second World War is more complicated. Because the generation of soldiers in the later war is not seen as

[112] Ibid., p. 163.   [113] See, for example, ibid., pp. 132ff and 166.
[114] Pfeifer, *Der deutsche Kriegsroman*, p. 105.   [115] Ibid.
[116] Ledig, *Die Stalinorgel*, p. 165.   [117] Ibid., p. 9.
[118] Remarque, *Im Westen nichts Neues*, p. 40.

innocent in the same way – they are not least accused of systematic involvement in atrocities – remembering their destruction is a politically more complex task. Ledig has one soldier state that 'we have all been betrayed'.[119] However, unlike Remarque, Ledig does not seem to be interested in generating sympathy for those who had to go through the hell of war. His novel is less about the soldiers' plight than, more fundamentally, about the futility and gruesomeness of war. As the major observes, he 'wanted to go to hell. And here it was. Complete with everything a sick mind could imagine.'[120] The 'betrayal' is thus both more ambiguous and more complete than that which Remarque may be describing. In the final scene of the book, the survivors of the battle attend a funeral. The army chaplain speaks of the comfort derived from the knowledge of salvation after death. The sergeant and the major leave during the funeral, discussing their 'secret' hope that this is true. As the major notes: 'It doesn't bear thinking about that we may be cheated even out of that.'[121] The only hope left is thus a dubious metaphysical one.

Ledig's representation of war is interesting, in this context, in at least three senses. Firstly, Ledig's representation of war as a senseless hell entails a comprehensive destabilisation of the idea of a 'good war' that seemed to be at the root of arguments, such as Kinkel's, supporting Bundeswehr deployments. Secondly, Ledig's work was 'rediscovered' in the late 1990s – apparently in response to Sebald's lecture series about the failure of German literature to engage with the experience of the bombing of German cities[122] – and republished in 2000. Thus it is part of a series of recent (re)publications which attest to a new interest in the war, notably at a time when the German military is involved in combat again. This seems to suggest that the public see novels as relevant to understanding war, but also that they know less about war than Kohl, for example, claimed: when they did know they did not care to read such books. Not only had everybody shared in the experience of the war in one way or another and therefore did not need to be told, people also simply did not want to be reminded of the war. The fate of Böll's *Der Engel schwieg* illustrates this. Böll was told by his publisher, after the novel had already been advertised in the 1950 catalogue, that people did not want to read about the war. Although the book was not even about the war but about the days immediately following Germany's unconditional surrender, it was only published posthumously in 1992.[123] Thirdly, Ledig's

---

[119] Ledig, *Die Stalinorgel*, p. 39.   [120] Ibid., p. 164.   [121] Ibid., p. 201.
[122] Hage, 'Die Angst'; Sebald, *Luftkrieg und Literatur.*
[123] Werner Bellmann, 'Nachwort', in: Heinrich Böll, *Der Engel schwieg* (Cologne: Kiepenheuer & Witsch 1992), pp. 195–7.

aim seems to be to tell how it 'really was', to re-create the war experience for those who had not been there. Ledig's effort to write again, late in his life – about the war in Bosnia – failed; he said that it 'didn't work. Too much distance. Fear has to be sitting on your own neck, you have to know that exactly.'[124] Ledig, in other words, appears to have been motivated by a desire to reveal the truth about war, and he notes 'having been there' as a condition for his writing.

Ledig does not discuss the question of memory but instead enacts the claim to authenticity that comes from 'having been there'. His writing is seen to imply 'a claim to truth';[125] it is driven by what Tachibana calls, in relation to early writing about Hiroshima and the Third Reich, the 're-creation of immediacy'.[126] Ledig, who had experienced the horror of battle, wanted to bear witness: he wanted to tell what it was really like. This 'bearing witness' turns to fiction, which is often construed to be the opposite of truth. This suggests, again, as discussed in relation to Sebald's claims in Chapter 3, that war cannot be represented simply 'as it was'; fiction – which makes no claim to accurately depict actual events – appears necessary to approach what may be considered the 'truth'. For example, the disorientation created by Ledig's narrative strategy perhaps might tell us more about what 'it was like' than a detailed historical account which may need to impose a meaning that was not available to those involved. Thus reading Ledig's novel raises the question of what it means to tell the truth about war, an issue explored further below. This question also appears in a different guise in Walser's novel *Ein springender Brunnen*.

Impossible authenticity: Walser's
Ein springender Brunnen

Martin Walser, an influential German novelist born in 1927, announced in the 1980s that he would 'demand of himself' a novel about his own experiences in the Second World War.[127] *Ein springender Brunnen*,[128] published in 1998, is apparently the result of this determination. What makes this novel intriguing is the interplay and contradiction between reflections on the problematic of memory and the bulk of the novel which seems to dismiss these difficult issues and, through detailed realistic description, entice the reader back into the past.

---

[124] Hage, 'Die Angst', 164.   [125] Ibid., 162; Hage, 'Nachwort', p. 203.

[126] Tachibana, *Narrative as Counter-Memory*, p. 7.

[127] Volker Hage, 'Königssohn von Wasserburg', *Der Spiegel*, 31, 27/07/98, 148.

[128] *Ein springender Brunnen* is a reference to Friedrich Nietzsche's phrase '[m]y soul is a gushing fountain' in *Also sprach Zarathustra: Ein Buch für Alle und Keinen* (Berlin: Walter de Gruyter & Co. 1968), p. 132.

The novel opens with a chapter on the 'Past as Present', as does each of the three parts of the book: 'As long as something is, it is not what it will have been. When something is over, one is no longer the one to whom it happened . . . Although the past, when it was the present, did not exist, it now imposes itself, as if it had existed in the way in which it imposes itself now.' In the collective past one can walk about 'as if in a museum', but not so in one's own past. Of our own past we 'only have what it reveals by itself.'[129] As Walser puts it, '[w]e survive not as those who we were but as those who we have become after we have been. When it is over. For it still is, even if [it is] over. Now is there more past or more present in being over?'[130] Walser is obviously deeply interested in memory and its relation to the present.

Ein springender Brunnen tells the childhood of Johann, who is 5 years old in 1932, at the start of the novel. I am here most interested in the third and final part of the book, which deals with the period of autumn 1944 to summer 1945. It is the first time the war becomes relevant to Johann and to Wasserburg, the small town on Lake Constance where the book is set. Johann is 17, writes poetry and constantly thinks about women and, having been brought up by a devoutly Catholic mother, in a rather roundabout way about sex and about his manhood. The military and war, as the ultimate sites for virility, are extremely important in his perception of himself as growing up, as following in the footsteps of his elder brother Josef. Johann has already taken over crucial parts of his mother's business since Josef has been drafted, first to the *Reichsarbeitsdienst*[131] and then into the military.

The second chapter of part three of the book is told as Johann's stream of consciousness whilst he is harvesting apples. He starts by contemplating that he is now able to carry a much bigger sack of apples on the ladder than he could when he was younger and that, because of this, he could not do the job barefoot any more. Therefore he thinks about his footwear. Currently, he is wearing the boots of the *Reichsarbeitsdienst*, but is hoping to soon exchange them for those of the *Gebirgsjäger* (mountain troops).[132] He is embarrassed about his uniform, which is that of the navy. He finds it 'exaggerated', 'almost ridiculous'. When he joins the proper military he never wants to be in the navy, never wants to have a cap without a shield. In view of the awful uniform, he doesn't comprehend how anyone could

---

129 Walser, *Ein springender Brunnen*, p. 9.
130 Ibid., p. 15. The idea that the past continues to exist even when it is over is expressed differently in Vonnegut's *Slaughterhouse 5*, discussed in Chapter 5.
131 A form of pre-military service in the Third Reich.
132 Walser, *Ein springender Brunnen*, p. 284.

volunteer for the navy at all.[133] Johann is also critical of his brother's uniform. The cap of the *Gebirgsjäger*, which he would get, is 'smarter'.[134]

Johann's interest in being able to wear the best uniform combines with his desire to be seen to be courageous. When his friend Adolf volunteers for the anti-aircraft batteries he finds the decision incomprehensible, but does not dare to ask the reason. In Johann's view, those 'who volunteered for anti-aircraft duties thereby confessed that they did not want to go to the front, that others should go to the front. Especially if Johann had not wanted to go to the front, he would never have admitted to that by signing up for the anti-aircraft batteries.'[135] Johann is desperate to join the military and keen to prove himself at the front.[136] He writes to his brother Josef on the Eastern front that he is hoping for his call-up to arrive soon.[137] Finally, in December 1944, when Josef has already been killed in action,[138] Johann reports for duty in Garmisch. He looks forward to skiing, walking in the mountains, long evenings in mountain cabins, lots of singing and, best of all, 'the most beautiful of all possible uniforms'.[139] He thinks of Friedrich Nietzsche's *Zarathustra* and, as he is skiing through heavy snowfall, Johann decides that nothing he is learning in the mountains could ever be relevant to war.[140] The incredible beauty of the landscape in the Alps makes it impossible to think that what he is doing is training for war. In any event, Johann never sees any action, because the war ends before his training is complete.

Thus problematic aspects of the German armed forces' conduct are only depicted either in Johann's reflection on hearsay or in his reports of what he has been told by specific people. His brother's letters, another source of information on the war, unsurprisingly contain no such descriptions.[141] In a POW camp, a lance-corporal confesses to Johann that as a member of the SA he took part in the persecution of Jews, and therefore he has to keep imitating dog barks at night to keep himself from wondering whether he will have to pay for it. Johann does not seem to understand what this man, who breaks down whimpering, tells him. He finds the man's smelly feet more repulsive.[142] On the topic of SS atrocities, Johann is more certain: 'There were rumours that the SS did not take prisoners in the East. Johann took this to be propaganda, because it just had to be unimaginable to still shoot someone who has given himself up to you as a prisoner . . . To consider something like this possible was despicable.'[143] Johann had, however, never been a fan of Nazism. Quite the contrary. He explains his own ability to be involved with the ideology,

---

[133] Ibid., p. 287.   [134] Ibid., p. 294.   [135] Ibid., pp. 311f.   [136] Ibid., p. 341.
[137] Ibid., p. 331.   [138] Ibid., pp. 340 and 347f.   [139] Ibid., p. 341.
[140] Ibid., pp. 352–4.   [141] Ibid., pp. 328–31.   [142] Ibid., pp. 357f.   [143] Ibid., p. 345.

such as in his military oath, by saying that he merely had to '[r]epeat and say out loud and promise what was none of his business'.[144] It was just another formula, like the act of contrition that Catholics say in the confessional. Johann's story also includes references to the effect the war had on civilian life, but only in a mediated way, because in his region 'they only dropped bombs on their way back which they had not been able to get rid of over the cities'.[145] He observes that there are a lot of women in town, each with two to four children: 'All city folk. Bombed out of their homes. Refugees.'[146] One family is now quartered on his mother's property, in the former stables.[147]

Despite Walser's announcement that he would write about his own experiences in the Second World War, *Ein springender Brunnen* is not a book primarily about the war. It is a novel about growing up, where the growing-up is done in particular political circumstances which in the end also involve war. Yet it is interesting as a depiction of the Second World War by a German. In a country where matters military were until recently regarded with the greatest of suspicion by most people, speaking about a young boy signing up in the Second World War because he fancied wearing a particular uniform and expected that doing so would confer manhood upon him is anything but politically correct. Johann, on his way back from Garmisch to Wasserburg, is even robbed of his gun, cigarettes and watch by ex-concentration camp inmates, still wearing the camp uniform marked as 'homosexual' by a pink triangle.[148] This scene in particular is left as bizarre, not contextualised through any commentary that might shed light on why it is there. Presumably, this lack of (political) contextualisation is, in Walser's view, due to what he calls the 'Urgesetz des Erzählens', the most basic rule about telling a story: *Perspektivität* (perspectivity),[149] or the freedom to choose a perspective and resist the use of any information that would not be 'visible' from that perspective.

Despite his belief in this basic rule, the text betrays Walser's concern about how his depiction of this period would be received. His musings on the 'past as present' at the beginning of the third part of the novel suggest as much. He writes that those 'who most ardently take trouble over the past are most in danger of considering what they have created to be what they have been looking for. We cannot admit that there is nothing but the present. For it does not really exist either.'[150] Thus whatever he may be writing about this past, Walser says, will always be more about the present, insofar as this present exists. Of course, he suggests, some

---

[144] Ibid., p. 351.   [145] Ibid., p. 290.   [146] Ibid., p. 296.   [147] Ibid.
[148] Ibid., p. 361.   [149] Walser, 'Dankesrede'.
[150] Walser, *Ein springender Brunnen*, p. 281.

people 'slip out of' their past in order to present a more favourable past. What he is particularly concerned about, however, is control over the past: 'In reality dealing with the past becomes more and more standard-ised decade after decade. The more standardised this dealing, the more what is presented as the past is a product of the present.' Thus the past becomes a fund from which one may pick and choose as one wishes. 'A past which is completely reconstructed [*erschlossen*], investigated, sani-tised, sanctioned, totally fit for the present. Ethically and politically cor-rected through and through.'[151] And finally, '[w]hatever our past may have been, we have liberated ourselves from everything which was such at the time that we do not want it any more now'.[152] It is the notion of *Vergangenheitsbewältigung* (coming to terms with the past) that Walser takes issue with, and if his story about Johann considering the mountain troops' uniform sexy or being robbed by ex-concentration camp inmates interferes with the dominant discourse on the past, that is fine by him. Thus he seems to endorse literature's function as counter-memory.[153] He claims a right to his memory, however subjective and indeed episte-mologically insecure, and however much in tension with what is, in the dominant political discourse, considered an appropriate memory.

Crucially, Walser's musings on 'the past as present' at the same time undermine any simplistic notion of revealing the truth about the past or bearing witness. Ledig's recourse to fiction in order to show what war was like already betrays the impossibility of simply telling it 'as it was'. Ledig's ruptured plot works against a singular narrative, and thus his book gives no simple answer to the question of what happened, what it was like. This destabilises the possibility of a monolithic or formulaic memory as is often enacted when referring to the 'experience' of the Second World War merely to underline the 'never again' mantra. The assault on this attitude in Walser's text is more subtle, but also more fundamental. The issue of memory – the way in which the present always already interferes with any telling of the past – is foregrounded. Thus the idea of a 'truth' about the past is a fiction, and not merely for the reasons identified in previous chapters; this truth is itself subject to change in time – this truth has a history. Moreover, we cannot recall what was as we experienced it then because we no longer are who we were, as Walser points out. It is this reflection on time, truth and memory which makes Walser's novel relevant beyond the specific story it tells. Taking seriously this aspect of the novel also makes it necessary to go beyond an interpretation that focuses on how Walser opposes public forms of memory against private

---

[151] Ibid., p. 282.   [152] Ibid., pp. 282f.
[153] Tachibana, *Narrative as Counter-Memory*, p. 1.

conscience in a bid to value the latter over the former.[154] This *may* be what Walser intended, although that, too, is doubtful; but it is certainly not all his text tells us.

Representing war and the political context

Ledig and Walser ostensibly represent the same war, but there is little the two novels have in common. *Die Stalinorgel* graphically depicts the horrors of war; it specialises in making as vivid as possible the situations faced by soldiers in the particular battle portrayed. *Ein springender Brunnen*, in contrast, never really gets around to the war at all. The main character misses the action. He only encounters war at the margins: he trains for war, receives reports about war from his brother and a fellow POW, observes his own desire to go to war and comments upon the influx of evacuees into his home town. In Ledig's text there is no narrator or other voice that comments upon events or contextualises them. In Walser's book there are lengthy reflections on 'the past as present', that is, on the problematic of remembering. Although these two novels thus treat the war in profoundly different ways, they have both been criticised for their alleged politics.

Despite its success in the 1950s, the critics find much to object to in accounts of the war such as Ledig's. Hermand refers to such writing as 'antimilitaristic "novels of cruelty" ['Romane der Härte'] which describe primarily the terrors of war'. He claims that they 'remain stuck in the portrayal of unreflected horror'[155] and complains that Ledig's *Die Stalinorgel* is '*only* about killing and being killed, about getting through or going under'.[156] Pfeifer, similarly, argues that the 'narrative attitude in places slides into the sarcastic; the attitude of the narrator to humanity is extremely distanced, the soldier has entirely become an object'. Pfeifer underlines this with the – false – claim that 'no names are mentioned in the entire novel' and the – largely correct – observation that military ranks are instead used to refer to people.[157] He argues that the 'shock therapy of the novel of cruelty falls flat, however, the style and the structure of the novel prove to be an obstacle to depicting the war . . . The cruel style is not a sensible means for expressing content other than a very trivial one: that the war was hard and cruel.'[158] This seems, however, in tension with Pfeifer's own judgement that Ledig's novels are 'among

---

[154] Schmitz, Helmut, *On Their Own Terms: The Legacy of National Socialism in Post-1990 German Fiction* (Birmingham: Birmingham University Press 2004), pp. 181–4.
[155] Hermand, 'Darstellungen', p. 36.   [156] Ibid., p. 37 (italics added).
[157] Pfeifer, *Der deutsche Kriegsroman*, p. 81.   [158] Ibid., pp. 82f.

the best that has been written about the war in the German language' because 'structural components and the building-blocks of content' work together to express 'the destructive senselessness and the absurdity of the friend–enemy relationship in war'.[159] Crucially, Pfeifer reaches his negative overall assessment because, in his view, *Die Stalinorgel* removes the war entirely from its historical context, and therefore cruelty is the *only* topic.[160] In other words, the criticism is that it is not enough to portray war as horrible; there is concern in particular about the lack of political contextualisation, that is, the failure to clarify the fact that the Second World War was not a war like any other but a genocidal war of aggression, a war that involved the systematic committing of atrocities.

The objection against the portrayal of the Second World War in *Die Stalinorgel* and, as will be shown, *Ein springender Brunnen*, seems to be that they focus on particular experiences and fail to portray their context. In other words, their representations zoom in on the particular and are therefore somehow not representative of what happened. This is, of course, the gist of the objection to German novels about the Second World War summarised in Chapter 1: they focus on particular experiences to the exclusion of other extremely significant aspects of the war and thus provide a dangerously depoliticised version of the war. This criticism was related to a general reluctance to engage with the political context of the war, made possible and to an extent justified by choosing main characters holding a low military rank. These characters are in no position to comment or reflect upon wider political issues; they merely attempt to get through the war as best they can. This particular choice of main characters also allows for an especially problematic exclusion, that of Wehrmacht atrocities. As the characters are not involved with wider policy questions, these crimes do not have to be mentioned unless the characters are themselves involved, which – unsurprisingly – they usually are not. Bance points out that:

German war novels about the Second World War are very rarely militaristic in nature; indeed, whatever the political colour of their authors, to a man they warn against the horrors of war and a renewal of war. Yet the effectiveness of the message must be in doubt when we consider how the emphasis of the warning is shifted from the sufferings, partly at *Wehrmacht* hands, of the victims of German aggression – above all the Jews, but also the more frequently mentioned partisans and the ordinary Russian population – to the miseries of the defeated Germans, thus feeding the Germans' post-war conception of themselves as the betrayed and exploited victims of a conspiracy imposed upon them by a demonic tyrant.[161]

---

[159] Ibid., p. 178.   [160] Ibid., p. 205.   [161] Bance, 'Brutalization of Warfare', p. 112.

In other words, war is horrible in these novels not because of the terrible atrocities committed by the Germans but because they themselves were exposed to hardship, suffering and indeed betrayal. Bance observes 'that curiously enough, the Army itself' is 'commonly seen as the repository of uprightness and pre-National Socialist values within an evil system' by writers dealing with the Second World War. This can sometimes 'offer almost complete detachment from implication in the black side of Germany's war, which is safely left to Hitler and his SS henchmen'.[162] If war crimes are mentioned at all, they are generally 'attributed to Nazi units, rather than to the army'.[163] There is criticism of the Prussian officer caste, but '[w]ar fiction reflects, as much as it contributes to, a German delusion of the post-war years that the Army was exempt from guilt for the crimes committed in the name of Germany'.[164] In sum, the 'majority of war novels imply at most only a hazy half-knowledge on the part of the fighting troops of the atrocities being carried out in the name of Germany'.[165] This implied lack of knowledge combines with what Bance refers to as the 'image of the unpolitical soldier' which 'had engraved itself upon the collective public memory, shared, and in part no doubt formed, by those who wrote fiction about the war'.[166] In other words, as noted in Chapter 1, German war literature is complicit in creating and maintaining the myth of the 'clean' Wehrmacht.

Thus, although representations of war such as Ledig's may enable us to imagine certain aspects of the war, they leave out extremely important elements. Inasmuch as there is a danger that the aspects that the novels do portray will be seen as representing what 'the war' was like, they create a politically problematic illusion. Thus Ledig's portrayal might be seen to be in tune with the side of the Wehrmacht debate that regards German soldiers as first and foremost victims of a horrible war. Before taking this problem further it is important to show how Walser's very different novel is seen to fall into the same trap. Walser's strategy of portraying only what was part of the direct experience of the boy whose childhood and youth he tells is seen as something of a political ploy: 'The richness of description conceals the desire to find normality in a time that could never be considered normal.'[167] Walser's nostalgic focus on the small town of Wasserburg, this suggests, excludes discussion of the system of National Socialism not only because the situation is seen through a boy's eyes but also because Walser seeks to focus on the normality of the past, thereby making it appear better, or more politically innocent, than it was.

---

[162] Ibid., p. 97.   [163] Ibid.   [164] Ibid., p. 98.   [165] Bance, 'Germany', p. 121.
[166] Bance, 'Brutalization of Warfare', p. 99.
[167] Thomas Steinfeld, 'Der Wanderfotograf', *Frankfurter Allgemeine Zeitung*, 26/09/98, V.

In Walser's case, this suspicion is not merely an outcome of reading *Ein springender Brunnen* but in addition takes account of his controversial criticism of how Germany deals with its past, not least in his acceptance speech for the 1998 Peace Prize of the German Book Trade. As noted in Chapter 2, Walser objected to what he considers to be a 'ceaseless representation of our disgrace' and spoke of his desire to 'look away'.[168] His speech was sharply criticised by Ignatz Bubis, then chairman of the Zentralrat der Juden in Deutschland (Central Council of the Jews in Germany), who called Walser's words 'intellectual arson'.[169] The ensuing debate revolved around the role of memories of the Third Reich and the Holocaust in German politics. This debate, and Walser's apparent interest in generating a more positive self-image of the German nation, might appear to be the obvious context within which Walser's literary work must be interpreted.[170] Barnouw notes, however, that the accusations against Walser were 'clearly absurd', in view of the actual content of his speech and of his contributions to engaging with the past over the years.[171] Yet it is not so simple. Although Walser, in the 1970s and 1980s, insisted on the continuing relevance of Auschwitz, he also noted that he is unable to correct his memory of his youth with the knowledge he has since acquired about the Third Reich.[172] The tension expressed so starkly in *Ein springender Brunnen* has always been there in his reflections on the past.

Reading Walser's work in the context of his alleged political convictions and goals is a limited approach, however, because it seems to miss the most interesting implications of Walser's reflections on memory: such a supposedly political reading of the novels fails to consider their political implications beyond assigning them a location on the Left–Right spectrum of politics. Walser's reflections on what it means to remember the past in fact seem to make much more difficult the kind of instrumental use of the past that is seen to be part of rightwing politics. Similarly, although Ledig does indeed exclude the political context, his representation of the war is not easily instrumentalised, because it resists the imposition of meaning. These issues are worth thinking through in detail.

---

[168] Walser, 'Dankesrede'. See also 'Das Gewissen ist nicht delegierbar', *Frankfurter Allgemeine Zeitung*, 12/10/98, 1.

[169] 'Was will Walser?', *Süddeutsche Zeitung*, 13/10/98, 15. See also 'Ignatz Bubis antwortet Martin Walser: Unterschwellig antisemitisch. Auszüge aus Rede zum 60. Jahrestag der Pogromnacht', *Süddeutsche Zeitung*, 10/11/98, 5.

[170] See, for example, Schmitz, *On Their Own Terms*, Chapter 6.

[171] Barnouw, *War in the Empty Air*, p. 18.

[172] Martin Walser, *Über Deutschland reden* (Frankfurt am Main: Suhrkamp 1988), pp. 24–31 and 76.

The truth of fiction

Ledig and Walser, each in their own way, tell stories of particular characters in the context of the Second World War. The critics seem to suggest,
however, that the truthfulness of these accounts is undermined by a lack
of contextualisation and that this is relevant, even though the texts are
fictional. This raises the question of the role of truth in fiction. Pfeifer
notes that the back covers of war books published in the first postwar
decades often announce that they show 'what it was really like'; this
was, in his view, a reaction to the exposure first to Nazi propaganda and
then Allied re-education.[173] Lothar-Günther Buchheim's war novel *Die
Festung* (*The Fortress*) is advertised, on its back cover, as 'more authentic
than any factual report'.[174] In other words, novels are offered as a form of
testimony about the authors' own experiences in the Second World War.
This attempt at or claim to authenticity is not just a reaction to what was
perceived as varying kinds of past propaganda: Buchheim's book carries
this claim on the back cover of the 1997 edition. Nor is this claim particular to German war novels: in his discussion of French texts on both world
wars, James Knibb notes that 'in discussions of war texts, the gauge of
"authenticity" almost always comes to be used'.[175] With respect to literature on the First World War, Holger Klein also claims that '[g]enerally,
war books were not looked on as "literature", not treated in the same way
as war critics treated other texts, but treated rather as *documents*'.[176] War
novels are read differently from other novels. Ulrich Baron and Hans-
Harald Müller, in their discussion of German novels about the Second
World War, point out that there was an 'emphatic claim to the "truth" in
the portrayal, although the authors did not claim to describe historically
verifiable events'.[177] They note that the question of how such a claim to
truth might be reconciled with the idea of fiction seemed to be less interesting to contemporary readers and critics than the question of whether
the author 'had really been there'.[178]

This idea of truth or authenticity based on the authors' own experiences is interesting not least because the irrepresentability of war is at

[173] Pfeifer, *Der deutsche Kriegsroman*, p. 77.
[174] Lothar-Günther Buchheim, *Die Festung* (Munich: Goldmann 1997).
[175] James Knibb, 'Literary Strategies of War, Strategies of Literary War', in: David Bevan
(ed.), 'Literature and War', *Rodopi Perspectives on Modern Literature* 3 (1990), 7.
[176] Holger Klein, *The Artistry of Political Literature: Essays on War, Commitment and Criticism*
(Lewiston: The Edwin Mellen Press 1994), p. 46.
[177] Ulrich Baron and Hans-Harald Müller, 'Die "Perspektive des kleinen Mannes" in der
Kriegsliteratur der Nachkriegszeiten', in: Wolfram Wette (ed.), *Der Krieg des kleinen
Mannes: Eine Militärgeschichte von unten*, 2nd edn (Munich: Piper 1995), p. 354.
[178] Ibid.

the same time a key theme of war fiction. For example, Grass's narrator in *Im Krebsgang* relies on assertions of personal experience but also says that 'I cannot describe it. No one can describe that.'[179] Similarly, in Vonnegut's *Slaughterhouse 5*, to be discussed in Chapter 5, the narrator explicitly notes that he 'had been there'[180] in the war and particularly at the destruction of Dresden. Yet he also discusses at length the impossibility of depicting this event. According to Rainer Emig, the heart of the problem of representations of war could be said to be 'to grasp with words a world that lies outside the imagination'.[181] However, if, as he notes, the central phrase of representations of war is 'words cannot express it', then the 'paradox of the phrase itself shows that a breaking out of representation is not possible'.[182] This is crucial; this issue has already arisen in previous chapters when the representability of the horrors of the air war and expulsions were considered. War may not be represented, but it nevertheless is. Language, although not equal to the job, is the best we have.

Emig pushes this problem further by considering in detail the claim to authenticity and the problem it poses. He notes that the 'seemingly most concrete component' on which narratives of war rely is the actual and the experienced.[183] Following Emig's arguments, there are two problems with this. Firstly, Emig raises the problem of zooming in on concrete occurrences. In his view, the radical focus on detail, here illustrated by Ledig's *Die Stalinorgel*, may actually make war disappear.[184] In other words, Emig considers that war is something more than just the sum of these experiences and that a focus on the trees may mean that we fail to see the wood. This is not unlike the critics' concern with the exclusion of the political context, although Emig seems more fundamentally concerned with any context that might give meaning to the detail, political or otherwise. Secondly, he points out that as soon as one uses the

---

[179] Grass, *Im Krebsgang*, p. 102.

[180] Vonnegut, *Slaughterhouse 5*, p. 49. See also Rainer Emig's discussion of authenticity in relation to *Slaughterhouse 5* outlined in Chapter 5.

[181] Rainer Emig, 'Augen/Zeugen: Kriegserlebnis, Bild, Metapher, Legende', in: Thomas F. Schneider, *Kriegserlebnis und Legendenbildung: Das Bild des 'modernen' Krieges in Literatur, Theater, Photographie und Film*, vol. I (Osnabrück: Universitätsverlag Rasch 1999), p. 19.

[182] Emig, *Krieg als Metapher*, p. 45. Emig here refers to Fussell, *The Great War and Modern Memory*, p. 186 who quotes Joseph Heller's *Catch-22* (London: Vintage 1994). He cites the ready-made postcard: 'Dear Mrs., Mr., Miss, or Mr. and Mrs.: Words cannot express the deep personal grief I experienced when your husband, son, father or brother was killed, wounded or reported missing in action.' *Catch-22*, p. 323.

[183] Emig, *Krieg als Metapher*, p. 249.

[184] Ibid., p. 172. Emig, however, raises this point in relation to representations on television and collections of personal items shown in exhibitions.

standard of authenticity in relation to war narratives the question that arises is whether the author has 'seen in this way' what he relates to us. Put differently, Emig asks 'how and whether one gets from experience to depiction, what must be considered in the process and what one must perhaps suppress and forget in order to *produce* authenticity'.[185] The last point makes clear the problem: whilst authenticity seems to mean 'simple' one-to-one representation, it is in fact produced. This production might necessitate, amongst other things, leaving things out. Walser, relying on his basic rule of telling a story, presumably regards Johann's – and his story's – failure to refer to the body of knowledge available on the Third Reich and Wehrmacht crimes as 'authentic'. It is, anyway, impossible to represent or report everything, much like it is impossible to remember everything about something.

Emig sees the 'great paradox of authenticity' thus: 'authenticity describes a single direct experience, but authenticity may on the other hand only be reached if this experience can successfully be related to other people'.[186] This process is therefore reliant on artificiality. It would, in Emig's view, be nonsensical to speak of 'objective seeing' in relation to representations of war, because this seeing always takes place against a background of meaning within which it makes sense.[187] It is impossible to look at war without already having imposed a context. War literature cannot opt for 'simple realism'. This would precisely obscure 'the artificiality of beginning, middle, end, problem and solution, friend and enemy, hero and coward'. Thus Emig suggests that it is important to point to the breaks in representations without, however, denying the urge of fiction to overcome those breaks.[188] In other words, it is significant to explore how war narratives fail to work or break down, even if the apparent aim is to obscure this failure.

This failure is certainly obscured when war books are advertised as simply telling us what it was like. Ironically, given that I have argued that both Ledig's and Walser's accounts undermine our trust in the possibility of obtaining the truth about the past, Ledig's *Die Stalinorgel* seems to be offered as a form of testimony: 'I will tell you what happened.' In some way, so is Walser's. Although Walser reflects upon the impossibility of such a claim – the past never was as it imposes itself now – his book actually draws us into the past. It creates an illusion of immediacy, though one that is different from Ledig's and exposed as something of a fraud in Walser's reflections on the 'Past as Present'. This performative contradiction may be seen as a break in the sense highlighted by Emig,

---

185 Emig, 'Augen/Zeugen', p. 16 (italics added).
186 Ibid., p. 21.   187 Ibid., p. 16.   188 Ibid., p. 22.

and thus worth thinking about. It is instructive to consider in this context Derrida's discussion of testimony. He reflects upon points similar to those that Emig raises as problems of authenticity in literature. Derrida, however, goes further in considering the political implications of the problem of testimony as he sees it. Derrida argues that:

I can only testify, in the strict sense of the word, from the instant when no one can, in my place, testify to what I do. What I testify to is, at that instant, my secret; it remains reserved for me. I must be able to keep secret precisely what I testify to; it is the condition of the testimony in a strict sense, and this is why one will never be able to demonstrate, in the sense of a theoretical proof or a determinate judgement, that a perjury or lie has taken place. Even an admission will not be enough.[189]

In other words, testimony relies on our singularity: I can testify only to what I have experienced myself and to what, by definition, no one else has. In this sense, the content of my testimony is a secret that cannot be judged right or wrong by others. However, the point of testimony is, of course, precisely communicating that which Derrida says is a secret and will always remain so.

Emig discussed this problem in relation to authenticity which, he argues, relies both on the irreducible singularity of the experience and the possibility of investing it with some objectivity, making it accessible to others. Testimony – like authenticity – is impossible. It is not that war fiction may not properly execute what we call testimony; it is that the structure of testimony with its tension between irreducible singularity and the corresponding requirement to make it publicly accessible makes it an impossible feat. Were testimony in the strict sense to be possible, it would have to be possible to repeat the same thing always: 'When I commit myself to speaking the truth, I commit myself to repeating the same thing, an instant later, two instants later, the next day, and for eternity, in a certain way.' In other words, the sentences of testimony 'must promise their own repetition and thus their own quasi-technical reproducibility'. However, this repetition inevitably 'carries the instant outside itself. Consequently, the instant is instantaneously, *at this very instant*, divided, destroyed by what it nonetheless makes possible – testimony.'[190] This problematic is underlined by Derrida's notion of iterability; whenever we articulate something, it is already a citation of something else, a parody, and therefore unfaithful to the original.[191] The repeatability implied by testimony is impossible, and this is illustrated, for our purposes, in Walser's thoughts on the past in the present. We may not repeat

---

[189] Derrida, *Demeure*, p. 30.   [190] Ibid., p. 33.   [191] Derrida, *Limited Inc*, p. 53.

the past in the same way always because we have already changed. Even if we wanted to tell the past as it was, this would be impossible.

War fiction often involves a claim to authenticity, the offer of truthful testimony; this is profoundly problematic. Yet, clearly, the alternative is not to resort to non-fiction and simply report. Emig's emphasis on 'meaning' as always intruding into what might be presented as objective observation makes clear the impossibility of merely reporting. The claim that Buchheim's novel is 'more authentic than any factual report' also suggests that fiction might be *necessary* to producing authenticity. In fact, mirroring the idea that war narratives ought to be authentic, there is a 'widespread view that the "essence" of war cannot be adequately expressed through the documentation of everyday experiences but only through literary construction'.[192] Baron and Müller point out that eyewitnesses like Ledig attempted to achieve objectivity not by describing the war from their own perspective but by 'introducing a multitude of different fictional perspectives'. As a consequence, the differences between genres – such as documentary literature versus fiction – came to be ignored.[193] These points echo Sebald's argument discussed in Chapter 3. Authenticity is not possible in any form of representation. Yet, although it is unable to provide the desired authenticity, fiction is still necessary to the representation of war.

Fiction might be important because it allows a different attitude towards meaning, one that allows it to resist rationalisation. It may at times tell the past in a way which avoids something that is too much, the retrospective closure imposed by historical narrative. Hayden White has suggested that the 'value attached to narrativity in the representation of real events arises out of a desire to have real events display the coherence, integrity, fullness, and closure of an image of life that is and can only be imaginary'.[194] This is related to Emig's observation that every war narrative inevitably involves an imposition of meaning. Although fictional accounts are also narratives, of course, they may resist the closure noted by White, which would ironically be 'fictitious' in the sense that the meaning given to events would not have been available to those involved at the time, an issue which is also expressed in Walser's assertion that the past never was as it now appears to be. As is apparent in the case of *Vergeltung*, the narrative of fictional accounts does not need to involve a coherent story that would produce some equally coherent meaning. Ledig's ruptured plot is an example of resisting 'meaning' that can only

---

[192] Baron and Müller, 'Perspektive des kleinen Mannes', p. 352.   [193] Ibid., p. 353.
[194] Hayden White, *The Content of the Form: Narrative Discourse and Historical Representation* (Baltimore: The Johns Hopkins University Press 1987), p. 24.

ever be imposed ex post facto. Pfeifer argues that in novels such as Ledig's one seems to be very close to the events, but he complains that this is all the meaning there is to these texts.[195] He fails to consider whether this might not be precisely the point. Ledig, even more so in *Vergeltung* than in *Die Stalinorgel*, seems to refuse any meaning being attached to war; his novels are an assault on the notion that war makes any sense. Although Walser, unlike Ledig, tells a coherent story, he seems also to want to resist carrying back today's meaning into past events.

On the other hand, fiction might be more able to represent an excess, something that goes beyond what historical narrative may capture, such as the failure of different narratives to neatly add up to 'the whole story', and also, significantly, emotions. According to Mulisch, 'a novel should not describe what happened but be itself something that happens – in the moment when one reads the book. That is the essential difference between art and non-art.'[196] That is, Ledig's re-creation of the chaos of battle is not just to tell us what it was really like: it is to move us to feel some of what it felt like. Despite the impossibility of authenticity, novels sometimes seem to give a good impression of what it 'was like'. Forte, a survivor of air raids, said about Ledig's depiction in *Vergeltung*: 'I can swear, this is what it was like.'[197] Clearly, in Forte's view, Ledig achieves an element of the re-creation of immediacy. Thus, although an authentic or truthful representation of the past seems impossible – it is not even clear what that would be – the past is apparently at times recognised in novels.

Walser, of course, objects that the past as we recognise it now, as it indeed imposes itself now, was never quite like that when it was the present. If he is right, it is not only unclear what authenticity might mean, it might also be worth considering how we retrospectively assign meaning to the past. As he says, we are 'in danger of considering what [we] have created to be what [we] have been looking for'.[198] Put differently, Walser is now presumably aware of the political circumstances under which a boy like Johann grew up, and so are his readers, but it does not seem clear whether the more 'authentic' representation of the past is one that acknowledges this retrospectively available context of what we now call the Third Reich, the Holocaust and the Second World War, or whether it is one that lets the character comment in now entirely inappropriate ways on events that may have appeared differently in the past. Johann, for example, refers to SA and SS crimes, but dismisses them in ways that may only be described as bizarre. On meeting a lance-corporal of the SA

[195] Pfeifer, *Der deutsche Kriegsroman*, p. 79.   [196] 'Tanz unter den Ruinen', p. 233.
[197] Forte, *Schweigen oder sprechen*, p. 53.   [198] Walser, *Ein springender Brunnen*, p. 281.

who confesses to his involvement in the persecution of Jews, Johann is more repelled by the man's smelly feet than anything else, and he simply dismisses as lies claims that the SS executed enemy soldiers whom they had captured.[199] Walser obviously does not offer a deep engagement with these atrocities. They are noted and quickly dismissed. The story moves on, unaffected by what has just been mentioned. It is easy to see why this is considered inappropriate. What is less obvious, however, is whether it is useful to see this in terms of misrepresenting the past and whether the solution to this representational lacuna is indeed to provide Johann or the narrator with all the insights that *Vergangenheitsbewältigung* was to highlight. It is unclear what precisely the nature of the inappropriateness is, and how, if at all, it might be remedied. Remembering or representing the full truth is not only impossible, it is also not necessarily the solution.

What is intriguing is that Walser recognises the impossibility of what he is doing. In a performative contradiction, he does exactly what he so elegantly reveals to be impossible: he entices us back into the past – his past – to walk around as if in a museum. He makes it appear as though he may tell the past as it was when it was the present. In order to make sense of this obvious contradiction between Walser's reflections on memory and the way he tells the story it is necessary to acknowledge that this is not a problem merely of rationality and truth. It has been shown that both politicians and writers who are survivors of the war refer to their experiences and the memories that haunt them. They apparently feel compelled to express what they might have recognised as inexpressible. They seem to feel not only an obligation to the dead but a strong sense that the events, however inexpressible, are relevant to the living. This was evident in the debate about Wehrmacht crimes.

Beyond truth? Emotion and ethics

In the Wehrmacht debate Dregger seemed to despair at today's Germans' inability to grasp just what the war was like. Given the impossibility not only of depicting war but also of representing the past as it was when it was the present, this inability is not surprising. Dregger does not speak about this, although his exasperation is perhaps a sign of having tried too many times to make others understand just what he remembers having experienced. Whatever the possibility of representation, getting across his view of the matter was clearly extremely important to Dregger. He insisted that the majority of soldiers had not been involved in crimes and were now retrospectively being tarnished by events they had no knowledge of

---

[199] Ibid., pp. 357f and 345.

or control over. He says that he feels moved to defend those many soldiers in the lower ranks who, for no particular reason, died when he did not.[200]

Thus, for Dregger, the grief for the many lives lost and the related wonder at his own survival are central; he therefore finds it inappropriate to focus on the Wehrmacht's involvement in crimes. His problem is similar to that of a veteran who was challenged by a young man in the queue for the Wehrmacht exhibition. The young man asserted that if the veteran said that he had not seen any crimes, he must be lying. One can perhaps not help having some sympathy with the veteran, who retorted: 'It's not on for you to tell me what I experienced.'[201] The young man's conviction that all soldiers would necessarily have witnessed atrocities committed by German troops was, in other words, pitched against a veteran's refusal to be told that his memories are lies because they did not involve such crimes. The temptation is of course to examine whether Dregger's and the veteran's asserted memories of the war are true, in the sense of asking whether they both indeed did not witness or participate in atrocities. Yet something else is significant that does not necessarily depend on the accuracy or otherwise of the memory articulated: they obviously feel strongly that they know precisely what they experienced and that their recollection is called into question by the wider assertion that the Wehrmacht committed crimes. This is perhaps experienced as especially hurtful in the context of the grief for those who are not in a position to account for their own experiences.

In other words, there seems to be a tension between larger statements on the war and some personal experiences as expressed in a variety of contexts, including political debate and literature.[202] This tension is also reflected in the unbridgeable gulf between Walser, who insists on his right to select his main character and stick to this character's potentially myopic vision of events, and his critics' assertion that this is tantamount to a suppression of the context of National Socialism. Walser's insistence on *Perspektivität* illustrates the problem: it is always possible to reject historical insights as not relevant because they are not what the character could have known or, in Dregger's case, not what he thinks he experienced. Dregger simply does not consider Wehrmacht atrocities relevant to his experiences, although in something of a contradiction he finds them dangerous, inasmuch as they might undermine the honour of the soldiers he served with. Walser's case is more complicated, in that he questions

---

[200] Deutscher Bundestag, *Plenarprotokoll*, 13/163, 13/03/97, 14710–14712.

[201] 'Es war Krieg, ich habe nichts zu verarbeiten', in: Prantl, *Wehrmachtsverbrechen*, p. 276.

[202] Some veterans of course confirm the crimes represented in the Wehrmacht exhibition. See, for example, Johannes Gründel, 'Der Krieg und die Schuld', in: Prantl, *Wehrmachtsverbrechen*, p. 149.

the epistemological status of his own memories; but, in the end, he too insists on telling it as he thinks it was.

Thus if there is concern about the appropriateness or political implications of such recollections of the past, it is necessary to acknowledge that apparently knowing about the context within which their memories are situated has not affected people like Dregger and Walser in the way in which one might have hoped it would.[203] So what *did* affect Dregger? Dregger was moved by other personal experiences and the emotions they aroused rather than by the conclusions of rigorous historical research. Schily is implacably opposed to Dregger's interpretation of the past, but Schily was repeatedly so overcome by emotion that he was unable to continue speaking.[204] Although Schily's brother, whom he portrayed as strongly opposed to National Socialism, was in the Wehrmacht, he fundamentally rejected the idea that Wehrmacht soldiers had fought in a good cause inasmuch as they had defended their fatherland. On the contrary, in Schily's narrative of his family only a partisan who fought against the Germans is depicted as having had a just cause. Schily clearly considers Wehrmacht soldiers such as his brother to have been involved in an unjustifiable enterprise; this crucially does not mean, however, that he callously dismisses their deaths. He is as emotionally involved as Dregger, and it was perhaps realising this that allowed Dregger to acknowledge Schily's intervention as something that could not be easily dismissed.

Despite their different understanding of events, both Dregger and Schily are emotionally involved: they grieve. Although Schily, born in 1932, is younger than Dregger by the margin that ruled him out from military service, they both have recollections of their own. It is sometimes taken for granted that those born after the war have a different relationship to this past, but Duve noted: 'This war haunts all of us – those who experienced it as soldiers or children and those who were born after its end.'[205] Dregger's worry that the exhibition on Wehrmacht crimes 'confuses the generation of sons and grandsons'[206] points to the belief that they are more removed from the events. Indeed, Nickels, a 'daughter' in this scheme, approaches the topic differently, but still within the context of personal experience and family history. She acknowledges the profoundly difficult situation that those who lived through the war were faced with and their continuing pain and distress, but also how younger Germans have been affected.[207] Her focus on these emotional aspects does not

---

[203] The question as to how later knowledge affects memories of earlier experiences is discussed in Chapter 5, p. 201.
[204] Deutscher Bundestag, *Plenarprotokoll*, 13/163, 13/03/97, 14714.
[205] Ibid., 14718.   [206] Ibid., 14712.   [207] Ibid., 14719f.

mean that she is willing to justify the Wehrmacht soldiers' behaviour. She explicitly rejects the exculpatory attitude that Dregger is accused of.

Whatever the outcome of the debate, the topic is of emotional significance not only to those who lived through the war. I have noted that literature may be seen as enabling us to feel or appreciate some of the emotion of the situations it depicts. Fiction does not merely tell a story: it affects us. Thus the point is not that literature is 'truer', but that it may put us into a different relationship with the events it depicts. The problem of the past is not merely a matter of what we know. In the Bundestag debate on the Wehrmacht exhibition those speakers who were able to move each other spoke not simply of events of the past but also showed how they themselves were affected. Of course, being emotionally involved does not lead to any particular political position, nor is it necessarily progressive – Dregger seems to have used his grief to justify his unwillingness to acknowledge the Wehrmacht's involvement in atrocities.

Interestingly, however, all speakers shared a deep-seated conviction that it was necessary to grasp the past, even if that was impossible. This might be attributed to their personal involvement. But why did they reveal their feelings in a political debate? Why did they consider not only the 'correct' memory of the Wehrmacht's war but also their emotions relevant to the present? Richard Kearney stresses the notion of 'narrative truth' where it comes to matters of historical trauma.[208] Yet the question of 'truth' or authenticity in war narratives gives rise to a paradox. As discussed in Chapter 3, despite the problems of seeking truth through fiction Sebald speaks of the necessity of 'an artificial view', as eyewitnesses would have been impaired in their capacity to think and feel.[209] Fictional representation is, or so the argument goes, both tied by the truth and necessary to telling the truth in the first place. Kearney further argues that '[e]very narrative bears some evaluative charge regarding the events narrated'.[210] In other words, the issue is not just that events might be fundamentally unrepresentable or that meaning is imposed on the events, but that doing so invariably entails a judgement. Dregger is worried about the condemnation of ordinary soldiers that he sees as involved in the story of Wehrmacht atrocities, Schily about the positive evaluation entailed by Dregger's representation. Hence both are concerned not merely with the truth but with the 'evaluative charge'.

Thus, as was already clear in Chapters 2 and 3, portrayals of German war experiences immediately raise not just questions about the truth but also questions about their status in ethical terms. Ledig's work

---

[208] Richard Kearney, *On Stories* (London: Routledge 2002), p. 47.
[209] Sebald, *Luftkrieg und Literatur*, p. 33.   [210] Kearney, *On Stories*, p. 155.

was apparently rediscovered in the context of Sebald's lecture series about the failure of German literature to deal with strategic bombing. As shown in Chapter 3, Sebald presumed in those lectures that he could judge the appropriateness of representations of war. This claim is in tension with any notion of poetic licence and also threatens literature's ability to function as counter-memory. So far I have represented this concern chiefly in terms of an impossible concern about the truth. There is, however, also an interesting blurring of concerns about truth into concerns about ethics. Walser's musings on the past as present render problematic the question of what might be considered a truthful representation of the Second World War, but Walser's apparent target is *judgements* made about such representations. Walser seems to be exercised chiefly by what he sees as the Left's desire to ensure that German memories of the Third Reich are appropriately related to the Holocaust. Sebald's intervention, which Walser incidentally rejected as 'absurd',[211] seems to suffer from the same problems: it judges representations of the past not merely in the context of the (anyway) tenuous notion of the truth but also in terms of their appropriateness. This entails an ethical evaluation. Walser seems concerned to question the benefits of judging representations of the past as to their ethical value. As discussed earlier, Walser is worried about the increasing standardisation of how we deal with the past. He rejects the notion of a 'past which is completely reconstructed [*erschlossen*], investigated, sanitised, sanctioned, totally fit for the present. Ethically and politically corrected through and through.'[212] He argues that we must confront the issue that the past may have been such that we do not find it acceptable now, and that we may never represent it without already introducing the present. He asks whether there is 'more past or more present in being over'.[213] What we may know about the 'truth' of the past is not only never quite the truth about the past, it is also not separate from ethics.

Objections against representations of the Second World War often concern ethical considerations rather than simply questions of the truth. Thus Ledig's depiction of the Eastern front is not seen as incorrect. It is not the facticity of the account that is disputed but its contextualisation, or rather, as the critics would have it, the lack thereof. May the hardships German soldiers experienced at the front be narrated without giving the whole context of the atrocities committed in the name of the Third Reich? The concern about the exclusion of the political context, although sometimes presented as one about 'the full truth', is about how Germans *should* remember. Thus the issue appears to be one of the ethics – and indeed

---

[211] Walser, 'Bombenkrieg', p. 130.
[212] Walser, *Ein springender Brunnen*, p. 282.   [213] Ibid., p. 15.

politics – of recalling the past in a particular way. This is where Walser's worry about an ethically corrected memory comes in. Yet the implications of his intervention are not straightforward, as he does not promote simply the right to speak out about how things were whether or not it fits in with approved notions of an ethical attitude towards the past, for Walser rejects the notion that there is a true memory which we could recover: he argues for his right to represent his memory – which he at the same time points out does not and cannot appeal to an unchanging truth that we might seek to recover.[214] The worry about ethics, about what should be remembered or how the past should be represented, seems to acknowledge that the problem, whatever it may be, cannot be solved with reference to the truth. This might be either because, for a range of reasons which have already been discussed, the truth is impossible to recall or represent, or because – and this is important – the truth does not hold the answer, or of course both. In other words, what is at issue is not simply whether representations or recollections are true to the events of the Second World War, but the question of how Germans should now relate to those events. This is a question that calls on a variety of ethico-political contexts, such as the legitimate concerns of the victims of the Third Reich and the fear of a re-emergence of rightwing politics, matters that have already been raised in the context of Grass's representation of Konrad in *Im Krebsgang* and the sixtieth anniversary commemorations of the destruction of Dresden, for example. There is a struggle to acknowledge and mourn the German victims without denying the ethical imperative that comes from an obligation towards those the Germans killed and tortured. Yet, as noted in Chapters 2 and 3, other political contexts may be relevant when recalling this past.

Representing war: the other political context

Germans are often considered to be biased against war; the 'never again war' principle is seen as the political expression of this attitude. This negative view of war arguably goes back to the immediate postwar years. Re-education in the Western sectors had been based on the shared responsibility of all Germans for Nazism and its crimes, and on the desire to ensure that the Germans would 'never again' wage war.[215] As Kettenacker points out:

---

[214] Note that this seems to be in tension with the simplistic political views in the context of which his work is often read.

[215] Susan L. Carruthers, 'Compulsory Viewing: Concentration Camp Film and German Re-education', *Millennium: Journal of International Studies* 3 (2001), 735.

Those who today complain about the lack of a will to wage war should be reminded that the stated key aim of the Allied re-education policy consisted precisely in curing the Germans once and for all of the supposed inclination to waging war: they were to learn that war was not a profitable undertaking. This policy was successful beyond all expectation, because, owing to the experiences of war, there was actually no need for further re-education.[216]

In other words, this aspect of re-education was a resounding success: the Germans were to learn that 'war' was bad, and apparently they did. Two points are important, however. Firstly, the Germans seem nevertheless to have been able to overcome this: their armed forces have taken part in a range of international military operations. It is significant to ask how such profound change was possible in a relatively short amount of time.[217] Secondly, the relative ease with which Germans have, despite their remaining aversion to war, returned to the use of force raises the question of whether war ever was as discredited as it appeared.

Kinkel's reframing of the Second World War presented the Allied war as something that had been good, that had allowed the Germans to be freed from tyranny and make a new start in a democratic context. In other words, whilst some wars are bad, and Germany's Second World War is a case in point, there *are* wars that are good. This is not entirely surprising. Although in 1946 Schmid had proclaimed that the Germans never again wanted anything to do with war and that if 'this insanity of war should break out, and if fate should want it that [their] land becomes a battle-field, then [they] shall simply perish and at least take with [them] the knowledge that [they] neither encouraged nor committed the crime',[218] there are indications that the Germans have never rejected war altogether. First of all, the establishment of the Bundeswehr already indicates that, although the Germans might have preferred to have nothing more to do with war, they were planning for the eventuality of war wanting something to do with them. Put differently, from 1955 on the Germans were sending their sons to the barracks again, even if they were intending, if at all possible, not to use their troops.[219] What is perhaps less obvious is that the myth of the 'clean' Wehrmacht also suggests that war is not rejected quite as unconditionally as one might think. The reason soldiers are seen to have been honourable is that they courageously defend their fatherland. This implies that such defence is good. There are therefore certain wars that are permissible. Thus, although it may have appeared

---

[216] Kettenacker, 'Vorwort des Herausgebers', p. 13.
[217] This change is traced in Zehfuss, *Constructivism*.
[218] Carlo Schmid, *Erinnerungen* (Bern 1979), p. 490, quoted in Abenheim, *Reforging the Iron Cross*, p. 43.
[219] See Bald, *Militär und Gesellschaft*, p. 91.

that the Germans rejected all wars for the suffering they cause, this was not the case. It is useful to recall that sometimes German participation in wars was rejected, but that these wars were otherwise held to be acceptable. Thus the German rejection of war turns out to be conditional. It is a rejection of the wrong kind of war only. Because throughout the Cold War the 'wrong kind of war' could apparently be equated with 'German war', there was an illusion of a complete rejection of war.

It may have appeared that peace was valued over war, as the Bundeswehr was not to be used and there was a strong aversion against war. That, however, was not the case, as has just been shown; rather, the Germans' Second World War was retrospectively re-evaluated. The Germans' war was no longer valued over that of their enemies. The soldiers' role that had been seen in terms of an honourable defence of the fatherland came to be seen as indirect support of and, in some cases, direct involvement with Nazi crimes. This message was reinforced by critical examinations of the role of the Wehrmacht itself, such as the historical work by Bartov and others[220] and, more recently, the exhibition on Wehrmacht crimes. Thus it was the relationship between the Germans' war and the enemies' war that was overturned: the Allies' war was good, that of the Germans bad.

Derrida explores how oppositions between such terms as male/female or nature/nurture – what he calls dichotomies – structure our thinking. Though both terms may appear to be on an equal footing, each pair is actually dominated by the first term. Although 'German war' versus 'Allied war' does not seem to be a proper dichotomy – it is obviously possible to be neither one nor the other – the understanding of war promoted by the logic of re-education and later (West) German self-representation involved something akin to what Derrida calls an overturning.[221] Thinking this through clarifies why the Germans' alleged aversion to war is not quite what it seems. The Germans had of course supported 'their' war. Yet the Germans' war was associated with an ideology that is now recognised as nothing short of evil and with unspeakable crimes committed in the name of Germany. Thus this 'normal' view of the world came to be under threat. The Allied war, in contrast, could retrospectively be associated with the constitution of the FRG. Thus, from a contemporary

---

[220] Omer Bartov, *Hitler's Army: Soldiers, Nazis, and the War in the Third Reich* (Oxford: Oxford University Press 1992); Bartov, *Germany's War*; Bartov, *The Eastern Front 1941–45: German Troops and the Barbarisation of Warfare*, 2nd edn (Basingstoke: Palgrave 2001); Christian Streit, *Keine Kameraden: Die Wehrmacht und die sowjetischen Kriegsgefangenen 1941–1945* (Stuttgart: Deutsche Verlags-Anstalt 1980).

[221] Derrida, *Positions*, p. 41. On overturning, see also Chapter 1, pp. 22–3.

German perspective, the enemies' war suddenly turns out to have been better than the war that had previously been valued by the Germans.

In other words, the 'normal' hierarchy came to be overturned. Yet this leaves in place the structure of the system which supports thinking in terms of the possibility of classifying wars as either good or bad. This is important, because we are dealing here not merely with the recognition that the German war had been 'bad', in terms both of cause and of conduct, but also with the corollary that the Allied war had been 'good', certainly in terms of outcome. This securing of the goodness of the Allied war against the background of the bad German war was central to Kinkel's reinterpretation, and this is addressed further in Chapter 6. Crucially, the possibility of a good war remained wide open, was in fact underlined. If war were to be rejected fundamentally, it would be necessary, in a second step, to achieve a displacement to begin thinking in terms of a concept that is not part of the previous system of thought.[222] An overturning, like the one achieved by re-education and *Vergangenheitsbewältigung*, is, on its own, not enough: it remains within the system. Thus, contrary to appearances, war was not fully delegitimised in the FRG. After the end of the Cold War, the argument that military activity which NATO allies approved of was good and hence required of the Germans[223] was able to slot into the system of thought that remained in place and led to an acceptance by the German government and increasingly also the public of the necessity and ethical value of participation in missions such as Operation Allied Force (in Kosovo in 1999). Despite attempts, at least at first, to construe Bundeswehr missions as 'not war',[224] this ultimately meant that the 'never again war' principle was eroded and reinterpreted. The overturning effected through re-education and later self-conceptions of the FRG had not intervened in the discourse to such an extent as to fundamentally change thinking about the use of force.

Value may still confidently be assigned to particular wars, as if they were circumscribable entities, as if they could be simply categorised as 'good' or 'bad'. Kinkel's analogy between Bundeswehr and Allied liberators was so appealing because the Allied war was recognised as good – the war that 'brought' democracy. The adverse consequences of this war have, as shown in Chapters 2 and 3, often been blanked out. Bringing these back in therefore makes a difference. This is where representations of war in novels can be useful. In the context of *Die Stalinorgel*, it is interesting

---

[222] See Derrida, *Positions*, pp. 42f.   [223] Zehfuss, *Constructivism*, esp. Chapter 2.
[224] Instead they were referred to as 'peace-making measures', 'coping with a crisis situation', the 'last resort', or even 'energetic prevention'. See 'Einsatz ins Ungewisse', *Der Spiegel*, 30/01/95, 71.

to think through how such a close-up encounter with the mayhem of battle affects us. It might disturb me to think that some ancestor of mine did not die a painless death as a result of a shot in the chest but might instead have been blown up alive or chopped up by machine-gun fire; but what is almost certainly going to confuse me about the FRG's military involvement abroad is the idea that this is what soldiers would be doing to others in my name. In other words, the supposedly politically lacking portrayal of war as a mess, both physical and moral – for example in *Die Stalinorgel* – works to undermine the possibility of instrumentalising the Second World War in order to present us with an abstract and supposedly ethical choice about war today.[225]

Because thinking about war after 1945 involved an overturning but no displacement, it was possible for the hierarchy to flip back into place, and for the Germans again to take up the practice of war. For some, of course, the overturning had not had any effect in the first place, as became clear in the debate surrounding Wehrmacht atrocities. Engaging with a multiplicity of memories may help to undermine the clear but simplistic distinctions that make it possible to value war as straightforwardly good. However, neither may we simply champion proper German remembering as a panacea to the difficult issues that arise in the context of war. Whilst such memories are useful to prevent abstracting from people's experiences and the trivial categorising that follows, memories may be deployed or even manipulated for particular political purposes. One important concern is the worry that dwelling on memories of war, with the suffering they recall, represents Germans as victims and thus provides the basis for a revisionism that seeks to dispose of German guilt.

Yet what is important is that the confrontation with concrete war memories, far from necessarily leading to a moral relativism that counts German bodies as against those killed by Germans, may help us to leave behind a system of thought that turns decisions about war into a choice between black and white, good war and bad war, and instead to recognise the complexity and uncertainty of the situation that calls for a responsible decision. This is crucial, for in the post-Cold War and certainly in the post-September 11 world it has increasingly become necessary to address the question of war. This question is not an easy one; it requires decisions about life and death. Decisions are necessary in this context precisely because things are rather less clear than the superficial

---

[225] One could imagine media other than literature achieving such a disturbance. However, given the often 'clean' representation of war on television today and complaints that 'live reporting breeds indifference', literature might be more important than it would at first appear. Bartov, *Germany's War*, p. 57. For a critique of visual representations of war, see also Susan Sontag, *Regarding the Pain of Others* (London: Penguin Books 2004).

categorisations suggest. Such a problem calls, according to Derrida, for responsibility:

> I will even venture to say that ethics, politics, and responsibility, *if there are any*, will only ever have begun with the experience and experiment of aporia. When the path is clear and given, when a certain knowledge opens up the way in advance, the decision is already made, it might as well be said that there is none to make: irresponsibly, and in good conscience, one simply applies or implements a program . . . The condition of possibility of this thing called responsibility is a certain *experience and experiment of the possibility of the impossible: the testing of the aporia* from which one may invent the only *possible invention, the impossible invention.*[226]

Thus thinking in detail about war, which is what those who have to make the choice undoubtedly do, reveals the condition of uncertainty within which choices have to be made. Literature is significant, because it provides one way of undermining the black-and-white categories which allow opposing the Allied war of liberation to the German war of expansion and extermination. It may remind us that, as Bucheli says of Grass's representations of the Second World War, 'you were perpetrator and victim in one'.[227] Ledig's *Die Stalinorgel* equally undermines neat distinctions between 'good' and 'bad' war, between perpetrators and victims. What is interesting is more generally that novels destabilise the unity of the signifier 'war'. Ledig's depiction of the battle over a hill close to Leningrad may support the notion that war is bad as such, in that war is represented as a senseless hell, but by linking this judgement to the specificity of the particular battle it works against the overturning we see in current politics. There is no 'good war' that could be opposed to what Ledig portrays: both sides to the war are inextricably linked through the mayhem and misery that the soldiers are exposed to.

Concluding thoughts

Two large themes emerge from the discussion in this chapter: firstly, the problematic status of truth and indeed its inadequacy in terms of addressing the questions that arise; and, secondly, the role of emotions. The chapter considered the debate surrounding the exhibition on Wehrmacht atrocities which, at least at first sight, appears to revolve around the question of the truth about the involvement of the Wehrmacht in crimes committed by the Third Reich. It also observed the related criticism that

---

[226] See, for example, Jacques Derrida, *The Other Heading: Reflections on Today's Europe*, Translated by Pascale-Anne Brault and Michael B. Naas (Bloomington: Indiana University Press 1992), p. 41.
[227] Bucheli, 'Die verspätete Erinnerung'. On a similar point, see also Jenny Edkins, 'Authenticity and Memory at Dachau', *Cultural Values* 5 (2001), 418.

German war novels exclude the political context and in particular the issue of Wehrmacht atrocities and therefore are complicit in the production and maintenance of the myth of the 'clean' Wehrmacht. The chapter questioned, however, what precisely this standard of truth-telling, which the novels are seen to fall short of, is based on. Through readings of the two novels the chapter made problematic the idea of telling the truth about the past, in particular because authenticity was revealed as *produced*. Specific, subjective experiences could be produced as authentic only as part of the production of a wider, 'objective' – and hence artificial – context. There was tension between the authenticity of a particular experience and the supposedly larger truth within which it ought to be contextualised. The Wehrmacht debate, as well as Walser's disagreement with his critics, could be read as a struggle over which of these is more important or 'truer': the personal, singular experience that is so keenly remembered or the wider context, involving Wehrmacht crimes and the system of National Socialism.

Against the thrust of this struggle my argument focused on the irresolvability of this tension. The so-called truth was shown to require its supposed opposite – fiction. Walser's reflections on the 'Past as Present' underlined the impossibility of recalling the past as it was. His thoughts on memory clearly demonstrated the futility of trying to go back to the past or expecting to be able to represent the past as it was. And yet, in a strangely contradictory move, Walser offers a richly realistic description of Johann's life, tempting readers to believe that they are being granted access to the past as it was when it was the present. One way of understanding this apparent paradox might be to see Walser as exposed to a tension: whilst he has rationally worked out the impossibility of going back to the past, this past – as it appeared to him at the time – is nevertheless important to him. In this spirit, we might understand *Ein springender Brunnen* as saying: 'What I am telling you is probably not true, but it is incredibly important to me.' In other words, the paradox of what Walser is doing – which he himself highlights – could be read as drawing attention to the necessity and inevitability of what nevertheless remains quite impossible: recalling the past.

Walser seems to offer his memory as something that disturbs politically correct versions of the past. In the Bundestag debate on Wehrmacht atrocities there were similar struggles over how to recall the past. Here what was most obvious was that this past affected the speakers emotionally. Whilst they were concerned about the truth of this past, Schily and Nickels in particular highlighted not what they know but how they feel about it. This, intriguingly, made possible a modicum of communication with Dregger, who claims to know something different about this past.

They all showed that they were deeply affected, that they mourned for lives that had been wasted and destroyed. Dregger's worry was about what he believed to be a lack of appreciation of the fate of ordinary soldiers, but he did not argue for more historical information. What he seemed to miss in others was rather his own emotional involvement. This raises the question of how the emotional would be part of the authentic, if it were possible. The violent argument over the Wehrmacht exhibition shows that the wider public also had feelings of one sort or another with respect to this past, but it also indicates that, whilst it is important not to deny the significance of emotions, they do not provide answers. In the case at hand, they seem instead to highlight the exasperation of being unable to find agreed and fruitful ways of dealing with the past.

Apart from a personal attachment to what one believes to know about the past, the issue was considered to be so profoundly significant because this particular past is seen as relevant to political choices today. Concerns were raised over the implications for the Bundeswehr of revealing Wehrmacht crimes, for example. What is more, the experience of the Third Reich is often deployed to answer ethico-political questions in the present. Chancellor Kohl indeed wanted to use the past as a 'compass' for the future.[228] Derrida's discussion of testimony as well as Emig's exploration of the implications of authenticity show that there are profound problems associated with the idea of remembering, of knowing about the past. The most obvious outcome of this reasoning is that any argument based on establishing what we should do on the basis of past experiences, such as we have seen in debates about Bundeswehr deployments, is problematic. The 'compass' or 'lessons' sometimes seen to be offered by the past turn out to be profoundly insecure. Walser's reflections on the past and the present add to this, for they fundamentally undermine the idea of the past as a repository of unchanging experiences from which we can draw lessons for the present. If we cannot know the past, if indeed the past changes with the present as Walser suggests, the compass is not an objective, outside tool that simply shows us the way.

It is instead, as I have argued, necessary to make decisions. The truth cannot be established, nor would it solve ethico-political questions such as how to remember or whether to use military force even if it could be established. What is important, however, is an awareness of the implications of the decision, and the failure of knowledge to determine its outcome. Significantly, the debates are not just about the past but also about political choices in the present. Literature may sometimes, by depicting issues in an unexpected or even objectionable way, produce a hesitation that

---

[228] Deutscher Bundestag, *Plenarprotokoll*, 04/10/90, 11/228, 18019.

arrests the automatism with which claims to knowledge are produced as solutions to ethical problems. The claim to remember is, as we have seen, often deployed in political debate as part of such automatism. At the same time, memory – because of its uncertainty – is always at risk of undermining its own power, producing the interruption necessary to confront the ethical. Examining memories and in particular their literary representations throws doubt on our ability to know for sure either what was or what we should do. Chapter 2 noted Derrida's argument that ethico-political questions are marked by a failure of knowledge, on its own, to be able to provide answers, and this apparently seems to be the case here. Such questions require instead a decision which cannot be determined simply by knowledge. They require the performance of responsibility, and responsibility cannot rely on knowledge. As previously noted, Derrida argues that 'it is necessary to know the most and the best possible, but between the widest, the most refined, the most necessary knowledge, and the responsible decision, an abyss remains, and must remain'.[229] What we know cannot, in a situation that requires responsibility, tell us what we should do; such situations are characterised precisely by competing ethical demands which cannot all be satisfied at the same time. Yet the point is not to issue some idealistic call for ethics, for making decisions rather than deploying knowledge. It is to reveal that we already do, all the time. The participants in the Wehrmacht debate made ethico-political judgements, as did Sebald when he judged the truthfulness of representations of the war. Crucially, so do those who claim that the 'lesson' of the past is that the FRG must now contribute to international military operations. What is at issue, then, is to highlight the way that the claim that policy choices rest on knowledge about the past obscures the fact that *decisions* are being made. It is not in the end about the truth of the past, but about the present and the future as a space for ethics.

---

[229] Jacques Derrida, *On Cosmopolitanism and Forgiveness*, Translated by Mark Dooley and Michael Hughes (London: Routledge 2001), p. 54.

5   Times of memory

Debates about political performances of memory and rituals of commemoration largely focus on what they construe as 'the past' and our present attitude to it: How, if at all, should Germans remember the Allied bombing of cities during the Second World War? What are the implications of particular versions of memory for the political present? How may 'the Germans' adequately imagine their own identity through such memories? Other difficult questions, for example, about truth, ethics and emotion, have been raised in the preceding chapters by exploring memories of the Second World War as they are articulated in novels. So far the argument has, however, bypassed any consideration of one of the most intriguing – and in some senses most obvious – aspects of memory: the question of temporality. Walser's assertion that we may not remember the past as it was when it was the present draws attention to this. That memories change over time is, of course, neither a surprisingly new nor a particularly controversial insight. Yet thinking through what this means for conceptions not only of memory but of temporality itself produces challenges to what appear to be deeply held assumptions. Memories disturb our conception of temporality, and this is crucial, because temporality is implicated in what we perceive to be ethical.

The present chapter starts by briefly considering memory and temporality, highlighting not only how uneasily memory seems to sit in the non-space between past and present but also how both modern physics and our experience pose challenges to a linear understanding of time. It explores Johnson's *Jahrestage*, in which I read the problematic of time as central. In *Jahrestage* different layers of time are inextricably linked but, crucially, it is not always clear where events and understandings fit into the overall chronology. This turns out not to be altogether different from problems that arise with respect to locating historical events on a timeline. Chapter 2 considered some of the debate over whether Germany was liberated by the Allies in the Second World War. Here, this issue is taken up from a different perspective by asking not *whether* Germany was liberated but *when*, a question that ultimately cannot be resolved. Linear temporality turns out to be unsatisfactory. The chapter also discusses Vonnegut's *Slaughterhouse 5*, which invents a non-linear notion of time in which the past continues to exist after, on a linear understanding, it is over.

Memory and temporality: between past and present?

Aleida Assmann highlights the fact that remembering works in a reconstructive way, that is, 'it always starts from the present and because of that there is inevitably a displacement, distortion [*Verformung*], misrepresentation [*Entstellung*], re-evaluation, renewal of what is remembered at the point in time when it is recalled'.[1] Thus there is, on the one hand, a temporal differentiation between when what is remembered took place – in the past – and when it is recalled – in the present, and yet, crucially, on the other hand, the present enters into memory at the point of recall. Thus memory, whilst 'about' the past, is inextricably linked to the present. The relevance of the present to memory is borne out by Alistair Thomson's fascinating study *Anzac Memories: Living with the Legend*. Thomson shows through a detailed analysis of interviews with former soldiers at different periods in time that 'our remembering changes in relation to shifts in the particular publics in which we live, and as the general public field of representations alters'.[2] Thomson is concerned with how personal memories are always situated within, and therefore affected by, larger public discourses. As these change so do personal memories. There is a temporal aspect to this argument: what people recall and tell about the past changes over time. Although the object of memory – in Thomson's case, the experiences of working-class Australian soldiers in the Second World War – is in the past, every time it is recalled, it is reconstructed in relation to the present. Thus memory is not *merely* about the past. Thomson notes rather that '[w]e compose our memories to make sense of our past *and* present lives'.[3] In other words, he draws attention to how memories are also about the present, inasmuch as they are a part of how we understand the present and ourselves in it. This is, of course, the apparent concern of work on memory that sees it as integral to productions of identity. The always ongoing debates in Germany about memories of the Third Reich similarly take it as a given that they are inextricably related to German

---

[1] Assmann, *Erinnerungsräume*, p. 29.
[2] Thomson, *Anzac Memories*, p. 9 quoting Graham Dawson and Bob West, '"Our Finest Hour"? The Popular Memory of World War Two and Struggles over National Identity', in: Geoff Hurd (ed.), *National Fictions: World War Two in British Film and Television* (London: BFI Publishing 1984), pp. 10–11.
[3] Ibid., p. 8 (italics added).

identity. This was evident, for example, in the *Historikerstreit*. In such an understanding, although the past constitutes the basis for memory, the focus is on the present. As Andreas Huyssen puts it:

The temporal status of any act of memory is always the present and not, as some naive epistemology might have it, the past itself, even though all memory in some ineradicable sense is dependent on some past event or experience. It is this tenuous fissure between past and present that constitutes memory, making it powerfully alive and distinct from the archive or any other mere system of storage and retrieval.[4]

Huyssen affirms the distinctness of past and present through the idea of a 'fissure'; the present plays a significant role, because memory itself occurs in the present. Far from retrieving an unchangeable past (as it has already and 'really' happened), memory is enacted in the present and is therefore marked by it. Huyssen's conception of memory thus seems to be presentist.

This impact of the present on memory raises serious questions. In Huyssen's conceptualisation, for example, a 'fissure' between past and present is asserted, but this fissure is at the same time seen as 'tenuous'. That past and present are thought of as separate but then conceptualised as inextricably related is also an intriguing aspect of Walser's reflections on the 'Past as Present'. Memory is not a form of mental time-travel: it does not allow us to go back to the past as it was. Walser observes that '[a]s long as something is, it is not what it will have been. When something is over, one is no longer the one to whom it happened . . . Although the past, when it was the present, did not exist, it now imposes itself as if it had existed in the way in which it imposes itself now.'[5] Thus the past does not exist before it is over; whatever may have existed when it was the present is not what is seen from the perspective of the present as the past. The present necessarily enters into any memory; it affects the past that is recalled. Again, 'the past' and 'the present' appear as distinct entities which are, however, inseparable, in that the present necessarily affects the past. Walser further reflects that '[w]e survive not as those who we were but as those *who we have become* after we have been. When it is over. *For it is still, even if* [it is] *over*. Now, is there more past or more present in being over?'[6] In *Das steinerne Brautbett* Mulisch similarly writes that 'we do not know any more how it was because we ourselves have changed and we would have to travel back to find out, but then again we would not be here and would not have changed'.[7] These thoughts highlight the

---

[4] Huyssen, *Twilight Memories*, p. 3.   [5] Walser, *Ein springender Brunnen*, p. 9.
[6] Ibid., p. 15 (italics added).   [7] Mulisch, *Brautbett*, p. 45.

fact that the question of temporality is more complex than is admitted by simply acknowledging that memory takes place in the present.

Although Walser speaks of 'the past' and 'the present' without questioning these concepts directly, two points are important. Firstly, the past, he says, imposes itself in a particular way in the present, but did not exist in this way when it is thought to have been the present. In other words, the past changes, or rather becomes available as 'the past' only retrospectively. Secondly, we are in Walser's reflections confronted with the undecidability of pastness and presentness. There can be no memory that is not affected by the present: we remember as who we are. At the same time, this present is affected by the past that we remember, firstly, because we *remember* and, secondly, because we remember as *who we have become*. This becoming is always influenced by 'the past' to which we are unable to return because we may remember only as who we have become. And yet, though we may not return to it, Walser claims the past still 'is', even if it never existed in this way in the first place. Following this aspect of undecidability in Walser's thoughts, conceptualising memory as in the present but about the past creates problems. In such a view, the past happens *before* the present, whilst memory is situated firmly *within* the present. Memories change precisely because they 'are' in the present; the past, however, remains the same. Walser's reflections raise doubts as to whether such a clear distinction between the past and the present is ever possible; the 'fissure' between past and present turns out to be more tenuous than Huyssen seems to acknowledge.

Unfortunately, Walser not only remains stuck in a terminology that seemingly accepts 'the past' and 'the present' as separate entities, but his thoughts on this matter also remain in the abstract. Indeed, in a performative contradiction, Walser, in the chapters that tell the story of Johann in *Ein springender Brunnen*, tempts us back into a world where the past seems unproblematically real and our present has not left any trace. Walser is criticised precisely for this, for not taking account of information acquired since the period of time in which the novel is set.[8] The Wasserburg of his youth thus appears hermetically sealed against later insights into the Nazi regime, for example through historical research. Present understandings appear to have had no influence, or so the criticism goes, on how Walser represents this past. This alleged lack of *Vergangenheitsbewältigung* (coming to terms with the past) sits nicely with the rightist political convictions of which he is accused, an issue noted in Chapter 4.

However, one might wonder why Walser would have included his reflections on the 'Past as Present' at all if the aim had been to delude the reader

---

[8] Steinfeld, 'Der Wanderfotograf'.

into the possibility of going back to the past, of rescuing the past from later knowledge, of forgetting the present. Even if Walser has in effect excluded his insights after the fact in favour of the perspective of the boy growing up at the time, this does not mean that the readers' present remains excluded. Indeed, one might argue that Walser relies precisely on the readers' present inevitably entering into any reading: he need not explicitly include *his* insights on the Third Reich because he expects readers to remember as who they have become, that is, amongst other things, as knowledgeable about the crimes of the Third Reich. Indeed, his reflections on memory might be seen to prompt the reader to recognise that such intrusions of present knowledge into the past are inevitable. Walser does not bother to clarify, for example, that Johann is wrong about the SS not possibly having simply shot prisoners; perhaps this is not because he seeks to exclude unpalatable events but because he expects us to know. One might argue that his faith in our knowledge is not enough, that the problematic of the Third Reich requires a more direct working-through, but it is worth considering that Walser's exclusion, even if intentional, even if motivated by rightist political convictions as some argue, can never be complete. Thus the critics' contention that Walser is in the business of sealing off the past against the present is interesting not so much for what it tells us about *Ein springender Brunnen* but for what appears to be an underlying assumption that this is possible, that the past has already happened and is therefore clearly distinct from the present. In other words, it is the critics' understanding of temporality that makes possible the idea of this sealing-off in the first place. Walser's reflections on memory with the implication of undecidability may be read to hint that this is problematic.

More generally, memory can be seen to subvert a neat distinction between past and present, and to introduce an element of undecidability between them, something that will become clearer in relation to Johnson's *Jahrestage*. Tachibana observes that Johnson 'removes the illusion that the past is a separate entity, apart from the present'.[9] Crucially, such undecidability should not arise within an understanding of temporality that sees the past as happening before the present. Although memories are conceptualised as being 'about' something that is considered past and therefore separate from the present, they are seen as intrinsically linked to the present. Therefore they change over time. This captures a profoundly interesting aspect of memory, but is an uncomfortable way of rendering not only memory but also temporality. Such conceptualisations – implicitly or explicitly – rely on distinguishing the past from the present; memory

---

[9] Tachibana, *Narrative as Counter-Memory*, p. 196.

then intriguingly occupies a bridging function. It is, in a sense, neither here nor there. This can be seen as a challenge not to memory and how we relate to it but to how we conceptualise the temporality within which memory is rendered. In other words, memory – with its ability to pierce the present with 'ghosts' from the past and, perhaps more importantly, with its effect on the past – seems to challenge our conception of time.

In his popular *A Brief History of Time*, Stephen Hawking seeks to explain the big questions of physics to ordinary readers; he does so in the context of the question of time. Hawking notes that:

Both Aristotle and Newton believed in absolute time. That is, they believed that one could unambiguously measure the interval of time between two events, and that this interval would be the same whoever measured it, provided they used a good clock. Time was completely separate from and independent of space. This is what most people take to be the commonsense view.[10]

In physics, such a view is outdated. As Hawking explains, the 'theory of relativity gets rid of absolute time'.[11] Yet, G.J. Whitrow observes, 'the idea that time is a kind of linear progression measured by the clock and calendar' in modern civilisation 'so dominates our lives that it seems to be an inescapable necessity of thought'.[12] This conception of time is often represented as an arrow on which different points in time – t1, t2 and so on – are marked. In this understanding, we may clearly tell whether t1 occurred before t2, and we can measure distances in time between t1 and t2. Crucially, if t1 occurred before t2, it is impossible to go 'back' from t2 to t1. This conception of time seems ingrained in our thinking. Clocks tell us what this 'physical' time is, and we are powerless to speed it up, slow it down or reverse it. It just is.

Thus we seem to carry on believing in time as something that exists 'out there', characterised by linearity, even though modern physics conceptualises time in more complex ways. It is important to note the caveats that physicists such as Hawking introduce. First of all, as Hawking notes, 'the concept of time has no meaning before the beginning of the universe'.[13] In other words, 'time' has a beginning; it does not just exist transhistorically. Secondly, modern physics does not operate on the basis of a notion of time that might be seen as 'common sense', but rather on a conception of spacetime. Thirdly, physicists also use a notion of 'imaginary' time in which there is no difference between the backward and forward

---

[10] Stephen Hawking, *A Brief History of Time: From the Big Bang to Black Holes* (New York: Bantam Books 1988), p. 18.
[11] Ibid., p. 33.
[12] G. J. Whitrow, *What Is Time?* (Oxford: Oxford University Press 2003), p. 1.
[13] Hawking, *Brief History of Time*, p. 8.

directions. Hawking indeed considers whether 'the so-called imaginary time is really the real time, and . . . what we call real time is just a figment of our imagination'. He concludes that 'it is meaningless to ask: which is real, "real" or "imaginary" time? It is simply a matter of which is the more useful description'.[14] In other words, physics does not support treating time as absolute and unidirectional. Whitrow, too, notes that the linear progression of time is not, as it appears to be assumed, an inescapable necessity of thought.[15]

Time also confronts us in less straightforward ways than the assumption of the obviousness and universal applicability of clock time suggests. The first point to note is that one of the reasons we need a clock to tell the time is that we do not always experience time as passing at the same speed. 'Time flies when you are having fun', after all. The reverse of this experience appears, for example, in Ledig's *Vergeltung*, which refers to the experience of time during an air raid. During the raid, Herr Cheovski thinks '[t]ime is passing. Time is passing for sure.'[16] An anonymous voice in the air-raid shelter observes that in the dark 'time passes more slowly'.[17] It is hardly surprising that when one is under a serious threat to one's life and utterly helpless, waiting for the raid to end, time would be experienced as slowed down. A different slowing-down, indeed stopping, of time is observed by Johnson in *Jahrestage*: the camps in which one of the main characters, Heinrich Cresspahl, is held by the Soviets were 'eternities that stood still'. Time stopped. The camp 'had become the world. The outside life did not come in.'[18] For time to elapse a social context is necessary, and this is lacking in the camp.

Such experiences of time are removed from the orderly, regular, inevitable ticking of clocks. Significantly, so-called clock time is not all there is. Rather, three challenges to treating clock time as the obvious basis for our thinking have been noted: physicists need different conceptions of time; we often experience time differently from clock time; and memory may be seen to play havoc with our securities about time. Assmann points out that where time plays no role, memory does not come to be discussed.[19] The reverse also seems to be the case. What is apparent in the novels discussed in this book is that where memory plays a role, temporality also becomes an issue. This is significant not least because many of the ways in which we understand and relate to the world are based on the linear conception of time, for example the idea of causality

[14] Ibid., p. 139.   [15] Whitrow, *What is Time?*, p. 1.
[16] Ledig, *Vergeltung*, p. 27.   [17] Ibid., p. 36.
[18] Uwe Johnson, *Jahrestage: Aus dem Leben von Gesine Cresspahl*, vols. I–IV (Frankfurt am Main: Suhrkamp Verlag 1970, 1971, 1973, 1983), p. 1297.
[19] Assmann, *Erinnerungsräume*, p. 95.

and the notion of drawing lessons from the past. Before these ideas can be examined it is necessary to further explore the problematic of memory and temporality, and Johnson's *Jahrestage* allows me to do so.

When we remember: Johnson's *Jahrestage*

Johnson's four-volume novel *Jahrestage: Aus dem Leben der Gesine Cresspahl (Anniversaries: From the Life of Gesine Cresspahl)* has been called the 'central German book of memory'.[20] D.G. Bond observes that '[w]riting is necessarily closely related to remembering, and this was particularly the case for Uwe Johnson'.[21] In *Jahrestage*, Gesine Cresspahl is a German woman in her mid-thirties who now – that is, in 1967/68 – lives in New York City with her 10-year-old daughter, Marie. Gesine, born in Mecklenburg in 1933, left the GDR in the 1950s to live first in West Germany and then the United States. Throughout *Jahrestage*, Gesine pieces together and narrates her life; she does so together with the 'comrade writer'. In this pursuit of memory, *Jahrestage* shifts between a narrative present in 1967/68 and the 'remembered time' from about 1931. There are numerous characters: relatives, friends, teachers, business contacts and so on in Gesine's past on the one hand, and her daughter, lover, colleagues and acquaintances in her current life on the other. To complicate matters, Gesine also hears voices of the dead from her past and has conversations with them.[22] Whilst readers are alerted to this by italicised script,[23] this remains confusing and obscure throughout. The voices are identified only implicitly, and they often speak Low German, a dialect that is quite impenetrable to outsiders.

Jahrestage is situated within the political situation in the USA and Germany in 1967/68 as reported by the *New York Times*. Gesine works in a Manhattan bank and is an avid reader of the *New York Times*, which she refers to as an 'aunt'. The paper represents her 'concept of an aunt': elderly, cultured, mildly disapproving, well-bred and therefore trustworthy.[24] The *New York Times* is explicitly the main source of information on political issues, mainly race relations in the USA, the Vietnam War, and the fate of former Nazis, including questions about their involvement

---

[20] Manfred Windfuhr, *Erinnerung und Avantgarde: Der Erzähler Uwe Johnson* (Heidelberg: Universitätsverlag Winter 2003), p. 15.

[21] D.G. Bond, *German History and German Identity: Uwe Johnson's* Jahrestage (Amsterdam: Rodopi 1993), p. 129.

[22] To be precise: not all the voices are of the dead. Gesine also seems to have such conversations with her old teacher Kliefoth, who is still alive. See, for example, Johnson, *Jahrestage*, p. 1177.

[23] However, some other conversations are also italicised.

[24] Johnson, *Jahrestage*, pp. 15 and 38–40.

in atrocities. These political issues provide the backdrop for questions of personal responsibility. How are Gesine and Marie, for example, to think about the Vietnam War, and what should they do? Thus, although readers only encounter war indirectly in *Jahrestage*, the labour of memory is inextricably related to the question of war. War is continually present, for example in Gesine's stories of a small town and village during the Second World War and in the frequent reports in the *New York Times* about the dead of the Vietnam War. *Jahrestage* is not a war novel, however, by any common interpretation of that term: there is no war 'story'. Marie is right when she says, 'You never make the war exciting, Gesine!'[25] Yet ethical issues that arise from war for ordinary citizens are crucial to *Jahrestage*.

These issues are contextualised within the story of Gesine's family and the war that *they* had been embroiled in. Gesine's father, Heinrich Cresspahl, emigrated from Germany to the UK in the 1920s. Despite his profound opposition to the regime that had in the meantime come to power in Germany, he later returned; his wife, Lisbeth, had not felt at home in Richmond and had gone back to Jerichow in Mecklenburg to give birth to their daughter, Gesine, in 1933. Eventually, Cresspahl agreed to settle in Jerichow with his family. His desire not to make his wife unhappy and to live with her and their daughter, even if this is possible only in Nazi Germany, is understandable. What is more puzzling is that although Cresspahl has a number of opportunities to leave Germany, notably after his wife's suicide, he decides to stay, despite being in no doubt that the regime would lead Germany into war. Gesine and her daughter struggle to understand this decision to remain in Germany. Moreover, Cresspahl eventually acts as a spy for the British. Marie – who grows up with US patriotism – profoundly objects to betraying one's country, even if the country is Nazi Germany. To some extent the excavation of memory in *Jahrestage* is an attempt to understand Cresspahl's decisions and to work out what, if anything, it all means in relation to how Gesine and Marie should act today, especially with respect to the Vietnam War.

It is necessary to outline how the book is constructed. Superficially, *Jahrestage* appears to represent a diary for the period 21 August 1967 to 20 August 1968, with entries for each date. However, quite apart from the explicit statement within *Jahrestage* that it is not a diary,[26] there are other textual clues that prevent such a simplistic interpretation. Firstly, much of the text is represented as conversations and oral narrative. Secondly, it is unclear who the narrator is. If *Jahrestage* was a fictional diary, Gesine would have to be the narrator. However, in places the narrator has information that Gesine is unaware of,[27] and the perspective is not

---

[25] Ibid., p. 986.   [26] Ibid., p. 1474.   [27] Ibid., p. 14.

always hers. When Gesine is described for the first time, the information presented is prefaced three times by 'I imagine'. The text reads, for example: 'I imagine: During the lunch break she reads again that yesterday afternoon . . .'[28] Gesine clearly is not the narrator here. The 'I imagine' also draws attention to Gesine's fictionality. The narrator does not report what s/he knows; instead, s/he imagines. Elsewhere, however, Gesine is presented as an independent personality who influences the process of narration. She interacts with someone whom she calls the 'comrade writer'. She makes reference to a contract between her and the writer,[29] and once notes that she has the writer 'in hand'.[30] It would, moreover, be possible to cite passages that are evidently told by Gesine or at least from her perspective. Indeed, the 'comrade writer', who is repeatedly mentioned in the text,[31] at one point asks, 'Who is telling this story anyway, Gesine[?]' only for Gesine to retort, 'Both of us. You hear that after all, Johnson.'[32]

This ambiguity of the narrator has generated discussion in the secondary literature. Colin Riordan, who also notes Gesine's shifts from 'I' to 'she' when she speaks of her remembered self,[33] calls it an 'idiosyncratic decentralization of narrative authority' or 'distributed narrative authority'.[34] Manfred Windfuhr notes the same phenomenon as 'polyphony', a reflection of the possibility of multiple views.[35] The shifting positions certainly make it harder for readers to simply identify; it requires them to think and, potentially, to doubt what they are being told.[36] Gesine does not construct her memories on her own but in conversation with the voices of the dead and with her daughter, and in the context of reports from the *New York Times*. She even tells them – in one way or another – *with* 'the comrade writer'. The problematic of representing remembering and Johnson's construction of an unusual narrator appear to be linked.

Gesine recounts her life and that of her family to her daughter, Marie. Sometimes this is a conversation in which Marie actively participates; sometimes Gesine is thought to speak the story onto tape 'for when [she

---

[28] Ibid., p. 12.   [29] Ibid., pp. 1426–8 and 1822.

[30] Ibid., p. 1638. See also Uwe Johnson, *Begleitumstände: Frankfurter Vorlesungen* (Frankfurt am Main: Suhrkamp 1980), p. 299.

[31] Johnson, *Jahrestage*, pp. 230, 253–7, 1039, 1075, 1426–8, 1638, 1657, 1726, 1766 and 1822.

[32] Ibid., p. 256.

[33] Colin Riordan, *The Ethics of Narration: Uwe Johnson's Novels from* Ingrid Babendererde *to* Jahrestage (London: The Modern Humanities Research Association 1989), p. 80.

[34] Ibid., pp. 3 and 76.

[35] Windfuhr, *Erinnerung und Avantgarde*, pp. 26f. See also Tachibana, *Narrative as Counter-Memory*, p. 247.

[36] Ibid., p. 189.

is] dead'.[37] However, even when Gesine is clearly depicted as the speaker, she tells Marie about events she cannot know of, something the child occasionally notices. Some of what Gesine did not know in the 'remembered time' she discovers through her conversations with the dead: chiefly her parents but also others she knew in her childhood. Gesine also notes that her stories often appear to her as a skeleton without flesh and that she conducts research in order to recount the past more vividly.[38] For example, she refers to consulting the 'Institute for the Cultivation of British Customs'. She similarly researches the precise weather conditions in Northern Germany at Easter 1938.[39] However, despite all the research there is a good deal that is asserted without any explanation of how this information is known. Although Gesine, if challenged, generally has an explanation for Marie, this does not mean that her explanations always hold.[40] In other words, although Gesine appears to offer her daughter and the reader knowledge about the past, the status of her memories as *truth* is always under threat. There is indeed no pretence that Gesine is telling it as it actually was. She tells her lover D. E. that 'Marie insists that I continue to tell her *how it may have been*'.[41] Gesine moreover notes that she 'never promised the truth'[42] and says to Marie, 'I only wanted to explain how it was. How it may have been.'[43] Thus Gesine freely admits that she is not telling what actually was. Indeed, Marie sometimes eggs Gesine on, saying: 'Tell me. You lie so beautifully.'[44] At other times, however, Marie is concerned about her mother's active manipulation for pedagogical effect. Yet Gesine insists that she is not in the business of *dichten* – that is, inventing as for poetry (*Dichtung*) – but that what she is doing is *erzählen*: telling, recounting, but also narrating.[45]

Marie at times interferes in Gesine's telling of the past. At one point she says that she does not like what is to come and asks whether Gesine could not change it.[46] When Gesine tells of Cresspahl being arrested by the Soviets, Marie is so keen that he should be innocent that she wants Gesine to make him so, even if that involves lying a little bit.[47] This is noteworthy in two respects. Firstly, Marie – who is otherwise concerned that Gesine does not have her on – wants Gesine to change the story without regard to what might be the truth. Secondly, Marie apparently already knows what she is about to be told, as otherwise she would not know to ask for changes. This makes no sense in the chronological unfolding of the story. Thus the reader's trust in the security of chronology is disturbed.

[37] Johnson, *Jahrestage*, p. 151.   [38] Ibid., p. 144.   [39] Ibid., p. 631.
[40] Ibid., pp. 151 and 859–62.   [41] Ibid., p. 143 (italics added).   [42] Ibid., p. 670.
[43] Ibid., p. 560.   [44] Ibid., p. 1651.   [45] Ibid., p. 832.   [46] Ibid., p. 296.
[47] Ibid., p. 1215.

Chronology also turns out to be a problem for how Gesine tells the story, a matter to which I turn below.

Gesine's main problem is the difficulty of reconstructing a period of time out of limited information. Memory fails Gesine. There are things she either never knew or does not remember. Gesine also admits the possibility of 'deceptive memory'[48] – that is, the possibility of remembering something that one never actually experienced in the first place. This concerns Gesine, for example, when she recognises the landscape of Denmark, a place she had never knowingly been before. Gesine also worries about the authenticity of her memories of Jakob, Marie's father:

And I don't trust what I know because it does not always show itself in my memory, then appears unexpectedly as an idea. Perhaps the memory makes out of itself the kind of sentence that Jakob said or perhaps said, could have said. Once the sentence is finished and in existence, the memory builds the others around it, even the voices of completely different people. That is what I am afraid of. All at once I hold a conversation in my thoughts about a conversation at which I was not present at all and the only aspect that is true about this is the memory of his intonation, how Jakob spoke.[49]

Johnson, moreover, leaves unresolved a contradiction between her memory and the writer's historical information with respect to Gesine's first port of call after leaving the GDR: 'Memory offers, insists on it, that she went to the refugee camp Marienfelde. The one who writes this would like to doubt whether this was already in use in July 1953.'[50] In all of these instances, we are confronted with the problem of memory. Johnson's book of memory unsurprisingly contains repeated reflection on this issue. Gesine, he writes, is not interested in 'going back into the past, the repetition of what was: to be in it again, to enter there again. That does not exist.'[51] According to Riordan, 'what might be termed authentic memory' is exposed as impossible in *Jahrestage*.[52] Underlining the impossibility of returning to the past, Gesine refers to her younger self as '[s]he, who I was'.[53] This draws attention to the issue, as also raised by Walser, that when we remember we no longer are who we were. Indeed, Johnson seems to put into practice what Walser reflects upon.[54] He says:

The depot of memory is precisely not designed for reproduction. It resists precisely the retrieval of an event. On inducement, on merely partial congruence, out of the blue absurd it voluntarily delivers facts, figures, foreign language, detached

---

[48] Ibid., p. 786.   [49] Ibid., p. 387.   [50] Ibid., p. 1853.   [51] Ibid., p. 63f.
[52] Riordan, *Ethics of Narration*, p. 99.   [53] For example, Johnson, *Jahrestage*, p. 1008.
[54] Bond, however, claims that Johnson also 'retains the realist illusion more or less consistently throughout'. *German History*, p. 92. Riordan similarly notes that 'Gesine directs her efforts towards remembering the past in a way which makes it as real as possible'. *Ethics of Narration*, p. 216.

gestures; if I hold out to it a tar-like, foul, still windy fresh smell, the secondary waft of Gustafsson's famous fish salad, and ask for content in place of the emptiness that once was reality, the feeling of being alive [*Lebensgefühl*], action; it will refuse to fill in. The blockade lets shreds, splinters, shavings trickle through so that they senselessly sprinkle the robbed and spaceless image, crush the trace of the scene that was sought so that we are blind with open eyes. That piece of the past, property through presence, remains hidden in a secret, locked against Ali Baba's password, cold, unapproachable, mute and tempting like a mighty grey cat behind window panes, seen from way below as if with children's eyes.[55]

Gesine later refers to memory as a cat: 'Independent, incorruptible, disobedient. And yet an agreeable companion when it shows up, even if it takes itself to be unattainable.'[56] Johnson clearly represents memory as beyond the control of the one who remembers. It is precisely her inability to control her memories that leads Gesine to be obsessed with the past. One of her central memories is of her mother standing by whilst the 4-year-old Gesine is about to drown in a rain barrel. Yet she cannot even recall whether her mother really was there at the crucial moment: 'When I want the memory, I cannot see her.'[57]

The idea of telling the family history to Marie is that she will not find herself in the same predicament of not knowing or being unable to recall important matters about her early life. Some of the story in *Jahrestage* is spoken by Gesine onto tape for Marie, on Marie's request, for when Gesine 'is dead'.[58] There are no such records for Gesine to rely on, no photos even. Cresspahl, she says, 'was secure in his memory [*Gedächtnis*]'.[59] Taking pictures only began with Gesine herself, and she asserts that she was the first in the family 'who feared forgetting'.[60] However, the reliance on Gesine's necessarily patchy and faulty memory – which Marie also suspects is being 'tuned' for pedagogical reasons – is ironic, inasmuch as Gesine, as we have seen, does not claim to tell the truth, nor does Marie trust that what Gesine tells her is the truth.

Questions of temporality and memory may be seen as central to reading *Jahrestage*. This is suggested by the title of the novel. As Windfuhr notes, *Jahrestage* (anniversaries) means the 365 days of the year that constitute the narrative present but also refers to '"commemoration days" [*Gedenktage*], looking back to the past'.[61] This would mean that the title alludes to two distinct temporalities, one that recounts the events of the year 1967/68 as they chronologically occur and another that recalls the past. Bond therefore claims that 'Johnson's *Jahrestage* uses both diachronic and synchronic narrative structures in its investigation

---

[55] Johnson, *Jahrestage*, pp. 63f.   [56] Ibid., p. 670.   [57] Ibid., p. 617.
[58] Ibid., p. 151.   [59] Ibid., p. 937.   [60] Ibid.; see also p. 227.
[61] Windfuhr, *Erinnerung und Avantgarde*, p. 15.

of history'.[62] This means that, on the one hand, time proceeds in a linear development; on the other, this linearity is disrupted by the principle of remembrance. Bond argues that the 'calendar denotes an attitude to history which entails both a sense of continuity – the passing of time – and the disruption of continuity which is necessary for remembrance'.[63] Through the calendar the present is confronted with the past.

What these commentators seem to suggest is that the two temporalities in *Jahrestage* are radically different from each other: one functions on the basis of linearity, whilst the other is circular, calling up specific memories according to particular, recurring dates. Yet Gesine does not remember events which happened, for example, in the same month of different years as belonging together. In fact, Gesine's recollection of the past is almost as linear as the rigidly structured narrative present, and Bond indeed notes that memory 'does not function in so neat a manner'.[64] Towards the beginning of the novel, Johnson himself writes that Gesine 'had searched for the year 1937 and again found nothing but a static, isolated fragment, such as the store of memory arbitrarily selects for her, kept in uncontrollable amounts, only from time to time sensitive to command and intention'.[65] If the fragments she finds are 'isolated', then they are not located within the linearity of a chronological order; her memory breaks out of this order.

Yet the representation of temporality in *Jahrestage* is less challenging than the commentators claim. Rather than two profoundly different times, there are, in effect, two linear temporalities that run at different speeds – the past that Gesine tells elapses much more quickly than the present – such that at the end of the novel both arrive at the same point in time. In Johnson's words, the cat was to be able to catch its own tail for once.[66] However, whilst this conjures up the idea of coming full circle and hence closure, the novel is actually open-ended. Gesine is to arrive in Prague on 21 August 1968, the day after *Jahrestage* finishes and, as readers – unlike Gesine – know, the day of the invasion by Warsaw Pact troops. Gesine is posted to Prague by her bank, which hopes to profit from a currency deal with the reform government, and Gesine, who for many reasons would prefer to stay in New York, agrees to the posting because she wants to give socialism a last chance. Readers know throughout that the Czechoslovakian reform project will fail. Johnson asserts that others might have been happy to be present in such a historical moment but that Gesine, despite not knowing of the Warsaw Pact intervention, is not, because she had 'experienced the future as the worst unalterability'.[67]

---

[62] Bond, *German History*, p. 37.   [63] Ibid., p. 98.   [64] Ibid., p. 95.
[65] Johnson, *Jahrestage*, p. 63.   [66] Johnson, *Begleitumstände*, p. 416.   [67] Ibid., p. 423.

And yet the novel is written towards this future as an opening. The closure that brings an end to Gesine's hopes – the events of 21 August 1968 – is not part of the novel, and thus the openness remains. Bond therefore notes that 'the future dominates the function of memory. This has to be the case if there is to be a place for political action.'[68] The element of surprise and unexpectedness that – as will be shown – Derrida construes as crucial to the idea of the future remains possible within the novel, despite the fact that readers bring to it the knowledge of historical closure and despite even Johnson's reference to the future as the 'worst unalterability'. Thus the supposed two temporalities of the calendar are not so radically different as the commentators suggest, but the most significant issue to arise from my reading of *Jahrestage* is nevertheless that of temporality. Gesine's remembering works against the rigid structuring of linear time, even though *Jahrestage* is presented within the structure of the calendar. This will be considered further after exploring an alternative way of interrogating linearity, Vonnegut's invention of a different conception of time in *Slaughterhouse 5*.

Different times: Vonnegut's *Slaughterhouse 5*

Vonnegut's *Slaughterhouse 5* was, like the first volumes of *Jahrestage*, written at the time of the Vietnam War. The novel starts, on the title page, by blurring the subject position of the narrator into the identity of the author. Kurt Vonnegut, Jr., is identified there as 'a fourth-generation German-American now living in easy circumstances on Cape Cod (and smoking too much)'.[69] For what is about to come, Vonnegut's or the narrator's status as 'German-American' is relevant because he is, in relation to the confrontations narrated in the novel, in some sense neither here nor there, or rather simultaneously both. He was a US soldier, but as a POW amongst the Germans and exposed to the bombing of Dresden. The assertion of identity on the title page also includes information that one might see as superfluous ('and smoking too much'), setting the pattern for a narrative that refuses to focus on what might, by some standards, be considered the essential. This apparent rejection of the essential may be linked to the proposition of an alternative temporality that is at the heart of the novel, for where linear time no longer exists, the notion of causality, for example – which helps identify what matters – no longer applies in the same way.

    Slaughterhouse 5 tells the story of Billy Pilgrim, but is framed by sections that give information about the narrator. We learn, still on the title page,

---

[68] Bond, *German History*, p. 80.　　[69] Vonnegut, *Slaughterhouse 5*, n.p.

that the German-American narrator 'as an American infantry scout, *hors de combat*, as a prisoner of war, witnessed the fire-bombing of Dresden, Germany, "the Florence of the Elbe," a long time ago, and survived to tell the tale'.[70] The narrator thus stakes his claim to be able to provide information about the raid on Dresden as a witness. In view of the alleged necessity, outlined in Chapter 4, of 'having been there' to be able to appropriately represent war in fiction the narrator seems to reassure us of his credentials. 'I was there',[71] he later says in confirmation of his privileged knowledge. Emig, in his analysis of *Slaughterhouse 5* discussed below, notes this 'promise of authenticity that is common to many war stories' implied in the stereotypical 'a long time ago' and 'survived to tell the tale'.[72] Yet the status of *Slaughterhouse 5* as a resource for knowledge about the past is immediately undermined: 'This is a novel', it continues, a reminder that the text is one of fiction. This already constitutes a challenge to the claim to authenticity just made. But it is worse: *Slaughterhouse 5* is a novel 'somewhat in the telegraphic schizophrenic manner of tales of the planet Tralfamadore, where the flying saucers come from. Peace.'[73]

Thus we are confronted with an unreliable narrator, preparing to speak in what is clearly an idiosyncratic way on what seems to require the greatest care: atrocity and human suffering in war. This impression is confirmed by the first two sentences of the novel: 'All this happened, more or less. The war parts, anyway, are pretty much true.'[74] What is phrased as an affirmation of authenticity actually undermines the reader's trust. After all, what we shall be told only happened 'more or less' and is merely 'pretty much' true, which does not inspire confidence. Nor does the comment 'As a trafficker in climaxes and thrills and characterization and wonderful dialogue and suspense and confrontations, I had outlined the Dresden story many times.'[75] The reference to climaxes draws attention to the requirements of fiction – making the tale interesting – rather than those of reporting facts on the basis of a claim to authenticity. At the same time, as Emig notes, the story of the novel is anticipated on the title page in the 'specifications' of Dresden and its destruction in an air raid.[76] In other words, we are told the outcome before hearing the story. In terms of 'climaxes' and 'thrills' this is the wrong move; the reader knows from the start what will happen. The narrative is thus precariously balanced between a supposedly authentic representation of an event we already know and the plot development of a novel.

---

[70] Ibid.   [71] Ibid., p. 49.   [72] Emig, *Krieg als Metapher*, p. 248.
[73] Vonnegut, *Slaughterhouse 5*, n.p.   [74] Ibid., p. 1.   [75] Ibid., p. 4.
[76] Emig, *Krieg als Metapher*, p. 248.

Emig observes that *Slaughterhouse 5* reflects upon itself and classifies itself as fiction. This leads to the 'first contradiction to the suggested authenticity of the reported war experience'.[77] Emig proposes to read Vonnegut's novel not as a modernist story that 'sees war as the fulfilment of an apocalypse but as a permanently present principle of repetition and penetration without beginning and end – and therefore without stable symbolic positions of meaning'.[78] He notes that the narrator starts by describing his original expectation that writing about the bombing of Dresden would be easy 'since all I would have to do would be to report what I had seen'.[79] Yet the narrator also describes himself as a 'trafficker in climaxes and thrills'.[80] Therefore, Emig argues, the authenticity problem of the novel derives in part 'from the obvious rivalry between facts and fiction. What "really" happened and has been seen by the subject that guarantees its authenticity can only be reported successfully . . . if the report follows fictional conventions . . . It is exactly these, however, that turn the apparently authentic, but in terms of narrative technique [*erzähltechnisch*] impossible, report into fiction again.'[81] Although the claim to authenticity is based on personal experience, the perspective of the other is necessary to confirm it. The narrator seeks to remember together with a friend, for example. Authenticity is located in the singularity of personal involvement, and yet the perspective of the other serves to confirm that the events were not merely experienced subjectively but 'really', objectively.[82]

The promise of authenticity, such as it is, is based on presence in the war zone. It becomes clear, however, that 'having been there' may not be enough to 'know' what has happened. The narrator – somewhat surprisingly – asserts that Dresden had been worse than Hiroshima but that he had not known this because there 'hadn't been much publicity'.[83] Having been there was not enough. Although, as noted in Chapter 3, keeping the damage caused in Dresden secret was hardly possible,[84] those present at the time may well not have appreciated the overall scale of the destruction. In other words, they might indeed not have 'known' what is now recognised as 'the bombing of Dresden'. Moreover, as Emig leads us to expect, the narrator needs confirmation of his memories. He asks for a friend's help 'remembering stuff'; he wants to visit him and 'drink and talk and remember'.[85] Remembering, in this representation, is a process, and one for which the narrator needs help. The friend is not keen on

---

[77] Ibid.   [78] Ibid., p. 249.   [79] Vonnegut, *Slaughterhouse 5*, p. 2.
[80] Ibid., p. 4.   [81] Emig, *Krieg als Metapher*, p. 250.
[82] Ibid., p. 251. See also Emig, 'Augen/Zeugen' and Chapter 4.
[83] Vonnegut, *Slaughterhouse 5*, p. 7.   [84] Ibid., p. 8.   [85] Ibid., p. 3.

this idea and claims that he cannot remember much, but he invites the narrator anyway. The narrator suggests to his friend that the climax of the book will be the trial and execution of a British soldier for stealing a teapot, because this event had been so ironic in the context of an entire city being burnt down.[86] As with the revelations on the title page, the reader is told the outcome long before the event actually occurs in the novel, thus undermining the build-up of suspense.

When the narrator and his friend get together, they fail to remember any 'good stories' that would make up a book.[87] This seems paradoxical, since readers nevertheless hold the book in their hands. What is being noted is therefore not so much the impossibility of writing the book as that the book is not a 'good story'. According to Hage, *Slaughterhouse 5* 'is about the difficulty of writing a novel as an eyewitness to the bombing of Dresden in February 1945'.[88] Indeed, Vonnegut makes the problem of writing about this topic central:

I would hate to tell you what this lousy little book cost me in anxiety and time. When I got home from the Second World War twenty-three years ago, I thought it would be easy for me to write about the destruction of Dresden, since all I would have to do would be to report what I had seen. And I thought, too, that it would be a masterpiece or at least make me a lot of money, since the subject was so big.[89]

However, much to the contrary, he not only finds it impossible to write the book but also discovers – once the book is written – that it is not a heroic tale of accomplishment in the face of adversity: 'There are almost no characters in this story, and almost no dramatic confrontations, because most of the people in it are so sick and so much the listless playthings of enormous forces. One of the main effects of war, after all, is that people are discouraged from being characters.'[90] Vonnegut points out that being bombed is a passive experience: 'As a survivor there is nothing one could be proud of.'[91]

He considers the book a 'failure'.[92] The narrator – and narrator and author are blurred in these comments – failed to write the story he had 'outlined many times'; he calls the actual book 'jumbled and jangled'. This is 'because there is nothing intelligent to say about a massacre. Everybody is supposed to be dead, to never say anything or want to say anything ever again. Everything is supposed to be very quiet after

---

[86] Ibid., p. 4.   [87] Ibid., p. 10.   [88] Hage, 'Berichte', p. 105.
[89] Vonnegut, *Slaughterhouse 5*, p. 2.   [90] Ibid., p. 119.
[91] 'Von allen Luftwaffen bombardiert', interview with Kurt Vonnegut, in: Hage, *Zeugen der Zerstörung*, p. 283.
[92] Vonnegut, *Slaughterhouse 5*, p. 16.

a massacre, and it always is, except for the birds.'[93] But it is not just that there is no one to speak: anything that might be said is both futile and trivial. The narrator notes: 'I have told my sons that they are not under any circumstances to take part in massacres, and that the news of massacres of enemies is not to fill them with satisfaction or glee.'[94]

Vonnegut represents the bombing very differently from Ledig and Mulisch, whose novels *Vergeltung* and *Das steinerne Brautbett* are discussed in Chapter 3. The narrator, who was a POW in Dresden at the time of the bombing, informs us that in 1967 he went back to Dresden, which he claims 'looked a lot like Dayton, Ohio, more open spaces than Dayton has. There must be tons of human bone meal in the ground.'[95] This oblique reference, in the second paragraph, to the large-scale destruction of buildings and loss of human life sets the tone for the novel. The descriptions of the destruction seem distanced, artificial: 'Dresden was like the moon now, nothing but minerals. The stones were hot. Everybody else in the neighborhood was dead. So it goes.'[96] Even more: 'One thing was clear: Absolutely everybody in the city was supposed to be dead, regardless of what they were, and that anybody that moved in it represented a flaw in the design. There were to be no moon men at all.'[97] Whereas Ledig and Mulisch present close-ups with all the horror this entails, Vonnegut seems to distance. Although atrocities and horrors are mentioned, the narrator seems detached, laconic, apparently unfeeling: 'And Billy had seen the greatest massacre in European history, which was the fire-bombing of Dresden. So it goes.'[98] Or: 'The Pole was a farm laborer who was being hanged for having had sexual intercourse with a German woman. So it goes.'[99] What the novel calls a 'massacre'[100] is referred to without explicit emotion and indeed without preparing the reader. The narrator says about a cab driver with whom he made friends when returning to Dresden, 'His mother was incinerated in the Dresden fire-storm. So it goes.'[101] The phrase 'So it goes' – a form of words that suggests emotional distancing, explored below – recurs time and again. It is as though the events in Dresden were not important.

Distancing is also achieved by reflecting on the writing process. The 'author' appears in the text several times, disturbing the boundary between fiction and 'reality',[102] a technique also used in Grass's *Im Krebsgang* discussed in Chapter 2. These reflections are not only about the possibility of writing about the bombing of Dresden but also about the possibility of writing an anti-war book. The attitude expressed in

---

[93] Ibid., p. 14.   [94] Ibid.   [95] Ibid., p. 1.   [96] Ibid., p. 129.   [97] Ibid., p. 131.
[98] Ibid., p. 73.   [99] Ibid., p. 113.   [100] Ibid., p. 14.   [101] Ibid., p. 1.
[102] Ibid., pp. 91 and 108.

Slaughterhouse 5 is critical of the war and its conduct. During the raid on Dresden, American fighter planes return to shoot at Billy and his fellow POWs: 'The idea was to hasten the end of the war.'[103] It is obvious that Americans shooting their fellow countrymen was unlikely to make a positive contribution to speeding up the conclusion of the war. The concrete question of whether *Slaughterhouse 5* is an anti-war book appears twice. In the first instance, the narrator claims to be unsure about this. 'I guess', he responds. He immediately admits that such a project is futile, much like writing an anti-glacier book: there would always be wars.[104] The wife of the narrator's friend similarly assumes that the book would not be anti-war, that it would script the narrator and his friend, who had been merely 'babies' at the time, into roles befitting 'Frank Sinatra and John Wayne or some of those other glamorous, war-loving, dirty old men. And war will look just wonderful, and we'll have a lot more of them.'[105] The narrator promises her that there would be no characters for John Wayne to play, and this is true. Indeed, as noted, the narrator claims that war discourages people from being characters.

Vonnegut seems to be driven by a need to write about the 'massacre', but he also addresses the question whether it is *permissible* to write about the bombing of Dresden in the face of German atrocities. The narrator tells a professor of his project and is lectured about 'concentration camps, and about how the Germans had made soap and candles out of the fat of dead Jews and so on'. The narrator's response suggests that he is exasperated by this attitude: 'I know, I know. I *know*.'[106] For him, obviously, the Germans' crimes do not mean that one has to remain silent on this particular crime against – mostly – Germans. Another – profoundly unpalatable – character, Professor Rumfoord, who is writing a history of the Army Air Force in the Second World War, asserts, 'It *had* to be done.'[107] Billy, the main character, does not dispute this necessity, though for reasons entirely different from Rumfoord's, namely the understanding of time that he has learnt from the Tralfamadorians.

Billy 'has come unstuck in time' such that he never knows which part of his life he will suddenly have to act in. For example, the first time Billy appears in the novel he has 'gone to sleep a senile widower and awakened on his wedding day'.[108] Billy has no control over his time travel and does not enjoy it. Billy's story starts with a brief account of his life, in what we would consider chronological order. After a plane crash in 1968, Billy talks of having come unstuck in time and having been kidnapped by a flying saucer in 1967,[109] though he had first, he claims, experienced this

---

103 Ibid., p. 131.   104 Ibid., p. 3.   105 Ibid., p. 11.   106 Ibid., p. 8.
107 Ibid., p. 144.   108 Ibid., p. 17.   109 Ibid., p. 18.

kind of time travel in 1944.[110] His absence had not been noticed on Earth, Billy explains, because the Tralfamadorians had kidnapped him 'through a time warp' which meant he was able to be there for years whilst only being away from Earth for a microsecond. Billy reports that he learnt on this other planet that '[a]ll moments, past, present, and future, always have existed, always will exist'.[111] As a result, it is, for example, 'silly' to cry over someone's death, for they are still very much alive in the past. Tralfamadorians, Billy explains, 'can look at all the different moments just the way we can look at a stretch of the Rocky Mountains'.[112] The idea that one moment follows another is 'just an illusion we have here on Earth'.[113] A Tralfamadorian would therefore be likely to comment 'So it goes' at the sight of a body and reflect that this person is merely in bad shape at this particular moment but 'just fine in plenty of other moments'.[114] What at first appears to be crude emotional 'distancing' is thus based on thinking within a different temporality.

There is one scene in which time is reversed. Billy watches a film on American bombers in the Second World War backwards,[115] thereby over-turning, of course, the relationships of what we see as cause and effect.[116] This reversal illustrates the implication of temporality in causality and hence conceptions of responsibility. Those who flew the bombers become 'gallant men' who 'flew backwards over a German city that was in flames. The bombers opened their bomb bay doors, exerted a miraculous mag-netism which shrunk the fires, gathered them into cylindrical steel con-tainers, and lifted the containers into the bellies of the planes.'[117] In this depiction, the bombers become a force for good for the Germans. Apart from this brief episode, Billy lives his life in forward motion; he just picks up at different points in time, some of which are in his 'past', and so – on a linear understanding that does not apply here – he has to go 'backwards' to get there.

The Tralfamadorian interpretation of time, according to which Billy experiences his life, has consequences for how one may look at the events. Billy has a 'memory of the future'.[118] Once, in a conversation with his daughter, he says, 'That isn't what happens next.'[119] Billy can remember different parts of his life that he has time-travelled to, even if they are in what – in an earthly understanding – would be the future. However, he cannot *change* the future, and therefore the Tralfamadorians claim that

---

[110] Ibid., p. 22.   [111] Ibid., p. 19.   [112] Ibid.; see also p. 62.
[113] Ibid., p. 19.   [114] Ibid., p. 20.   [115] Ibid., pp. 53f.
[116] This is pushed further by Martin Amis, *Time's Arrow, Or the Nature of the Offence* (London: Penguin Books 1992).
[117] Vonnegut, *Slaughterhouse 5*, p. 53.   [118] Ibid., p. 76; see also p. 109.
[119] Ibid., p. 95.

there is no such thing as free will.[120] Because they look at all moments simultaneously, there is – in this reading – no scope for freedom or change. It is not just a 'what will be will be' but a 'what will be already is': hence the recurring image of bugs in amber,[121] stuck, unable to move. In other words, our notion of freedom is seen to rely on a linear notion of time. Billy says, in a speech supporting pacifism, 'I myself have seen the bodies of schoolgirls who were boiled alive in a water tower by my own countrymen, who were proud of fighting pure evil at the time.'[122] But the Tralfamadorians merely laugh at him. In their view of events, there is nothing you can do to stop them. Whatever will happen has always happened because the 'moment is *structured* that way'.[123] Catastrophic events cannot be averted; Tralfamadorians merely spend time looking at pleasant moments rather than horrible ones.[124] Billy likes the Tralfamadorian conception of time. He expects to be able to comfort people by telling them 'the truth about time'.[125] The Tralfamadorians had not caused Billy to come unstuck in time but they had been 'able to give him insights into what was really going on'.[126]

The Tralfamadorian concept of time fundamentally disturbs our understanding of the atrocities at Dresden; our understandings of morality or ethicality depend on conceptions of temporality. Linear time is relied on in order to assess responsibility. This was also clear in the discussions, outlined in Chapter 3, that stressed that Germany had started it, had dropped bombs on cities first, thereby diminishing the Allies' culpability in having done so later. Moreover, in this reading of time 'So it goes' is not simply a move of emotional distancing. A changed understanding of time leads to a different view of massacre. The dead are merely in 'bad shape' at this particular moment. This might be an unpalatable way of looking at the matter, as it implies that the killing of thousands was not such a big problem; but the point is that by looking at it from this changed perspective, we may be able to understand our own view better. The way in which Vonnegut plays on our understandings of time – far-fetched and irritating though we may find them – alerts us to the significance of temporality. In other words, Vonnegut's memories are written as 'a story of time'.[127] Time thus again appears as crucial to memory. What is perhaps most worrisome about Tralfamadorian time is that there is no future in the sense of an openness: what will be already is. That this is judged problematic – Jones, for example, is worried that

---

[120] Ibid., p. 62.   [121] Ibid., pp. 55 and 61.   [122] Ibid., p. 84.   [123] Ibid.
[124] Ibid., p. 85.   [125] Ibid., p. 20.   [126] Ibid., p. 22.
[127] Peter G. Jones, *War and the American Novelist: Appraising the American War Novel* (Columbia: University of Missouri Press 1976), p. 217.

in 'Vonnegut's universe there is no free will, and war is an inevitable by-product of the intercourse among nations'[128] – reveals that this openness, which is often associated with risk and danger, is also potentially fruitful.

Tensions of time

Both *Jahrestage* and *Slaughterhouse 5* illustrate in different ways the inescapability of the past, which indeed is not (simply) past. Gesine is convinced that it is vital to know one's past: hence, for example, the recording of her family's story on tape for her daughter. But she also hears voices from the past, and they prevent her from escaping those memories she might not wish to recall. Billy Pilgrim is unable to shed the past in a different way. His understanding of the Tralfamadorian concept of time leads him to believe that the past persists; he might at any point have to act 'back' in his own past.

Memory and chronology: Gesine's troubles

In *Jahrestage*, it seems clear that the past – especially that of the Third Reich – is not becoming less important over time. The past of the Third Reich is not sealed against the present but immediately relevant to Gesine and Marie. As Bond observes, for 'Johnson there can be no forgetting, and this . . . makes him both arguably dated and yet also acutely relevant today'.[129] Interestingly, Johnson's novel does not simply issue a demand that we remember, such as perhaps the one in Federal President von Weizsäcker's famous 1985 speech. Instead it works through the related inescapability and impossibility of remembering and the inevitable relevance of memory. It is useful to recall Assmann's observation that '[u]nlike memorising, remembering is not an intentional act; one remembers or one simply does not remember. It would probably be more correct to say that something remembers one.'[130] It is clear that, although Gesine wants to remember, she does not necessarily wish to remember everything she remembers. For example, the voices from the past remind her of events she would rather forget, and she says about the way the voices keep talking to her: 'I do not want it.'[131] She is annoyed that remembering is beyond her control. Johnson's image of memory as a cat further illustrates the uncontrollability of memory. It is like a cat in that it is '[i]ndependent, incorruptible, disobedient. And yet an

[128] Ibid., p. 222.   [129] Bond, *German History*, p. 211.
[130] Assmann, *Erinnerungsräume*, p. 29.   [131] Johnson, *Jahrestage*, p. 1539.

agreeable companion when it shows up.'[132] However, whether memory is an 'agreeable companion' seems to depend. Gesine remembers, for example, that her mother did not attempt to rescue her when she was about to drown.[133] Although Gesine is able to understand that her mother did not want to live with the responsibility for the war started by the Third Reich and presumably wanted to spare her daughter that responsibility,[134] this memory remains profoundly uncomfortable for Gesine. The memories discussed here – of Allied strategic bombing, the expulsions from the East or, indeed, Wehrmacht atrocities – are also unwelcome.

One might want to say, therefore, that such memories haunt us. Woods notes that 'our presence is traced through with the manifestation of ghosts from the past: America and its Vietnam; the Industrial West and its ecological problems; South Africa and the avatars of *apartheid*; Europe and Bosnia; England and Ireland . . . the list goes on'.[135] It certainly does, and it is surprising that the spectre of the Second World War and the Holocaust are not on Woods's list. Derrida, who is interested in what he calls '*hauntology*', a logic of haunting,[136] points out that scholars have not made ghosts a serious subject of inquiry:

A traditional scholar does not believe in ghosts – nor in all that could be called the virtual space of spectrality. There has never been a scholar who, as such, does not believe in the sharp distinction between the real and the unreal, the actual and the inactual, the living and the non-living, being and non-being ('to be or not to be,' in the conventional reading), in the opposition between what is present and what is not, for example in the form of objectivity. Beyond this opposition, there is, for the scholar, only the hypothesis of a school of thought, theatrical fiction, literature and speculation.[137]

Memory, however, finds itself between what might be seen as the real and the unreal. It draws attention to the undecidability not only of pastness and presentness but also of real and unreal. Even if it could be solved, the problem of what really 'was' in the past would not resolve the problematic of memory, because memory is affected by the present, and indeed by intervening memories. At the same time, the ghosts of memory have real effects. This is what we see in the use of memories in political debate, such as in order to support or reject military action. In *Jahrestage*, Gesine conceptualises her responsibility with respect to the Vietnam War in relation to her memory of her family's actions with respect to the Second World War. However, the two ethico-political situations are not the same, and Johnson explicitly rejects any comparison.

---

[132] Ibid., p. 670.   [133] Ibid., pp. 64f and 616–18.
[134] Ibid., p. 618.   [135] Woods, 'Spectres of History', p. 109.
[136] Jacques Derrida, *Specters of Marx: The State of Debt, the Work of Mourning, and the New International*, Translated by Peggy Kamuf (New York: Routledge 1994), p. 10.
[137] Ibid., p. 11.

The problem of comparison – and hence comparability – arises in particular because Johnson interweaves the history of the Third Reich with the narrative present. One may ask whether Johnson is trying to compare the political situation in the USA in 1967/68 with that in Germany 1933–45. For example, is Johnson, by telling them together, implying that persecution in the Third Reich and the Second World War on the one hand and racism in the USA and the Vietnam War on the other are comparable? This concern arises because Johnson jumps from one to the other. For example, on the occasion of Gesine's visit to the beach, he observes that black people are not welcome to buy houses or use the beach in the village in New Jersey and without further comment moves to the question of the position of Jews in relation to the beach near Jerichow, her home town in Germany, before and during the Third Reich.[138] However, Gesine explicitly argues *against* any comparison. She tells of the treatment she received from the other villagers when her father was installed as mayor first by the British and then the Soviet occupation forces. Marie believes she is meant to think of how she and her friends respond to the only black girl in her class, but Gesine tells her not to compare.[139]

Riordan notes 'Gesine's antipathy (shared by Johnson) to *Vergleichung* with its implications of sameness and consequent inaccuracy'.[140] *Jahrestage* can be read to reject simplistic comparison in favour of the need to make decisions in each ethico-political situation. The question of personal responsibility is crucial. Cresspahl's spying for the British, for example, presents an ethical problem. Marie does not accept that it is permissible to betray one's country just because it is in the wrong, for the USA is also in the wrong with respect to Vietnam.[141] Cresspahl was, according to Gesine, forced and bribed by the British into working for them because they had discovered that he still owned undeclared money in the UK, an offence punishable by up to ten years' imprisonment under German law at the time. However, the ethical core of the problem, as Gesine presents it, is not that Cresspahl was acting under duress and could thus be excused; rather it is that he maintained his freedom by acting for his own reasons – his desire to hurt the Nazis – and keeping them to himself, 'Blackmailed and bought off and safe. Only that he had decided for himself and reliably kept his freedom.'[142] This, interestingly, is parallel to Gesine's attitude towards her posting to Prague. She, too, is pressed and bribed because she would not easily find another job in a bank if she refused this opportunity, but she again acts for her own secret

[138] Johnson, *Jahrestage*, p. 7.   [139] Ibid., p. 1048.
[140] Riordan, *Ethics of Narration*, p. 151; *gleich* is the German for 'same'.
[141] Johnson, *Jahrestage*, pp. 809f.   [142] Ibid., p. 814.

motive, namely her desire to see a new version of socialism succeed in Czechoslovakia.

As Bond points out, the 'problem of individual integrity is the central ethical issue in *Jahrestage*, and above all, in the story of Gesine Cresspahl's life'.[143] The issue is not just Cresspahl's responsibility in the Third Reich, but Gesine's and Marie's in the narrative present. This comes out most clearly in relation to the Vietnam War. Many of the 'chapters' associated with particular days of the year refer to this war, in particular to the reporting about it in the *New York Times*. There is a struggle between Gesine and Marie – who is socialised into US patriotism at school – about this war and about what are sensible and appropriate forms of protest against it. This is, because of the set-up of the novel, inevitably read together with the Second World War and the 'failure' of Gesine's family to prevent it. Cresspahl, Gesine's father, saw the war coming. Lisbeth, her mother, felt herself drawn into a responsibility for it that she could not bear; she committed suicide. Unsurprisingly, Gesine feels compelled to find a better way of dealing with the current war and her inevitable responsibility for it because she is part of the system. Thus the past belongs not only to the past: the past enters into the present.

Events in the present prompt Gesine, as one would expect, to remember the past, but she maintains a largely chronological order in her story about the past. The tension between the acknowledgement that memory functions outside clear linear temporality – one need only recall the representation of memories as 'fragments' – and the generally strict chronological order of Gesine's recollections makes *Jahrestage* appear profoundly constructed. Gesine is extremely keen on chronology, although memory fails to obey it. Marie once asks whether the Robert Papenbrock who returned after having been missing abroad for twenty years was the real Robert. Gesine insists on telling the event as it appeared at the time, reserving information on whether he truly was Robert for later, and asks rhetorically whether Marie wants her to tell the story 'muddled up in time'.[144] Marie agrees to wait for the answer to her question until Gesine, in her presentation of the order in which events occur, arrives at the moment when the information becomes available. However, Marie at the same time observes that she does 'not sort that Jerichow according to years' but rather according to people.[145] Marie does not work from a timeline, as indeed is only to be expected if she is told the 'fragments' that are memories.

In her reaction to Marie, Gesine claims for herself the obvious chronological order of events, which responding to Marie's query would

---

[143] Bond, *German History*, p. 40.   [144] Johnson, *Jahrestage*, p. 561.   [145] Ibid.

'muddle up'. However, it is worth noting that in this instance she bases the chronology on when things were *known* rather than when they *occurred*, although such a distinction is of course problematic. Even if one insists on telling the story chronologically, another chronology would be possible. In another instance, Gesine opts for the other possibility. She reports that her uncle Alexander Paepcke refused an order to set a group of Jews to work because there were children amongst them – presumably because he wanted no part in their maltreatment, though this is not said – and describes his career in the army afterwards. She notes that she knows this 'from the time after the war',[146] but she tells it in the context of the last time she saw Alexander, on a holiday, before he was killed in the war. In other words, she inserts the 'later' information into the chronology of unfolding events. Crucially, Gesine in this case seems to explicitly object to representing the events according to the chronology she had insisted on with respect to Robert, based on what was known to her at the time; this would somehow be wrong. She says that 'of this summer the memory knows . . . the holidays. It was not like that.'[147] So here the later information is confronted with Gesine's memory and in effect challenges it. The later knowledge does not achieve a correction of memory – her memory still recalls the pleasantness of the holiday – but the 'It was not like that' suggests that the later information is superior, in some way more true. In other words, it acts as a supplement; whilst on the one hand it functions as a surplus, on the other it 'adds only to replace'.[148] Whilst Gesine refused to disrupt what she sees as the chronological order in relation to the story about Robert, she does precisely that in the latter example: her later knowledge intrudes into the past in the process of telling it.

The problematic of chronology and its implication in the question of responsibility perhaps come out most clearly with respect to Gesine's conversations with the dead. The voices are treated as an obvious part of Gesine's reality until well into the fourth volume of *Jahrestage*. They just happen, and are not discussed. However, in mid-July 1968, with her impending departure to Prague appearing ever more problematic, Gesine writes to a professor at the Research Institute for Psychoanalysis in Frankfurt am Main: 'In principle I would like to consider myself normal. The exception: I hear voices.'[149] She has done so since she was 32 years old, but does not recall an immediate cause. She adds: 'I do not want it. Nevertheless I reach (sometimes almost completely) into past situations

[146] Ibid., p. 956.   [147] Ibid.
[148] Jacques Derrida, *Of Grammatology*, Translated by Gayatri Chakravorty Spivak, Corrected edn (Baltimore: The Johns Hopkins University Press 1998), p. 145.
[149] Johnson, *Jahrestage*, p. 1539.

and speak with people from that time like I used to at that time. This happens in my head, without my control. Even dead people speak with me as if in my present.' What particularly bothers her is that her own position in these conversations shifts: 'So I hear myself speak not only from the subjectively real (past) place, but also from the place of the subject who is today 35 years old.'[150] This shift turns her into a partner who she could not have been at the time. Put differently, she feels responsible for events that occurred when she was only a child and did not have the means to interfere. In this sense, it is hard to argue with Marie's assertion, referring to Gesine's interest in Marie's attitude towards the Vietnam War, 'You did not stop your war, now you want me to do it for you!'[151]

But the real issue is that Gesine is uncomfortable because she is out of time: her conversations with the dead are anachronistic and thus pose insurmountable problems with respect to her personal responsibility. Gesine ends her letter by asking: 'Is this an illness? Should I adapt my professional responsibilities? Should the child be protected from me?'[152] The response arrives roughly one month and 300 pages later. It is signed 'A. M.', suggesting a reference to Alexander Mitscherlich, the co-author of *Die Unfähigkeit zu trauern* (*The Inability to Mourn*).[153] The professor of psychoanalysis suspects that injuries and losses, starting with her mother's suicide, are continuing to have an effect. This 'disowning by the mother' is 'unfinished', has not been dealt with.[154] Gesine, he argues, has a tendency to securitise which she might wish to examine in light of her current circumstances.[155] The temporal problematic is interesting here. What Gesine is concerned about is not talking to the dead as such but that through these dialogues she is placed as an adult into situations that she experienced as a child, leading to a profound feeling of inadequacy due to her inability, at the time, to live up to the responsibility she would have had if, at the time, she had been the adult she is now.

This problem arises because her memories and the voices disturb the chronology, despite Gesine's best efforts to enforce clarity in it. Chronology was unachievable in her telling of memory. It was not even clear what chronology means; two different versions appear possible, as illustrated by the stories about Robert and Alexander. In the first case, Gesine rejects introducing later information into the timeline. Yet, with respect to her recollection of the holiday with Alexander, she does precisely that. In this

---

[150] Ibid.   [151] Ibid, p. 494.   [152] Ibid., p. 1541.
[153] See Bond, *German History*, p. 138; Riordan, *Ethics of Narration*, p. 107. See Alexander Mitscherlich and Margarete Mitscherlich, *Die Unfähigkeit zu trauern: Grundlagen kollektiven Verhaltens*, 17th edn (Munich: Piper 2004).
[154] Johnson, *Jahrestage*, p. 1856.   [155] Ibid., pp. 1856f.

case, Gesine insists that her memory remains the same, despite the later information, but that this is not how it really *was* – which rather suggests that the memory has changed as well. She is unable to recall the pleasure of the holiday now without at the same time thinking of what 'really was' at the time. The supplementary information has insinuated itself into the space of her earlier recollection. The event indeed seems to have changed: it was not the pleasant holiday she once thought it was, and one rather wonders where this leaves the linearity of time. In other words, the interference of later information with what we thought we knew about the past is in some ways an embarrassment to linear time; it makes it difficult to locate events on a timeline.

Memory and chronology: when was 'liberation'?

Crucially, Gesine is not alone with such problems. The implications of notions of temporality can be developed by exploring an example, returning to a problematic first raised in Chapter 2: how the end of the Second World War is to be remembered in Germany. There I noted that a group of politicians of the conservative to right-wing end of the spectrum published an advertisement in the *Frankfurter Allgemeine Zeitung* that exhorted readers to guard 'against forgetting'.[156] The group around Dregger of the CDU sought to remember that 8 May 1945 had meant not only the end of the National Socialist tyranny but also the beginning of expulsions, oppression in the East and the division of the country.[157] According to Dubiel, they had been provoked by the clear assessment of 8 May as a 'day of liberation' in the plans for the main 1995 commemorations. The publication of the advertisement marked the beginning of a controversy about the interpretation of 8 May.[158] Chapter 2 showed that the parameters of remembering versus forgetting within which this debate was conducted were unhelpful. Here I reconsider this issue from the vantage point of temporality.

There has always been a struggle over how to remember the end of the Second World War.[159] Articulations of the memory of 8 May 1945 have, as one would expect, changed over time.[160] At first, the date was not part of the official schedule of commemorations; it was only acknowledged by

---

[156] '8. Mai 1945 – Gegen das Vergessen', *Frankfurter Allgemeine Zeitung*, 07/04/95, 3.
[157] Dubiel, *Niemand ist frei*, p. 263.   [158] Naumann, *Krieg als Text*, p. 21.
[159] The end of the Second World War was of course not in May 1945. However, the end of the war for Germany was, and it is this 'end' that is at issue here.
[160] See Jeffrey K. Olick, 'Genre Memories and Memory Genres: A Dialogical Analysis of May 8, 1945. Commemorations in the Federal Republic of Germany', *American Sociological Review*, 64 (1999), 381–402.

the Federal Government in 1965.[161] Furthermore, as Dubiel points out, in the 1970s it was not possible in West Germany 'to articulate publicly the ambivalence of the date, more precisely: the possibility of seeing in it primarily the liberation'.[162] In other words, at that time the end of the war was seen as anything but liberation. 'Defeat' was the most prominent alternative description, though 'collapse' was a term current at the end of the war.

In 1970, von Weizsäcker addressed the mixed feelings linked to 8 May in the Germans' public and private consciousness, foreshadowing elements of his famous speech fifteen years later.[163] He noted:

Our experiences regarding 8 May do not correspond one with another. Everyone experienced it in their own way. One person returned home, the other lost his *Heimat*. This one was liberated, for that one captivity started. Some were embittered by shattered illusions, others grateful for the gift of a new beginning. For many of us 8 May has shaped our consciousness like no other date. Others have no interest at all in this date.[164]

Von Weizsäcker thus appealed to people not to try to make 'their personal experiences a standard for everyone'.[165] In 1985, in his speech as federal president that was to become influential, von Weizsäcker elaborated on these themes in a more receptive environment, though there was still considerable resistance to his ideas.[166] Accordingly, his speech was considered a 'sensation' at the time: no politician had previously acknowledged the responsibility of the Germans for their Nazi past with such 'insistence and historical precision'.[167] Apart from this crucial acceptance of responsibility for the crimes of the Nazi regime, it was, according to Naumann, one particular sentence by von Weizsäcker that 'stuck in the collective memory: "8 May was a day of liberation"'.[168] This declaration of belief profoundly influenced future assessments of the date. Given a choice between 'liberation' and 'defeat', in 1985 the majority – 58 per cent overall – even claimed that they had experienced the day as 'liberation' *in 1945*.[169] In 1995, the idea of liberation appeared dominant. A media initiative, for example, proclaimed that '[f]reedom is celebrating its birthday'.[170] This provoked the appeal 'Against forgetting'.

---

[161] Naumann, *Krieg als Text*, p. 228.   [162] Dubiel, *Niemand ist frei*, p. 134.
[163] Ibid., p. 135.
[164] Von Weizsäcker in Deutscher Bundestag, *Plenarprotokoll*, 6/51, 1970, 2567 quoted in Dubiel, *Niemand ist frei*, p. 135.
[165] Ibid.   [166] Langenbacher, 'Changing Memory Regimes', 53.
[167] Dubiel, *Niemand ist frei*, p. 208.   [168] Naumann, *Krieg als Text*, p. 232.
[169] Elisabeth Noelle-Neumann, 'Ein Volk, gebeutelt und gezeichnet', *Die Zeit*, 10/05/85, 7.
[170] Naumann, *Krieg als Text*, p. 232.

Serious points can be raised against the interpretation of 8 May 1945 as a day of liberation; the advertisement campaign made use of that. Scholars have noted the hardship expellees experienced and the implications of this for the idea of 'liberation'. Michael Schwartz argues that part of the ambivalence of 8 May is that the forced expulsions of 14 million Germans, of whom 2 million are thought to have died in the process, must be considered. He points out that the meaning of the date is therefore 'not exhausted' by the idea of liberation.[171] Moeller similarly notes that for many expellees 'the liberation of Europe, celebrated by the Allies, meant only "liberation" from possessions, homes, and, in some cases, loved ones'.[172] Others point to the GDR and claim that only West Germans were 'liberated' in 1945, whilst East Germans found themselves with a different kind of dictatorship.

The controversy over the interpretation of 8 May has always been seen as a struggle between the Right and the Left. Therefore commentators were intrigued that 'Right' and 'Left' ideas about the end of the war seemed to have swapped sides by 1985. Or, to put it differently, both sides changed their assessment of what constitutes an appropriate memory over time. In the immediate postwar years the Left insisted on a German 'defeat' out of which grew the responsibility to improve. The Right – without using the word 'liberation' – represented the end of the war as the Allies taking a heavy burden off the shoulders of the Germans who had been 'abused' or 'seduced' by Hitler.[173] Later, however, the Left focused on the fate of the victims of National Socialism and the political change towards liberal democracy (despite the worry about the extent of political continuity), thus labelling the end of the war 'liberation'. The Right, in contrast, stressed the division of the country and therefore the consequences and indeed sacrifices entailed by 'defeat'.[174] The Left, Naumann explains, focused on the bankruptcy of the *regime*, the Right on the costs for the *nation*. Given the extensive popular support for the regime, however, these alternative interpretations are symmetrical to each other, and both offer an implicit apology. 'Liberation' reinterprets the Germans as the victims of National Socialism; 'defeat' stresses the burden for the Germans and in this way seems to reduce German responsibility.[175]

Dubiel notes that even in 1995 'the dispute about whether 8 May 1945 was a day of liberation or of defeat dominated the consciousness of the public'.[176] He observes that it was addressed in the overwhelming majority of commemorative speeches.[177] Both sides were stuck in a

---

[171] Schwartz, 'Vertreibung und Vergangenheitspolitik', 177.
[172] Moeller, *War Stories*, p. 71.   [173] Naumann, *Krieg als Text*, pp. 277f.
[174] Ibid., p. 278.   [175] Ibid.   [176] Dubiel, *Niemand ist frei*, p. 52.   [177] Ibid., p. 264.

binary frame of reference – 'liberation' versus 'defeat' – and Naumann argues that they remained so even when they attempted to break out of it.[178] He points out that the most common counter-argument that stressed the interrelationship between the two did not change the basic premises.[179] What linked these interpretations was that they both tended to view 'the historic we-community [*Wir-Gemeinschaft*] as an object of the circumstances, some as the sufferer [*Leidensträger*] of "defeat" and "new oppression", the others as those on whom the hopes of "liberation" from outside were pinned'.[180] This controversy over 'liberation' or 'defeat' is thus set to continue; there does not seem to be a way of thinking outside the categories offered. The role of temporality in setting up the issue is significant. Both sides assume that there is an event in the past – coming to a close on 8 May 1945 (or indeed 9 May)[181] with the unconditional surrender of the German Reich to the Allies – that might be interpreted in different ways. In other words, in tune with conceptualisations of memory discussed above, this interpretation construes the remembered event – 8 May 1945, or rather the events coming to an end on this day – as in the past; the memory of it, however, is in the present and therefore subject to change. Changing political circumstances in the FRG led to different ways of remembering. Overall, it appears that there has been a shift away from remembering the end of the war as defeat towards remembering it as liberation. Both interpretations share the assumption that it 'was' one or the other.

If 'liberation' is an appropriate way of remembering this past, one would have to assume that the events coming to a conclusion on 8 May 1945 *have always been* liberation. A number of interesting points come into view by looking at this within the context of temporality. Firstly, if liberation refers to the deliverance of an oppressed people, whilst defeat connotes the wrestling-down of a people that supported its government, then the two are incompatible.[182] This is certainly how the controversy treats them. In this case, if the events coming to a close in May 1945 had always been liberation, there would never have been defeat. In other words, although the Nazi regime lost the war, the Germans – in this interpretation – did not: they were liberated by the Allies. Secondly, this does not seem to be how events appeared in 1945. Many Germans referred to

---

[178] Naumann, *Krieg als Text*, p. 279.   [179] Ibid., p. 286.   [180] Ibid., p. 288.

[181] A second document of surrender was signed in Berlin-Karlshorst for the Soviet Union on 9 May. In Germany, the surrender in Reims before the Western Allies – signed on 7 May but effective from 8 May – is treated as the 'real' surrender. Ibid., pp. 236f.

[182] Barnouw, however, points out that many Germans would have experienced the events as both liberation *and* defeat. *War in the Empty Air*, p. 112.

the situation as *Zusammenbruch* ('collapse') at the time.[183] Although Norbert Frei points out that *Zusammenbruch* was a 'comfortable metaphor that disguised individual responsibility',[184] this does not mean that it was not what people experienced: after all, the collapse was one not merely of a country's military but of a regime and its entire ideology which many people had previously believed in. This might also be called defeat. In either case, although there certainly were those who were genuinely liberated, liberation seems not to have been at the forefront of the Germans' minds at the end of the war. Neither were they offered liberation. The declaration of the Yalta Conference in February 1945 stated the 'unalterable intention to destroy German militarism and Nazism and to create the guarantee that Germany would never again be in a position to break world peace'.[185] Indeed, although the stated aim was not to destroy the German people, but to give them a chance to return to a place within the community of nations in the future,[186] US President Franklin D. Roosevelt clarified in a memo to his Joint Chiefs of Staff that he was 'not willing at this time to say that we do not intend to destroy the whole German nation'.[187] The American declaration that they were coming as a 'victorious army, not as liberators' was frequently cited in connection with commemorations of 8 May in Germany in 1995.[188]

Thus in 1945 liberation was neither offered nor accepted. And yet from today's perspective it appears that liberation has taken place; retrospectively, it has been. So 8 May 1945 is remembered as a day of liberation. This raises problems. As shown at the beginning of this chapter, what I called the presentist conception of memory locates memory firmly in the present in which it is produced; the memory may then change over time, which is what appears to have happened here. However, this leads to a difficulty. If the past happened before the present and cannot be affected by the present, *either* our current understanding of the end of the Second World War as liberation is wrong (and if it is right, previous memories would have been wrong) *or* the events amounted to liberation even when no one looked at them in that way. Both seem uncomfortable options: in the one case we have to accept an alternative interpretation that faces the same problem, in the other we have to assume that liberation could

[183] Heinrich Jaenecke, 'Die Stunde Null', *Geo Epoche* (9/2002), 29.
[184] Norbert Frei, *Vergangenheitspolitik: Die Anfänge der Bundesrepublik und die NS-Vergangenheit* (Munich: Deutscher Taschenbuch Verlag 1999), p. 128.
[185] 'Amtliche Verlautbarung über die Konferenz von Jalta vom 3. bis 11. Februar 1945 (Auszug)', Reprinted in Clemens Vollnhals, with Thomas Schlemmer (eds.), *Entnazifizierung: Politische Säuberung und Rehabilitierung in den vier Besatzungszonen 1945–1949* (Munich: Deutscher Taschenbuch Verlag 1991), p. 97.
[186] Ibid., p. 98.   [187] Quoted in Bower, *The Pledge Betrayed*, p. 124.
[188] Naumann, *Krieg als Text*, p. 211.

have taken place without anyone knowing, something that certainly sits uncomfortably with liberal and conservative ideas about freedom.

Following Gesine's logic with respect to her telling of Robert's re-appearance, liberation would take its place in the chronology when it was understood as such: somewhere around 1985, perhaps. This is awkward if 'the past' happened indisputably before the present. Following Gesine's thinking with respect to the last holiday with Alexander, we would perhaps continue to remember May 1945 as 'collapse' or 'defeat', but appreciate at the same time that 'really' it was 'liberation', in which case liberation would have happened in 1945. Much as Gesine's recollection of the holiday is affected by learning of the extermination of Jews and Alexander's small act of resistance, our understanding of 8 May 1945 could be affected by knowledge of the FRG's success as a liberal democracy. At the time, this would not have been known. Indeed, if the Morgenthau plan with its forced transformation of Germany into an agrarian society had been implemented,[189] we might not have been able to speak of 'liberation' now. As Walser notes, we remember as who we have become. That is, in May 1945 it was impossible to know whether this was 'liberation'; whether it would be depended on the future. Hence it would not have been liberation then, but it is now. In other words, in this view the events would have *become* liberation, retrospectively, only once people interpreted them in this way; but then it appears that the past itself changed retrospectively. This, again, is an uncomfortable view of the matter within a linear notion of time. Thus memory seems to be an embarrassment to our notion of temporality.

Thinking time differently

It is interesting, therefore, to examine the implications of thinking time differently. Vonnegut attempts this in *Slaughterhouse 5*. He challenges our notion of time by working with an alternative, Tralfamadorian time. In this conception of time, every moment persists. Tralfamadorians 'can look at all the different moments just the way we can look at a stretch of the Rocky Mountains'.[190] Although the context is different, one is reminded of Walser's comment that the 'past still is, even if [it is] over'. Billy, who starts out with a 'commonsense' linear conception of time, has a confusing life because he has 'come unstuck in time'. Coming from a linear time perspective, he is exposed to involuntary time-travel: he moves

---

[189] Grayling, *Among the Dead Cities*, p. 159. For the argument that the 'Morgenthau plan' was not as it is remembered, see Olick, *In the House*, part I.
[190] Vonnegut, *Slaughterhouse 5*, p. 19; see also p. 62.

up and down the arrow of time. He experiences his life as not obeying the linearity that he expects. Instead, Billy may at any moment find himself at any time in his life. He is able to remember the future – something that is normally prohibited – but he is unable to change future events.

Taking their cue from Hawking's question 'Why do we remember the past, and not the future?',[191] Peter Middleton and Tim Woods discuss time and memory in relation to Hawking's *A Brief History of Time*. They submit that 'the way he answers the question underlines the degree to which modern physics has upset ordinary conceptions of time, and has elicited literary and philosophical attempts to understand the consequences for everyday life in time'.[192] Hawking explains that the 'arrow of time' that distinguishes the future from the past and thus gives a direction to time may be seen as reflected, for example, in the increase of disorder, or entropy. According to Hawking, there are 'at least three different arrows of time', thermodynamic, psychological and cosmological, and the first two arrows 'necessarily always point in the same direction'.[193] Hawking, interestingly, once argued that the universe would eventually collapse back into itself and that this 'would mean that the contracting phase would be like the time reverse of the expanding phase. People in the contracting phase would live their lives backwards: they would die before they were born and get younger as the universe contracted.'[194] Although Hawking has now changed his mind about this, Middleton and Woods observe that '[p]hysics and mathematics appear to allow for temporal reversibility' and that this is a 'seeming asymmetry between physics and experience'.[195] The laws of science, to quote Hawking, 'do not distinguish between the forward and backward directions of time'.[196]

According to Middleton and Woods, Hawking's narrative of science and time itself relies on *two* temporalities:

The time of history, discovery, subjective reasoning and the social relations of scientists affected by wars, nationality, institutions and the media of communication, is constantly signalled to the reader through dates and other markers. This time is constantly surpassing the shortcomings of the past in its future-oriented passage of development, prediction and results, while the other, ahistorical, time or detemporalised existence, has no rhetorical displays to indicate its importance, and is simply presented implicitly as an assumed condition of the known, law-governed material processes discovered within the first sort of time.[197]

[191] Hawking, *Brief History of Time*, pp. 143f.
[192] Peter Middleton and Tim Woods, *Literatures of Memory: History, Time and Space in Postwar Writing* (Manchester: Manchester University Press 2000), p. 122.
[193] Hawking, *Brief History of Time*, p. 145.   [194] Ibid., p. 150.
[195] Middleton and Woods, *Literatures of Memory*, p. 123.
[196] Hawking, *Brief History of Time*, p. 152.
[197] Middleton and Woods, *Literatures of Memory*, p. 125.

The second time is fundamental, and it 'produces a division between the eternity of physical law and the history of material activity'.[198] Thus Hawking, in his narrative of science, actually reproduces an unreflected notion of time 'out there', separate from social activity. As Middleton and Woods point out, there is 'nothing unusual about Hawking's deployment of these two temporalities. This is the standard scientific world picture, and it has been enormously influential.' What they find interesting, however, is that 'Hawking's book inadvertently demonstrates what has been so disturbing about modern physics of time and space – its claim to authoritative control over the imagination of social time and its relation to the past.'[199] They give examples of how the notion of relativity was seen to affect ideas of time in the wider public, show how scientists fed these linkages and explain that the:

theory of relativity seemed to ascribe temporal difference entirely to perspective, which could be understood as a merely subjective limitation added to the mathematically formulable objective reality of a spacetime which already contained the future alongside the past. Kurt Vonnegut's amusing spoof on the popular image of the time of the new physics in *Slaughterhouse Five* shows how disturbing the idea has been. It also implicates the new physics in the failures of social memory.[200]

Middleton and Woods note that the narrator of *Slaughterhouse 5* construes the book as a failure

because it is so inadequate to the unique horror of the fire-bombing, but can only measure this failure by showing the reader that the advanced scientific discourse of spacetime which ought to be the best means of writing about the new experiences of the century, appears absurd and renders its possessors mad in the eyes of the ordinary world.[201]

So, they continue, 'Vonnegut's parody of relativity can be read as no more than a dismissal of the relevance of science to the crises of modernity, but it suggests another reading as well. Perhaps modern memory's sometimes uncontrollable *Nachträglichkeit* does result from changes to the locatability of the past resulting from the new temporalities of science.'[202] Whether or not the new temporalities of science bear any direct relation to this, it certainly appears difficult to locate 'the past', which anyway is unlike what it was when it was thought to be the present, because the present always enters into this past. Memory is always belated, *nachträglich*; we recall retrospectively what appears to have been in a way that it never was. Crucially, what appears to have been may change, with all the implications for linear temporality already discussed.

---

[198] Ibid.   [199] Ibid., p. 126.   [200] Ibid., p. 127.   [201] Ibid.   [202] Ibid., p. 128.

Vonnegut's novel explicitly picks up the idea of spacetime, but other novels also engage this idea. In *Das steinerne Brautbett*, Corinth suggests expressing time as space, much like we express space as time when we speak of something being an hour away.[203] He also contemplates the idea that the soul has a different relationship to space and time from that of the physical body. The soul, he thinks, 'travels by horse'. Because he travelled to Dresden by plane, this means that his soul would arrive months after him, and he would have to do without it for the duration. He would 'have to manage without himself for months, like he managed without himself for years after the war'.[204] In other words, Corinth is not sure whether his soul can keep up with the speed of developments around him, in particular – apparently – whether it is able to process quickly enough experiences such as the ones he had in the war. Thus his experience of time and space becomes heterogeneous. In *Jahrestage*, too, the inextricable relation of time and space is an issue; more specifically, time and space are rhetorically conflated, as Riordan notes.[205] Gesine is once woken up by Marie with the words, 'Gesine, wake up. Where have you been [?]' Gesine – conflating time and space – replies, 'A few years ago.'[206] The same occurs in relation to memory, which is at one point described as reporting 'as the present at the location where [Gesine's lover] now stays',[207] as if the matter was one of spatial distance.

Billy is, of course, estranged from his environment through his time-travelling, a common theme in the genre of science fiction. Assmann asserts that this 'playful aura of strangeness' allows Vonnegut to approach the war experience whilst simultaneously distancing himself from it.[208] Where the recalling of memories, for example together with his friend, fails, the experimental character of the idea of time-travel allows Vonnegut to confront his experience of the war. However, by focusing on the distancing implied by Billy's time-travelling, Assmann loses sight of the other side of the coin. Billy may appear distanced from his environment owing to his frequent 'trips' to another time. But he is also very much 'there' in a different time. He only appears distanced to those who operate according to the earthly illusion of linear time.

This is reminiscent of the narrator's criticism of his mother in Grass's *Im Krebsgang*, discussed in Chapter 2. Tulla experiences the events of the sinking of the *Gustloff* as 'out of time' and permanently present. Tulla, much like Billy, though without the science-fiction implications, finds herself in a time different from the one her environment expects her to

[203] Mulisch, *Brautbett*, p. 44.   [204] Ibid., p. 27.
[205] Riordan, *Ethics of Narration*, p. 106.   [206] Johnson, *Jahrestage*, p. 120.
[207] Ibid., p. 1806.   [208] Assmann, *Erinnerungsräume*, p. 289.

be in. Paul is convinced that this being stuck in time is what stops her from working through the ethical issue of the sinking of the *Gustloff*. Yet Middleton and Woods argue, in relation to Pat Barker's work (which they liken in this respect to Billy Pilgrim's 'unpredictable temporal swoops and forays'), that '[a]nachronism becomes a necessary measure of the working-through and ethical relation to history'.[209] In other words, being 'out of time' or at the 'wrong' point in time, notwithstanding the worry about the lack of free will, may be crucial for coming to terms with ethico-political issues. Gesine certainly experiences the question of responsibility vis-à-vis the Third Reich as particularly acute because she is out of time and re-experiences situations from childhood as an adult.

Even within *Slaughterhouse 5* and much less with respect to how we think more generally, there is no question of dispensing with linear temporality. Woods notes that in *Slaughterhouse 5* temporality 'is not treated . . . in a linear fashion, because the present moment embeds within it pretensions and retensions of the past and future'.[210] As we have seen, Billy notes that '[w]hen a Tralfamadorian sees a corpse, all he thinks is that the dead person is in a bad condition in that particular moment, but that the same person is just fine in plenty of other moments'.[211] Thus Woods draws attention to how the novel constitutes a challenge to the idea that time is naturally and necessarily linear: 'Vonnegut's aim is to allow human actions to be freed from the ideology of linear temporality with its model of the road and life-as-a-straightforward-journey, arranging temporality more as a rhythmic time which abandons the teleology, the transcendence and the putative neutrality of linear time.' In the Tralfamadorian view, 'all times are always present and absent'. However, as Woods points out, this does not represent a complete abandonment of linear temporality: 'after all, the Tralfamadorian is *dead*. Time is linear, too'.[212] Tralfamadorian time is at the same time linear and non-linear. The point 'is not that one can do away with concepts of linear temporality, but one has to recognize that linear temporality is *not the only way* that temporality can be thought: linear concepts need to be supplemented with non-linear concepts'.[213] Billy, of course, remarks upon what he experiences as different, namely that, as Woods puts it, 'temporal linearity is an earthly illusion'. Woods relates this to 'Vonnegut's powerful pacifist fictional narrative' that 'ushers in the political and ethical importance of conceiving history and its othernesses'.[214] This conclusion is then almost diametrically opposed to Jones's worry, cited above, that

---

[209] Middleton and Woods, *Literatures of Memory*, p. 117.
[210] Woods, 'Spectres of History', 107.   [211] Vonnegut, *Slaughterhouse 5*, p. 20.
[212] Woods, 'Spectres of History', 107.   [213] Ibid.   [214] Ibid., 117.

Vonnegut's idea of Tralfamadorian time makes free will impossible and war therefore inevitable, implying that Vonnegut gets rid of politics and ethics.

Woods claims instead that 'Vonnegut's dynamic non-linear narrative dramatizes the moment when the flow of history is arrested by a configuration which shocks the present into releasing the affirmative and emancipatory thinking of the messianic'.[215] The messianic, in Derrida's thinking, on which Woods draws, refers to 'the event that cannot be awaited *as such*, or recognized in advance therefore, to the event as the foreigner itself, to her or to him for whom one must leave an empty place, always, in memory of the hope – and this is the very place of spectrality'.[216] Woods notes that 'the future holds spectrality within it as well, as it swims blurringly into the present and hints at possible alternative trajectories for the present. It is a form of opening oneself to the impossible and making it possible in its very impossibility.'[217] The question of the impossible possibility is, in Derridean thought, the question of ethics.

The future of ethics

Some of what has been developed in this chapter in relation to memory – specifically as represented in novels – may be linked to the implications of Derrida's thought in relation to time. Derrida is widely known to critique what he calls the 'metaphysics of presence'.[218] That is, he questions the way in which Western thinking is based on the possibility of presence. According to Derrida, pure presence is impossible. Jonathan Culler explains this by discussing the flight of an arrow. At any given instant, the arrow is in a particular place; it is never in motion. And yet, Culler argues, we 'want to insist, quite justifiably, that the arrow *is* in motion at every instant from the beginning to the end of its flight, yet its motion is never present at any moment of presence. The presence of motion is conceivable, it turns out, only insofar as every instant is already marked with the traces of the past and the future.' Motion therefore requires that the present instant be 'a product of relations between past and future. Something can be happening at a given instant only if the instant is already divided within itself, inhabited by the nonpresent'.[219] To put this differently, each moment contains retensions of the past and pretensions of the future; pure presence is impossible.

[215] Ibid.   [216] Derrida, *Spectres of Marx*, p. 65.
[217] Woods, 'Spectres of History', 110.   [218] Derrida, *Of Grammatology*, p. 49.
[219] Culler, *On Deconstruction*, p. 94.

Thus it is necessary to go beyond the mutual exclusivity of presence and absence that, Derrida argues, is central to Western thought but deeply problematic. To do so, Derrida introduces the idea of *différance*. *Différance* is intrinsically related to the French for difference, *différence*. Both sound the same, but the 'a' signals the active character of *différance*, which plays on the two meanings of the French word *différer*: to differ and to defer. *Différance*, on the one hand, means something not being identical or being other, discernible. On the other hand, it refers to a 'temporal or temporizing mediation or a detour that suspends the accomplishment or fulfillment of "desire" or "will"', and equally effects this suspension in a mode that annuls or tempers its own effect.'[220] *Différance* always has more than one meaning, and these may not be reduced to one another. *Différance*

is a structure and a movement no longer conceivable on the basis of the opposition presence/absence. *Différance* is the systematic play of differences, of the traces of differences, of the *spacing* by means of which elements are related to each other. This spacing is the simultaneously active and passive . . . production of the intervals without which the 'full' terms would not signify, would not function.[221]

Différance, in other words, highlights the movement of delay, detour or postponement inherent in signification, but it also produces differences. As such it makes possible oppositional concepts, for example, sensible/intelligible, intuition/signification, nature/culture.[222]

Derrida notes that the 'present is that from which we believe we are able to think time, effacing the inverse necessity: to think the present from time as différance'.[223] In the thinking Derrida criticises the 'past is a former present, the future an anticipated present, but the present simply is: an autonomous given'.[224] Thus he challenges the familiar linear relationship from the past, which once was the present, to the future, which will become the present. The present is not only dominant in this conception; it is, Derrida argues, conceptualised as pure, distinct from both past and present. This is not only revealed as problematic by Derrida but also leads to tensions in our thinking of time, certainly in relation to memory. Walser and Johnson in particular think through in their novels how the past and the present are inextricably linked, how they seep into each other; the difficulties raised by the idea of linearity were also apparent in relation to memories of 'liberation'. Yet Derrida also argues that our linear conception of time is crucially significant. He speaks of the linearity of 'the traditional concept of time' as 'an entire organization

---

[220] Jacques Derrida, *Margins of Philosophy*, Translated, with additional notes, by Alan Bass (Chicago: The University of Chicago Press 1982), p. 8.
[221] Derrida, *Positions*, p. 27.   [222] Ibid., pp. 8f.
[223] Derrida, *Of Grammatology*, p. 166.   [224] Culler, *On Deconstruction*, p. 95.

of the world and of language'.[225] Thus, much like Vonnegut's rendering of Tralfamadorian time, Derrida's argument acknowledges the profound significance of the linearity of time in our thinking. His thought also seeks to open up the possibility, however, of imagining the world in ways that are not locked in by this inevitable – but impossible – linearity and its implications.

Derrida draws attention to how memory is not just about the past or indeed the present. In *Memoires for Paul de Man* he observes:

> The memory we are considering here is not essentially oriented toward the past, toward a present deemed to have really and previously existed. Memory stays with traces, in order to 'preserve' them, but traces of a past that has never been present, traces which themselves never occupy the form of presence and always remain, as it were, to come – come from the future, from the *to come*.[226]

Thus, firstly, the past 'has never been present'. This formulation, which decidedly challenges thinking that regards the past as a former present and the future as a present to be, recalls ideas that we have already seen expressed, for example by Walser and Johnson. Secondly, and perhaps more importantly, the traces of the past that has never been are yet to come and are thus associated with the future. This is perhaps counter-intuitive, although linking memory to the future is not uncommon. In the debate on Wehrmacht atrocities, for example, Defence Minister Rühe underlined the significance of looking 'at our past critically in order to draw the right lessons for the future'.[227] For Geißler, the whole point of remembering was to shape the future in the right way.[228] Derrida, however, expresses something more fundamental by linking memory with the future.

When Derrida argues that the 'new cannot be invented without memory or repetition',[229] this must be read within the context of Derrida's conceptualisation of the future. Derrida distinguishes two meanings of 'the future'. On the one hand, the 'future is that which – tomorrow, later, next century – will be. There's a future which is predictable, programmed, scheduled, foreseeable.'[230] This is presumably the future that politicians are referring to when they underline the need to remember the past in order to learn lessons for the future: the possibility of planning is assumed. There is, however, Derrida explains, another future:

> there is a future . . . to come which refers to someone who comes whose arrival is totally unexpected. For me, that is the real future. That which is totally unpredictable. The Other who comes without my being able to anticipate their arrival.

---

[225] Derrida, *Of Grammatology*, p. 85.   [226] Derrida, *Memoires*, p. 58.
[227] Deutscher Bundestag, *Plenarprotokoll*, 13/163, 13/03/97, 14721.   [228] Ibid., 14726.
[229] Derrida, *Negotiations*, p. 238.
[230] Derrida in Kirby Dick and Amy Ziering Kofman, *Derrida* (Jane Doe Films 2003).

So if there is a real future behind this other known future, it's l'avenir in that it's the coming of the Other. When I am completely unable to foresee their arrival.[231]

Thus Derrida is interested in the future to come, in the future which may not be anticipated and which therefore offers possibilities we are not able to imagine. As he says, an 'event is only possible when it comes from the impossible. It arrives *as* the coming of the impossible, where a "perhaps" deprives us of all assurance and leaves the future to the future.'[232] Thus an event is the unexpected, it involves a moment of surprise;[233] it is not the routine unfolding of a course we may predict. This, of course, means that such an event may be seen as dangerous, threatening: before it arrives we do not know what it will be.

Derrida argues, however, that we must not seek to overcome this unpredictability: 'The coming of the event is what cannot and should not be prevented; it is another name for the future itself.'[234] Already in *Of Grammatology*, Derrida set out his work as 'a way of thinking that is faithful and attentive to the ineluctable world of the future which proclaims itself at present, beyond the closure of knowledge. The future can only be anticipated in the form of an absolute danger.'[235] Yet, according to Derrida, 'without risk, there is nothing'.[236] Crucially, the ethical is not possible without risk. As was shown in Chapter 2, the ethical is inextricably connected, for Derrida, with the moment of decision. It is a crucial characteristic of such a decision that it moves towards that which cannot be known: 'Even if one knows everything, the decision, if there is one, must advance towards a future that is not known, that cannot be anticipated.'[237] In contrast, where we apply knowledge, where a programme simply unfolds, ethico-political decisioning is not possible.

Jones's concern that Vonnegut's Tralfamadorian world excludes free will, and that therefore war comes to be inevitable, highlights that how we conceptualise time has an impact on our understandings of ethics and politics. In Tralfamadorian time we may not change anything, because the future already is, and therefore ethics and politics become meaningless. In other words, our conceptions of ethics and politics require that time is linear: there must be a past on the basis of which we make decisions in the present for the future. It is the linearity between past, present and future that makes responsibility (so conceived) possible. The trouble with this is that this conception of time – however natural it may seem – does not actually seem to work, certainly in relation to memory. In the context of the question of whether Germans were liberated at the end of the

---

[231] Derrida in ibid.   [232] Derrida, *Negotiations*, p. 344.   [233] Ibid., p. 96.
[234] Ibid., p. 94.   [235] Derrida, *Of Grammatology*, pp. 4f.
[236] Derrida, *Negotiations*, p. 238.   [237] Ibid., p. 231.

Second World War, linearity posed serious problems. It was impossible to say when such liberation was supposed to have taken place, something one ought to have no trouble with on the basis of linear time. Chronology turned out to be much more problematic than the notion of linear time suggests.

Therefore it is interesting to work through the implications of thinking time differently. Whilst in Jones's view Vonnegut makes free will impossible and thus closes off the possibility of ethics, Woods relates Vonnegut's non-linear narrative to the Derridean idea of the messianic, that is, the unexpected. The messianic highlights Derrida's notion of the 'real' future as the to-come, which we do not expect and therefore cannot plan for. Thus the future, rather than being merely that which will turn into the present, is the space for the new, for that which we cannot deal with on the basis of knowledge alone, that is, ethico-political decisioning. The future poses a risk, but a risk that enables us to face ethico-political questions. Crucially, the future in the Derridean sense is not just what comes after the present; it is not just that which will be the present in the future: it is only the experience of the aporia that allows 'for the future, it allows the future to arrive *as* a future (and not a future present) and so allows for the future of the decision (a future in which decisions can "take place" and decisions in which the future is not anticipated)'.[238]

In their commemorative speeches in 1995, both Chancellor Kohl and Federal President Herzog attempted to offer ways out of the interpretative impasse regarding the question of how 8 May 1945 was to be interpreted. Kohl asserted that, for him, 8 May 1945 had been a day of liberation, but that there are 'no restrictions on memory'.[239] He further said that no one may determine how people remember; 8 May needed 'space for many feelings'.[240] In other words, no common interpretation of the date should be enforced, and everyone should be free to remember as they wished. Herzog went further in offering what he framed as a new way of looking at the matter. He claimed that the question of 'liberation' or 'defeat' was not fruitful. He suggested instead that 8 May 1945 had 'opened a gateway to the future'. This, according to Naumann, is the key phrase of Herzog's speech.[241] Herzog insisted that as a member of the younger generation he retrospectively sees this day as one on which 'a gateway to the future was opened. It followed terrible sacrifices and involved terrible sacrifices, but it was still a gateway to the future.'[242] Naumann observes that in

---

[238] Ibid., p. 233.   [239] Naumann, *Krieg als Text*, p. 22.
[240] *Welt am Sonntag*, 23/04/95 quoted in ibid., p. 275.   [241] Ibid., p. 262.
[242] Roman Herzog, 'Return to the Future: Speech by the Federal President in Berlin on 8 May 1995', in: *Remembrance and Perpetual Responsibility* (Bonn: Press and Information Office of the Federal Government 1995), 21.

this argument the 'pathos of the future absorbs the past'.[243] Yet the real trouble with Herzog's future is that it is already in the past. Although he speaks of the future in the sense of a space for new possibilities, we already know what they were. There is no longer any risk. As such, the 'gate to the future' sounds suspiciously like a different way of framing 'liberation', implying as it does that this gate had previously been closed. Herzog's future is not the future as the to-come: we already know where the gate led.

Something like this often happens when politicians speak of the future: they immediately inform us that they know what this future requires, thereby closing down the space for the future as the to-come. Recently, this has been most evident in the USA's acknowledgement that the kinds of thing they want to know in relation to security can never be known,[244] and the simultaneous attempts to know and impose control, most obviously in the war against Iraq.[245] President Bush is sometimes credited with saying that 'the future will be better tomorrow', but this is most probably an urban myth. What Derrida's thought implies is not only that we have no way of knowing whether the future will be better because the future is a realm of risk but also that the future – as far as it exists – is not a future present but rather the irreducibly risky space for ethics that must be seized now.

Concluding thoughts

This chapter has explored problems that arise in relation to the nexus of linear temporality and memory. It started out by noting that although a linear conception of time might appear to be natural, even inescapable, such an understanding of temporality seemed not only insufficient in terms of accounting for our experience of time but was also challenged by modern physics. Walser's assertion, discussed in Chapter 4, that we cannot remember the past as it was when it was the present, not least because we no longer are who we were, had already highlighted the fact that memory and temporality are intertwined. This chapter has argued that conceptions of memory that rendered memory as *in* the present but *about* the past seemed to capture something significant about the phenomenon, but were in the end unable to account for how past and present intersect in memory. Through the readings of the issue of temporality in

---

[243] Naumann, *Krieg als Text*, p. 262.

[244] Most famous are, of course, Rumsfeld's remarks about the 'unknown unknowns'. See Donald Rumsfeld, *NATO Press Conference*, 06/06/02.

[245] On this, see also Jenny Edkins and Maja Zehfuss, 'Generalising the International', *Review of International Studies* 31 (2005), 451–72.

Johnson's *Jahrestage* and Vonnegut's *Slaughterhouse 5*, the question of the time of memory was further examined and then related to the issue of the liberation of Germany.

Memory proved to be an embarrassment to chronology. Gesine's determinedly linear story about her family's past runs into problems. She herself defines chronology in different ways with respect to different subjects, using on one occasion the order of events as they seemed to her to have happened at the time and on another understandings influenced by later information. She is unable to enforce the clear linear development that she aims for, not least because it is not clear what it would mean to do so. What is more, she finds herself 'out of time', inasmuch as she does not only remember as 'who she has become' but also feels compelled to assess her own behaviour in the past as though she had already been who she is now. She worries that this may reflect a mental illness. This insertion of her current subjectivity into the past makes her feel responsible for events in her childhood in a way in which she could only have been if she had then been an adult. Her later understanding of the political situation in which she grew up has supplemented her relation to her childhood experiences. Such a supplement is on the one hand a surplus: Gesine already knew what happened in the past. Yet at the same time it replaces what was: Gesine can no longer understand the situation as she did before. Thus her conception of herself as responsible is inextricably linked with temporality, but at the same time it challenges linearity.

This nexus of time and ethics also comes to be apparent in Vonnegut's *Slaughterhouse 5*. Vonnegut introduces a non-linear concept of time in which the past continues to exist indefinitely. Thus it makes no sense, for example, to be upset about death, as the dead are still alive in other moments that continue to be present. Vonnegut's main character has a memory of the future, indicating that the future, too, already exists and that it remains permanently the same. This means, arguably, that free will is impossible: what will happen already has, and Billy can do nothing about it. Thus, by implication, responsibility disappears. This, again, underlines the way that our conceptions of time and responsibility are intimately linked. However, Woods and Middleton suggest that Vonnegut's idea of Tralfamadorian time does not get rid of responsibility, but instead offers a different vantage point on events. Being 'out of time' or at the 'wrong' point in time may thus be a productive endeavour that enables us to re-evaluate events and our relation to them. It calls for renewed efforts at conceiving the Other, the unexpected. In other words, it makes it necessary to understand the problematic of speaking of the past as an ethico-political problem that, again, cannot be solved merely with reference to knowledge or the truth. That the unexpected lurks within memory – within that which ought to be in the past and hence untouched by anything new – underlines that memory is never merely about the past or even the present, but concerns the future.

The chapter has changed the perspective on the question of whether Germany was liberated by asking, assuming that it was, *when* this is supposed to have been. This discussion revealed that the insecurities of time that we encountered in the fictional representations of the past and memory also occurred with respect to this political event. In particular, it was impossible to locate 'liberation' on a timeline. Little would be gained by being able to do so; the point is, however, that if time was linear, and if memory was about the past, we ought to have no trouble with this. That we do highlights not only that memory is an embarrassment to linear temporality – that it is all but impossible to satisfactorily conceive memory within such an understanding of time – but also that the problem may not be the phenomenon of memory but our unthinking acceptance that time is natural, even, unidirectional. 'Liberation', on which Kinkel's powerful argument about the ethical significance of military deployments hangs, turns out to be not just problematic, but an idea that may be deployed to disturb beliefs that are treated as self-evident truths on which our understanding of ethics – and in particular of responsibility – seems to rest.

6   Memory, uncertainty, responsibility

This book has explored how German memories of the Third Reich and the Second World War have been articulated in a variety of contexts. It has highlighted what one might call the double implication of speaking of the past. On the one hand, the book has examined the closures in such discourses, how they seem to rule out potential objections, thoughts and queries, in particular those that question how the past came to be the past in the first place. On the other hand, and crucially, the book has followed up how the invocation of memory inevitably offers opportunities to challenge the closures that are being produced, in particular when tensions are made visible. These tensions might at times be related to something as simple as the existence of a variety of memories of the past, but they also indicate that remembering retrospectively conjures up a past that never quite existed in this way when it was the present. In this final chapter, I draw out the wider implications of this argument, implications not only in relation to the particular political situation explored but also to wider questions about war and the practice of scholarship. Thus, rather than tying everything together into a neat bundle of conclusions that have already been shown, this chapter opens the arguments up to new questions, implications and challenges.

Challenges of memory

This book started by observing how the past was spoken of in debates about whether the FRG should use its military for anything other than strictly defensive purposes. Memories of the Second World War and its effects were prominent in arguments about the use of force. They formed an important part of the production of the political context within which choices about this issue were made. The horror of war was, for example, cited as relevant, as was, however, the value of war against oppression.

In the debates about the use of force, the past and the alleged memories of it were referred to only telegraphically: in a limited number of words. Lambsdorff described war, without further explanation, as the 'father of all horrors'.[1] Vogel, even more cryptically, merely noted that he knew 'what war means'.[2] Ullmann referred to his experience of being bombed as decisive for his rejection of air raids against Iraq, without, however, describing it.[3] Similarly, there were references to the Wehrmacht 'causing havoc' in the Balkans that remained in the abstract. All this might suggest that there was no need to elaborate, that Germans know what is meant when 'the war' is mentioned. From a closer examination two issues emerge, however: firstly, some argue that Germans remember less of the war than the frequent invocations of memory suggest, and secondly, and more importantly, articulations of war memories are extremely controversial, despite being presented as an obvious, shared point of reference. Both issues were particularly apparent when the shorthand references to the horror of being bombed and the matter of the Wehrmacht having 'wreaked havoc' were read together with, respectively, the public debates on strategic bombing and Wehrmacht atrocities.

Given the consensus that Germans believe war to be hell, one may dismiss the relevance, in practical terms, of the particular details of such an attitude; all that matters is the reluctance to use force, as evident again in the overwhelming rejection of the Iraq war. I argue below, however, that there is a significant difference between the generalised view that 'war is hell' and the ability to imagine or understand the particular ways in which war is hell. The debates within Germany about how the community should relate to the past of the Second World War suggest as much. The discussions set off by Sebald's lecture series on the failure of German literature to portray the impact of strategic bombing and by Friedrich's controversial *Der Brand* confronted people with vivid detail about the destruction and the particular – often gruesome – ways in which people died. These debates were, however, shown to be constrained by concerns over how it is appropriate for the Germans to remember; they prove to be stuck on this issue. Novels were thus explored as another site of memory: one that should, in principle, not be limited by political considerations, and one that includes reflections upon the articulations of memory it presents. From this examination emerged a number of challenges.

Memory seems to be inextricably related to what we call the truth. We appear to know because we remember. The claim to remember implies that what is offered is the truth about a past that is in some intimate way connected to those who are doing the remembering. Ricoeur notes that '[t]o memory is tied an ambition, a claim – that of being faithful to

---

[1] Deutscher Bundestag, *Plenarprotokoll*, 12/3, 17/01/91, 51.   [2] Ibid., 47f.
[3] Quoted in Bölsche, 'So muss die Hölle aussehen', pp. 21f.

the past'.[4] An apparent commitment to the truth of the past was evident in otherwise diverse articulations of memory, such as von Weizsäcker's speech on the fortieth anniversary of the end of the Second World War in Europe and the conservative campaign 'against forgetting'. They spoke of the need to face the truth and the problem that important truths had been denied or obscured. Similarly, novels that depict the war often invoke the idea that the author was 'there', at the events portrayed, in order to underline the authenticity of the representation. Ledig highlighted the significance of this by admitting his inability to write about Bosnia; he said that he could not do it because there was '[t]oo much distance'.[5] Vonnegut's *Slaughterhouse 5* also acknowledges this convention by noting that the narrator had been 'there'[6] at the bombing of Dresden, even if the novel then proceeds to undermine any trust in the authenticity of the story. Despite this apparently intimate connection of truth and memory, however, a series of problems became apparent through the representations of and reflections on memory in the novels examined.

Chapter 5 stressed the nexus of memory and temporality. The idea of a memory of the past seemed to both rely on linear time and challenge it. The temporal ambiguity of memory is apparent; it is ostensibly about a past that has already been, but is itself thought to be located in the present. Huyssen emphatically argues that the 'temporal status of any act of memory is always the present'.[7] This seems to be a problematic way, however. Within a linear understanding of temporality, which might simply not be adequate to capture the phenomenon, memory seems to be precariously suspended *between* the present and the past. We do not remember the past as it was when it was the present. The retrospective assertion by Germans that they experienced 8 May 1945 as 'liberation' might be seen as a case in point; the issue was also explored in novels such as Walser's *Ein springender Brunnen* and, in particular, Johnson's *Jahrestage*. Walser notes that '[a]lthough the past, when it was the present, did not exist, it now imposes itself as if it had existed in the way in which it imposes itself now'.[8] Johnson writes that Gesine is not interested in 'going back into the past, the repetition of what was: to be in it again, to enter there again. That does not exist.'[9] This, however, leaves us with a temporal conundrum, for if the past was not as we experience it now when it was the present, then memory retroactively *produces* – in the present – something that is necessarily already past and therefore appears to already have existed.

---

[4] Ricoeur, *Memory, History, Forgetting*, p. 21.   [5] Hage, 'Die Angst', 164.
[6] Vonnegut, *Slaughterhouse 5*, p. 49. See also Rainer Emig's discussion of authenticity in relation to this novel outlined in Chapter 5, pp. 190–1.
[7] Huyssen, *Twilight Memories*, p. 3.   [8] Walser, *Ein springender Brunnen*, p. 9.
[9] Johnson, *Jahrestage*, p. 63.

In Chapter 4, Walser's reflections on 'the past as present' were considered. He reflects on the issue of when the past becomes the past as we remember it. He also appears to contemplate how this is related to subjectivity. In other words, he reflects not merely on what is remembered and the problem of how it comes to appear as it now does but also on who is doing the remembering and how this subject comes to be. Thus not only is it an illusion that the past was as we now remember it when it was the present but we also remember, Walser points out, 'as who we have become'.[10] We do not remember as who we were when that which is remembered seems to have taken place, in the past. As Mulisch observes, 'we do not know any more how it was because we ourselves have changed and we would have to travel back to find out, but then again we would not be here and would not have changed'.[11] Indeed, the main character of Johnson's *Jahrestage*, Gesine, worries about her sanity precisely because she at times feels an impossible identity between her current and her remembered self, putting her into the impossible position of having to respond to what was as who she has become. As she puts it, 'So I hear myself speak not only from the subjectively real (past) place but also from the place of the subject who today is 35 years old.'[12] Significantly, Gesine's insertion of her current self into the past means that she identifies her past behaviour as a failure because she did not respond – as a child – in the way in which she now – as an adult – might have. Moreover, who we have become is related to what we remember; our memories are part of what makes us who we are. In sum, the past becomes the past retrospectively, when we remember, when we speak of it, and then we no longer are who we were when we imagine that this past was the present. Ricoeur observes in a similar vein that '[i]n remembering something (*se souvenant de quelque chose*), one remembers oneself (*on se souvient de soi*)'.[13] Both the past and the subject who remembers it are produced in the articulation of memory.

This complicates the matter of remembering 'the truth', as does recognising that it is actually impossible to remember everything. Derrida points out that a 'limitless memory would . . . be not memory but infinite self-presence'.[14] In Chapter 2, the significance of forgetting for memory was highlighted. If 'total recall' were possible, we would be in the past again, which is precisely what we are not when we remember. Nevertheless, remembering the truth is an aim cherished by politicians, novelists and indeed the public. Politicians claim to take the past and its lessons into

---

[10] Walser, *Ein springender Brunnen*, p. 15.   [11] Mulisch, *Brautbett*, p. 45.
[12] Johnson, *Jahrestage*, p. 1539.   [13] Ricoeur, *Memory, History, Forgetting*, p. 96.
[14] Derrida, *Dissemination*, p. 109.

account in their political choices or to face the truth in commemorations; novelists promise to depict how it 'really was'. Both acknowledge the important status of the truth in our thinking, and yet the truths they speak of are very different. Politicians typically offer 'the truth', which may then be seen to offer guidance or necessitate a response. This is illustrated by the exception to the rule, von Weizsäcker's acknowledgement in his 1985 speech that there are many possible stories to tell about the end of the war in Europe, that different people experienced this event in different ways. Of course, von Weizsäcker immediately shied away from the implications of this acknowledgement and asserted instead that all Germans had to remember 8 May 1945 as liberation, even if their experiences had been of being imprisoned or losing their home. Novelists construe memory differently; they admit, not least, the possibility of multiple memories without resolving them into one. In Mulisch's *Das steinerne Brautbett*, for example, the couple in the pub and Corinth have different memories of what is ostensibly the same event in the past, the bombing of Dresden, but neither is identified as more 'right' than the other. Grass, too, weaves together different memories of the sinking of the *Gustloff* in a way that suggests their possibility and legitimacy, although he does portray Konrad's memory as unacceptable. The 'truth' might involve such multiplicity which at the same time proves a challenge to the notion that the Second World War is – or should be – remembered in a particular way. Speaking of the past as if it had to be recalled in a particular way, as Kinkel did, for example, sets up a context; other possibilities of imagining the world are delegitimised. Yet this move may be destabilised by memories which are out of tune with what is asserted. Such instrumental arguments have thus been revealed as problematic. Crucially, 'the' German memory does not exist. There is no agreed, acceptable Second World War memory; there could not be. Most obviously, memories will differ depending on perspective. The experience of civilians in the Southern German countryside was different from that of those in the cities of the industrial areas further north, for example, and both of those different again from that of the soldiers.

Yet the problem is more fundamental. Ledig's *Die Stalinorgel*, with its close-up view of the battle, or Mulisch's *Das steinerne Brautbett*, with its unforgiving depiction of the carnage caused by the firestorm in Dresden, do not just tell what was: they attempt to draw the reader into feeling some of the confusion, horror and despair that is part of 'what it was like'. Friedrich's *Der Brand* seems to do something similar, and this is instructive chiefly for the swift rejection in the public debate of such 'sentimentality' in recalling strategic bombing. What is spoken of as memory does not just produce a past: it touches us. Thus memory cannot be grasped within the context of a narrowly conceived rationality; it is in part significant because of the emotions attached to it and aroused by it. There is a quality to memory beyond what may be simply described. A significant part of what the war 'was like' is what it felt like, a dimension that Grass's Tulla identifies as important. For her, any acceptable representation of the sinking of the *Gustloff* has to 'come from the heart'.[15] As a result, memories may be to some extent inexpressible; this was reflected upon in the novels, for example Grass's *Im Krebsgang* but also Vonnegut's *Slaughterhouse 5*.[16] The horror of what went on inside the sinking ship cannot, Grass writes, 'be grasped by words'.[17] It is impossible to 'grasp with words the thousand-fold dying',[18] and even Tulla has no words for it.[19] Forte argues that it is a mistake to think that it is possible to put everything into words. There is, he says, 'horror beyond language, an unspeakable terror'.[20] Thus although he remembers the horror of being repeatedly exposed to air raids, he feels unable to communicate his memory to others.

Ironically, despite the impossibility of expression, there are numerous articulations of memory. The point is not so much that the story cannot be told; it always is. But the memory – be it of an unspeakable horror or of something else – may never entirely be grasped by language. This also means that the act of expression effects an alteration. Through each expression memory changes: it becomes a variation of what has come before. Memory does not merely change over time because the social context does; it necessarily changes in and through its articulation. It always relates not only to the past and present but also to previous expressions of memory. Put differently, articulations of memory involve what Derrida calls iterability. Iterability 'supposes a minimal remainder . . . in order that the identity of the selfsame be repeatable and identifiable *in, through* and even *in view* of its alteration. For the structure of iteration . . . implies *both* identity *and* difference.'[21] Derrida explains this in the context of signification; it must be possible to recognise a sign whilst assigning it a different signification according to the situation. So it is with memory: it changes every time we invoke it, and yet there must be a remainder for us to recognise that it is 'that' memory again. It never returns twice in exactly the same way, but neither does it wholly change or go away. The process might also be understood to be one of 'grafting', where different texts and contexts are written onto and into each other.[22]

[15] Grass, *Im Krebsgang*, p. 94.   [16] See Chapter 5.
[17] Grass, *Im Krebsgang*, p. 136; but see p. 132.   [18] Ibid., p. 139.
[19] Ibid., pp. 136 and 157.   [20] Forte, *Schweigen oder sprechen*, p. 33.
[21] Derrida, *Limited Inc*, p. 53.   [22] See Culler, *On Deconstruction*, p. 134.

It is important to acknowledge that as we articulate it, memory already changes. In that sense, there will never be *a* memory for us to know. This means that memory cannot be tracked down; memory never just simply 'is'. It is impossible to write a sentence in which memory – or German memory – 'is', though we routinely do, and I certainly have done in this book. Memory is always threatened. It is liable to change as soon as we think about it. It is its very precariousness and ambiguity that highlights the tension between the notion of memory and such claims to knowledge about the past – memories – as are offered with considerable certainty in political debate. This contradiction is at the root of the potential of memory to draw our attention to the uncertainties with which we live. At the same time, it is perhaps this precariousness that provokes the desire to agree and share 'a' memory. We saw this in the couple 'agreeing' that their child died at the beginning of the raid in Mulisch's *Das steinerne Brautbett* and indeed in Germans agonising over the correct way to remember the Second World War.

The iterability of memory challenges the implicit and simplistic assumption that Germans remember the horror of the Second World War in the particular ways referred to in the debates on Bundeswehr deployments. Yet although it is difficult to grasp what memory actually 'is', or indeed what it means to say that particular people 'have' certain memories at a given time, memory is significant. Speaking of memories produces a past and a corresponding subjectivity; it also appeals to feelings. Questions about memories of the past and their political significance are not questions merely about what was in the past. With the possible exception of the debate on Wehrmacht atrocities, there was indeed no suggestion in any of the nevertheless highly controversial debates that anything that was said to have happened had not.[23] Nevertheless, objections were often phrased in terms of the truth, for example in terms of acknowledging the full truth. The idea that Germans must remember that they triggered the bombing of cities is of this variety. It asserts that a certain piece of information must be acknowledged, as if this would resolve the problems. Yet at the same time the concern really seems to be about the politics/ethics of representing certain memories. The apparent issue is how the Germans *should* remember. There are two problems with this. Firstly, it is not clear how telling anyone how to remember something is actually meant to work. Secondly, the question of how Germans should remember is hardly a question that can be – or is – answered with reference solely to the truth of the past, even if such a thing existed.

---

[23] One might also note Friedrich's reference to shrunken bodies here. See Chapter 3, p. 88.

Concern about the impropriety of Germans recalling the horrific deaths of civilians exposed to bombing is not based on such accounts being untrue, but rather on worries about their ethical and political implications. The problem is therefore not so much that we cannot know the truth but that, being so busy trying to establish the truth, we lose sight of the fact that the truth does not actually hold the answer to the question we are asking.

The spectre of horror

Memory is continuously claimed, invoked, performed and articulated, in particular by politicians on behalf of the community. Von Weizsäcker and Herzog did so at commemorative occasions, Kinkel and others in the debates about military involvement abroad. And yet, despite the effort invested in promoting particular versions of memory, memory always remained to an extent beyond control. Other articulations, such as those offered by the novels examined above, remained possible, reappeared without warning and were, at times, politically unwelcome. One might say with Johnson that memory behaves like a cat, coming and going without waiting for approval. However, whilst it may sometimes, like a cat, be an 'agreeable companion', at other times it may be more like a ghost or spectre, an unwelcome reminder of something uncomfortable, unfinished. The memory of the Second World War in Germany seems to be more like the latter; it has haunted Germans.

Remembering war: politics of guilt

Some memories of war are horrific, and this book has engaged with representations of war that confront such horror directly. Ledig describes a woman burning 'like a torch'[24] and a squad leader being 'barbecued',[25] but also a soldier shot to bits, flattened by a tank and subsequently blown up.[26] Mulisch writes of people throwing themselves into the flames to die more quickly and beating others to death to put them out of their misery.[27] Such Second World War memories are unwelcome to some not just because they are reminders of cruel deaths but also because of their alleged political implications. Because of the problematic of guilt and responsibility, it might be attractive to 'forget' certain aspects of the war. On the one hand, the crimes committed by Germans and in the name of Germany during the Third Reich were horrific and some in

[24] Ledig, *Vergeltung*, p. 10.   [25] Ibid., p. 128.   [26] Ledig, *Die Stalinorgel*, pp. 7f.
[27] Mulisch, *Brautbett*, p. 73.

Germany either still fail to acknowledge them or may prefer no longer to be reminded. The Germans' own suffering, on the other hand, poses a different problem. Memories of the horrors that Germans were exposed to are seen to provide material for those who wish to deny or reduce the Germans' responsibility for the crimes of the Third Reich. Put differently, there is concern that such memories could be used for unacceptable political purposes.

This anxiety has to be understood in the context of Germans' attitudes immediately after the war, when the view that the Germans had been victims first of Hitler and then of Allied warfare and re-education was prominent. As noted before, Moeller argues that memories in particular of the suffering of refugees and expellees from the East and POWs were an integral part of the FRG's founding myth.[28] Arguably, remembering this suffering today is different, given that the Germans' responsibility for the crimes of the Third Reich is readily acknowledged by all but the extreme Right and given that 'the Germans' are no longer the same Germans as before, although there are still echoes of the attitude Moeller describes. It is impossible to escape this context. Even those who distance themselves from previous and parallel memories that construe the Germans as victims acknowledge its existence by doing so. Federal President Herzog's assertion that commemorating the dead of the Dresden firestorm is not about offsetting one set of victims against another shows, above all, that this context is always there.

Put differently, the context for Germans' memories of the war is not only the past that is remembered, their ancestors' crimes, but also previous failures to acknowledge them and the resulting worry that Germans will go back to this exculpatory attitude. Thus one might think that if Germans no longer remembered, for example, that German civilians were brutally killed, they would then not have to worry about how to do so appropriately, something that is difficult given the context of the atrocities committed by Germans at the time. Yet this clashes with the imperative to remember. Facing up to the truth, acknowledging the full truth about the Third Reich, has been seen as extremely significant. The logical development of remembering the truth about atrocities by Germans is precisely remembering the truth about atrocities against Germans, but this causes concern.

In fact, not remembering the suffering of Germans is not an option and never has been. Not least due to the scars on urban environments, it is impossible to hide the profound impact of the war on Germany and its civilians. Whilst the sensitivities surrounding the issue were sometimes

---

[28] Moeller, *War Stories*.

read as evidence of a taboo, they also show that memories never disappeared. Memories of the horror of war have been maintained throughout the postwar period and not only within the private sphere of some families. Many towns and cities have always held commemorative ceremonies on the anniversaries of bombing raids. Books – both historical and literary – have been written and films made that have addressed the suffering in war. Expellee organisations have always been politically active in the FRG, promoting not least their – deeply controversial – version of memory. Moreover, Second World War memories, however contentious they may be, continue to haunt not only those who were actually 'there'. As Duve noted, this 'war haunts all of us – those who experienced it as soldiers or children and those who were born after its end'.[29] The memories keep coming back, and they unsettle.

This failure of memories to simply disappear and the commitment to the truth, which requires remembering not only their crimes but also their suffering, apparently leave Germans exposed to potentially unwelcome implications. Right-wing instrumentalisation of memories in political debate makes use of just this and is therefore difficult to counter on the grounds of truth. Perhaps unfortunately, the Neo-Nazis' claim that the destruction of Dresden was an instance of 'Allied bombing terror' is not incorrect. The city was bombed by the Allies, and this caused considerable terror amongst the population, as did the entire bombing campaign against German cities. Although there are exaggerations in what Neo-Nazis claim, this is not actually the problem. 'Allied bombing terror' is rejected not just as an unwarranted reproach against the Allies who have now become 'friends and partners' but also – and crucially – as Nazi terminology; it is therefore the ideological baggage seen to be attached to this characterisation that is fiercely rejected by many Germans, not least survivors of the bombing of Dresden.

This book has discussed precisely memories of suffering in the war to the exclusion of other aspects of the period of the Third Reich. Wehrmacht atrocities have been mentioned, but the focus has been on the horrors Germans were exposed to. Some might argue therefore that my argument plays into the hands of an unpalatable right-wing politics; clearly, I do not think it does. Above all, memories that have the potential of making Germans appear as victims of the Second World War are both unavoidable and significant, however unwelcome they may be. Some of the problems surrounding this issue are illustrated in the figures of Konrad and Paul in Grass's *Im Krebsgang* and their respective attitudes to memory. Forgetting turns out to be an impossible, if on the surface

[29] Deutscher Bundestag, *Plenarprotokoll*, 13/163, 13/03/97, 14718.

attractive, option, and one which Grass seems finally to reject, despite Paul's despair over the inescapability of memory. Paul observes at one point that one should never have remained silent 'about so much suffering merely because one's own guilt was overpowering and one's admitted remorse urgent all these years', that one should never have left the 'avoided topic' to the right-wingers.[30]

Memories of German suffering are indeed intriguing: they seem to unsettle. There is a tension between the commitment to remember and the alleged – and feared – political implications of doing so, given these memories. In the discussions of memories of strategic bombing and the flight and expulsion of Germans from the East there seemed to be a consensus that construing Germans as victims was unacceptable. There was disagreement, however, about whether recalling the suffering or even commemorating the dead, which was increasingly acknowledged as important, would automatically fall into this trap. In the debate on Wehrmacht atrocities, Dregger and Steinbach[31] construed soldiers as victims. Dregger objected to what he regarded as a memory of soldiers as perpetrators which did not consider that 'soldiers have always been victims of war'.[32] He was duly identified as a political fossil who had not changed his views since the 1950s. However, whilst Dregger's views are problematic, it is difficult to take issue with his basic point about soldiers. There were soldiers who were victims precisely in the way Dregger asserts: their lives were taken away from them as citizens of the Reich called up for military service. They had not in some way deserved to die, certainly not more so than other citizens.

The issue then is that, although there is widespread agreement that it would be unthinkable and outrageous to think of Germans as having been victims of the Second World War, it seems to be problematic to insist that some Germans were not, in some way, victims of the war. Both the Neo-Nazis and Dregger feed off this tension. Dregger concludes from the allegation of Wehrmacht atrocities that the claim is that soldiers had not been victims. Drawing attention to their lack of control over the outbreak and conduct of the war, he alleges that most Wehrmacht soldiers – like soldiers in general – *were* victims: they were acted upon and suffered. Yet, in the terms of the debate, either the soldiers were perpetrators or they were victims; they cannot have been both. As I observed in Chapter 3, this categorisation of victims versus perpetrators is less than helpful. In this context, it enables the shift from acknowledging that some soldiers suffered 'undeservedly' to the wider and dubious assertion that 'the

---

[30] Grass, *Im Krebsgang*, p. 99.
[31] Deutscher Bundestag, *Plenarprotokoll*, 13/163, 13/03/97, 14719.   [32] Ibid., 14710.

Germans' – or, in this case, Wehrmacht soldiers – were victims of the Second World War and not perpetrators. Therefore I argued that it was crucial to admit that the categories are actually not, as they are presented, mutually exclusive but that it is possible to be both simultaneously. Nickels drew attention to this when she argued that men like her father were victims in some way, but that this did not excuse their behaviour.[33]

The debate about Second World War memories has failed to acknowledge this possibility; it has remained stuck on the issue of avoiding the impression that Germans might have been victims. This is unfortunate. Firstly, this categorisation keeps leading us into a dead end. Some Germans were 'victims' some of the time in some ways. The insistence, despite this, on the framing which opposes and clearly distinguishes perpetrators and victims plays into the hands of those who would like to construe all Germans as victims, for – in this dysfunctional framing – if one German was a victim, they all were and, what is more, they cannot then have been perpetrators. In other words, the framing that is meant to counter right-wing versions of the past in fact supports the possibility of them. Secondly, the worry about this issue has made the right-wing abuse of memory central, which gives disproportionate weight to what are after all minority views. Thirdly, and most problematically, it turns the struggle with the far Right into one about the accuracy of memories rather than about their political positions. This is not to say that the far Right does not peddle untruths. It is rather to say that the ground for argument is chosen unwisely: truth is, in the end, not the issue.

There are at least three reasons for this. Firstly, it is possible to have political influence without being right. Thus, being shown to be wrong does not necessarily undermine the political position in question. Indeed, far Right articulations of Second World War memory underline this, as, whether they are right or wrong, they affect the context within which other such memories are articulated. Secondly, and crucially, the obsession with the correctness of memory stops debate. Barnouw has noted the 'near-impossibility of discussing rationally the German experience of that war: its shadowy past presence in German memory . . . has provoked the notorious, bitterly hostile, intertwined debates and controversies over a morally and then politically correct collective remembrance of collective guilt'.[34] Thirdly, the truth would not solve the problem. The truth, which is anyway a highly problematic notion, certainly in relation to memory, does not provide the answer to how the Germans ought to remember. The problem is in fact thinking that the question of memory and of right-wing politics is something that can or should be resolved by the

---

[33] Ibid., 14720.   [34] Barnouw, *War in the Empty Air*, p. 11.

truth, once and for all. How to remember the past is a political question and as such requires a decision, a decision which precisely might not be right. The best that can be done is to take that risk and acknowledge it. The concern that becomes visible in public debates about memory in Germany has largely been to work out an 'appropriate' relation to the past for the Germans. Yet this problematic must be confronted differently, because this approach has excluded consideration of other contexts, such as the politics of memory in relation to war today.

Remembering war: politics of war

Ironically, although memories are controversial and in the end cannot be pinned down, they are extremely significant. This is not only because we imagine ourselves – as political communities, too – through memory, but also because memory is relevant to the political imagination in other ways. Second World War memories were invoked in German political discourse to underline claims about the horror of war and thus to argue against proposals to use military force. Yet such memories were also used to argue *for* the use of force, in particular through the memory of Allied liberation. In this memory, the heroic deed of the Allied soldiers is central, and German soldiers are represented as having an opportunity to accomplish the same today on behalf of others. This move, made by Foreign Minister Kinkel in justifying a 1995 Bundeswehr deployment to Bosnia, could be seen as problematic because it obscures aspects of the past; it takes the focus away from the Wehrmacht and therefore from the involvement of German soldiers in atrocities. The link between German soldiers today and German soldiers of the past – who committed crimes – is severed; instead today's German soldiers are likened to the Allied liberators.

This move could then be seen as making German crimes less prominent, forgetting them even. However, my argument shows the impossibility and ineffectiveness of arguing simply for remembering the truth. To put it differently, I have argued that this elision of Wehrmacht atrocities is *not* in any simple way problematic, because remembering is better than forgetting – indeed both are implicated in each other. Yet leaving out or concealing Wehrmacht atrocities has political implications: it supports the use of armed force by the German state. It does so in tandem with a further, at least equally important, concealment in Kinkel's reframing of the Second World War. The analogy between Bundeswehr troops and Allied soldiers is attractive because the latter are seen as heroic liberators. This not only ignores that it is problematic to speak, simply, of Germany's liberation, an issue discussed in Chapters 3 and 5, but also crucially relies on seeing the Allied Second World War as a 'good war'. The impact of this war on civilians is concealed in the process.

The idea of the glorious Second World War has been powerful recently, well beyond Germany. In view of the implications of this war for civilians, this memory of the glorious war is sanitised. The recognition that they fought a 'good war' may be reassuring to individual Allied soldiers and their families, though one suspects it is cold comfort to those who were there and remember what it entailed. Ledig certainly has little time for the claim that soldiers 'did not die in vain'.[35] However, memory is not merely about the past but has serious implications for the future. There is something much larger at stake in such memory than comfort for individuals. Although this issue is perhaps more complex in the case of Germany, the state legitimises itself precisely through heroic memories of struggle, obscuring the fact that the community only comes into being retrospectively, through such commemorative narratives.[36] The state also legitimises specific courses of action, in particular war in its own defence, through such memories. In other words, such articulations of memory are part of the performance of state sovereignty.

The Germans are not on their own in recalling the Second World War as a relevant context in political debate. The US administration, for example, attempted to liken the war against Iraq to the Second World War and more specifically to the 'liberation' of Germany and Japan.[37] The appeal to Second World War memories started in the immediate aftermath of September 11, when the US administration likened the events of September 11 to the attacks on Pearl Harbor.[38] Such references to the past do not merely serve to make sense of events, they are designed to elicit specific responses today. The comparison suggested usually remained implicit, and is limited. The attack on Pearl Harbor led to the USA entering the Second World War, or so the argument goes, which ended in victory for the USA and its Allies. The *topos* of this reference seems to be one of heroism, of 'being on the right side', of defending not only one's country but civilisation. President Bush claimed that US troops today were 'commissioned by history to face freedom's enemies',

---

[35] Ledig, *Vergeltung*, p. 10.

[36] Jenny Edkins, 'Remembering Relationality: Trauma Time and Politics', in: Duncan S. Bell (ed.), *Memory, Trauma and World Politics* (Basingstoke: Palgrave 2006), pp. 99–115.

[37] Dao, 'Experts debate'; Representative Skelton, in United States Department of Defense, *Testimony of Secretary of Defense Rumsfeld*. For more on this, see Maja Zehfuss, 'Derrida's Memory, War and the Politics of Ethics', in: Madeleine Fagan et al. (eds.), *Derrida: Negotiating the Legacy* (Edinburgh: Edinburgh University Press 2007), pp. 97–111.

[38] Secretary Donald Rumsfeld, in United States Department of Defense, *Testimony of Secretary of Defense Rumsfeld*.

that they were fighting 'for the security of our people and the success of liberty'.[39]

In 2002, on the occasion of the celebrations of the liberation of France, which Bush attended, French President Chirac, who was later seen to be at loggerheads with Bush over this topic, made a telling link between the Second World War and the 'war on terror'. The values for which the soldiers had fought in the Second World War were, according to Chirac, under threat again today.[40] Such claims about the defence of Western values seem to be politically more powerful than the limits of the analogy. The failure of the analogy was perhaps most obvious when Bush claimed that '[l]ike the Second World War, our present conflict began with a ruthless, surprise attack on the United States'.[41] This was surely 'news to the Poles',[42] as the *Guardian* dryly noted. The parallel did not work; comparability was not given. That, however, was not the point. These 'comparisons' are not what historians might accept as a proper analogy, but invocations of memory. Such a memory practice is not a question of historical knowledge; pointing out the differences between Pearl Harbor and September 11 would in many ways miss the point. Whilst calling upon memory touches on knowledge of the past – on what are represented as facts – it does so in ways which appeal to the emotions, such as pride in a shared identity. Some of the glory of the Second World War – which has been portrayed as 'the "Mother" of all just wars'[43] – was clearly meant to rub off on the 'war on terror'. Historical 'detail' could not deter Bush from exploiting the emotional attachment to Second World War memories as a successful and heroic war in the name of freedom.

The tactic of calling on memory and thereby implicitly or even explicitly likening the 'war on terror' to the Second World War went into overdrive as the sixtieth anniversary of the Allied invasion of Normandy approached. President Bush, for example, explained in a graduation speech at the US Air Force Academy that the following weekend he would 'go to France for the ceremonies marking the 60th anniversary of D-Day, at a place where the fate of millions turned on the courage of thousands. In these events we recall a time of peril, and national unity,

---

[39] George W. Bush, 'We're Fighting to Win – And Win We Will', Remarks by the President on the USS *Enterprise* on Pearl Harbor Day, www.whitehouse.gov/news/releases/2001/12/print/20011207.html

[40] Chirac cited in Michaela Wiegel, 'Wo das 20. Jahrhundert aus der Dunkelheit in das Licht trat', *Frankfurter Allgemeine Zeitung*, 28/05/02, 3.

[41] George Bush, Speech at Air Force Academy Graduation, Falcon Stadium, 02/06/04, www.whitehouse.gov/news/releases/2004/06/print/20040602.html

[42] 'Past and present', *Guardian*, 04/06/04, 25.

[43] Barnouw, *War in the Empty Air*, p. 9, see also p. 149, and Grayling, *Among the Dead Cities*, p. 210.

and individual courage. We honor a generation of Americans who served this country and saved the liberty of the world.' He continued, making a link between that generation and today's troops: 'Each of you receiving a commission today in the United States military will also carry the hopes of free people everywhere.' Although Bush acknowledged that in some ways the current conflict is different and 'unique', the 'goal of this generation', he said, was 'the same: We will secure our nation and defend the peace through the forward march of freedom.' Finally, he asserted that 'our will is strong. We know our duty. By keeping our word, and holding firm to our values, this generation will show the world the power of liberty once again.'[44] Through the supposed defence of freedom, the parallel is established. And this, given memories from the Allied perspective of the Second World War as they are invoked by Bush, goes a considerable way towards justification. With these appeals to the Second World War, the US administration seems to deploy memory to attempt to escape the ethical questions involved. They obscure the contradictory imperatives, for example over the protection of lives, to which we are exposed in the decision of whether and how to lead a war.[45] If the war against Iraq is like the liberation of Germany and Japan, then the right course of action is a foregone conclusion: it is then obviously right to fight for freedom.

This 'comparison' was, however, noted as problematic by the critics of the 'war on terror'. In 2004, the French government – which was opposed to the war against Iraq – did not want France's liberation hijacked by the US administration's attempts to legitimise its war. According to the *Guardian*, advisers 'close to Jacques Chirac' expressly warned 'that any reference to Iraq during the 60th anniversary of the Allied invasion of France . . . would be ill-advised and unwelcome'.[46] As a result, the speeches at the commemoration ceremony did not mention the 'war on terror', though Bush noted that 'our alliance of freedom is still needed today' and Chirac implicitly criticised Bush by observing that 'our two countries, our two peoples have stood shoulder to shoulder in the brotherhood of blood spilled, in the defense of a certain ideal of mankind, of a certain vision of the world – the vision that lies at the heart of the United Nations Charter'.[47] In Chirac's representation, doubts over the

[44] Bush, Air Force Academy Graduation.
[45] For someone highlighting the problematic of a decision in the context of a contradictory imperative, see, for example, Joseph Fischer (Bündnis 90/Die Grünen) in Deutscher Bundestag, *Plenarprotokoll*, 13/248, 16/10/98, 23141. See also Zehfuss, *Constructivism*, pp. 234f.
[46] Kim Willsher, 'Anniversary anxiety', *Guardian*, 02/06/04, 14.
[47] Remarks by President Bush and President Chirac on marking the 60th Anniversary of D-Day, The American Cemetery, Normandy, France, 06/06/04, www.whitehouse.gov/news/releases/2004/06/print/20040606.html

comparability of the two wars are central, with the latter violating the principles defended by the former.

However, parallels were, at the same time, still being drawn, in particular by the US administration. This suggests that the analogy – however transparently faulty – was considered politically effective. Crucially, Chirac's intervention only disputes one of its fundamental assumptions, namely the comparability of the two wars. What Chirac and others did not question was whether the Allied Second World War had indeed been 'good'. It is precisely the idea of investing the 'war on terror' with some of the glory of the Second World War that makes the analogy so attractive to supporters of the war. This book has focused on memories which undermine the unproblematic categorisation of the Allied Second World War as a good war[48] and argued that this is significant in relation to war today. The Germans' memory of the Second World War as catastrophic and the bombing of cities as a form of terror may go some way towards explaining why they have not bought into Bush's rhetoric on the 'war on terror'.

Remembering war: challenges

Simon Schama has been sharply critical of the Second World War memorial dedicated in Washington on 29 May 2004, drawing attention to its failure to account for experiences even on the Allied side. According to Schama, we should not 'embalm the memory in stone-faced reverence in the manner of the banal neo-classical monument just opened on the Mall in Washington DC, with its meaninglessly feeble euphemisms for sacrifice and slaughter'. In fact, he added that 'the last thing we need, 60 years on, are platitudes in marble'.[49] Significantly, Schama locates the reason for the current monumentification in the present war: 'How the memory craves the reassurance of the Good War . . . while we're in the middle of a bad one.'[50] In other words, Schama points out how the invocation of memory itself – designed to underline the moral validity of the 'war on terror' – ironically points up the moral uncertainty that it is meant to conceal.

Thus Schama argues that the recourse to memory betrays our ethical insecurity: we seek refuge in what we think we know, in the moral certainties of what appears to us a less complicated time. Memory

---

[48] Olick asserts that '[w]e commonly remember World War II as "the Good War"', without clarifying who 'we' might be or what 'World War II' signifies in this context. *In the House*, p. 33.

[49] Simon Schama, 'If you receive this, I'll be dead', *The Guardian G2*, 28/05/04, 4.

[50] Ibid., 3.

retrospectively conjures up a past which we seem to be able to grasp, unlike the present, with its confusing uncertainties, which appears to be constantly in flux. But the use of memory as a source of moral certainty ignores the problem that memory seems to never fully obey such designs. Schama uses letters from soldiers involved in the D-Day landings as counter-memory, to illustrate that the war was not simply glorious; he describes the letters as 'a moving antidote to empty monumental platitudes'.[51] In other words, just like German memories, memories of the war on the Allied side turn out to be diverse and painful. They are not simply of a heroic fight for freedom, as Bush invokes them. This becomes clear, as well, through reading Vonnegut's *Slaughterhouse 5* and becoming aware of his inability to quite articulate the horror of Dresden. Similarly, in Mulisch's *Das steinerne Brautbett* a former US soldier is physically marked for life by his wartime experiences and haunted by his memories; indeed, he eventually breaks down. This book has focused on the German perspective. It has, if one may put it this way, looked at those at the receiving end of the good war. Chapter 3 gave considerable space to illustrating what today we would perhaps call 'collateral damage': the deaths of civilians in bombing raids on German cities. Although Friedrich's *Der Brand* also displays an intriguing interest in the technicalities of death, one of the aspects that I have highlighted about the novels on the theme of strategic bombing was that they did not avoid a close-up engagement with how people died. People were depicted as ripped to bits by explosions, set alight, barbecued in tarmac. The images conjured up by the painstakingly detailed descriptions would not be shown on television in Western countries. Perhaps unsurprisingly, given the context of the crimes of the Third Reich, some are worried that dwelling on such unpalatable detail invests the topic with emotionality.

The way in which 'emotionality' is immediately criticised as obviously pernicious, discussed in Chapter 3, is interesting. Emotion, it appears, has to be avoided. Friedrich's book is charged with being 'melodramatic'.[52] Boog, in particular, worries that *Der Brand* leaves 'the reader in an emotionally heated empty space'.[53] The emotional heat from novels such as *Vergeltung* and *Das steinerne Brautbett* seems to be even stronger, inasmuch as the horror is both more vivid and more personal in the context of a novel, though the space is perhaps less empty. Mulisch raises the ethical questions of the air war more directly, but does not, of course, offer an answer. Ledig's political contextualisation may appear minimal, although I have argued that there is more of it than some critics assert.

---

[51] Ibid., 4.   [52] Langenbacher, 'Changing Memory Regimes', 60.
[53] Boog, 'Ein Kolossalgemälde', p. 133.

Nevertheless, the republication of *Vergeltung*, with its focus on the sense-lessness and cruelty of death, probably underlines the wider concern that sentimentality is becoming the only way in which both strategic bombing and the expulsions from the East are being addressed at all. Inter-estingly, in such arguments the affective dimension is derided as senti-mentality. Even Winkler, who considers that 'sentimentalisation' may be necessary,[54] uses this terminology. Although one would have reservations about Germans wallowing in self-pity over the Second World War, the worry that any expression of memories in the public sphere which calls up emotions is somehow dangerous seems bizarre.

Naumann complains that in the context of strategic bombing there is little expression of shame on the German side in relation to the failure to stop this senseless dying by bringing the war to a quicker conclusion.[55] This seems to mean that shame – an emotion if ever there was one – would be appropriate, whereas the kind of emotion allegedly induced by Friedrich's *Der Brand* – presumably grief and probably anger – would not. To put it differently, emotions that do not challenge the accepted repre-sentation of the Second World War – in particular that the responsibility lies with the Germans both for starting it and conducting it in a criminal way – are to be desired, whereas those that are potentially in conflict with this story are derided. Yet it is impossible to explain away the grief and anger; that the Germans started the war and conducted it in a criminal way does not mean that they will not have feelings about their dead. Her-zog, in his speech on the fiftieth anniversary of the bombing of Dresden, underlined the necessity and legitimacy of mourning. Those present had come together, he said, 'first and foremost to mourn, to lament the dead – an expression of emotion dating back to the beginnings of civilization'.[56] Herzog's mourning, of course, produces a particular German memory of 'Dresden' and with it a vision of community. Although the horror of the past can only be overcome together with other nations, and although Herzog calls for going beyond simplistic understandings of the past 'in terms of states and nations',[57] he necessarily invokes the German 'we', the 'we' that can only find peace through acknowledging its past mis-takes but also, crucially, mourning its own victims. It seems problematic to dismiss the Germans' right to and need for such carefully contextu-alised mourning. Yet Herzog creates the impression that mourning had in some way been forbidden. He objected to the Germans' 'mourning being seen as an attempt to square the suffering of the victims of crimes com-mitted by Germans against people of other nations, and against fellow

---

[54] Winkler, 'Nun singen sie wieder', p. 105.   [55] Naumann, *Der Krieg als Text*, p. 70.
[56] Herzog, 'Dresden', p. 5.   [57] Ibid., p. 8.

countrymen, with the suffering of German victims of war and expulsion'.[58] Whether or not mourning has actually ever been seen in this way, the Federal President, speaking for his people, asserts that it has.

Thus the issue of emotions in relation to German Second World War memories is complex. On the one hand, they are unavoidable, and it might even be seen as unnatural if they did not come to be articulated. On the other hand, when emotions come to be central, as they allegedly do in Friedrich's *Der Brand*, this triggers strong reactions. These seem to suggest that emotions – 'sentimentality' – are to be rejected as such or at any rate must not challenge our rational understandings of the past. Thereby they appear to enforce a problematic distinction between the emotional and the rational, privileging the latter. The question of the emotional and the rational is too large to be appropriately addressed here. Two points seem important, however. Firstly, the suggestion that the emotional may be distinguished from the rational and that the emotional must be subordinated to the rational, that is, our knowledge of German crimes, for example, is one-sided. The appeals to memories of the heroic fight for freedom suggest instead the opposite, namely its centrality, for they, too, play on emotions. Secondly, what seems to be important in this particular context is that the sidelining of the emotional is part of the problem. We seem unsure how to deal with it, even how to analyse it, and therefore it seems safer to exclude it from the proper business of (understanding) war and politics. That, however, means excluding an important aspect of difficult situations: is it not precisely how we *feel* about, for example, killing children that makes us squirm over decisions related to war? Carol Cohn famously opens her 'Wars, Wimps, and Women' with a scene in which a (male) physicist realises, in a discussion of nuclear strategy, what it means to speak of 'only' 30 million dead – as compared with 36 million dead – in modelling a particular attack and blurts out his distress. His colleagues evidently find this inappropriate; the room falls silent, and no one reacts or even looks at the physicist, making him feel 'like a woman'.[59] Cohn thus locates the emphasis on the rational in a gendered discourse and power struggle, where men have the upper hand and women find it difficult to participate owing to their inability or unwillingness to focus exclusively on the rational. The exclusion of emotions is revealed as fundamental for professional conduct in the strategic defence community; admitting

---

[58] Ibid., p. 6.
[59] Carol Cohn, 'Wars, Wimps, and Women: Talking Gender and Thinking War', in: Miriam Cooke and Angela Woolacott (eds.), *Gendering War Talk* (Princeton University Press 1993), p. 227.

emotions would 'distort the process required to think well about nuclear weapons and warfare'.[60] Cohn notes that

weapons' effects may be spoken of only in the most clinical and abstract terms, leaving no room to imagine a seven-year-old boy with his flesh melting away from his bones or a toddler with the skin hanging down in strips. Voicing concern about the number of casualties in the enemy's armed forces, imagining the suffering of the killed and wounded young men, is out of bounds.[61]

The idea that Germans should not concentrate on their civilian dead, much less on the gruesome detail of how some of them died, because it leads to a distorted representation of the Second World War, with problematic political consequences, is similar.

Crucially, it does not seem to be enough to ask about how many die as so-called collateral damage; it matters how they did. Grass writes in his *Im Krebsgang*, 'But what do numbers tell?'[62] It is not just that we may never know the number of the dead but that it is simply not enough to know it. If we are more affected by the idea of someone being ripped apart or burnt alive than of their receiving a single bullet wound to the chest, then we must know as much as possible about the ways of dying when we confront the question of war. Anything else seems to be nothing but an evasion of what is most disturbing. Perhaps, in order to let this issue touch us, we do need art. The screenings of atrocities in Iraq by Al-Jazeera, showing them in gory detail, certainly did not seem to open up the ethico-political question but rather to close it down. Mulisch notes that a 'novel should not describe something that has happened, but itself be something that happens – in the moment when one reads the book'.[63] As noted earlier, Ledig's *Die Stalinorgel*, for example, seems to produce emotions in the reader: confusion, fear, despair. Mulisch further claims that literature is not about learning about *reality* – for that one might read non-fiction books – but about learning about oneself.[64] It is about thinking through the situation and what one might have done in it – or, I might add, what one feels about what was done in it. This experience of reading adds another dimension to the question of war – which therefore appears to become more 'real'. Admitting emotions makes the question more uncomfortable, indicating that what is traditionally conceptualised as 'knowledge' alone does not provide a satisfactory way forward. However, neither does generating emotions by television footage. There is no distance there, no uncertainty, just another unproblematic 'known'. Such footage merely confronts the viewer with an outrage. In contrast,

---

[60] Ibid., p. 231.   [61] Ibid., p. 232.   [62] Grass, *Im Krebsgang*, p. 104.
[63] 'Tanz unter den Ruinen', p. 233.   [64] Ibid.

memories, especially as represented in literature, at the same time as drawing us into (grasping) emotions, already involve a distance – they are fictional – and therefore offer scope for reflection. The issue is not one of simple empathy. The memories that haunt us may mark an opportunity to engage with the dilemmas of war in a less offhand fashion, both because we are drawn in more closely and because they give us reason to be more reflective.

The spectre of the Holocaust

My argument has made Kinkel's reinterpretation of the Second World War central, although the issue was more complex. The FRG does not, of course, simply use its military abroad because of this rhetorical move in relation to memory.[65] Yet the invocation of memory has been crucial in terms of winning political support and legitimacy. There is a larger issue. We are told, not only in Germany, to engage in wars that are likened to the Second World War, for the defence of Western values, even of civilisation. There is also an increasing division between Western countries that have the technology to fight from a distance, whose populations will not be affected by the wars in which their armies are involved (what Colin McInnes has, somewhat unconvincingly, termed 'spectator-sport war')[66] – and those countries where the wars are raging and that are on the receiving end of, for example, air strikes. It is in the context of air strikes today that it seems inappropriate to dismiss questions about precisely how people die in war and did die in the Second World War. In other words, it is because looking back at the Second World War implies looking forward at other wars that there is something more at stake than the Germans' responsibility for the crimes of the Third Reich and concern for their victims. The failure to engage with the 'how' of death allows us to suppress what 'collateral damage' really means and as a result the emotions we might feel in relation to fellow human beings' suffering. Bringing together our memories of horrific deaths in past wars with our current military deployments may make us feel uncomfortable, but there is nothing wrong with that. In fact, feeling uncomfortable may precisely prompt us to ask questions. The horror of war always lurks beneath the surface, whatever story – or memory – may be told about war. Heribert Prantl notes in relation to Wehrmacht crimes that memory is arguably

---

[65] For a detailed analysis of this issue, see Zehfuss, *Constructivism*.

[66] McInnes, *Spectator-Sport War*. The image of 'spectator-sport war' glosses over what it seems designed to point out, namely the asymmetry of recent warfare involving the West. Sporting fixtures tend to involve supporters off the pitch on both sides; in 'spectator-sport war' this is true only for one side, whilst the other lives on the battlefield.

like 'liberation' in the sense that it is impossible to 'simply proclaim it'.[67] He continues:

For future generations [*einen nachgeborenen Menschen*] memory has to be more than what parents and grandparents have recounted. More than what you read and learnt at school. Memory – that is, the restlessness that seizes you when you stand in front of the pictures in the Wehrmacht exhibition, when you leaf through the catalogue of this exhibition again and again and pause. Memory is a whole personal translation [*Umsetzung*] of history. Memory means: sensing what these pictures mean for you in a very personal way. Memory also means to understand that history is not as far away as commemoration days and anniversaries might lead you to suspect. Memory makes impossible the disposal of the past. And the restlessness that appears with this memory is salutary.[68]

The restlessness Prantl refers to comes from the confrontation with the horror of the crimes committed by his ancestors. This is crucial in relation to German memories of the Second World War. Whilst the horror of war has been stressed in this book, the Holocaust has been deliberately excluded. There has been no discussion at all of concentration camps or even the maltreatment and murder of POWs. The problematic of atrocities committed by the Wehrmacht has occasionally been raised but – other than in Chapter 4 – not in detail. Hence one might argue that this book has given a skewed picture of the Second World War: it has excluded at least what comes under the heading of German crimes and atrocities, in particular what we have come to call 'the Holocaust'. One could therefore say that I have failed to address the particular problem of the Second World War, something that German fiction is also accused of.[69] This made the Second World War look like any other war, a war that led to suffering and casualties amongst both civilians and soldiers on all sides, a war that entailed cruelty and horror but, inasmuch as war is seen to be a normal occurrence, nothing out of the ordinary.

War and the Holocaust

The Holocaust is thought to set Germany's Second World War apart from any other war. As Bartov puts it:

Never before, or after, has a state decided to devote so many of its technological, organizational, and intellectual resources to the sole purpose of murdering every single member of a certain category of people in a process that combined the

---

[67] Prantl, 'Einleitung', p. 20.   [68] Ibid., p. 21.
[69] Pfeifer, *Der deutsche Kriegsroman*, pp. 82f. See also Chapter 1, pp. 16–20.

knowledge acquired in mass industrial production with the experience of waging total war.[70]

On this basis Germany's war is thought to have been unique. I showed in Chapter 4 that the implication of the Wehrmacht in the Holocaust is still contentious for the public, though not for historians. In other words, some would like to separate the war from the Holocaust in much the way I have done so far, but for very different reasons. Bartov confirms what was argued in Chapter 4, namely that what 'many Germans found hard to take was that the exhibition [on Wehrmacht crimes] demonstrated in the most graphic manner the complicity of Wehrmacht soldiers in the Holocaust and other crimes of the regime, especially in the occupied parts of the Soviet Union and Yugoslavia'.[71] The German people's reluctance to accept this, their willingness to buy into the legend of the 'clean' Wehrmacht, is perhaps not surprising. The Wehrmacht represented the people; the Wehrmacht meant everyone, or at least their father, brother, uncle.

However, looking at the Second World War minus the Holocaust and other atrocities committed by the Third Reich is actually difficult. Although there is no simple cause-and-effect relationship, both the flight and expulsion from the East and the Allied strategic bombing against German cities invite questions about the Germans' own conduct prior to these events. Moreover, Kinkel's analogy of Bundeswehr troops and Allied liberators most strongly highlights the Wehrmacht's failure to provide an adequate tradition with which to identify.[72] The reference to the Allied liberators in order to support Bundeswehr deployment is necessary because there are no German armed forces that Kinkel could invoke as a role model. That the analogy was used to overcome the Kohl doctrine, the idea that German soldiers could not be deployed to the Balkans where the Wehrmacht had wreaked havoc, underlined the fact that this was about more than previous opposition in war. In other words, the issue of atrocities, of the Holocaust, creeps into Second World War memories. This is illustrated by Chancellor Schröder's speech at the German–French commemoration in Caen, marking the sixtieth anniversary of D-Day. Schröder paid tribute to the 'soldierly courage' shown there for the 'liberation of Europe', but noted at the same time that Normandy had been the scene of 'infinite suffering and ten thousand-fold sacrifice [*Opfer*]'. He noted that the French people's memory of 6 June 1944 differed from that of the Germans, but that they led to the same desire for peace. He

---

[70] Bartov, *Germany's War*, p. 135.   [71] Ibid., p. xi.
[72] This failure had been noted by Defence Minister Rühe. See Chapter 4, p. 138.

recalled the Germans' awareness that they had caused the war, and their resulting responsibility before history.[73]

On the one hand, Schröder distinguished between the Allied soldiers who had paid 'the highest price for freedom' and the Germans who died because they had been sent into a 'murderous campaign for the oppression of Europe'. On the other hand, he claimed that in death they were united through 'the grief of their parents and wives, their siblings and friends'. In other words, Schröder stressed the similarity of soldiers in war. Yet he specifically commemorated the citizens of Oradour-sur-Glane, murdered by the Waffen-SS on 10 June 1944, drawing attention – if briefly – to the criminality of the German war. Schröder claimed that he did not represent the 'old Germany of those dark years', but rather the country that had found its way back into the community of peoples.[74] In terms of present issues, he noted that, despite the horrors of war, Germans could not be pacifists, because they knew that soldiers had been necessary to overthrow Hitler. At the same time, he claimed, Germans were not prepared to use military means 'lightly', though where military intervention was necessary Germany did not 'shirk from its responsibility for peace and human rights'.[75] Thus Schröder hinted at the ambiguity in terms of political implications of Second World War memories: though the experience certainly may have led to an abhorrence of war, he argues that pacifism is not the lesson, because war was needed to dispose of the Nazi regime. This argument is of course by now familiar from Kinkel's successful justification of the deployment to Bosnia.

Schröder's speech was called '[p]erhaps the most moving of all the speeches of the day'[76] in the *Independent*. Yet it illustrates many of the problems with German Second World War memories. Schröder attempted to acknowledge German guilt whilst at the same time construing individual soldiers as similar to their French counterparts. He also distanced the Germany of today from the Germany of the Third Reich and noted the difficult balance Germany now seeks to strike in terms of a 'responsible' use of the military. These are, on the one hand, reasonable points. On the other, they may be seen as amounting to a simultaneous acknowledgement and rejection of responsibility: Germany was responsible, but not the Germans; Germany was responsible, but Germany is no longer that Germany. These moves, and their implications, are problematic. Schröder's simultaneous in- and

---

[73] Gerhard Schröder, Rede bei den deutsch-französischen Feierlichkeiten zum 60. Jahrestag des 'D-Day' in Caen, 06/06/04, www.bundesregierung.de
[74] Ibid.   [75] Ibid.
[76] John Lichfield, Terri Judd and Cahal Milmo, 'The last march', *Independent*, 07/06/04, 4.

exclusion of the topic of atrocities is perhaps most interesting. He specifically included the massacre at Oradour: 'I also commemorate the citizens of Oradour. They became victims of an unleashed, inhuman Waffen-SS sixty years ago.'[77] Then he moved on to a different subject. He shied away from naming what happened at Oradour and, despite mentioning the Waffen-SS as the perpetrators, he chose the passive voice. The Waffen-SS is also, in the speech, not related to the Germans in any way. There is no mention of German memories in this context, and the Waffen-SS is certainly not commemorated. Schröder opposes ordinary German soldiers, who were much like their French counterparts even if they served the wrong cause, to the Waffen-SS, who committed crimes that, however, are not named. Thus the atrocities remain in a profound sense excluded, and certainly detached from the Germans, despite being noted.

Schröder thus goes back to the dichotomy between good Wehrmacht and bad other armed units such as the SS and SD that was revealed as false in the debate surrounding the exhibition on Wehrmacht crimes. Although not everyone agreed, Janßen summed up the outcome of the controversy thus: 'Wehrmacht and Holocaust – these could hitherto not belong together. After this exhibition such a distinction is no longer possible.'[78] As Bubis, then chairman of the Central Council of the Jews in Germany, pointed out, '[i]f the Wehrmacht had remained as clean as the myth claims, the murder of European Jews would have gone off much less perfectly, and there would have been many more survivors.'[79] Schröder's exclusion of the Waffen-SS from official memory is familiar from the Bitburg controversy, though he does tentatively include their crimes. In 1985 US President Ronald Reagan was invited by Chancellor Kohl to commemorate soldiers killed in the Second World War at Bitburg Cemetery.[80] Reagan, by accepting the invitation, 'agreed to honor a German military cemetery', a controversial step not merely because he had previously declined to visit a concentration camp, though he eventually went to Bergen-Belsen.[81] A controversy ensued as to whether this visit to Bitburg was appropriate, particularly when it transpired that there were not only graves of Wehrmacht soldiers but also graves of soldiers from the Second SS Panzer division 'Das Reich', which committed the

---

[77] Schröder, Rede bei den deutsch-französischen Feierlichkeiten.
[78] Janßen, 'Als Soldaten Mörder wurden', p. 30.
[79] Ignatz Bubis, 'Entmenschlichte Zeit', in: Prantl, *Wehrmachtsverbrechen*, p. 186.
[80] Geoffrey H. Hartman, 'Introduction: 1985', in: Geoffrey H. Hartman (ed.), *Bitburg in Moral and Political Perspective* (Bloomington: Indiana University Press 1986), p. 5.
[81] Hartman, 'Introduction', p. 2. The story is told slightly differently in Olick, 'Genre Memories', 393f.

massacre at Oradour, at that cemetery.[82] Some were predictably enraged that the commemoration seemed to include perpetrator groups. Jan-Holger Kirsch, however, points out that the assumption that 'historical memory means an identification with the remembered persons' is misleading.[83] In other words, the controversy about the visit to Bitburg Cemetery was premised at least in part on the idea that by commemorating the Second World War over the graves of Wehrmacht soldiers – and, more problematically, Waffen-SS soldiers – the Germans, and indeed Reagan, would in some way identify with them and therefore even signal approval of their actions.

An official act of commemoration is normally designed precisely to create community and therefore obscures rather than highlights any possible tensions. Yet the desire to exclude the Waffen-SS from commemoration is as problematic as its inclusion would be. Inclusion would invariably be seen as honouring the Waffen-SS, and therefore the perpetrators of atrocities. However, exclusion retrospectively, and artificially, removes the Waffen-SS from the community that invented it. By implication this also removes the atrocities that are ascribed to the Waffen-SS from their relation to Germans more generally. If this move succeeds, German identity emerges as less problematic – a result that the opponents of the Bitburg visit sought to avoid. This is problematic not only because, in Bartov's words, the 'attempt to differentiate between the Wehrmacht and the SS, between the fighting at the front and the death camps in the rear, presents a wholly false picture of the historical reality'.[84] Crucially, it is also problematic because laying the Holocaust at the door of such units as the Waffen-SS, the SS, the SA and the SD makes it possible to implicitly rescue the Wehrmacht from any embroilment in the Holocaust, at least in the public imagination. The problem with this was highlighted by Heinrich Graf von Einsiedel in the debate about the Wehrmacht exhibition: 'There is a gang of gangsters who decide to rob a bank and it splits itself up into two groups. Some storm the bank and shoot somebody there; the others cover this from outside. Those are the honest ones.'[85] Von Einsiedel thus insists that it is impossible to distinguish the good Wehrmacht from the bad SS, much like one would not distinguish between the bank robbers because some happened to cover 'only' from

---

[82] The controversy is collected in Geoffrey Hartman (ed.), *Bitburg in Moral and Political Perspective* (Bloomington: Indiana University Press 1986).

[83] Jan-Holger Kirsch, *'Wir haben aus der Geschichte gelernt': Der 8. Mai als politischer Gedenktag in Deutschland* (Cologne: Böhlau Verlag 1999), p. 94.

[84] Bartov, *Germany's War*, p. 14.

[85] Heinrich Graf von Einsiedel, in 'Die schwierige Frage nach der Schuld', in: Prantl, *Wehrmachtsverbrechen*, p. 305.

outside. Schily's argument in his contribution to the Wehrmacht debate, discussed in Chapter 4, is similar to von Einsiedel's. After talking about several members of his family who had served on the German side, he insists it was only his wife's father – a Jewish partisan in Russia – who had risked his life for a just cause, because he had fought an army that was protecting the gas chambers, that was leading a war of extermination, that, in other words, did at least not stop others from committing mass murder but in actual fact was involved in it.[86] Crucially, rescuing the Wehrmacht from involvement in the Holocaust not only implicitly detaches the Germans in general from such involvement but also rescues war as such; the ordinary military and its war emerge as 'clean'.

War and the defence of the fatherland

The myth of the 'clean' Wehrmacht has been exceptionally successful. Heer and Naumann note that the Wehrmacht started 'spinning' its story immediately after its defeat in the war.[87] The basis for saving the Wehrmacht's reputation was the idea that it had been an apolitical institution that merely carried out orders.[88] This legend was accepted and promoted even outside Germany.[89] That is, the *war* had only been tarnished by the Nazi system inasmuch as other groups – such as the SS and the SD – committed atrocities. German soldiers may at times have used what appears excessive violence to those who did not have to experience the cruelty of the war, especially on the Eastern front, but the idea was that they were not systematically involved in Nazi crimes. Bartov notes that the view in Germany that any war is hell paradoxically 'legitimized the actions of German soldiers in the war as being in no way essentially different from those of all other soldiers'.[90] In particular, the danger from the East was construed as barbaric, which meant in turn that the Wehrmacht had acted bravely and honourably in defending the fatherland. A number of factors therefore contributed to making this myth acceptable and convenient, amongst them the Germans' desire to rescue the Wehrmacht from any implication in the Holocaust. Moreover, the context of the Cold War also made it possible to construe the Eastern front retrospectively as a defensive bulwark against communism. More fundamentally, the legend is based on the unproblematic assumption that not only is war acceptable as such but also defending the fatherland is automatically to be valued. Benz indeed points out that the conviction that one has fought

[86] Deutscher Bundestag, *Plenarprotokoll*, 13/163, 13/03/97, 14714.
[87] Heer and Naumann, 'Einleitung', p. 32.
[88] See, for example, Bartov, *Hitler's Army*.   [89] Bartov, *Germany's War*, p. 64.
[90] Ibid., p. 12.

in a just cause for the fatherland is part of the strategies of justification that later became necessary.[91]

Dregger, who still defended the Wehrmacht against any criticism in the 1997 Bundestag debate, insisted that soldiers have always been victims, that they had no influence over the outbreak of the Second World War or indeed its criminal conduct. He described '[m]ost of the German soldiers' as having 'risked life and limb for their country' and having had to 'bear infinite misery'.[92] In other words, they had merely been defending their fatherland, an honourable cause if ever there was one. Dregger enlisted the support of French President François Mitterand to prove that German soldiers had been honourable. Mitterand had said at the celebrations of the fiftieth anniversary of the end of the war that 'the uniforms and even the ideas that at that time lived in the heads of the soldiers who died in such great numbers mean little to [him] in this context. They were brave. They accepted the loss of their life for a bad cause. But their attitude had nothing to do with that. They loved their fatherland.'[93] Schröder's assertion at the celebrations of the sixtieth anniversary of D-Day that the German soldiers had been similar to their French counterparts seems to recall Mitterand's assessment. All this implies that defending one's country is an honourable cause, even when the country is Nazi Germany. Some even worry that questioning the image of the Wehrmacht as 'clean' undermines 'Germany's ability to defend itself [*Wehrfähigkeit*]',[94] presumably because it challenges the absolute validity of the imperative of defending one's country. The FRG's still troubled relationship towards Wehrmacht deserters[95] confirms the value with which the idea of the defence of the state is invested above other considerations.

In this context, the insistence on the absolute value of the defence of one's country may be related to a need for Germans to salvage something. In other words, the Wehrmacht – everybody's father, brother, uncle – had to be good, even when the crimes of the regime and the German people's political responsibility for them were acknowledged. This struggle is ongoing; units such as the Waffen-SS and the SD are still often seen as responsible for the atrocities, although it is clear that it makes no sense to separate them so clearly from the Wehrmacht. Perhaps unsurprisingly, this struggle over who precisely is responsible for atrocities tends

---

[91] Benz, no title, p. 31.
[92] Deutscher Bundestag, *Plenarprotokoll*, 13/163, 13/03/97, 14710.
[93] Quoted ibid., 14710f. See also Theodor Waigel (CDU/CSU) ibid., 14727. For two slightly different versions of Mitterand's words, see Naumann, *Krieg als Text*, p. 263.
[94] Rebentisch, no title, p. 58.
[95] Ullrich, 'Den Mut haben, davonzulaufen'.

to be regarded as a German problem. And in many ways it is. There are, however, two points to be noted. The first concerns how the Germans' uniquely bad war becomes the backdrop against which the goodness of the Allied war can be secured; the other relates to the difficulty of actually distinguishing war from other, supposedly less legitimate, forms of violence.

The evilness of the German war is the background against which the goodness of the Allied war could be secured.[96] The Allies' war was so glorious precisely because the German war had been aggressive, genocidal and opposed to Western values. The Allies liberated the Germans and thereby made the new democratic beginning possible.[97] Hence the Allied war was good. Thus the Germans' rejection of war was not, and never could have been, complete; it was a rejection merely of 'bad' war, and that, for the time being, had been synonymous with German war. This is why Kinkel was able to introduce a shift. If the Germans remembered the Second World War chiefly from their country's perspective, they were bound to see it as a catastrophe. If, however, they were able to remember it with regard to its outcome and indeed from the perspective of the Allied contribution that had been vital to making the constitution of the FRG possible, then the same war begins to have positive connotations. This reframing of the Second World War is problematic, however. By focusing on the long-term outcome – the free, democratic FRG – it discounts people's experiences of the war. Kinkel's argument says little about war itself and thereby safeguards its status as a circumscribable entity which may be ethically judged in an abstract way. It does not engage with particular effects of the war on people, be they civilians or soldiers, Germans or non-Germans. From such a perspective, war may appear to be good. However, unsurprisingly, any closer engagement with these issues shows that matters are not so simple. Memories have the potential to threaten such categorical judgements as those implied in Kinkel's story.

Moreover, in much the same way that some Germans would like to see the committing of atrocities restricted to the Waffen-SS or at least to a long-vanished version of Germany, it is comfortable to assume that this problematic is one that only concerns Germans. In other words, there is an implicit assumption that no parallel exists between the German Second World War and, for example, any current wars that Western countries fight because of what these countries are: they would not commit such atrocities. The singularity of the Second World War lies in Germany's

---

[96] Carruthers, 'Compulsory Viewing', 733. See also Maja Zehfuss, 'Writing War, against Good Conscience', *Millennium: Journal for International Studies* 33 (2004), 91–121.

[97] Deutscher Bundestag, *Plenarprotokoll*, 13/48, 30/06/95, 3957.

criminal conduct; it was about the Third Reich being a genocidal regime. The German Second World War was bad because it was the Third Reich that conducted it.[98] This argument, of course, protects 'war' from implication in 'atrocities'. The argumentational strategy of the legend of the 'clean' Wehrmacht relies on the widely accepted assumption that war is a legitimate and indeed civilised form of conduct that may be clearly distinguished from the Holocaust and the barbarism on the Eastern front. There is, in this argument, a world of difference between two uniformed groups fighting each other and the uncontrolled slaughter of defenceless civilians. This may appear obvious, but the clarity of the distinction is disturbed by exploring the problem more closely.

War and the spectre of its Other

War is a funny thing. In war, the injunction against taking life is not only suspended with respect to particular groups of others but killing even turns into an imperative. Of course, war is thought to be not *about* the killing.[99] It is rather, we are reminded, 'the continuation of politics by other means';[100] that is, war is about accomplishing certain political goals, survival even, and in that sense the killing is incidental. War to defend ourselves – or rather our fatherland – is not only permissible, it is imperative. Those who are seen to undermine this goal, such as deserters or even those critical of the armed forces in wartime, typically attract severe criticism.

War and death

There is always a danger that, in looking at war in terms of what it is thought to accomplish, death and suffering in war are put to one side as mere by-products, that, in other words, killing is put to one side in order to focus on what is supposed to be central about war. This has been shown to be at work in different contexts and at different levels. The Germans' recent interest in Second World War memories, in

---

[98] Note Susan Buck-Morss's argument that after September 11 ontological arguments such as '[b]ecause the US is a civilised nation, it does not violate human rights' have taken over from epistemological ones such as '[b]ecause the US does not violate human rights, it is a civilised nation'. *Thinking Past Terror: Islamism and Critical Theory on the Left* (London: Verso 2003), p. 64.

[99] For the argument that killing is central, see Joanna Bourke, *An Intimate History of Killing* (London: Granta 1999) and Dave Grossman, *On Killing: The Psychological Cost of Learning to Kill in War and Society* (New York: Little, Brown 1995), p. 93.

[100] Carl von Clausewitz, *Vom Kriege*, 3rd edition (Munich: Ullstein Taschenbuchverlag 2002), p. 44.

particular the death and suffering of civilians, has led to concern that they might be moving to the Right politically. Memories of the suffering and death of German civilians during the Second World War are seen to be an inappropriate occupation because they are thought to have the potential to lead Germans to conclude that they have been wronged. Novels, like Ledig's *Vergeltung*, which focus on the human misery caused by air raids against German cities are criticised for failing to grasp the particularity of the Second World War, meaning its association with Nazi ideology and the Holocaust. It is, or so the argument goes, crucial that we acknowledge that the barbarity of the Nazi regime is central. German civilians and their suffering do not matter so much. They may be put to one side without much loss of understanding. My doubts on this matter – and the potential of memories articulated in literature to underline them – are clear. What is particularly worrying is that creating a supposedly appropriate relation to the past seems to trump any consideration of how the approved memory affects the political imagination beyond the immediate question of remembering the Third Reich and the Second World War and commemorating the victims.

There is a strange inconsistency in claiming the central importance of remembering the Holocaust whilst suggesting that it is preferable not to dwell on the suffering of Germans themselves. The suspicion – underlined by Schama's suggestion that Americans now turn to the Second World War as a time of moral clarity – is that acknowledging that Germans – however guilty they may have been – suffered in the war just like everyone else does not merely affect what is considered an appropriate relation to the past, it also muddies the moral waters. The clear line between German perpetrators and non-German victims becomes more difficult to draw. Thus the fear with respect to the past is that this could serve to deduct something from German guilt, that others could also (appear to) have had responsibility for unpleasant matters. Moreover, under no circumstances are Germans to share a category with their victims; they may therefore not be remembered as 'victims'. The trouble is, however, that the supposed moral clarity of the past – enforced by placing consideration of the suffering and death of Germans beyond the pale – is in danger of being translated into a programme for the future, in particular in relation to war.

If it was possible to fight a good war against the Third Reich, liberating Germany and indeed Western Europe, with merely insignificant – for Germans are to ignore it – collateral damage, then it may just be possible to do so again, perhaps indeed in Iraq. Thus how the Second World War is remembered affects how war is imagined today. The possibility of imagining a good war is achieved by putting to one side consideration of the suffering of those on the side of the perpetrators. This invariably excludes a range of questions, for example whether killing in war is not itself an atrocity, whoever may be killed. In other words, the problem with excluding as insignificant the deaths and suffering of Germans is not primarily that German civilians who were expelled from their homes, raped and killed in atrocious ways ought to be commemorated and mourned, nor is it what kind of a German identity will be produced through the memories of these events. It is instead significant to recognise that if we do not acknowledge their plight – on the grounds of their guilt – it makes it all the easier to ignore the plight of 'enemy' civilians in war today, to lack the imagination to picture people's suffering in war.[101] Remembering that people were burnt alive and ripped to pieces as a result of strategic bombing is an opportunity; being too polite to say so means that we miss a chance to remind ourselves of what may be happening to those exposed to our bombs in Kosovo, Afghanistan and Iraq. This is problematic. Even if the German Second World War was unique because of its implication in the Holocaust, this is not a good reason to ignore the ways in which it was like any other war, in particular in terms of the effects it had on civilians. Indeed, even if warfare may have fundamentally changed since the Second World War, people ripped apart by bombs still die, and in ways we do not want to see.

Generally, how people die is put to one side, whether they are soldiers or civilians. It is not normally shown on Western television, for example. We are merely told the numbers of dead, though which deaths get counted is political.[102] Sometimes we are shown bodies, but not how they died.[103] This is precisely what is so disturbing about some of the novels discussed in this book. Ledig does not avert his gaze when a soldier is ripped apart by machine-gun fire, flattened by a tank and subsequently blown up. He does not spare us the detailed description of people barbecued or burning like a torch. Mulisch also brutally zooms in on people with their hair and clothes burnt off, too distressed to notice that their child has slipped from their hands into the river in the general mayhem. That we are not normally shown such pictures as are conjured up by Ledig's and Mulisch's descriptions suggests not so much that they are not important but that they are: it would be too upsetting. It is more comfortable not to know. Friedrich's *Der Brand* engages, amongst other things, precisely with the question of how people actually died in the air raids: how many were

---

[101] For a similar point, see Barnouw, *War in the Empty Air*, xii.

[102] Maja Zehfuss, 'Subjectivity and Vulnerability: On the War with Iraq', *International Politics* 44 (2007), 58–71.

[103] The November 2004 footage of a US Marine shooting a defenceless Iraqi at close range was an exception; in the UK it was shown only on Channel 5.

killed by the impact of rubble? How many were ripped apart by the blast itself? How many burnt? How many suffocated? Friedrich, of course, was accused of being sentimental, producing an inappropriate emotionality. Whilst there clearly are problems with Friedrich's book, this accusation is intriguing because it contains a dismissal, for, following such thinking, the emotional, as I observed above, must be put to one side in order to be rational. Ironically, this means that a certain kind of knowledge is delegitimised in the name of rationality, exposing incidentally as false the distinction between the rational and the emotional. Presumably, we are supposed to focus on other, more central, facts. And yet these facts are excluded precisely because they are so central, because there is no war without killing and dying, because we find it painful to be confronted with this in such a vivid manner.

War and atrocity

Earlier I observed the attempts to save the Wehrmacht's reputation by separating the 'war' from atrocities and in particular the Holocaust. The argument that the German Second World War was unique stresses its inextricable relationship with the Holocaust; the Holocaust is what makes it unique. This claim seems to be problematic. Obviously, it rests on the idea that the Holocaust was unique; I do not want to enter that debate here. My concern rather is that focusing on the uniqueness of the German Second World War reinforces the dubious distinction between war and atrocity. This is more problematic than is admitted. It is obvious that the Wehrmacht cannot be cleared of responsibility for the Holocaust by drawing attention to its military professionalism and 'apolitical' role. The Wehrmacht itself found that the boundary between war and atrocity was hard to enforce, that it was difficult to make troops understand that they were to massacre civilians when ordered to do so but that they were not to plunder and kill as a recreational activity.[104] Once war is led in a criminal way, it is difficult to see how one can expect soldiers to obey rules at all.

Yet the problem is more fundamental. Even though Bush rallies the troops in the 'war on terror' with the idea of heroism and saving civilisation, the boundary between war and its supposed other – illegitimate violence such as torture, rape and massacre – is not merely porous: atrocity seems to lurk *within* war. Even the heroic Allied liberators of the Second World War, for one reason or another, conducted air raids on towns, even in France, thereby directly endangering civilians, sometimes

---

[104] Bartov, *Hitler's Army*, Chapter 3; Bartov, *The Eastern Front*, Chapter 4.

'friendly' civilians.[105] Moreover, historian Richard Overy pointed out in a newspaper article following the publication of photos showing the abuse of prisoners at Abu Ghraib prison that '[s]ince the 1940s, all instances of asymmetrical warfare – where local populations have sustained irregular campaigns against an occupying army – have occasioned a brutal, sometimes atrocious, response'. He therefore argues that the 'term used to describe the terrible behaviour of German forces in the Soviet Union, the "barbarisation of warfare", can be transferred to many other contexts, though none as grim and murderous'.[106] What is important is not only that the barbarity of German forces may differ only in degree but also that our shock at discovering that Western soldiers have been committing atrocities in Iraq is oddly misplaced: 'The mistreatment of prisoners, common in Iraq as in occupied Russia or Vietnam, has horrified world opinion. But it is the standard behaviour of troops under pressure, fighting a war whose purpose is hard for them to understand.'[107] Overy highlights the fact that it is not only pressure in the war situation that contributes to this but also how the enemy is portrayed. He draws a direct parallel between the US administration's depictions of 'terrorists' and Nazi propaganda:

The 'terrorist' – this was, of course, the term used by the Nazis to describe the resistance movements throughout occupied Europe – has become a generic, demonised fanatic, capable in the popular imagination of the worst atrocities. The effect has been to dehumanise the alleged enemy in Iraq, just as German propaganda dehumanised the Bolshevik commissar in 1941, and permitted their mistreatment and execution.[108]

Overy concedes that there is a difference inasmuch as 'unlike German soldiers in 1941, coalition soldiers are supposed to be subject to discipline if they mistreat prisoners', but he nevertheless sees the outrage shown by President Bush and Prime Minister Tony Blair over the atrocities at Abu Ghraib as 'disingenuous'.[109]

We have been confronted with news of torture and murder by US and UK forces in Iraq. These are, we are told, the exceptions, despicable acts committed by the few who got it all dreadfully wrong. It is an issue of 'the unspeakable behaviour of a handful of Americans'.[110] As Bush put it in a radio address, 'the abuse and humiliation meted out to

---

[105] See, for example, John Lichfield, 'The day Allied bombers destroyed my home town', *Independent*, 05/06/04, 8–9.
[106] Richard Overy, 'Like the Wehrmacht, we've descended into barbarity', *Guardian*, 10/05/04, 16.
[107] Ibid.   [108] Ibid.   [109] Ibid.
[110] Bruce Anderson, 'It's a sad end to a fine career, but for the good of his country Mr Rumsfeld has to go', *Independent*, 10/05/04, 29.

Iraqi prisoners in the jail were the "actions of a few"'.[111] The difference between these excesses of coalition forces and Saddam's regime was that soldiers would be prosecuted. However, it soon became clear that the 'hopeful notion – that the abuse was perpetrated by a few "bad apples" in the US military establishment – no longer holds'.[112] Rather, Red Cross spokesman Roland Huguenin-Benjamin revealed that 'the organisation has found "a general pattern of mistreatment of detainees" in Iraq's prisons'.[113] According to Rosa Ehrenreich Brooks, formerly a senior adviser on human rights to the State Department, the 'attitude that was communicated started from the highest levels and was sent on down the chain. It created an overall climate in which adversaries were dehumanised, the distinction between suspect and known perpetrator was effaced, and the overall message was that international law or domestic niceties get in the way of doing quote "what we had to do"'.[114] Susan Sontag equally argues that the 'torture of prisoners is not an aberration. It is a direct consequence of the doctrines of world struggle with which the Bush administration has sought to fundamentally change the domestic and foreign policy of the US.' This is the case because the 'endless "war on terror" inevitably leads to the demonising and dehumanising of anyone declared by the Bush administration to be a possible terrorist: a definition that is not up for debate'.[115] Thus the attempt to exclude the atrocities perpetrated at Abu Ghraib and elsewhere as insignificant to the 'war on terror' because they are only the excesses of the few does not entirely succeed.

Yet the implications of the 'bad apple' argument are interesting. Gary Younge claims that the soldiers who have been court-martialled for atrocities at Abu Ghraib 'are being used to symbolise not all that is wrong with war but the only thing that is wrong'.[116] In other words, by excluding their behaviour from what war is, not only this particular war but also war more generally emerges as – at least potentially – good. Younge suggests that 'the White House keeps pointing at [Lyndie] England and her six colleagues to bear the moral burden for their immoral war', for 'England's brutality is explained away not as the logical continuum of the occupation but as a contradiction to it'.[117] This is presumably what allowed General Richard Myers to claim in the middle of the controversy, 'We absolutely

---

[111] Luke Harding, 'Actions of a few, or a policy from the top?', *Guardian*, 17/05/04, 5.
[112] Suzanne Goldenberg, 'US forces taught torture techniques', *Guardian*, 14/05/04, 4.
[113] 'British soldiers are just as much to blame for abusing Iraqi prisoners as Americans', *Independent*, 10/05/04, 28.
[114] Quoted in Goldenberg, 'US forces taught torture techniques', 4.
[115] Susan Sontag, 'What have we done?', *Guardian* G2, 24/05/04, 4.
[116] Gary Younge, 'Blame the white trash', *Guardian*, 17/05/04, 15.   [117] Ibid.

have the high moral ground.'[118] This argumentational strategy is not so different from the claim that some Wehrmacht soldiers may well have been involved in atrocities, but that the Wehrmacht as an institution was not, and that such barbarity was largely down to other armed units. It is interesting to recall that the attempt to rescue the reputation of the Wehrmacht was based on the validity of its basic aim of defending the fatherland. There are echoes of this in US Secretary of Defense Donald Rumsfeld's insistence that US forces are fighting the threat of terrorism, and that these alleged atrocities have to be seen in this context. He forcefully argued that the abuse at Abu Ghraib did not 'rank up there with chopping someone's head off on television'.[119] Part of the point here is presumably that abuse is less serious than killing; but given that US and UK forces have also been accused of unlawful killing – in relation to deaths in custody, for example – this is not the whole story. The difference, one suspects, is that the coalition forces' cause is legitimate; and this cause, in the eyes of the US administration, derives at least in part from the right and imperative to defend one's country.

The possibility of construing war as good depends not least on what is seen as its purpose. The defence of the fatherland is still often assumed to be right per se. Ledig, in his *Vergeltung*, notes however that '[f]atherland, heroism, tradition, honour are hollow phrases'.[120] He does not, however, take this discussion any further. Johnson, in his *Jahrestage*, dissects this problem in more detail, approaching it from the other end, the question of whether it is permissible – or even imperative – to betray one's country when the country is in the wrong. Marie, of course, fiercely objects to this idea and hence is deeply troubled that her grandfather spied for the British. Such questions were not raised in debates between politicians over the 'war on terror', however. The US administration continuously appeals to the need to defend the country; it is not necessary to validate this idea itself. We may argue about *how* our fatherland is to be defended but not – other than as academics – about *whether* we should do so in the first place. Crucially, it was this that allowed the Wehrmacht and its troops to be portrayed as honourable, and to draw attention away from its crimes.

The justification of fighting on behalf of the fatherland brings us back, of course, to the implications of memories of heroism, noted above. The state, I observed, legitimises itself through heroic memories of

---

[118] Quoted in Rory McCarthy, 'I'm a survivor, insists Rumsfeld', *Guardian*, 14/05/04, 4.
[119] Quoted in 'Rumsfeld says terror outweighs jail abuse', *Washington Post*, 11/09/04, A4.
[120] Ledig, *Vergeltung*, p. 106.

struggle.[121] This, however, means that the argument is circular: commemoration invests dying with a heroism that serves to constitute and confirm the community and that in turn legitimises dying in the first place. Soldiers are not to have died in vain; therefore the defence of the fatherland must be good. Those who criticise the legitimacy of ongoing wars are often seen as 'betraying' the troops; this is presumably because they draw attention to the fact that claims about the heroic defence of the fatherland are based on nothing but themselves. In other words, the problem is not that we may disagree over whether particular acts are useful for defending the state; rather, it is that the state comes to be constituted in its defence and through the memories thereof. The lack around which the legitimation of war revolves is concealed.

This raises the even bigger question of war and its justification, which is not something that can be addressed here, though one point should be noted. My argument that it is important to confront the horror of how people die in war might be read to imply that it would be all right if they were killed more cleanly. Similarly, one might wonder whether war would be acceptable if atrocities could be excluded; if we could make war as civilised as it is supposed to be, it would be all right. However, this would not only be impossible. Rather, even if such a 'clean' war were possible, it would not be desirable. The opposition between war and 'painless' killing of properly identified people on the one hand and atrocity and gruesome deaths on the other appears to be not just false. In fact, it would repay investigating how far it would be useful to understand killing – even in war, even where it is condoned by the rules of war – as a form of atrocity. Soldiers are killed in war as representatives of their states; their singularity is already effaced by their status. The killing is, in other words, supposedly not personal. But the dying is, of course, always personal: no one can die in my place. As Derrida observes, '[m]y irreplaceability is . . . conferred, delivered, "given," one could say, by death'.[122] In Derrida's view, mortality and responsibility are linked: '[i]t is from the site of death as the place of my irreplaceability, that is, of my singularity, that I feel called to responsibility. In this sense only a mortal can be responsible.'[123] The implication of this is that no 'justification' for war could ever take away the responsibility for killing, for wiping out the other's singularity that can never be replaced. Nickels indeed draws attention to this when she argues that no justification would help the men who had killed in war;

[121] Edkins, 'Remembering Relationality'; see also Edkins, *Trauma and the Memory of Politics*.
[122] Jacques Derrida, *The Gift of Death*, Translated by David Wills (Chicago: The University of Chicago Press 1995), p. 41.
[123] Ibid.

they would not stop hurting because of it.[124] Thus it seems less than clear that war and the supposedly justifiable killing that happens as part of it can be distinguished satisfactorily from illegitimate violence.[125] It is not simply that there are traces of atrocity within the killing that war justifies; the argument that killing was done due to war also does not seem to necessarily put at ease those who actually had to carry it out, suggesting that – as a justification – it does not work.

Speaking of war and memory: uncertainty and responsibility

War, its permissibility and implications are pressing ethico-political problems. In Germany, these are often contextualised with memories of the Second World War. This book has explored articulations of Second World War memories both in the political debate regarding the use of force and beyond. It has examined how invocations of memories are meant to work and how they fail to do so. Thus thinking about what it means to speak of the past and of memory has offered an opportunity to reveal unacknowledged assumptions which threaten the very possibility of deploying the past in the way in which it is nevertheless deployed. In particular, although memory invokes a past as though it already exists, the past is produced and continually reproduced in such articulations of memory. As a result of this argument, the present book has not revealed how the Germans do or should remember the Second World War, nor has it determined just how their war memories really influence the Germans' decision-making on war. On the contrary, this book has challenged what appeared to be obvious. It has pursued questions about how we remember, about how remembering is related to conceptions of truth, of subjectivity, of time and of ethics. It has challenged, for example, the boundary between remembering and forgetting, the distinction between truth and fiction, and the necessity and adequacy of the linear conception of time. In other words, it has put a bewildering complexity in the place of some well-defined, if slightly unsatisfactory, knowledge about the Germans' attitudes to and memories of war. It has not argued for a particular alternative. In this final section, I offer some more general observations about memory, uncertainty and responsibility in order to show why this failure to re-impose order through a clear interpretation is not a flaw in the argument but precisely what is important.

[124] Deutscher Bundestag, *Plenarprotokoll*, 13/163, 13/03/97, 14720.
[125] This problem has, of course, been raised by others. See, for example, Robert L. Holmes, *On War and Morality* (Princeton University Press 1989) and Richard Norman, *Ethics, Killing and War* (Cambridge: Cambridge University Press 1995).

Second World War memories were read as a significant reference point in arguments about the use of military force in Germany. This, I claimed, was both more interesting and more problematic than was acknowledged. Politicians referred to the past in order to contextualise and support their political choices; they displayed certainty both about what the past was and about how it mattered for the decisions they were about to take. This, perhaps, is to be expected. They hope to persuade others, and displays of certainty may help. After all, memories of past wars are used to justify and support current wars, and not just in Germany. To put it differently, not least because of memory's close association with identity memory may be instrumentalised in politics. Whether it is pride in accomplishments or resentment over the losses and suffering endured, war memories may be seen as generating particularly strong emotions, and these may be used to propel people to some future action. The constant invocation of the Good War and the generation that fought in it by the Bush administration is, in that sense, not entirely different from references in Serbia to the Battle of Kosovo Field in 1389 or indeed from the calling-up of the horrors of war and Nazism within the context of presenting a particular military deployment as being able to help other people avoid such hardship. All are employed to mobilise support. The strength of the emotion may carry people over the abyss that separates the past from the future, what has been from what should – or will – be done. Crucially, this often involves presenting a narrow, one-sided version of memory that excludes a range of experiences as irrelevant. The failure to make the misery and suffering created precisely by the Good War part of the memories that are used in support of today's deployments makes war appear better than it is.

Yet the politics of memory might be seen to be a double-edged sword, for memory, despite its significance for the collective, for the invention of political community, at the same time remains open to multiple interpretations: everybody is, to some extent, an expert. Thus an articulation of memory almost invites the feeding-in of what Woods calls 'noise':[126] other ways of remembering the past and therefore, potentially, other ways of acting politically in the present. At first sight this is a point about the content of memory, the need to admit a multiplicity of different ways of remembering the past. Crucially, however, Woods suggests that fictional literature might provide such 'noise', and this is what I have explored, in particular because literature reflects upon itself, upon the implications of its articulations of memory. Fiction also offers a different way of writing the past, one which does not seek simply to argue something but to affect readers. As a result, expressions of memory in literature

---

[126] Woods, 'Spectres of History', p. 119.

have the potential to make the exclusions discussed above – for example of death and atrocity in war – harder; they may confront us with the Other, thus undermining the possibility of dismissing the Other's death as 'collateral damage'. They may confront us with how the realisation of the Other's suffering affects us not just intellectually but in other ways as well. They may confront us also with the difficulty of distinguishing war from its supposed opposite, illegitimate violence such as atrocities and torture. Far more fundamentally, they may confront us – if we pay attention – with the inherent ambiguity and uncertainty of some of the things we are most sure of. It is no longer quite so clear even what it means to remember or whether matters were as straightforward in the past as we now may think they were, for even if the bombing of German cities retrospectively made perfect sense as part of the fight against Nazism that was the Second World War – and it is not clear that it did – it seems that, at the time, matters are more likely to have been a confusing shambles akin to the current 'war on terror'. It all may make sense now, but it does so because through our memory we produce a past that never quite existed in that way.

As a result, the moral certainty which Schama suspects people may be seeking in the monumentification of the Second World War when – it appears retrospectively – Good and Bad were easy to distinguish is an illusion. The 'noise' fed back into images of the past through acknowledging a multiplicity of memories is thus significant. In the debate resulting from recent German interest in strategic bombing, Cora Stephan asserted that the realisation that the Allies also did things we might not approve of does not serve to exculpate the Germans:

A 'But the others also . . .' does not exonerate, on the contrary: it robs us of the conception of the Good and Right. That is sad, and yet at the same time an anchor for current and future policy – for it demands turning away from moral self-righteousness [*Selbstgewissheit*] which believes its means to be justified because of the horribleness of the enemy.[127]

Thus Stephan sees as crucial precisely that good and bad become less clearly distinguishable – or rather that it becomes clear that they have always been mixed up in each other. Thus, whilst Schama observes that we turn to memory at the point of insecurity, to find a certainty that seems to be unavailable in the present, Stephan notes that the noise of multiplicity and ambiguity reveals that memory cannot deliver the moral certainty that is sought, and that this is no bad thing. Her worry is that the illusion of a clear demarcation between good and bad feeds a

---

[127] Stephan, 'Wie man eine Stadt anzündet', p. 101.

self-righteousness that may serve as a justification for violence. Appeals to the clarity of the moral stakes in the Second World War have certainly come to be deployed in justifications for the use of military force, in particular the Iraq war.

The desire for moral clarity is pronounced in the particular context of the German discourse not least because of the context of the Third Reich and the Holocaust. That is, what is at issue in the public debates over Second World War memories is the appropriate attitude to the past. Germans are, above all, not to construe themselves as victims. Whilst any exculpatory attitude towards the past of the Third Reich would be inappropriate and offensive, the particular framing of German perpetrators versus non-German victims seems dysfunctional. It is not least an oversimplification that is easily exposed as such and may be exploited politically by the Right. What is more, this particular oversimplification may be useful in establishing an inoffensive relationship towards this horrendous past; but it also makes it difficult to acknowledge the horrors of being bombed, something that is significant, given current military operations. Thus, ironically, the desire to correctly remember the crimes of the Third Reich makes it difficult to remember the implication of the Allies' bombing of German cities. The 'truth' turns out to be more problematic an issue than is comfortable. What is more, the certainty sought by appealing to memory does not seem to be available from remembering the past. The underlying, profound uncertainty, traced throughout this book, cannot be explained away, either by somehow properly conceptualising memory or indeed by leaving memory out of the analysis and focusing on other aspects of the decision-making process. Indeed, it is necessary to acknowledge the uncertainty that is involved in both making the political choices at issue here and analysing them as a scholar.

When the question is whether or not to go to war, we are confronted with what Derrida calls an aporia: faced with decisions about life and death, we do not know what to do. Ethico-political questions, I showed in Chapter 2, arise under such conditions, and they require a response that is beyond knowledge. They require us to decide *even though* we do not and cannot know the right way forward. We agonise over the decision. Moreover, the decision, whatever it will be, will not be ethically satisfactory. It is impossible to determine a 'correct' decision by using knowledge. Derrida sees aporetic situations as calling us to responsibility. Responsibility, in Derrida's conception, only becomes possible beyond knowledge:

responsibility can only be taken – and a decision, and an act of freedom – where one does not know, whatever one's knowledge (and one must know, it is always better to know), the decision is made where knowledge as such does not dictate the rules or norms from which we would need, in short, but to unfold the program of action or draw the consequences. Thus, it is always in a dilemma and a certain non-knowledge (*non-savoir*) as to what it would be best to do, it is at the moment when two contradictory imperatives are in competition, that a responsible freedom can be exercised as such.[128]

Knowledge is of course necessary for a responsible decision, but it is never enough.[129] This impossibility of discovering the 'right way' through knowledge and then choosing the ethically correct course of action through the application of this knowledge makes us, apparently, nervous. We find ourselves exposed to profound uncertainty. The recourse to memory interestingly often occurs at this point. This might be seen as a retreat to familiar territory, a search for reassurance: we ascertain that 'we' know and share the 'lessons' of the past. In particular, when we wage war, we appear to have no time for moral uncertainty. However, as I have argued, matters are not straightforward: the reassuring certainty of memory is always under threat. Thus referring to memory might *conceal* an uncertainty, but it does not resolve it. This uncertainty is related not least to the absolute unknowability of what is to come, of what Derrida calls the future. Memory and the future – or memory and the aporia of being faced with ethico-political questions – are inextricably linked.

Derrida points out that attempting to escape uncertainty through imposing control is not merely impossible but undesirable, for 'without risk, there is nothing'.[130] He exhorts us to realise that we must live with risk. And he is not alone. The alleged lack of risk in Vonnegut's conceptualisation of temporality in *Slaughterhouse 5* in fact led to accusations that he was taking free will out of life and therefore the possibility of change, of making things better. One may be suspicious about the idea of 'making things better', but the basic point that for there to be responsibility or an ethico-political problem there has to be risk, something that cannot be addressed with knowledge alone, is also expressed in Derrida's rendering of the future as the space for the ethical. As he observes, '[e]ven if one knows everything, the decision, if there is one, must advance towards a future that is not known, that cannot be anticipated'.[131] The future that Derrida refers to here is not 'an anticipated present';[132] rather, it is '[t]hat which is totally unpredictable'.[133] It is this unpredictability which is so distressing, especially if the question we face is one of war, one of death.

[128] Derrida, *Negotiations*, pp. 210f.   [129] Derrida, *Gift of Death*, p. 24.
[130] Derrida, *Negotiations*, p. 238.   [131] Ibid., p. 231.
[132] Culler, *On Deconstruction*, p. 95.   [133] Derrida in Dick and Kofman, *Derrida*.

Because of the seriousness of the question of war, in particular its association with death, risk is as inevitable as it is unwelcome. Thus we would perhaps rather bypass our responsibility to decide and instead rely on knowledge. Knowledge incurs our trust, and it nicely takes away the agonising: if we know what is right, we may embark on this course of action in good conscience. This, however, means that in fact we act irresponsibly; we give ourselves over to the illusion that responsibility has been taken care of when we have actually shied away from the very question. The point is that there is no knowledge that may make just or responsible the blowing-up of civilians abroad, for example in order to protect other civilians. We may nevertheless decide to do so. Yet if we do, for whatever reasons, relying on whatever knowledge, the contradictory imperative that derives from the competing claims to life – which is precisely what made the question so difficult in the first place – will not have gone away. It is only when we delude ourselves into believing that it was all about the correct application of some knowledge – perhaps that they were harbouring terrorists – that we may lull ourselves into good conscience. Thus it is crucial that the uncertainty involved is acknowledged. If we decide to risk others' lives in the name of our security, it is fundamentally important that we are aware that we are responsible for their deaths, if they occur, that there is nothing, and certainly no knowledge, that may take this responsibility away from us.

The attraction of knowledge means not only that we would like to rely on it when faced with difficult questions but also that we would like to produce – and as scholars may be called upon to produce – knowledge that would help us through the aporia of, in this case, decisions about war. The way we often speak of war and memory makes assumptions that allow us to produce what appears to be secure knowledge about the past which may then be applied to political questions in the present. This is an issue not just for us as members of political communities but also as scholars. As scholars we are in danger of being complicit in this process inasmuch as our business is the production of knowledge that is regarded as in some way secure, acknowledged as arrived at in approved ways by other experts in the field. Of course, scholarship at the same time has a critical faculty: it may question such beliefs as cannot be proved in this way. Yet it seems extremely important that we do not merely reject particular knowledges as false through the process of scholarship but that we also remain aware – and acknowledge our awareness – of the uncertainty which *invariably* marks what we say and of the inadequacy of knowledge, however it may be produced, in the face of ethico-political questions.

Therefore it seems to me that it is worth attempting to write in a different way, with less confidence that either we know or that knowing is actually the point. Not only is it doubtful that we are able to establish the truth; the truth may also not hold the answer to the kind of question that is being asked. Whatever we may be writing about will necessarily already appear to be in the past. It gives rise precisely to the kind of ambiguities discussed in this book and in particular to the problem of retroactivity. We write as though something existed in the past which, however, is only produced as we write it; when it supposedly was the present 'the past' cannot have been quite like it appears now. We write as though we know what it means to know about the past. Literature illustrates vividly that both knowing and knowing what knowing means is much more complicated. Novels require the active participation of the reader; they do not easily give up their meaning. Whilst academic work has a different aim and requires us to be precise about what we argue, we would do well to acknowledge that we do not argue what we argue because we are certain. As we offer ways of thinking about the world which have political implications we need to think about these with the greatest possible care, although they are not, in the end, under our control.

Schmid, in his plea against war cited at the beginning of this book, speaks of his conviction that Germans would rather die than fight and 'at least take with [them] the knowledge that [they] neither encouraged nor committed the crime'.[134] His message is stark: Germans would prefer death over the guilt incurred by any kind of involvement in war, even if they had no hand in 'the insanity of war' breaking out and even if their country should turn into a battlefield. Death is preferable because Schmid presents simply perishing as an alternative to being implicated, to incurring guilt. He is, of course, not suggesting that simply dying is an easy option, but he seems to be saying that it is the only certain way of escaping complicity in the horror of war, the only way to make sure we neither encourage nor commit the crime. Schmid offers a radical but certain way out of responsibility for war. The desire to do the right thing and to escape complicity is understandable in the German context, perhaps even laudable. Schmid's certainty is tempting, even though it requires the price of perishing; but it does not work. In contrast to certainty such as Schmid's I have argued that we are exposed to profound uncertainty when we confront ethico-political questions, such as the question of war. It is in recognising and acknowledging this uncertainty and the related

---

[134] Carlo Schmid, *Erinnerungen* (Bern: 1979), p. 490, quoted in Abenheim, *Reforging the Iron Cross*, p. 43.

inevitability of complicity – such that even simply perishing does not afford a way out, does not allow us to take with us 'the knowledge that we neither encouraged nor committed the crime' – that we may find the courage to embrace our difficult responsibility that, both in politics and in scholarship, has to be confronted without the apparent safety net of knowledge.

Bibliography

'8. Mai 1945 – Gegen das Vergessen', *Frankfurter Allgemeine Zeitung*, 07/04/95, 3.

'8. Mai 1945 – Gegen das Vergessen', *Frankfurter Allgemeine Zeitung*, 28/04/95, 3.

'8. Mai 1945 – Gegen das Vergessen', *Frankfurter Allgemeine Zeitung*, 05/05/95, 3.

Abenheim, Donald, *Reforging the Iron Cross: The Search for Tradition in the West German Armed Forces* (Princeton University Press 1988).

Adams, Tim, 'Germany's conscience', *Observer*, 10/02/02, 25.

'Alles Vorherige war nur ein Umweg', interview with Dieter Forte, in: Volker Hage, *Zeugen der Zerstörung: Die Literaten und der Luftkrieg: Essays und Gespräche* (Frankfurt am Main: S. Fischer Verlag 2003), pp. 151–74.

'Als das Ghetto brannte', interview with Marcel Reich-Ranicki, in: Volker Hage, *Zeugen der Zerstörung: Die Literaten und der Luftkrieg: Essays und Gespräche* (Frankfurt am Main: S. Fischer Verlag 2003), pp. 235–46.

Amis, Martin, *Time's Arrow, Or the Nature of the Offence* (London: Penguin Books 1992).

'Amtliche Verlautbarung über die Konferenz von Jalta vom 3. bis 11. Februar 1945 (Auszug)', Reprinted in Clemens Vollnhals, with Thomas Schlemmer (eds.), *Entnazifizierung: Politische Säuberung und Rehabilitierung in den vier Besatzungszonen 1945–1949* (Munich: Deutscher Taschenbuch Verlag 1991), pp. 96–8.

Anderson, Benedict, *Imagined Communities: Reflections on the Origin and Spread of Nationalism*, Revised edition (London: Verso 1991).

Anderson, Bruce, 'It's a sad end to a fine career, but for the good of his country Mr Rumsfeld has to go', *Independent*, 10/05/04, 29.

Antze, Paul and Michael Lambek (eds.), *Tense Past: Cultural Essays in Trauma and Memory* (New York: Routledge 1996).

Assmann, Aleida, *Erinnerungsräume: Formen und Wandlungen des kulturellen Gedächtnisses* (Munich: Verlag C.H. Beck 1999).

Assmann, Jan, *Das kulturelle Gedächtnis: Schrift, Erinnerung und politische Identität in frühen Hochkulturen* (Munich: Verlag C.H. Beck 2002).

Augstein, Franziska, 'Rumsfelds Logik', *Süddeutsche Zeitung*, 18–19/01/03, 13.

Aust, Stefan and Stephan Burgdorff (eds.), *Die Flucht: Über die Vertreibung der Deutschen aus dem Osten* (Stuttgart: Deutsche Verlags-Anstalt 2002).

Bald, Detlef, *Militär und Gesellschaft 1945–1990* (Baden-Baden: Nomos Verlags-gesellschaft 1994).

Bamm, Peter, *Die unsichtbare Flagge* (Frankfurt am Main: Fischer Bücherei 1957).

Bance, A.F., 'The Brutalization of Warfare on the Eastern Front: History and Fiction', in: Ian Higgins (ed.), *The Second World War in Literature* (Edinburgh: Scottish Academic Press 1986), pp. 97–114.

'Germany', in: Holger Klein (ed.) with John Flower and Eric Homberger, *The Second World War in Fiction* (London: Macmillan 1984), pp. 88–130.

Barnouw, Dagmar, *The War in the Empty Air: Victims, Perpetrators and Postwar Germans* (Bloomington: Indiana University Press 2005).

Baron, Ulrich and Hans-Harald Müller, 'Die "Perspektive des kleinen Mannes" in der Kriegsliteratur der Nachkriegszeiten', in: Wolfram Wette (ed.), *Der Krieg des kleinen Mannes: Eine Militärgeschichte von unten*, 2nd edn (Munich: Piper 1995), pp. 344–60.

Bartov, Omer, *The Eastern Front 1941–45: German Troops and the Barbarisation of Warfare*, 2nd edn (Basingstoke: Palgrave 2001).

Germany's War and the Holocaust: Disputed Histories (Ithaca: Cornell University Press 2003).

Hitler's Army: Soldiers, Nazis, and the War in the Third Reich (Oxford: Oxford University Press 1992).

Bastian, Till, *Furchtbare Soldaten: Deutsche Kriegsverbrechen im Zweiten Weltkrieg*, 2nd edn (Munich: Verlag C.H. Beck 1997).

Beevor, Antony, *Stalingrad*, Translated by Klaus Kochmann (Munich: Goldmann 2001).

Bellmann, Werner, 'Nachwort', in: Heinrich Böll, *Der Engel schwieg* (Cologne: Kiepenheuer & Witsch 1992), pp. 195–212.

Benz, Wolfgang (ed.), *Die Vertreibung der Deutschen aus dem Osten: Ursachen, Ereignisse, Folgen*, updated edn (Frankfurt am Main: Fischer Taschenbuch Verlag 1995).

no title, in: Hans Günther Thiele (ed.), *Die Wehrmachtsausstellung: Dokumentation einer Kontroverse* (Bonn: Bundeszentrale für politische Bildung 1997), pp. 30–2.

Berger, Thomas U., *Cultures of Antimilitarism: National Security in Germany and Japan* (Baltimore: The Johns Hopkins University Press 1998).

Beste, Ralf et al., 'Abenteuer Nahost', *Der Spiegel*, 21/08/06, 24–7.

Bet-El, Ilana R., 'Unimagined Communities: The Power of Memory and the Conflict in the Former Yugoslavia', in: Jan-Werner Müller (ed.), *Memory and Power in Post-War Europe: Studies in the Presence of the Past* (Cambridge: Cambridge University Press 2002), pp. 206–22.

Bickerich, Wolfram, 'Die Moral blieb intakt', in: Stephan Burgdorff and Christian Habbe (eds.), *Als Feuer vom Himmel fiel: Der Bombenkrieg in Deutschland* (Munich: Deutsche Verlags-Anstalt 2003), pp. 202–10.

Biermann, Wolf, 'Brachiale Friedenliebe', *Der Spiegel*, 24/02/03, 144–7.

Bilke, Jörg Bernhard, 'Flucht und Vertreibung in der deutschen Belletristik', *Deutsche Studien* 32 (1995), 177–88.

Böll, Heinrich, *Wo warst du, Adam?* *und Erzählungen* (Cologne: Friedrich Middelhauve Verlag 1967).

Bollmann, Ralph, 'Im Dickicht der Aufrechnung', in: Lothar Kettenacker (ed.), *Ein Volk von Opfern? Die neue Debatte um den Bombenkrieg 1940–45* (Berlin: Rowohlt 2003), pp. 137–9.

Bölsche, Jochen, 'So muss die Hölle aussehen', in: Stephan Burgdorff and Christian Habbe (eds.), *Als Feuer vom Himmel fiel: Der Bombenkrieg in Deutschland* (Munich: Deutsche Verlags-Anstalt 2003), pp. 18–38.

'Bombenkrieg macht alle gleich', in: Stephan Burgdorff and Christian Habbe (eds.), *Als Feuer vom Himmel fiel: Der Bombenkrieg in Deutschland* (Munich: Deutsche Verlags-Anstalt 2003), pp. 141–50.

Bond, D.G., *German History and German Identity: Uwe Johnson's Jahrestage* (Amsterdam: Rodopi 1993).

Boog, Horst, 'Ein Kolossalgemälde des Schreckens', in: Lothar Kettenacker (ed.), *Ein Volk von Opfern? Die neue Debatte um den Bombenkrieg 1940–45* (Berlin: Rowohlt 2003), pp. 131–6.

Bourke, Joanna, *An Intimate History of Killing* (London: Granta 1999).

Bower, Tom, *The Pledge Betrayed: America and Britain and the Denazification of Postwar Germany* (New York: Doubleday & Company 1982).

'British soldiers are just as much to blame for abusing Iraqi prisoners as Americans', *Independent*, 10/05/04, 28.

Brumlik, Micha, Hajo Funke and Lars Rensmann, 'Einleitung', in: Micha Brumlik, Hajo Funke and Lars Rensmann, *Umkämpftes Vergessen: Walser-Debatte, Holocaust-Mahnmal und neuere deutsche Geschichtspolitik* (Berlin: Verlag Das Arabische Buch 1999), pp. 6–12.

Umkämpftes Vergessen: Walser-Debatte, Holocaust-Mahnmal und neuere deutsche Geschichtspolitik (Berlin: Verlag Das Arabische Buch 1999).

Bruner, M. Lane, *Strategies of Remembrance: The Rhetorical Dimensions of National Identity Construction* (Columbia: University of South Carolina Press 2002).

Bubis, Ignatz, 'Entmenschlichte Zeit', in: Heribert Prantl (ed.), *Wehrmachtsverbrechen: Eine deutsche Kontroverse* (Hamburg: Hoffmann und Campe 1997), pp. 181–6.

Bucheli, Roman, 'Die verspätete Erinnerung', *Neue Zürcher Zeitung*, 09–10/02/02, 63.

Buchheim, Lothar-Günther, *Das Boot* (Munich: Piper Verlag 1973).

Die Festung (Munich: Goldmann 1997).

Buck-Morss, Susan, *Thinking Past Terror: Islamism and Critical Theory on the Left* (London: Verso 2003).

Burgdorff, Stephan and Christian Habbe, 'Vergleichen – nicht moralisieren', interview with Hans-Ulrich Wehler, in: Stephan Burgdorff and Christian Habbe (eds.), *Als Feuer vom Himmel fiel: Der Bombenkrieg in Deutschland* (Munich: Deutsche Verlags-Anstalt 2003), pp. 42–6.

(eds.), *Als Feuer vom Himmel fiel: Der Bombenkrieg in Deutschland* (Munich: Deutsche Verlags-Anstalt 2003).

Buruma, Ian, *Wages of Guilt: Memories of War in Germany and Japan* (London: Vintage 1995).

Bush, George W., 'We're Fighting to Win – And Win We Will', Remarks by the President on the USS *Enterprise* on Pearl Harbor Day, www.whitehouse.gov/news/releases/2001/12/print/20011207.html Speech at Air Force Academy Graduation, Falcon Stadium, 02/06/04, www.whitehouse.gov/news/releases/2004/06/print/20040602.html

Carruthers, Susan L., 'Compulsory Viewing: Concentration Camp Film and German Re-education', *Millennium: Journal of International Studies*, 3 (2001), 733–59.

Cohen-Pfister, Laurel, 'The Suffering of the Perpetrators: Unleashing Collective Memory in German Literature of the Twenty-First Century', *Forum of Modern Language Studies* 41 (2005), 123–35.

Cohn, Carol, 'Wars, Wimps, and Women: Talking Gender and Thinking War', in: Miriam Cooke and Angela Woolacott (eds.), *Gendering War Talk* (Princeton: Princeton University Press 1993), pp. 227–46.

Collins English Dictionary, 3rd updated edn (Glasgow: HarperCollins Publishers 1994).

Connelly, Mark, 'Die britische Öffentlichkeit, die Presse und der Luftkrieg gegen Deutschland, 1939–1945', in: Lothar Kettenacker (ed.), *Ein Volk von Opfern? Die neue Debatte um den Bombenkrieg 1940–45* (Berlin: Rowohlt 2003), pp. 72–92.

Cooper, Alice H., 'When Just Causes Conflict with Acceptable Means: The German Peace Movement and Military Intervention in Bosnia', *German Politics and Society* 15 (1997), 99–118.

Culler, Jonathan, *On Deconstruction: Theory and Criticism after Structuralism* (London: Routledge 1983).

Dao, James, 'Experts debate meaning of regime change', *New York Times*, 22/09/02.

'Das Gewissen ist nicht delegierbar', *Frankfurter Allgemeine Zeitung*, 12/10/98, 1.

'Das hatte biblische Ausmaße', interview with Walter Kempowski, in: Volker Hage, *Zeugen der Zerstörung: Die Literaten und der Luftkrieg: Essays und Gespräche* (Frankfurt am Main: S. Fischer Verlag 2003), pp. 187–99.

'Der Fisch und die Bomben', interview with Monika Maron, in: Volker Hage, *Zeugen der Zerstörung: Die Literaten und der Luftkrieg: Essays und Gespräche* (Frankfurt am Main: S. Fischer Verlag 2003), pp. 211–21.

Derrida, Jacques, *Acts of Literature*, Edited by Derek Attridge (London: Routledge 1992).

'Autoimmunity: Real and Symbolic Suicides', in: Giovanna Borradori, *Philosophy in a Time of Terror: Dialogues with Jürgen Habermas and Jacques Derrida* (Chicago: The University of Chicago Press 2003), pp. 85–136.

Demeure: Fiction and Testimony, in Maurice Blanchot, *The Instant of my Death*/Jacques Derrida, *Demeure: Fiction and Testimony*, Translated by Elizabeth Rottenberg (Stanford: Stanford University Press 2000).

Dissemination, Translated by Barbara Johnson (London: Athlone Press 1981).

'Letter to a Japanese Friend', in: David Wood and Robert Bernasconi, *Derrida and Difference* (Coventry: Parousia Press 1985), pp. 1–8.

Limited Inc (Evanston: Northwestern University Press 1988).

Margins of Philosophy, Translated, with additional notes, by Alan Bass (Chicago: The University of Chicago Press 1982).

Memoires for Paul de Man: The Wellek Library Lectures at the University of California, Irvine, Revised edn, Translated by Cecile Lindsay, Jonathan Culler, Eduardo Cadava and Peggy Kamuf (New York: Columbia University Press 1989).

Negotiations: Interventions and Interviews 1971–2001, Edited and translated by Elizabeth Rottenberg (Stanford: Stanford University Press 2002).

Of Grammatology, Translated by Gayatri Chakravorty Spivak, Corrected edn (Baltimore: The Johns Hopkins University Press 1998).

On Cosmopolitanism and Forgiveness, Translated by Mark Dooley and Michael Hughes (London: Routledge 2001).

Points . . . Interviews, 1974–1994, Edited by Elisabeth Weber, translated by Peggy Kamuf and others (Stanford: Stanford University Press 1995).

Positions, Translated and annotated by Alan Bass (London: Athlone Press 1987).

Specters of Marx: The State of Debt, the Work of Mourning, and the New International, Translated by Peggy Kamuf (New York: Routledge 1994).

The Gift of Death, Translated by David Wills (Chicago: The University of Chicago Press 1995).

The Other Heading: Reflections on Today's Europe, Translated by Pascale-Anne Brault and Michael B. Naas (Bloomington: Indiana University Press 1992).

and Bernard Stiegler, *Echographies of Television: Filmed Interviews*, Translated by Jennifer Bajorek (Cambridge: Polity Press 2002).

'Deutsche "Tornados" sollen in Bosnien zum Schutz der europäischen Eingreiftruppe eingesetzt werden', *Süddeutsche Zeitung*, 27/06/95, 1.

Deutscher Bundestag, *Drucksache*, 13/7162, Bonn, 11/03/97.

Plenarprotokoll, 11/228, Berlin, 04/10/90, 18015–18083.

Plenarprotokoll, 11/235, Bonn, 15/11/90, 18819–18859.

Plenarprotokoll, 12/2, Bonn, 14/01/91, 21–43.

Plenarprotokoll, 12/3, Bonn, 17/01/91, 45–55.

Plenarprotokoll, 12/5, Bonn, 30/01/91, 67–93.

Plenarprotokoll, 12/151, Bonn, 21/04/93, 12925–13002.

Plenarprotokoll, 12/240, Bonn, 22/07/94, 21165–21218.

Plenarprotokoll, 13/48, Bonn, 30/06/95, 3953–4044.

Plenarprotokoll, 13/76, Bonn, 06/12/95, 6631–6708.

Plenarprotokoll, 13/163, Bonn, 13/03/97, 14625–14770.

Plenarprotokoll, 13/248, Bonn, 16/10/98, 23127–23176.

Plenarprotokoll, 14/187, Berlin, 19/09/01, 18301–18343.

Plenarprotokoll, 14/198, Berlin, 08/11/01, 19281–19487.

Plenarprotokoll, 14/202, Berlin, 16/11/01, 19855–19916.

Dick, Kirby and Amy Ziering Kofman, *Derrida* (Jane Doe Films 2003).

'Die Deutschen an die Front', *Der Spiegel*, 04/02/91, 18–22.

'Die Diskussion in der Arbeitsgruppe 1', in: Hans Günther Thiele (ed.), *Die Wehrmachtsausstellung: Dokumentation einer Kontroverse* (Bonn: Bundeszentrale für politische Bildung 1997), pp. 76–101.

'Die Diskussion in der Arbeitsgruppe 2', in: Hans Günther Thiele (ed.), *Die Wehrmachtsausstellung: Dokumentation einer Kontroverse* (Bonn: Bundeszentrale für politische Bildung 1997), pp. 122–52.

'Die Lebensuhr blieb stehen', interview with Wolf Biermann, in: Volker Hage, *Zeugen der Zerstörung: Die Literaten und der Luftkrieg: Essays und Gespräche* (Frankfurt am Main: S. Fischer Verlag 2003), pp. 135–50.

'Die schwierige Frage nach der Schuld', in: Heribert Prantl (ed.), *Wehrmachtsverbrechen: Eine deutsche Kontroverse* (Hamburg: Hoffmann und Campe 1997), pp. 300–5.

Diner, Dan, *Der Krieg der Erinnerungen und die Ordnung der Welt* (Berlin: Rotbuch Verlag 1991).

(ed.), *Ist der Nationalsozialismus Geschichte? Zu Historisierung und Historikerstreit* (Frankfurt am Main: Fischer Taschenbuch Verlag 1987).

Domansky, Elisabeth, 'A Lost War: World War II in Postwar German Memory', in: Alvin H. Rosenfeld (ed.), *Thinking about the Holocaust: After Half a Century* (Bloomington: Indiana University Press 1997), pp. 233–72.

Dorff, Robert H., 'Normal Actor of Reluctant Power? The Future of German Security Policy', *European Security* 6 (1997), 56–69.

'Dresden setzt Zeichen gegen Rechtsextremismus', *Süddeutsche Zeitung*, 14/02/05, 1.

Dubiel, Helmut, *Niemand ist frei von der Geschichte: Die nationalsozialistische Herrschaft in den Debatten des Deutschen Bundestages* (Munich: Carl Hanser Verlag 1999).

Dückers, Tanja, *Himmelskörper* (Berlin: Aufbau-Verlag 2003).

Edkins, Jenny, 'Authenticity and Memory at Dachau', *Cultural Values* 5 (2001), 405–20.

'Remembering Relationality: Trauma Time and Politics', in: Duncan S.A. Bell (ed.), *Memory, Trauma and World Politics: Reflections on the Relationship between Past and Present* (Basingstoke: Palgrave 2006), pp. 99–115.

Trauma and the Memory of Politics (Cambridge: Cambridge University Press 2003).

and Maja Zehfuss, 'Generalising the International', *Review of International Studies* 31 (2005), 451–72.

Eichwede, Wolfgang, no title, in: Hans Günther Thiele (ed.), *Die Wehrmachtsausstellung: Dokumentation einer Kontroverse* (Bonn: Bundeszentrale für politische Bildung 1997), pp. 33–4.

'Einsatz ins Ungewisse', *Der Spiegel*, 30/01/95, 68–79.

Emig, Rainer, 'Augen/Zeugen: Kriegserlebnis, Bild, Metapher, Legende', in: Thomas F. Schneider (ed.), *Kriegserlebnis und Legendenbildung: Das Bild des 'modernen' Krieges in Literatur, Theater, Photographie und Film*, vol. I (Osnabrück: Universitätsverlag Rasch 1999), pp. 15–24.

Krieg als Metapher im zwanzigsten Jahrhundert (Darmstadt: Wissenschaftliche Buchgesellschaft 2001).

'Es war Krieg, ich habe nichts zu verarbeiten', in: Heribert Prantl (ed.), *Wehrmachtsverbrechen: Eine deutsche Kontroverse* (Hamburg: Hoffmann und Campe 1997), pp. 275–77.

'Europäische Truppe schützen und stützen', *Süddeutsche Zeitung*, 27/06/95, 5.

Evans, Richard J., 'The New Nationalism and the Old History: Perspectives on the West German *Historikerstreit*', *Journal of Modern History* 59 (1987), 761–97.

Felman, Shoshana and Dori Laub, *Testimony: Crises of Witnessing in Literature, Psychoanalysis, and History* (New York: Routledge 1992).

Finkelstein, Norman G. and Ruth Bettina Birn, *A Nation on Trial: The Goldhagen Thesis and Historical Truth* (New York: Henry Holt 1998).

Forte, Dieter, *Schweigen oder sprechen*, Edited by Volker Hage (Frankfurt am Main: S. Fischer 2002).

Frei, Norbert, *Vergangenheitspolitik: Die Anfänge der Bundesrepublik und die NS-Vergangenheit* (Munich: Deutscher Taschenbuch Verlag 1999).

Frevert, Ute, 'Geschichtsvergessenheit und Geschichtsversessenheit revisited: Der jüngste Erinnerungsboom in der Kritik', *Aus Politik und Zeitgeschichte* B40–1 (2003), 6–13.

Friedrich, Jörg, *Der Brand: Deutschland im Bombenkrieg 1940–1945* (Munich: Propyläen Verlag 2002).

Fromme, Friedrich Karl, 'Was bleibt: die Schuld', in: Heribert Prantl (ed.), *Wehrmachtsverbrechen: Eine deutsche Kontroverse* (Hamburg: Hoffmann und Campe 1997), pp. 79–81.

Fussell, Paul, *The Great War and Modern Memory* (Oxford: Oxford University Press 1975).

Garrett, Stephen A., *Ethics and Airpower in World War II: The British Bombing of German Cities* (New York: St Martin's Press 1993).

Gehorsam bis zum Mord? Der verschwiegene Krieg der deutschen Wehrmacht – Fakten, Analysen, Debatte, ZEIT-Punkte 3 (1995).

Genscher, Hans-Dietrich, Speech at the 45th General Assembly of the UN, in: Presse- und Informationsamt der Bundesregierung, *Bulletin*, 115, 27/09/90, 1201–6.

Gertz, Bernhard, no title, in: Hans Günther Thiele (ed.), *Die Wehrmachtsausstellung: Dokumentation einer Kontroverse* (Bonn: Bundeszentrale für politische Bildung 1997), pp. 105–6.

Geyer, Michael, 'The Place of the Second World War in German Memory and History', Translated by Michael Latham, *New German Critique* 71 (1997), 5–40.

Gillessen, Günther, 'Die Ausstellung zerstört nicht eine Legende – sie baut eine neue auf', in: Heribert Prantl (ed.), *Wehrmachtsverbrechen: Eine deutsche Kontroverse* (Hamburg: Hoffmann und Campe 1997), pp. 164–71.

'Kritische Bemerkungen zur Ausstellung "Die Verbrechen der Wehrmacht"', in: Hans Günther Thiele (ed.), *Die Wehrmachtsausstellung: Dokumentation einer Kontroverse* (Bonn: Bundeszentrale für politische Bildung 1997), pp. 85–91.

Giordano, Ralph, 'Ein Volk von Opfern?', in: Lothar Kettenacker (ed.), *Ein Volk von Opfern? Die neue Debatte um den Bombenkrieg 1940–45* (Berlin: Rowohlt 2003), pp. 166–8.

Goldenberg, Suzanne, 'US forces taught torture techniques', *Guardian*, 14/05/04, 4.

Grass, Günter, *Die Blechtrommel* (Darmstadt: Luchterhand Literaturverlag 1989).

Die Rättin (Darmstadt: Luchterhand 1986).

Hundejahre (Neuwied am Rhein: Luchterhand 1963).

Im Krebsgang (Göttingen: Steidl 2002); translated as *Crabwalk*, Translated by Krishna Winston (London: Faber and Faber 2003).

Katz und Maus (Frankfurt am Main: Luchterhand Literaturverlag 1988).

Grayling, A. C., *Among the Dead Cities: Was the Allied Bombing of Civilians in WWII a Necessity or a Crime?* (London: Bloomsbury 2006).

Greiner, Gottfried, no title, in: Hans Günther Thiele (ed.), *Die Wehrmachtsausstellung: Dokumentation einer Kontroverse* (Bonn: Bundeszentrale für politische Bildung 1997), pp. 35–40.

Groehler, Olaf, *Bombenkrieg gegen Deutschland* (Berlin: Akademie Verlag 1990).

Grossman, Dave, *On Killing: The Psychological Cost of Learning to Kill in War and Society* (New York: Little, Brown 1995).

Gründel, Johannes, 'Der Krieg und die Schuld', in: Heribert Prantl (ed.), *Wehrmachtsverbrechen: Eine deutsche Kontroverse* (Hamburg: Hoffmann und Campe 1997), pp. 149–52.

Habbe, Christian, 'Mit dem Rechen des Todes', in: Stephan Burgdorff and Christian Habbe (eds.), *Als Feuer vom Himmel fiel: Der Bombenkrieg in Deutschland* (Munich: Deutsche Verlags-Anstalt 2003), pp. 151–60.

'Vorwort', in: Stephan Burgdorff and Christian Habbe (eds.), *Als Feuer vom Himmel fiel: Der Bombenkrieg in Deutschland* (Munich: Deutsche Verlags-Anstalt 2003), pp. 9–10.

and Hans-Ulrich Stoldt, 'Tief in jedem Hinterkopf', interview with František Černý, in: Stefan Aust and Stephan Burgdorff (eds.), *Die Flucht: Über die Vertreibung der Deutschen aus dem Osten*, 2nd edn (Stuttgart: Deutsche Verlags-Anstalt 2002), pp. 126–32.

Hage, Volker, 'Berichte aus einem Totenhaus', in: Stephan Burgdorff and Christian Habbe (eds.), *Als Feuer vom Himmel fiel: Der Bombenkrieg in Deutschland* (Munich: Deutsche Verlags-Anstalt 2003), pp. 101–14.

'Die Angst muß im Genick sitzen', *Der Spiegel*, 04/01/99, 160–4.

'Königssohn von Wasserburg', *Der Spiegel*, 27/07/98, 148–50.

'Nachwort', in: Gert Ledig, *Vergeltung* (Frankfurt am Main: Suhrkamp Verlag 2001), pp. 201–11.

'Das tausendmalige Sterben', in: Stefan Aust and Stephan Burgdorff (eds.), *Die Flucht: Über die Vertreibung der Deutschen aus dem Osten* (Stuttgart: Deutsche Verlags-Anstalt 2002), pp. 39–47.

'Unter Generalverdacht', *Der Spiegel*, 08/04/02, 178–81.

Zeugen der Zerstörung: Die Literaten und der Luftkrieg: Essays und Gespräche (Frankfurt am Main: S. Fischer Verlag 2003).

Halbwachs, Maurice, *On Collective Memory*, Edited, translated and with an introduction by Lewis A. Coser (Chicago: The University of Chicago Press 1992).

Harding, Luke, 'Actions of a few, or a policy from the top?', *Guardian*, 17/05/04, 5.

Hartman, Geoffrey H., 'Introduction: 1985', in: Geoffrey H. Hartman (ed.), *Bitburg in Moral and Political Perspective* (Bloomington: Indiana University Press 1986), pp. 1–12.

(ed.), *Bitburg in Moral and Political Perspective* (Bloomington: Indiana University Press 1986).

Hawking, Stephen, *A Brief History of Time: From the Big Bang to Black Holes* (New York: Bantam Books 1988).

Heer, Hannes, 'Von der Schwierigkeit, einen Krieg zu beenden: Reaktionen auf die Ausstellung "Vernichtungskrieg. Verbrechen der Wehrmacht 1941 bis 1944"', *Zeitschrift für Geschichtswissenschaft* 45 (1997), 1086–1100.

and Klaus Naumann, 'Einleitung', in: Hannes Heer and Klaus Naumann (eds.), *Vernichtungskrieg: Verbrechen der Wehrmacht 1941–1944* (Hamburg: Hamburger Edition 1995), pp. 25–36.

Walter Manoschek, Alexander Pollak and Ruth Wodak (eds.), *Wie Geschichte gemacht wird: Zur Konstruktion von Erinnerungen an Wehrmacht und Zweiten Weltkrieg* (Vienna: Czernin Verlag 2003).

Helbig, Louis Ferdinand, *Der ungeheure Verlust: Flucht und Vertreibung in der deutschsprachigen Belletristik der Nachkriegszeit*, 3rd edn (Wiesbaden: Harrasowitz Verlag 1996).

Heller, Joseph, *Catch-22* (London: Vintage 1994).

Hermand, Jost, 'Darstellungen des Zweiten Weltkrieges', in: Jost Hermand (ed.), *Literatur nach 1945 I: Politische und regionale Aspekte* (Wiesbaden: Akademische Verlagsgesellschaft Athenaion 1979), pp. 11–60.

Herzog, Roman, 'Dresden – A Warning for the Future: Speech by the Federal President in Dresden on 13 February 1995', in: *Remembrance and Perpetual Responsibility* (Bonn: Press and Information Office of the Federal Government 1995), 5–9.

'Return to the Future: Speech by the Federal President in Berlin on 8 May 1995', in: *Remembrance and Perpetual Responsibility* (Bonn: Press and Information Office of the Federal Government 1995), 17–23.

Hillgruber, Andreas, *Zweierlei Untergang: Die Zerschlagung des Deutschen Reiches und das Ende des europäischen Judentums* (Berlin: Siedler 1986).

Hirsch, Helga, 'Flucht und Vertreibung: Kollektive Erinnerung im Wandel', *Aus Politik und Zeitgeschichte* B40–1 (2003), 14–26.

'Historikerstreit': Die Dokumentation der Kontroverse um die Einzigartigkeit der nationalsozialistischen Judenvernichtung (Munich: Piper 1987); translated as *Forever under the Shadow of Hitler? Original Documents of the* Historikerstreit, *the Controversy Concerning the Singularity of the Holocaust*, Translated by James Knowlton and Truett Cates (Atlantic Highlands, NJ: Humanities Press 1993).

Höges, Clemens et al., 'Die verdrängte Tragödie', in: Stefan Aust and Stephan Burgdorff (eds.), *Die Flucht: Über die Vertreibung der Deutschen aus dem Osten* (Stuttgart: Deutsche Verlags-Anstalt 2002), pp. 51–65.

Holmes, Robert L., *On War and Morality* (Princeton: Princeton University Press 1989).

Hooper, John, 'Günter Grass breaks taboo on German war refugees', *Guardian*, 08/02/02, 16.

Horsley, William, 'United Germany's Seven Cardinal Sins: A Critique of German Foreign Policy', *Millennium: Journal of International Studies* 21 (1992), 225–41.

Huyssen, Andreas, 'Present Pasts: Media, Politics, Amnesia', *Public Culture* 12 (2000), 21–38.

Twilight Memories: Marking Time in a Culture of Amnesia (New York: Routledge 1995).

'Ignatz Bubis antwortet Martin Walser: Unterschwellig antisemitisch: Auszüge aus Rede zum 60. Jahrestag der Pogromnacht', *Süddeutsche Zeitung*, 10/11/98, 5.

Illies, Florian, *Generation Golf: Eine Inspektion* (Berlin: Argon 2000).

Jacobsen, Hans-Adolf, 'Zur Rolle der Wehrmacht im Rußlandfeldzug 1941–1944', in: Hans Günther Thiele (ed.), *Die Wehrmachtsausstellung: Dokumentation einer Kontroverse* (Bonn: Bundeszentrale für politische Bildung 1997), pp. 48–50.

Jaenecke, Heinrich, 'Die Stunde Null', *Geo Epoche* (9/2002), 28–30.

Janßen, Karl-Heinz, 'Als Soldaten Mörder wurden', in: Heribert Prantl (ed.), *Wehrmachtsverbrechen: Eine deutsche Kontroverse* (Hamburg: Hoffmann und Campe 1997), pp. 29–36.

Joffe, Josef, 'Abschied von der "Kohl-Doktrin"', *Süddeutsche Zeitung*, 16/12/94, 4.

Johnson, Uwe, *Begleitumstände: Frankfurter Vorlesungen* (Frankfurt am Main: Suhrkamp 1980).

Jahrestage: Aus dem Leben von Gesine Cresspahl, vols. I–IV (Frankfurt am Main: Suhrkamp Verlag 1970, 1971, 1973, 1983).

Jones, Peter G., *War and the American Novelist: Appraising the American War Novel* (Columbia: University of Missouri Press 1976).

Kaiser, Gerhard, 'Aufklärung oder Denunziation?', in: Heribert Prantl (ed.), *Wehrmachtsverbrechen: Eine deutsche Kontroverse* (Hamburg: Hoffmann und Campe 1997), pp. 52–60.

Kattago, Siobhan, 'Representing German Victimhood and Guilt: The Neue Wache and Unified German Memory', *German Politics and Society* 16 (1998), 86–104.

Kearney, Richard, *On Stories* (London: Routledge 2002).

Kettenacker, Lothar, 'Vorwort des Herausgebers', in: Lothar Kettenacker (ed.), *Ein Volk von Opfern? Die neue Debatte um den Bombenkrieg 1940–45* (Berlin: Rowohlt 2003), pp. 9–14.

(ed.), *Ein Volk von Opfern? Die neue Debatte um den Bombenkrieg 1940–45* (Berlin: Rowohlt 2003).

Kinkel, Klaus, 'Peacekeeping missions: Germany can now play its part', *NATO Review* 42/5 (1994), 3–7.

'Verantwortung, Realismus, Zukunftssicherung', *Frankfurter Allgemeine Zeitung*, 19/03/93, 8.

Kirsch, Jan-Holger, *'Wir haben aus der Geschichte gelernt' Der 8. Mai als politischer Gedenktag in Deutschland* (Cologne: Böhlau Verlag 1999).

Kirst, Hans Hellmut, *08/15* (Munich: Wilhelm Goldmann Verlag n.d.).

Klein, Holger, *The Artistry of Political Literature: Essays on War, Commitment and Criticism* (Lewiston: The Edwin Mellen Press 1994).

Klußmann, Uwe, 'Attacke des Jahrhunderts', in: Stefan Aust and Stephan Burgdorff (eds.), *Die Flucht: Über die Vertreibung der Deutschen aus dem Osten* (Stuttgart: Deutsche Verlags-Anstalt 2002), pp. 69–70.

Knibb, James, 'Literary Strategies of War, Strategies of Literary War', in: David Bevan (ed.), 'Literature and War', *Rodopi Perspectives on Modern Literature* 3 (1990), 7–24.

Knischnewski, Gerd and Ulla Spittler, 'Memories of the Second World War and National Identity in Germany', in: Martin Evans and Ken Lunn (eds.), *War and Memory in the Twentieth Century* (Oxford: Berg 1997), pp. 239–54.

Knopp, Guido, *Stalingrad: Das Drama* (Munich: C. Bertelsmann 2003).

Kohl, Helmut, Message on the day of German unification on 3 October 1990 to all governments in the world, in: Presse- und Informationsamt der Bundesregierung, *Bulletin*, 118, 05/10/90, 1227–8.

Kohler, Berthold, 'Nachkriegszeiten', *Frankfurter Allgemeine Zeitung*, 14/09/04, 1.

Koshar, Rudy, *Germany's Transient Pasts: Preservation and National Memory in the Twentieth Century* (Chapel Hill: The University of North Carolina Press 1998).

Kurbjuweit, Dirk et al., 'Fehlbar und verstrickt', *Der Spiegel*, 21/08/06, 46–66.

LaCapra, Dominick, *History and Memory after Auschwitz* (Ithaca: Cornell University Press 1998).

Langenbacher, Eric, 'Changing Memory Regimes in Contemporary Germany?', *German Politics and Society* 21 (2003), 46–68.

Langer, Lawrence L., *The Holocaust and the Literary Imagination* (New Haven: Yale University Press 1975).

'Länger verheddern', *Der Spiegel*, 02/10/95, 36–8.

Ledig, Gert, *Die Stalinorgel* (Frankfurt am Main: Suhrkamp Verlag 2000).

Vergeltung (Frankfurt am Main: Suhrkamp Verlag 2001).

'Lehrer loben die Wehrmacht-Ausstellung', in: Heribert Prantl (ed.), *Wehrmachtsverbrechen: Eine deutsche Kontroverse* (Hamburg: Hoffmann und Campe 1997), pp. 315–17.

Lichfield, John, 'The day Allied bombers destroyed my home town', *Independent*, 05/06/04, 8–9.

Terri Judd and Cahal Milmo, 'The Last March', *Independent*, 07/06/04, 1 and 4.

Limbach, Jutta, 'Rede zur Eröffnung der "Wehrmachtsausstellung" in Karlsruhe am 10.1.97', in: Heribert Prantl (ed.), *Wehrmachtsverbrechen: Eine deutsche Kontroverse* (Hamburg: Hoffmann und Campe 1997), pp. 61–5.

Maier, Charles S., *The Unmasterable Past: History, Holocaust, and German National Identity* (Cambridge, MA: Harvard University Press 1988).

Margalit, Avishai, *The Ethics of Memory* (Cambridge, MA: Harvard University Press 2002).

McCarthy, Rory, 'I'm a survivor, insists Rumsfeld', *Guardian*, 14/05/04, 4.

McCrisken, Trevor B. and Andrew Pepper, *American History and Contemporary Film* (New Brunswick: Rutgers University Press 2005).

McInnes, Colin, *Spectator-Sport War: The West and Contemporary Conflict* (Boulder: Lynne Rienner Publishers 2002).

Meiers, Franz-Josef, 'Germany: The Reluctant Power', *Survival* 37 (1995), 82–103.

Middleton, Peter and Tim Woods, *Literatures of Memory: History, Time and Space in Postwar Writing* (Manchester: Manchester University Press 2000).

Mitscherlich, Alexander and Margarete Mitscherlich, *Die Unfähigkeit zu trauern: Grundlagen kollektiven Verhaltens*, 17th edn (Munich: Piper 2004).

Moeller, Robert G., 'On the History of Man-Made Destruction: Loss, Death, Memory, and Germany in the Bombing War', *History Workshop Journal* 61 (2006), 103–34.

War Stories: The Search for a Usable Past in the Federal Republic of Germany (Berkeley: University of California Press 2001).

Mommsen, Hans, 'Moralisch, strategisch, zerstörerisch', in: Lothar Kettenacker (ed.), *Ein Volk von Opfern? Die neue Debatte um den Bombenkrieg 1940–45* (Berlin: Rowohlt 2003), pp. 145–51.

'Wie die Bomben Hitler halfen', in: Stephan Burgdorff and Christian Habbe (eds.), *Als Feuer vom Himmel fiel: Der Bombenkrieg in Deutschland* (Munich: Deutsche Verlags-Anstalt 2003), pp. 115–21.

Mosse, George L., *Fallen Soldiers: Reshaping the Memory of the World Wars* (Oxford: Oxford University Press 1990).

Mulisch, Harry, *Das steinerne Brautbett*, Translated by Gregor Seferens (Frankfurt am Main: Suhrkamp Verlag 1995).

Müller, Jan-Werner, 'Introduction: The Power of Memory, the Memory of Power and the Power over Memory', in: Jan-Werner Müller (ed.), *Memory and Power in Post-War Europe: Studies in the Presence of the Past* (Cambridge: Cambridge University Press 2002), pp. 1–35.

Münkler, Herfried, 'Den Krieg wieder denken: Clausewitz, Kosovo und die Kriege des 21. Jahrhunderts', *Blätter für deutsche und internationale Politik* 44 (1999), 678–88.

'Moralphilosophie auf dem Kriegspfad', *Blätter für deutsche und internationale Politik* 47 (2002), 1335–44.

Über den Krieg: Stationen der Kriegsgeschichte im Spiegel ihrer theoretischen Reflexion (Weilerswist: Velbrück Wissenschaft 2003).

Musial, Bogdan, 'Bilder einer Ausstellung: Kritische Anmerkungen zur Wanderausstellung "Vernichtungskrieg: Verbrechen der Wehrmacht 1941 bis 1944"', *Vierteljahreshefte für Zeitgeschichte* 47 (1999), 563–91.

Naumann, Klaus (a), 'Erinnern, lernen – nichts kopieren', in: *Gehorsam bis zum Mord? Der verschwiegene Krieg der deutschen Wehrmacht – Fakten, Analysen, Debatte, ZEIT-Punkte* 3 (1995), 87–90.

Naumann, Klaus (b), *Der Krieg als Text: Das Jahr 1945 im kulturellen Gedächtnis der Presse* (Hamburg: Hamburger Edition 1998).

Neumann, Klaus, *Shifting Memories: The Nazi Past in the New Germany* (Ann Arbor: The University of Michigan Press 2000).

Neumann, Thomas W., 'Der Bombenkrieg: Zur ungeschriebenen Geschichte einer kollektiven Verletzung', in: Klaus Naumann (ed.), *Nachkrieg in Deutschland* (Hamburg: Hamburger Edition 2001), pp. 319–42.

Nietzsche, Friedrich, *Also sprach Zarathustra: Ein Buch für Alle und Keinen* (Berlin: Walter de Gruyter & Co. 1968).

Unzeitgemäße Betrachtungen (Stuttgart: Alfred Kröner Verlag 1964).

Noack, Hans-Joachim, 'Die Deutschen als Opfer', in: Stefan Aust and Stephan Burgdorff (eds.), *Die Flucht: Über die Vertreibung der Deutschen aus dem Osten* (Stuttgart: Deutsche Verlags-Anstalt 2002), pp. 15–20.

Noelle-Neumann, Elisabeth, 'Ein Volk, gebeutelt und gezeichnet', *Die Zeit*, 10/05/85, 7.

Norman, Richard, *Ethics, Killing and War* (Cambridge: Cambridge University Press 1995).

Norris, Margot, *Writing War in the Twentieth Century* (Charlottesville: University Press of Virginia 2000).

Nutz, Walter, 'Der Krieg als Abenteuer und Idylle: Landser-Hefte und triviale Kriegsromane', in: Hans Wagener (ed.), *Gegenwartsliteratur und Drittes Reich: Deutsche Autoren in der Auseinandersetzung mit der Vergangenheit* (Stuttgart: Reclam 1977), pp. 265–83.

Olick, Jeffrey K., 'Genre Memories and Memory Genres: A Dialogical Analysis of May 8, 1945 Commemorations in the Federal Republic of Germany', *American Sociological Review* 64 (1999), 381–402.

In the House of the Hangman: The Agonies of German Defeat, 1943–1949 (Chicago: The University of Chicago Press 2005).

Overy, Richard, 'Die alliierte Bombenstrategie als Ausdruck des "totalen Krieges"', in: Lothar Kettenacker (ed.), *Ein Volk von Opfern? Die neue Debatte um den Bombenkrieg 1940–45* (Berlin: Rowohlt 2003), pp. 27–47.

'Like the Wehrmacht, we've descended into barbarity', *Guardian*, 10/05/04, 16.

'Past and present', *Guardian*, 04/06/04, 25.

Pfeifer, Jochen, *Der deutsche Kriegsroman 1945–1960: Ein Versuch zur Vermittlung von Literatur und Sozialgeschichte* (Königstein/Ts.: Scriptor 1981).

Prantl, Heribert, 'Einführung', in: Heribert Prantl (ed.), *Wehrmachtsverbrechen: Eine deutsche Kontroverse* (Hamburg: Hoffmann und Campe 1997), pp. 231–3.

'Einleitung', in: Heribert Prantl (ed.), *Wehrmachtsverbrechen: Eine deutsche Kontroverse* (Hamburg: Hoffmann und Campe 1997), pp. 9–25.

(ed.), *Wehrmachtsverbrechen: Eine deutsche Kontroverse* (Hamburg: Hoffmann und Campe 1997).

Press Conference by Jamie Shea and Brigadier General Giuseppe Marani, *NATO Press Conferences*, 15/04/99 (www.nato.int/kosovo/press/p990415a.htm).

'Pressemitteilung des Hamburger Instituts für Sozialforschung vom 24.4.97', in: Heribert Prantl (ed.), *Wehrmachtsverbrechen: Eine deutsche Kontroverse* (Hamburg: Hoffmann und Campe 1997), pp. 215–18.

Radvan, Florian, 'Nachwort', in: Gert Ledig, *Die Stalinorgel* (Frankfurt am Main: Suhrkamp Verlag 2000), pp. 203–29.

Raulff, Ulrich, 'Untergang mit Maus und Muse', *Süddeutsche Zeitung*, 05/02/02, 13.

Rautenberg, Hans-Werner, 'Die Wahrnehmung von Flucht und Vertreibung in der deutschen Nachkriegsgeschichte bis heute', *Aus Politik und Zeitgeschichte* B53 (1997), 34–46.

Rebentisch, Ernst, no title, in: Hans Günther Thiele (ed.), *Die Wehrmachtsausstellung: Dokumentation einer Kontroverse* (Bonn: Bundeszentrale für politische Bildung 1997), pp. 55–9.

Reemtsma, Jan-Philipp, 'Die wenig scharf gezogene Grenze zwischen Normalität und Verbrechen', in: Heribert Prantl (ed.), *Wehrmachtsverbrechen: Eine deutsche Kontroverse* (Hamburg: Hoffmann und Campe 1997), pp. 187–99.

Remarks by President Bush and President Chirac on marking the 60th Anniversary of D-Day, The American Cemetery, Normandy, France, 06/06/04, www.whitehouse.gov/news/releases/2004/06/print/20040606.html

Remarque, Erich Maria, *Im Westen nichts Neues*, Edited by Brian Murdoch (London: Routledge 1984).

Ricoeur, Paul, *Memory, History, Forgetting*, Translated by Kathleen Blamey and David Pellauer (Chicago: The University of Chicago Press 2004).

Riehl-Heyse, Herbert, 'Die Geister einer Ausstellung', in: Heribert Prantl (ed.), *Wehrmachtsverbrechen: Eine deutsche Kontroverse* (Hamburg: Hoffmann und Campe 1997), pp. 236–43.

Riordan, Colin, *The Ethics of Narration: Uwe Johnson's Novels from Ingrid Babendererde to Jahrestage* (London: The Modern Humanities Research Association 1989).

Roth, Günther, no title, in: Hans Günther Thiele (ed.), *Die Wehrmachtsausstellung: Dokumentation einer Kontroverse* (Bonn: Bundeszentrale für politische Bildung 1997), pp. 67–73.

Rumsfeld, Donald, *NATO Press Conference*, 06/06/02.

'Rumsfeld says terror outweighs jail abuse', *Washington Post*, 11/09/04, A4.

Schama, Simon, 'If you receive this, I'll be dead', *Guardian G2*, 28/05/04, 3–4.

Schirrmacher, Frank (ed.), *Die Walser-Bubis-Debatte: eine Dokumentation* (Frankfurt am Main: Suhrkamp 1999).

Schlant, Ernestine, *The Language of Silence: West German Literature and the Holocaust* (New York: Routledge 1999).

Schmidt-Klingenberg, Michael, 'Wir werden sie ausradieren', in: Stephan Burgdorff and Christian Habbe (eds.), *Als Feuer vom Himmel fiel: Der Bombenkrieg in Deutschland* (Munich: Deutsche Verlags-Anstalt 2003), pp. 47–60.

Schmitz, Helmut, *On Their Own Terms: The Legacy of National Socialism in Post-1990 German Fiction* (Birmingham: University of Birmingham Press 2004).

Schneider, Jens, 'Eine Kultur der Erinnerung', *Süddeutsche Zeitung*, 14/02/05, 3.

'Im brüchigen Rahmen der Erinnerung', *Süddeutsche Zeitung*, 10/02/05, 3.

Schneider, Peter, 'Deutsche als Opfer? Über ein Tabu der Nachkriegsgeneration', in: Lothar Kettenacker (ed.), *Ein Volk von Opfern? Die neue Debatte um den Bombenkrieg 1940–45* (Berlin: Rowohlt 2003), pp. 158–65.

Schreiber, Gerhard, 'Dokumente einer Vergangenheit, die ehrlich angenommen werden muß', in: Heribert Prantl (ed.), *Wehrmachtsverbrechen: Eine deutsche Kontroverse* (Hamburg: Hoffmann und Campe 1997), pp. 172–7.

Schröder, Gerhard, 'Erklärung von Bundeskanzler Gerhard Schröder zum 60. Jahrestag der Zerstörung Dresdens', 13/02/05, www.bundeskanzler.de.

Rede bei den deutsch-französischen Feierlichkeiten zum 60. Jahrestag des 'D-Day' in Caen, 06/06/04, www.bundesregierung.de

Schwab-Trapp, Michael, *Kriegsdiskurse: Die politische Kultur des Krieges im Wandel 1991–1999* (Opladen: Leske und Budrich 2002).

Schwartz, Michael, 'Vertreibung und Vergangenheitspolitik: Ein Versuch über geteilte deutsche Nachkriegsidentitäten', *Deutschlandarchiv* 30 (1997), 177–95.

Schwarz, Ulrich, 'Überall Leichen, überall Tod', in: Stephan Burgdorff and Christian Habbe (eds.), *Als Feuer vom Himmel fiel: Der Bombenkrieg in Deutschland* (Munich: Deutsche Verlags-Anstalt 2003), pp. 70–84.

Schwendemann, Heinrich, 'Tod zwischen den Fronten', in: Stefan Aust and Stephan Burgdorff (eds.), *Die Flucht: Über die Vertreibung der Deutschen aus dem Osten*, 2nd edn (Stuttgart: Deutsche Verlags-Anstalt 2002), pp. 71–82.

Sebald, W.G., *Luftkrieg und Literatur: Mit einem Essay zu Alfred Andersch* (Munich: Carl Hanser Verlag 1999); translation published as *On the Natural History of Destruction*, translated by Anthea Bell (London: Penguin Books 2004).

Seidler, Franz W., 'Pauschale Verurteilung verunglimpft einzelne', in: Heribert Prantl (ed.), *Wehrmachtsverbrechen: Eine deutsche Kontroverse* (Hamburg: Hoffmann und Campe 1997), pp. 87–9.

Seifert, Heribert, 'Rekonstruktion statt Richterspruch', in: Lothar Kettenacker (ed.), *Ein Volk von Opfern? Die neue Debatte um den Bombenkrieg 1940–45* (Berlin: Rowohlt 2003), pp. 152–7.

Shandley, Robert R. (ed.), *Unwilling Germans? The Goldhagen Debate* (Minneapolis: University of Minnesota Press 1998).

Sofsky, Wolfgang, 'Die halbierte Erinnerung', in: Lothar Kettenacker (ed.), *Ein Volk von Opfern? Die neue Debatte um den Bombenkrieg 1940–45* (Berlin: Rowohlt 2003), pp. 124–6.

Sommer, Theo, 'Die Diktatur des Krieges', in: *Gehorsam bis zum Mord? Der verschwiegene Krieg der deutschen Wehrmacht – Fakten, Analysen, Debatte*, ZEIT-Punkte 3 (1995), 5.

Sontag, Susan, *Regarding the Pain of Others* (London: Penguin Books 2004). 'What have we done?', *Guardian G2*, 24/05/04, 2–5.

Sontheimer, Michael, 'Schillerndes Ungeheuer', *Der Spiegel*, 02/12/02, 56–7.

Spiegel, Hubert, 'Das mußte aufschraiben!', *Frankfurter Allgemeine Zeitung*, 09/02/02, 56.

Stargardt, Nicholas, 'Opfer der Bomben und der Vergeltung', in: Lothar Kettenacker (ed.), *Ein Volk von Opfern? Die neue Debatte um den Bombenkrieg 1940–45* (Berlin: Rowohlt 2003), pp. 56–71.

Stegelmann, Katharina, 'Ein Riesenspaß, ein Alptraum', in: Stephan Burgdorff and Christian Habbe (eds.), *Als Feuer vom Himmel fiel: Der Bombenkrieg in Deutschland* (Munich: Deutsche Verlags-Anstalt 2003), pp. 215–19.

Steinfeld, Thomas, 'Der Wanderfotograf', *Frankfurter Allgemeine Zeitung*, 26/09/98, V.

Stephan, Cora, 'Wie man eine Stadt anzündet', in: Lothar Kettenacker (ed.), *Ein Volk von Opfern? Die neue Debatte um den Bombenkrieg 1940–45* (Berlin: Rowohlt 2003), pp. 95–102.

Stephan, Rainer, 'Wenn alle nach der Ehre fragen', in: Heribert Prantl (ed.), *Wehrmachtsverbrechen: Eine deutsche Kontroverse* (Hamburg: Hoffmann und Campe 1997), pp. 271–5.

Streit, Christian, *Keine Kameraden: Die Wehrmacht und die sowjetischen Kriegsgefangenen 1941–1945* (Stuttgart: Deutsche Verlags-Anstalt 1980).

Stumfall, Florian, 'Wie Deutsche diffamiert werden', in: Heribert Prantl (ed.), *Wehrmachtsverbrechen: Eine deutsche Kontroverse* (Hamburg: Hoffmann und Campe 1997), pp. 251–3.

Stürmer, Michael, 'Geschichte in geschichtslosem Land', in: *'Historikerstreit'. Die Dokumentation der Kontroverse um die Einzigartigkeit des nationalsozialistischen Judenvernichtung* (Munich: Piper 1987), pp. 36–8.

Tachibana, Reiko, *Narrative as Counter-Memory: A Half-Century of Postwar Writing in Germany and Japan* (Albany: State University of New York Press 1998).

'Tanz unter den Ruinen', interview with Harry Mulisch, in: Volker Hage, *Zeugen der Zerstörung: Die Literaten und der Luftkrieg: Essays und Gespräche* (Frankfurt am Main: S. Fischer Verlag 2003), pp. 223–34.

Thomson, Alistair, *Anzac Memories: Living with the Legend* (Melbourne: Oxford University Press, 1994).

Timm, Uwe, *Am Beispiel meines Bruders*, 3rd edn (Cologne: Kiepenheuer & Witsch 2003).

Trenkner, Joachim, 'Wieluń, 1. September 1939: "Keine besondere Feindbeobachtung"', in: Lothar Kettenacker (ed.), *Ein Volk von Opfern? Die neue Debatte um den Bombenkrieg 1940–45* (Berlin: Rowohlt 2003), pp. 15–23.

Ude, Christian, 'Rede zur Eröffnung der "Wehrmachtsausstellung" am 24. Februar 1997 in der Ludwig-Maximilians-Universität', in: Heribert Prantl (ed.), *Wehrmachtsverbrechen: Eine deutsche Kontroverse* (Hamburg: Hoffmann und Campe 1997), pp. 255–64.

Ulrich, Bernd, *Stalingrad* (Munich: Beck 2005).

Ullrich, Volker, 'Den Mut haben, davonzulaufen', *Gehorsam bis zum Mord? Der verschwiegene Krieg der deutschen Wehrmacht – Fakten, Analysen, Debatte*, ZEIT-Punkte 3 (1995), 64–9.

'Weltuntergang kann nicht schlimmer sein', in: Lothar Kettenacker (ed.), *Ein Volk von Opfern? Die neue Debatte um den Bombenkrieg 1940–45* (Berlin: Rowohlt 2003), pp. 110–15.

United States Department of Defense, *Testimony of U.S. Secretary of Defense Donald Rumsfeld before the House Armed Services Committee regarding Iraq (Transcript)*, 18/09/02.

'U.S. Policy towards Iraq: Administration Views', *Hearing before the Committee on International Relations, House of Representatives*, 107th Congress, 2nd session, 19/09/02, Serial No. 107–117.

'Vertrag über die abschließende Regelung in bezug auf Deutschland', reprinted in: *Grundgesetz für die Bundesrepublik Deutschland*, 51st edn (Munich: C.H. Beck'sche Verlagsbuchhandlung 1993), pp. 107–14.

'Von allen Luftwaffen bombardiert', interview with Kurt Vonnegut, in: Volker Hage, *Zeugen der Zerstörung: Die Literaten und der Luftkrieg: Essays und Gespräche* (Frankfurt am Main: S. Fischer Verlag 2003), pp. 281–6.

Von Clausewitz, Carl, *Vom Kriege*, 3rd edn (Munich: Ullstein Taschenbuchverlag 2002).

Von Krockow, Christian Graf, 'Zwei Pole, die das Verhängnis bargen', in: Heribert Prantl (ed.), *Wehrmachtsverbrechen: Eine deutsche Kontroverse* (Hamburg: Hoffmann und Campe 1997), pp. 153–9.

Von Scheven, Werner, 'Gibt es eine Traditionslüge? – Die Wehrmacht in Rußland und die Tradition der Bundeswehr', in: Hans Günther Thiele (ed.), *Die Wehrmachtsausstellung. Dokumentation einer Kontroverse* (Bonn: Bundeszentrale für politische Bildung 1997), pp. 125–35.

Von Weizsäcker, Richard, 'Zum 40. Jahrestag der Beendigung des Krieges in Europa und der nationalsozialistischen Gewaltherrschaft', 08/05/85, www.dhm.de.

Vonnegut, Kurt, *Slaughterhouse 5, or The Children's Crusade: A Duty-Dance with Death* (London: Vintage 2003).

Wagener, Hans, 'Soldaten zwischen Gehorsam und Gewissen: Kriegsromane und -tagebücher', in: Hans Wagener (ed.), *Gegenwartsliteratur und Drittes Reich: Deutsche Autoren in der Auseinandersetzung mit der Vergangenheit* (Stuttgart: Reclam 1977), pp. 241–64.

Walser, Martin, 'Bombenkrieg als Epos', in: Lothar Kettenacker (ed.), *Ein Volk von Opfern? Die neue Debatte um den Bombenkrieg 1940–45* (Berlin: Rowohlt 2003), pp. 127–30.

'Dankesrede zur Verleihung des Friedenspreis des Deutschen Buchhandels in der Frankfurter Paulskirche', 11/10/98, www.dhm.de.

Ein springender Brunnen (Frankfurt am Main: Suhrkamp 2000).

Über Deutschland reden (Frankfurt am Main: Suhrkamp 1988).

Die Verteidigung der Kindheit (Frankfurt am Main: Suhrkamp 1991).

Walzer, Michael, *Just and Unjust Wars: A Moral Argument with Historical Illustrations*, 2nd edn (New York: Basic Books 1992).

'Was will Walser?', *Süddeutsche Zeitung*, 13/10/98, 15.

Wehler, Hans-Ulrich, 'Einleitung', in: Stefan Aust and Stephan Burgdorff (eds.), *Die Flucht: Über die Vertreibung der Deutschen aus dem Osten* (Stuttgart: Deutsche Verlags-Anstalt 2002), pp. 9–14.

'Wer Wind sät, wird Sturm ernten', in: Lothar Kettenacker (ed.), *Ein Volk von Opfern? Die neue Debatte um den Bombenkrieg 1940–45* (Berlin: Rowohlt 2003), pp. 140–4.

Wette, Wolfram, 'Ein Hitler des Orients? NS-Vergleiche in der Kriegspropaganda von Demokratien', *Gewerkschaftliche Monatshefte* 45 (2003), 231–42.

'Jude gleich Partisan', in: Heribert Prantl (ed.), *Wehrmachtsverbrechen: Eine deutsche Kontroverse* (Hamburg: Hoffmann und Campe 1997), pp. 37–43.

and Gerd R. Ueberschär (eds.), *Stalingrad: Mythos und Wirklichkeit einer Schlacht* (Frankfurt am Main: Fischer 1997).

White, Hayden, *The Content of the Form: Narrative Discourse and Historical Representation* (Baltimore: The Johns Hopkins University Press 1987).

Whitrow, G.J., *What is Time?* (Oxford: Oxford University Press 2003).

Wiedmer, Caroline, *The Claims of Memory: Representations of the Holocaust in Contemporary France and Germany* (Ithaca: Cornell University Press 1999).

Wiegel, Michaela, 'Wo das 20. Jahrhundert aus der Dunkelheit in das Licht trat', *Frankfurter Allgemeine Zeitung*, 28/05/02, 3.

Willms, Johannes, 'Außer Thesen nichts gewesen', *Süddeutsche Zeitung*, 16/11/00, 15.

'Die glorreiche Provokation', *Süddeutsche Zeitung*, 22/11/00, 15.

Willsher, Kim, 'Anniversary anxiety', *Guardian*, 02/06/04, 14.

Windfuhr, Manfred, *Erinnerung und Avantgarde: Der Erzähler Uwe Johnson* (Heidelberg: Universitätsverlag Winter 2003).

Winkler, Willi, 'Nun singen sie wieder', in: Lothar Kettenacker (ed.), *Ein Volk von Opfern? Die neue Debatte um den Bombenkrieg 1940–45* (Berlin: Rowohlt 2003), pp. 103–9.

Winter, Jay, *Sites of Memory, Sites of Mourning: The Great War in European Cultural History* (Cambridge: Cambridge University Press 1995).

'Wir haben eine neue Rolle übernommen', interview with Volker Rühe, *Der Spiegel*, 16/10/95, 24–7.

Wodak, Ruth, '"Wie Geschichte gemacht wird" – zur Enstehung und zu den Absichten eines Projekts', in: Hannes Heer, Walter Manoschek, Alexander Pollak and Ruth Wodak (eds.), *Wie Geschichte gemacht wird: Zur Konstruktion von Erinnerungen an Wehrmacht und Zweiten Weltkrieg* (Vienna: Czernin Verlag 2003), pp. 7–11.

Woods, Tim, 'Mending the Skin of Memory: Ethics and History in Contemporary Narratives', *Rethinking History* 2 (1998), 339–48.

'Spectres of History: Ethics and Postmodern Fictions of Temporality', in: Dominic Rainsford and Tim Woods (eds.), *Critical Ethics: Text, Theory and Responsibility* (Basingstoke: Macmillan 1999), pp. 105–21.

Wyschogrod, Edith, *An Ethics of Remembering: History, Heterology, and the Nameless Others* (Chicago: The University of Chicago Press 1998).

Young, James E., *The Texture of Memory: Holocaust Memorials and Meaning* (New Haven: Yale University Press 1993).

Younge, Gary, 'Blame the white trash', *Guardian*, 17/05/04, 15.

Zehfuss, Maja, *Constructivism in International Relations: The Politics of Reality* (Cambridge: Cambridge University Press 2002).

'Derrida's Memory, War and the Politics of Ethics', in: Madeleine Fagan et al. (eds.), *Derrida: Negotiating the Legacy* (Edinburgh: Edinburgh University Press 2007), pp. 97–111.

'Forget September 11', *Third World Quarterly* 24 (2003), 513–28.

'Subjectivity and Vulnerability: On the War with Iraq', *International Politics*, vol. 44 (2007), 58–71.

'Writing War, against Good Conscience', *Millennium: Journal for International Studies* 33 (2004), 91–121.

Index

8 May 1945 32, 33, 40–1, 203–8, 217–18, 223, 225
  see also liberation

Abu Ghraib 255–7
Afghanistan 6, 7, 68, 253
Altmann, Elisabeth 5
ambiguity
  highlighted by memory 261
  highlighted by novels 123, 261
  of memory 2, 10, 71, 227, 261
  of political implications of memory 245
  of temporality of memory 223
  of understandings of the end of the
    Second World War 104–5
amnesia 63, 82
anti-war novel 15, 144, 193–4
apology, for the past 18, 71, 115, 128
aporia, 171, 217, 262–3, 264
appropriateness
  of emotionality 254
  of memory 12, 14, 41, 64, 65, 71, 73,
    111, 122, 150, 163, 222, 229, 252
  of relation to past 65, 233, 252, 262
  of representations of past 45, 59, 83,
    161, 165
artificiality, necessity of 84, 157, 164, 172
Assmann, Aleida 21, 37, 39, 55, 63, 123,
    176, 181, 197
atonement 95
atrocities
  of Bosnians 70
  and Bundeswehr deployments 35
  committed by Germans 28, 48, 153,
    165, 194, 229, 243, 244
  depiction of 14
  failure to depict 17, 29, 141
  against Germans 46, 51, 61, 70, 196,
    229
  in Iraq 241, 255
  killing in war as 253
  Nazi 6, 64, 121, 127, 183

question of Wehrmacht involvement 11,
    231
  responsibility for 249
  simultaneous in- and exclusion of 245–6
  and war 30, 91, 152, 190, 193, 250,
    254–9, 261
  Wehrmacht 69, 70, 126, 129–41, 145,
    162, 164, 198, 230, 233, 243
    debate about 19, 28, 111, 170, 171,
      172, 215, 222, 227, 231
    exclusion of 152
    forgetting of 38, 69
  see also Wehrmacht crimes, exhibition on
Augstein, Franziska 116
Auschwitz 7, 54, 89, 100, 103, 117, 154
authenticity
  claim to 105, 146, 155–7, 189–92, 223
  and the emotional 173
  of experience 84
  of literature 155–7, 159
  of memory 186
  of reporting 19
  impossibility of 158, 160
  paradox of 157, 164
  production of 155–7, 159, 172
  and testimony 158

Balkans 8, 9, 11, 30, 31, 32, 69, 81, 129,
    139, 222, 244
Bamm, Peter 19
Bance, Alan 16, 17, 18, 19, 152
Barker, Pat 212
Barnouw, Dagmar 27, 54, 112, 154, 232
Baron, Ulrich 155, 159
Bartov, Omer 6, 63, 69, 70, 128, 168, 243,
    247, 248
Basic Law 6, 8
bearing witness 42, 47, 49, 51, 52, 54, 59,
    146, 150
  see also testimony
Benz, Wolfgang 136, 138, 248
Berger, Thomas U. 6, 127

Bet-El, Ilana R. 37
Bickerich, Wolfram 77
Biermann, Wolf 117
Bitburg controversy 135, 246
Blair, Tony 255
Böll, Heinrich 18, 83, 143, 145
Bölsche, Jochen 78, 116, 118
bombing, area 79
bombing of German cities 77–9, 87–92
    as causing terror 230, 237
    difficulty of remembering 262
    as focus of memories 28, 29, 41, 175
    as part of fight against Nazism 261
    questions invited by 244
    related to Iraq war 12
    representation in literature 16, 81–7, 145
    representing Germans as victims of 111
    and ways of dying 238
bombing, strategic 76
    cause of 99
    emotions evoked by remembering 123,
        226, 239
    and Germans as victims 231
    implicit comparison with crimes of
        Third Reich 89
    interest in 67
    limitation of memory of 222
    memories of, linked to contemporary
        wars 29, 68, 116–21
    questions invited by 244
    representation in literature 165
    uncertainties about 115
    unwelcome memory of 198
    and ways of dying 238
Bond, D.G. 182, 187, 188, 189, 197, 200
Boog, Horst 88, 90, 108, 238
Bosnia
    Bundeswehr deployments to 5, 6, 8, 12,
        34, 41, 69, 126, 127, 233, 245
    genocidal politics in 35, 139, 198
    Second World War in 69, 70
    war in 9, 10
Bubis, Ignatz 115, 154, 246
Bucheli, Roman 66, 171
Buchheim, Lothar-Günther 17, 155, 159
Buruma, Ian 26
Bush, George W. 117, 118, 218, 235, 237,
    254, 255

Cambodia 68
causality 93, 95, 181, 189, 195
certainty
    as always under threat 122, 263
    disturbed by novels 20
    of ethical categorisation 96

illusion of 74
importance of undermining 74
inability of memory to deliver 3
memories offered with 227, 260
memory as source of 261, 262
moral 27, 237, 261
undermining of 121
Schmid's 265
Sebald's 82
underlined by memory 2
Chirac, Jacques 235, 236
chronology
    as significant 93
    memory as challenging 50, 188,
        197–203, 219
    problem of 175, 185, 200–3, 217
    see also temporality; time
civilians, killed in air raids 78, 82
Cohen-Pfister, Laurel 112
Cohn, Carol 240
Cold War 4, 18, 68, 101, 168
collapse 94, 204, 207, 208
coming to terms with the past, see
    Vergangenheitsbewältigung
commemoration
    of bombing of cities 79–81, 82, 113,
        114, 165, 166, 230
    as concealing forgetting 39
    and controversiality of memories 2, 41,
        175, 203, 205, 217
    and Germans as victims 66, 92, 93, 229,
        230
    and German suffering 110
    and perpetrator groups 244–8
    political significance of 22
    as producing community 72, 228, 234,
        247, 258
    and the truth 225
    and value of remembering 34, 35
community
    appropriate relation to past of 140, 222
    as an object of circumstances 205, 206
    imagined 22, 93
    invocation of 34, 81
    memories as part of production of 48,
        64, 72, 233, 234, 247, 258, 260
    of memory 47
    memory articulated on behalf of 228
    and production of knowledge 264
    of the suffering 122
    see also commemoration
Connelly, Mark 77
counter-memory 19, 20–1, 150, 161–4,
    238
Culler, Jonathan 22, 213

culpability
  feeling of 5, 127
  of Allies 196
Czechoslovakia 200

damage, collateral 116, 119, 127, 238,
    242, 252, 261
D-Day 13, 235, 238, 244, 249
de Mendelsohn, Peter 83
decision, necessity of 4, 29, 73, 75, 123,
    170, 173, 199, 233
deconstruction, general strategy of 22
defeat 10, 13, 104, 204, 205, 206, 208, 217
denazification 92
Derrida, Jacques
  on deconstruction 22
  on différance 214
  on fiction 23–6
  on future 189, 214, 215–16, 217, 218,
    263
  on forgetting 63
  on haunting 198
  on iterability 158, 226
  on knowledge 73–4, 174, 262
  on memory 63, 215, 224
  on the messianic 213, 217
  and overturning 168
  on presence 213
  on reading 23, 24, 25
  on responsibility 24, 73–4, 171, 258, 262
  on testimony 24, 158–9, 173
  on time 213–15
  on undecidability 24, 74
différance 214
disgrace 39, 54, 66, 154
displacement, Derridean 22, 169, 170
distancing 44, 58, 193, 195, 196, 211
Domansky, Elisabeth 27
Dönitz, Grand Admiral Karl 54
Dregger, Alfred 5, 38, 132–4, 135, 138,
    140, 141, 161–4, 172, 203, 231,
    249
Dresden
  50th anniversary of bombing of 34, 76,
    79–81, 109, 229, 239
  60th anniversary of bombing of 114,
    165, 166
  death toll in 113
  fictional representation of bombing of
    101–8, 109, 123, 156, 189–97, 211,
    223, 225, 238
  instrumentalisation of bombing by
    Neonazis 113, 230
  links to war today of bombing of 116,
    117, 118

people killed in shelters in 109
remembrance in 80–1
results of bombing of 82
survivors of bombing of 113, 122, 230
Dubiel, Helmut 34, 47, 92, 94, 133, 135,
    203, 205
Duve, Freimut 5, 12, 135, 138, 140, 163,
    230

Eastern front 9, 58, 89, 141, 148, 165,
    248, 251
Edkins, Jenny 22
effect, emotional 88
Ehrenreich Brooks, Rosa 256
Eichwede, Wolfgang 136, 137
Emig, Rainer 14, 155–7, 158, 159, 173,
    190–2
emotion 242
  ability of fiction to express 56
  acknowledgement of 81, 217
  false distinction from the rational of 254
  generated by memories 121, 123, 226,
    235, 242, 260
  lack of 55, 193
  relation to engagement with war today of
    29
  relation to ethics and truth of 29, 161–6
  shown in political debate 134, 137, 140,
    172
  supporting certainty 122
  towards memories 121
  within the Bundeswehr 138
  see also effect, emotional; emotionality;
    empathy; grief; guilt; identification,
    emotional; mourning; pain;
    sentimentality; shame
emotionality 81, 93, 123, 132, 136, 238,
    239, 254
empathy 12, 57, 119, 120, 121, 242
England, Lyndie 256
Evans, Richard J. 6
exculpating, of Germans 26, 109, 110,
    164, 229, 262
exoneration 66, 92, 117, 135
  possibility of 39, 95
expellee organisations 42, 47, 230
expulsion
  difficulty of representing 45–6
  and German identity 111
  impossibility of representing 155
  and memory of liberation 31, 32, 41, 69,
    205
  and mourning 80, 240
  question of appropriate memory of 72,
    231

expulsion (*cont.*)
  question of reasons for 71, 244
  representation in fiction 41–55
  and sentimentality 90, 238
  suppression of memory of 62, 78
  unwelcome memory of 198
  and war 68
  worries about turn to memory of 65
  see also suffering; victims

fatherland
  defence of 137, 163, 167, 248, 257–8
  dying for 98
  fighting for 11
  love of 133, 249
  see also Wehrmacht, myth of 'clean'
Federal Constitutional Court 8
fiction
  and authenticity 159, 189–92
  blurring of boundary of 44, 57–8, 193
  criticism of 16, 18–20, 155
  effect of 164, 241, 260
  freedom of 19, 25, 109
  impossibility of distinguishing from
      non-fiction 24
  and memory 73
  necessity of 20, 24, 29, 56, 146, 159,
      164, 172
  perception of war through 14
  as political weapon 26
  reflexivity of 24, 59, 73
  as testimony 20, 24, 146
  see also literature
First World War 15, 52, 144, 155
Fischer, Joschka 7, 70
forgetting
  of air war 78, 86, 101, 123
  campaign against 31, 32, 33, 34, 41, 61,
      69, 70, 203, 204, 223
  common sense definition of 63
  concealment of 39, 71
  danger of 28, 41
  ease of 61
  inevitability of 71
  impossibility of 48, 197, 230
  necessity of 37–40, 63, 157
  as part of remembering 28, 33, 40–1,
      63–4, 71, 72, 224, 233, 259
  of war 27, 228
  see also memory
Forte, Dieter 85, 99, 113, 123, 160,
      226
Foucault, Michel 21
France 9, 235, 236, 254
Frei, Norbert 207

Frevert, Ute 89, 132
Friedrich, Jörg 87–92, 109, 116, 117, 222,
      225, 238, 239, 240, 253
future
  memory of the 195, 209, 219
  as space for ethics 174, 217, 218, 263
  as the unexpected 189, 215–16, 217,
      263
  see also memory

GDR 45, 46, 52, 55, 61, 102, 108, 117,
      182, 186, 205
Geißler, Heiner 139, 140, 215
genres 24, 57, 159, 211
Genscher, Hans-Dietrich 1
Gertz, Colonel Bernhard 138
Gillessen, Günther 136
Giordano, Ralph 93
Glotz, Peter 127
Goebbels, Joseph 117
Goldhagen, Daniel Jonah 114
Good War, The 13, 29, 237, 238, 260
grandchildren, generation of 67, 132, 133,
      163
Grass, Günter 6, 28, 33, 41–55, 57, 61–3,
      64–7, 70, 72–3, 74, 85, 91, 117,
      156, 166, 171, 193, 211, 225, 226,
      230, 241
Great Britain 9
Grief 162, 163, 164, 239, 245
Groehler, Olaf 91
guilt
  attempts to obscure or reduce 46, 48,
      67, 96, 153, 170, 252
  collective 231, 232
  and disgrace 66
  complexity of 108
  about feelings 107
  and Germans as victims 76, 252, 253
  of involvement in war 265
  memory of 13, 34, 99, 110, 126, 228,
      245
  of the Nazi regime 76
  overpowering 62, 231
Gulf War, 1991 1, 4, 12, 68
Gysi, Gregor 70

Häfner, Gerald 139
Hage, Volker 16, 73, 78, 84–6, 89, 97, 99,
      100, 192
Halbwachs, Maurice 68, 116
Harpprecht, Klaus 15
hauntology 198
Hawking, Stephen 180–1, 209–10
healing 81, 125

Heer, Hannes 131, 132, 133, 137, 248
Helbig, Louis Ferdinand 45, 48
Hermand, Jost 14, 18, 151
Herzog, Roman 34, 36, 79–81, 87, 90,
    109, 110, 114, 117, 122, 217, 228,
    229, 239
Heuer, Jens-Uwe 5
Heuss, Theodor 31, 32
Historikerstreit 33, 38, 60, 111, 114,
    177
history, three types of 37
Hitler 92, 103, 104, 118, 129, 133, 153,
    205, 229, 245
  war without 7
Holocaust
  bombing as response to 96, 100
  bringing back in of 30
  commemorations of 34
  context of 160, 262
  denial of 114
  German identity after the 135
  Germans' responsibility for 44, 92,
    135
  legacy of 6, 127
  and literature 20, 21, 252
  meaning of 89
  memory of 33, 35, 37, 38, 61, 63, 90,
    154, 165, 198, 252
  relation to flight from the East 66
  setting aside of 26–8, 110, 243
  victims of 65
  Wehrmacht involvement in 137, 243–8,
    251, 253, 254
Holocaust memorial 39, 115
Huguenin-Benjamin, Roland 256
Hussein, Saddam 121, 256
Huyssen, Andreas 35, 37, 40, 177, 178,
    223

identification
  emotional 119, 120, 121
  of the reader 18, 142, 143, 184
  with the group of the remembered 64,
    247
  with victims 60, 119
identity
  German 80, 91, 111, 112, 115, 144,
    175, 177, 247, 253
  and memory 64, 111, 112, 176, 235,
    253, 260
immediacy
  recreation of 29, 100, 146, 160
  illusion of 157
imperative to remember 36, 40, 60–3, 71,
    74, 122, 229

innocence 58, 66, 94, 95, 110, 145
innocents 9, 119
instrumentalisation
  of bombing of Dresden 113
  of memories 2, 56, 72, 73, 120, 122,
    230, 260
  of past 69, 140, 154, 170, 225
Iraq 31, 32, 241, 252, 255
  war against 6, 12, 13, 29, 76, 79,
    116–21, 218, 222, 234, 236, 262
Ireland 198
iterability 158, 226, 227

Janßen, Karl-Heinz 131, 139, 246
Japan 20
  liberation of 13, 76, 234, 236
Johnson, Uwe 30, 175, 179, 181, 182–9,
    197–203, 214, 215, 219, 223, 228,
    257
Jones, Peter G. 196, 212, 216

Kasack, Hermann 83
Kearney, Richard 164
Kempowski, Walter 85
Kettenacker, Lothar 91, 92, 94, 166
Kinkel, Klaus 7, 9, 12, 34–5, 41, 69, 70,
    71, 76, 145, 167, 169, 220, 225,
    228, 233, 242, 244, 245, 250
Kirsch, Jan-Holger 247
Kirst, Hans Hellmut 16
Klein, Holger 155
Knibb, James 155
knowledge
  claim to 105, 122, 174, 190, 227
  closure of 216
  delegitimation of 254
  failure of 3, 73, 173
  historical 113, 235
  impossibility of 56, 58, 71, 74
  inadequacy of 3, 74, 121, 123, 217, 219,
    241, 262, 263
  memory as 12, 74, 122
  security of 73, 264
  shared 92
  as solution 3, 71, 74, 171
Kohl doctrine 8, 9, 11, 34, 35, 69, 70, 126,
    129, 244
Kohl, Helmut 1, 5, 6, 12, 35, 145, 173,
    246
Kosovo 6, 10, 12, 35, 68, 121, 253, 260
Kuwait 31, 32

Lambsdorff, Otto Graf 4, 133, 221
Langenbacher, Eric 90
Lebanon 7

Ledig, Gert 16, 29, 77, 94, 96–101, 107,
    109, 110–11, 123, 126, 141–6, 150,
    151–2, 153, 154, 155, 156, 157,
    159, 160, 164, 165, 171, 181, 193,
    223, 225, 228, 234, 238, 241, 252,
    253, 257
liberation
  by Allies 9, 10, 12, 34, 41, 76, 171, 175,
    250
  of Europe 244
  of France 235, 236
  of Germany and Japan 13, 76, 234, 236
  memory of 12, 30, 32, 33, 35, 41, 104,
    120, 203–8, 214, 216, 217, 220,
    223, 225, 233
  see also 8 May 1945
liberators, heroic 9, 10, 29, 69, 115, 120,
    169, 233, 244, 254
Limbach, Jutta 136
linearity, see temporality; time
literature
  association with war of 14
  complicity in myth of 'clean' Wehrmacht
    of 19, 153, 172
  as counter-memory 21, 150, 165
  function of 19, 20, 25
  necessity of 24, 83–4
  relation to memory of 21
  significance of 71–5, 112, 123, 171, 173,
    241, 252, 260, 265
  see also fiction

manipulation, of memory 37, 56, 62, 170
Mann, Thomas 93, 95
Margalit, Avishai 36, 37
Maron, Monika 86
McInnes, Colin 242
memorials 22, 39, 77, 237
  see also Holocaust memorial
memory
  abuse of 56, 63, 113, 232
  affective 49, 55
  authentic 186
  collective 21, 26, 100, 112, 139, 153,
    204
  communities of 47
  cultural 37
  deceptive 186
  desire to escape 53, 61, 62
  ethics of 36
  individual 37
  instrumentality of see
    instrumentalisation, of memory
  as knowledge see knowledge, memory as
  lack of 42, 83

  as linked to future 64, 115, 138, 139,
    140, 173, 215, 234, 252, 260
  multiplicity of 41, 55–9, 72, 73, 120,
    121, 122, 170, 225, 260
  official 20, 21, 39, 47, 111, 247
  personal 176
  public 43, 47, 79, 150, 153
  refusal of 38
  site of 3, 222
  standardisation of 150, 165
  and uncertainty 2–4, 174
  unavoidability of 21, 61, 62, 64, 108,
    231, 240
  waning of 7, 61
  see also manipulation
memory boom 35, 39
memory work, active 39
Merz, Friedrich 7
messianic, the 213, 217
Middleton, Peter 209–10, 212, 219
Mitscherlich, Alexander 202
Mitterand, François 133, 249
Moeller, Robert G. 27, 43, 47, 92, 110,
    205, 229
Mommsen, Hans 77, 119
mourning 56, 80, 90, 114, 116, 122, 134,
    140, 166, 173, 239, 253
Mulisch, Harry 15, 29, 77, 101–8, 109,
    110, 123, 160, 177, 193, 224, 225,
    227, 228, 238, 241, 253
Müller, Hans-Harald 155, 159
Müller, Kerstin 7
Münkler, Herfried 119, 121
Myers, General Richard 256

NATO 16, 66, 169
Naumann, Klaus 34, 79–80, 92, 93, 95,
    96, 131, 139, 204, 205, 206, 217,
    239, 248
Naumann, Klaus (Inspector General) 138
Nazi terminology 89, 109, 230
Neo-Nazism 51, 52, 54, 56–7, 60, 67, 113,
    230
Neumann, Klaus 33
never again war 1, 5, 7, 81, 126, 128, 150,
    166, 169
Nickels, Christa 134, 141, 163, 172, 232,
    258
Nietzsche, Friedrich 37–8, 40, 64, 148
Norris, Margot 14, 48
Nossack, Hans Erich 14, 82

Olick, Jeffrey K. 115
overturning 22, 28, 40, 168–9, 170, 171
Overy, Richard 255

pacifism 196, 212, 245
pain 82, 123, 124, 126, 134, 135, 163
painfulness, of memory 28, 29, 66, 108,
    121, 124, 134, 231, 238
past
    disposing of 33, 38, 61, 243
    ethical representation of 21
    as imposing itself 21, 147, 157, 160,
        177, 178
    inescapability of 60, 172, 197
    obsession with 11, 13, 79, 187
    as present 147, 149–51, 157, 165, 172,
        177, 178, 223
    shared 2, 41, 140
peace movement 4
Peace Prize of the German Book Trade 38,
    154
Pearl Harbor 234
perpetrators
    commemoration of 247
    Germans as 65, 70, 92, 108–15, 127,
        135, 262
    moral emancipation of 34
    people of 46, 84, 87
    society of 65
    soldiers as 29, 231
    suffering on side of 253
    Waffen-SS as 246
    see also victims
Pfeifer, Jochen 14, 16, 17–19, 144, 151,
    155, 160
plot 62, 150, 159, 190
Poland 94
Prantl, Heribert 131, 242
presence, metaphysics of 213

Raulff, Ulrich 44
Reagan, Ronald 246
Rebentisch, Ernst 249
reconciliation 33, 36, 37
redemption 34, 36, 94
re-education 6, 155, 166, 168–9, 229
Red Army 11, 47, 123
Reemtsma, Jan Philipp 132, 136
Reich-Ranicki, Marcel 25, 99
relativism
    historical 89
    moral 115, 170
Remarque, Erich Maria 15, 143, 144
representation
    appropriateness of 45, 83, 165
    ethical 21
    impossibility of 14, 56–7, 59, 86, 155,
        164
responsibility

of Allies 99, 252
    escape from 18, 265
    of Germans 67, 93, 138
        for bombing 99
        in contemporary international politics
            59
        for the Holocaust 44, 92, 135
        to improve 205
        for their past 67, 204, 245
    reduction of 205
    for Second World War 239
    for the Third Reich 65, 67, 160, 229,
        242, 249
    to use military 3, 7, 30, 32, 76, 245
    individual 207
    personal 132, 183, 199, 202, 203
    of reader 24, 25, 58
    of scholars 4, 30, 266
    and temporality 195, 196, 201–2, 212,
        216, 219, 220
    of Wehrmacht 137, 254
    see also Derrida, on responsibility
Ricoeur, Paul 57, 222, 224
Riordan, Colin 186, 197, 199, 211
Roosevelt, Franklin D. 207
Rühe, Volker 138, 215
Rumsfeld, Donald 257
Russia 134, 248, 255
Rwanda 35, 139

SA 148, 160, 247
sacrifice 94, 205, 217, 237, 244
salvation 34, 81, 145
Schama, Simon 237, 252, 261
Scharping, Rudolf 35, 69, 70
Schily, Otto 134, 163, 164, 172, 248
Schlant, Ernestine 18, 128
Schmid, Carlo 5, 128, 167, 265
Schmidt, Arno 83
Schneider, Jens 113
Schneider, Peter 84, 91, 95
Schreiber, Gerhard 131
Schröder, Gerhard 6, 114, 117, 244–6, 249
Schwab-Trapp, Michael 4
Schwartz, Michael 205
SD 131, 246, 247, 248, 249
Sebald, W.G. 77, 81–7, 89, 100, 101, 104,
    109, 145, 146, 159, 164, 165, 174,
    222
Seifert, Heribert 115
self-righteousness 96, 261
sentimentality 81, 82, 90, 108, 123, 128,
    143, 225, 239, 240, 254
Serbia 11, 139, 260
shame 66, 96, 110, 123, 239

silence 15, 43, 51, 61, 62, 82, 86, 103,
        131
singularity 112, 158, 190, 191, 250, 258
Sofsky, Wolfgang 95, 125
Solms, Hermann-Otto 8
Somalia 6
Sommer, Theo 138
Sontag, Susan 256
Soviet Union 45, 47, 61, 92, 244, 255
South Africa 36, 198
spacetime 180, 210
spectrality 198, 213
Spiegel, Hubert 65
SS 70, 131, 135, 136, 148, 153, 160, 179,
        246, 247, 248
Stalingrad, battle of 26, 42
Stargardt, Nicholas 94, 116
Steinbach, Erika 231
Stephan, Cora 91, 96, 261
Stern, Carola 116
Stiegler, Bernard 63
Stürmer, Michael 38
subjectivity 219, 224, 227, 259
suffering
    depiction of 18, 25, 65, 83
    Germans' focus on 28, 45, 47, 65, 79,
        109, 121, 230
    and German identity 112
    reason for 40
    in the Second World War 43, 65, 79,
        93, 126, 127, 153, 252
    human dimension of 90
    memory of 10, 28, 61, 62, 74, 92, 99,
        170, 229, 230, 231, 252, 260
    of people in war 1, 5, 12, 99, 168, 190,
        191, 241, 242, 243, 253
    senseless 94
    of soldiers in war 231, 243
    see also victims; community, of the
        suffering
supplement 201, 203, 219

taboo 25, 28, 43, 48, 50, 51, 61, 62, 78,
        79, 82, 87, 136, 230
Tachibana, Reiko 20, 21, 100, 146,
        179
temporality
    alternative 189, 195
    circular 188
    conception of 29, 175, 179, 196, 203,
        208, 210, 212, 263
    question of 175, 178, 181, 187, 223
    representation of 188
    significance of 196, 206
    see also time

terror
    of Allied bombing 86, 94, 114, 230, 237
    beyond language 86, 113, 226
    of expulsion 32, 41
testimony 3, 20, 24, 84, 155, 157–9, 173
    see also bearing witness
Thomson, Alistair 176
time
    absolute 180
    arrows of 180, 209
    clock 180, 181
    conception of 29, 181, 208–13, 216, 259
    Derrida on 213–15
    layers of 30, 175
    linearity of
        inescapability of 181, 218
        naturalness of 30, 216, 218, 220
        relationship to causality of 181, 189,
            195
        relationship to ethics of 30, 196, 216,
            219
        relationship to freedom of 196
    imaginary 180
    memories changing over 175, 176, 179,
        207, 226
    memory as challenge to conception of
        180, 189, 208, 216, 218–20, 223
    narrative 43
    out of 49, 202, 212, 219
    question of 180, 219
    real 181
    reversed 194, 195–7
    reversibility of 209
    Tralfamadorian 194, 195–7, 208, 212,
        215, 216, 219
    truth changing over 150
    see also linearity
time travel 177, 194, 195, 208, 211
truth
    about past 34, 36, 71, 150, 157, 165,
        172, 174, 222
    appeals to 82
    claim to 105, 146, 155, 225
    conception of 127, 259
    desire to reveal 146
    and ethics 165, 219, 220, 227
    ethics of 29
    of fiction 155–61
    full 32, 71, 161, 165, 227, 229
    ideal of 83
    inadequacy of 171, 173, 232, 262, 265
    narrative 164
    necessity of fiction to telling 24, 29, 146,
        164, 172
    see also authenticity; truthfulness

Truth and Reconciliation Commission 36
truthfulness 24, 40, 83, 155, 174

Ude, Christian 141
Ullmann, Wolfgang 117, 222
uncertainty
   highlighted by memory 140, 227
   inevitability of 4, 71, 72
   lack of 241
   literature as highlighting 123
   of memory 174
   moral 237, 263
   of numbers 56, 78, 113
   and repoliticisation 75
   and responsibility 74, 170, 259–66
   significance of 30
   and recourse to memory 2–4, 259, 261
Undecidability 24, 25, 74, 178, 179
United Kingdom 82, 87, 95, 183,
   199
UNPROFOR 9
UN Security Council 8–10

Vergangenheitsbewältigung 20, 60, 150,
   161, 169, 178
Verheugen, Günter 5
victimhood 29, 47, 48, 65, 80, 92–6, 115
victims
   civilians as 66, 137
   counting up of groups of 46, 53, 65–6,
      79, 92, 96, 114, 144, 229, 239
   of conditions 17
   danger of Germans construing
      themselves as 46, 85
   dignity of 137
   duty towards 33, 36
   empathy with 4
   focus on Germans as 90
   expanding category of 114
   Germans construed as 27, 28, 29, 45,
      65, 66, 76, 79, 86, 91, 108–15, 117,
      170, 205, 229, 230
   of historical injustice 34
   humanity as 144
   mourning for 114, 166, 239
   people of 87, 93
   and perpetrators in one 66, 108–15,
      122, 171, 252
   problem of representing Germans as 48,
      84, 99
   soldiers as 18, 133, 135, 137, 140, 144,
      153, 231–2, 249
   unacceptability of Germans construing
      themselves as 47, 122, 231, 262
   see also expulsion; suffering; victimhood

Vietnam 255
Vietnam War 182, 183, 189, 198, 199,
   200, 202
Vogel, Hans-Jochen 4, 222
von Clausewitz, Carl 89
von Einsiedel, Heinrich Graf 247
von Krockow, Christian Graf 19
von Weizsäcker, Richard 33, 36, 40, 41,
   61, 71, 72, 122, 197, 204, 223, 225,
   228
Vonnegut, Kurt 15, 30, 74, 77, 107, 156,
   176, 189–97, 208, 210, 211, 213,
   215, 216, 219, 223, 226, 238, 263

Waffen-SS 103, 135, 244–8, 249, 250
Wagener, Hans 15, 16–17
Waigel, Theo 141
Walser, Martin 29, 38–9, 84, 85, 91, 115,
   126, 146–51, 153, 155, 157, 158,
   159, 160, 161, 162, 165, 166, 172,
   173, 175, 177–9, 186, 208, 214,
   215, 218, 223
war of extermination 11, 66, 89, 129, 134,
   137, 248
war
   aversion against 6, 15, 127, 167, 168
   as disaster 4, 237, 250
   futility of 15, 18, 145
   good 145, 169, 170, 171, 234–7, 250,
      252
   as hell 6, 29, 70, 99, 100, 101, 128, 142,
      145, 171, 222, 248
   rejection of 1, 4, 8, 81, 121, 127, 168,
      222, 250
   return of 68, 117
   senselessness of 16, 81, 95, 100, 101,
      117, 142, 145, 152, 171
   see also Good War, The
Wehler, Hans-Ulrich 88, 90
Wehrmacht
   commemoration of 246
   conduct in the Balkans of 8, 9, 11, 30,
      70, 129, 222, 244
   conduct on Eastern front of 9, 11,
      58, 71
   as fighting for the country 131, 133,
      163, 248
   implication in Holocaust of 244, 246,
      247, 248, 254
   links with Bundeswehr of 9, 28, 137–40,
      173, 244
   memory of 164
   myth of 'clean' 11, 15, 19, 20, 27, 131,
      135, 139, 153, 167, 172, 244, 246,
      248, 251

Wehrmacht (*cont.*)
  as 'the people in arms' 136, 137, 244,
    249
  praise of accomplishments of 15
  see also atrocities
Wehrmacht crimes, exhibition on
  Bundestag debate about 38, 129, 132–5,
    138, 139, 140, 164, 172
  as critical examination of the
    Wehrmacht's role 168, 244
  debate about 29, 126, 129–41, 171, 173,
    246, 247
  and intergenerational conversations 162,
    242
  outcry about 11, 70
  see also atrocities
Wette, Wolfram 7, 131

White Russia 11
White, Hayden 159
Whitrow, G.J. 180
Windfuhr, Manfred 184, 187
Winkler, Willi 90, 239
Woods, Tim 21, 198, 209–10, 212–13,
    217, 219, 260
wounds 6, 8, 81, 127
  of memory 124, 126

Yad Vashem 33
Younge, Gary 256
Yugoslavia 69, 70, 244
  former 8–9, 10, 35, 37, 69

Zwerenz, Gerhard 5, 11, 127, 133,
    137

For EU product safety concerns, contact us at Calle de José Abascal, 56–1°,
28003 Madrid, Spain or eugpsr@cambridge.org.

www.ingramcontent.com/pod-product-compliance
Ingram Content Group UK Ltd.
Pitfield, Milton Keynes, MK11 3LW, UK
UKHW042153130625
459647UK00011B/1317